Understanding Everyday Racism

SAGE SERIES ON
RACE AND ETHNIC RELATIONS

Series Editor:
JOHN H. STANFIELD II
College of William and Mary

This series is designed for scholars working in creative theoretical areas related to race and ethnic relations. The series will publish books and collections of original articles that critically assess and expand upon race and ethnic relations issues from American and comparative points of view.

SERIES EDITORIAL BOARD

Volumes in this series include

Understanding Everyday Racism

An Interdisciplinary Theory

Philomena Essed

SAGE PUBLICATIONS
The International Professional Publishers
Newbury Park   London   New Delhi

For information address:

 SAGE Publications, Inc.
2455 Teller Road
Newbury Park, California 91320

SAGE Publications Ltd.
6 Bonhill Street
London EC2A 4PU
United Kingdom

SAGE Publications India Pvt. Ltd.
M-32 Market
Greater Kailash I
New Delhi 110 048 India

Printed in the United States of America

Library of Congress Cataloging-in-Publication Data

Essed, Philomena, 1955-
    Understanding everyday racism: an interdisciplinary theory/
Philomena Essed.
        p.   cm.—(Sage series on race and ethnic relations; v. 2)
    Includes bibliographical references and index.
    ISBN 0-8039-4255-9.—ISBN 0-8039-4256-7 (pbk.)
    1. Racism.   2. Prejudices.   3. Race relations—Research—
Methodology.   I. Title.   II. Series.
HT1521.E78   1991
305.8—dc20   91-22025
                                                                             CIP

FIRST PRINTING, 1991

Sage Production Editor: Michelle R. Starika

Contents

84604

Foreword

This fascinating study by Dr. Philomena Essed of the University of Amsterdam promises to break new theoretical ground in research on African-descent women in Western high-technology societies. It is an interdisciplinary analysis of gendered social constructions of racism as experienced by samples of African-descent women in the United States and in the Netherlands. *Understanding Everyday Racism* is a revised version of Dr. Essed's doctoral dissertation, which has been the center of a widely publicized debate in the Netherlands because it so skillfully pierces dominant "polite Dutch culture" and exposes the cultural and political contours of Dutch styles of gendered racism. Her ideas about racism as experienced by African-American women are just as illuminating.

I hope that what Dr. Essed has written will stimulate much needed creative and comparative theory building in social scientific research on African-descent women's experiences with racism in Western high-tech societies.

John H. Stanfield II
Series Editor

Preface

Euro-American culture contains an awkward balance between racist and nonracist tendencies. Throughout history there have been people subscribing to racist beliefs, but there have also been oppositional groups. This book represents oppositional views of Black women. It reports results of a cross-cultural investigation of racism. I have analyzed reconstructions of reality gathered in interviews conducted with African-American women in California and with Black Surinamese women—first-generation immigrants in the Netherlands. Whereas most other studies of racism have a macro orientation, little attention has been paid to its everyday manifestations. The experienced reality of racism one finds in novels or autobiographies of Black authors is hardly visible in the social sciences. This study examines crucial, but largely neglected, dimensions of racism: How is racism experienced in everyday situations? How do Blacks recognize covert expressions of racism? What knowledge of racism do Blacks have, and how is this knowledge acquired? Through the accounts of Black women about their daily racial experiences, this study problematizes and reinterprets many of the meanings and everyday practices the majority has come to take for granted. Moreover, it presents a new approach to the study of racism based on the concept of "everyday racism." Such an approach requires an interdisciplinary framework. Therefore, I try to combine daily experiences of individuals with a more structural account of racism within a theoretical framework that integrates developments in such disciplines as macro- and microsociology, social psychology, discourse analysis, race relations theory, and women's studies.

Although the interviews were held in the Netherlands and the United States, there are reasons to assume that the results have a more general nature and also hold true for other White-dominated societies. A general feature of these societies is the fact that the superiority of Euro-American culture is taken for granted. Although in many of these countries the language of cultural tolerance suggests increasing equality among different racial and ethnic groups, this is not the case. On the contrary the idea of tolerance is inherently problematic when applied to hierarchical group relations. This will be illustrated by examples from the Netherlands, where tolerance is generally assumed to be a prevailing national attitude.

Racism not only operates through culture, it is also the expression of structural conflict. Individuals are actors in a power structure. Power can be used to reproduce racism, but it can also be used to combat racism. This study shows how power, operative in everyday situations, perpetuates racial and ethnic oppression. Note, however, that I focus on racist practices, not on individuals. To talk about "to be or not to be a racist" simplifies the problem. Although individuals are the agents of racism, my concern is practices and their implications, not the psyche of these individuals.

This study examines more specifically racism among Whites with higher education. This is important when we assume that, the more opportunities people have to gain information about racism and the more authority they have by virtue of their social positions, the more responsible they are for the racist implications of their practices. Dominant group members are, however, generally inclined to deny racism. Therefore, the definition of the situation, and more specifically who defines whether situations are racist, is at the heart of this study. These questions are addressed through an analysis of the knowledge and perceptions of Black women.

This book is a reworking of a Ph.D. thesis. Because of space limitations I had to cut out, in this commercial edition, pages of the text. As a result some of the technical details of the methodological underpinning of this study could not be included. For those who are really interested in seeing more of it, however, I indicate in the text, at relevant points, those places where additional material is available (which, upon request, can be obtained from me).

This study is part of an ongoing project on Black perceptions of Whites, which I started in the beginning of the 1980s. I reported on this subject, among others, in my book *Everyday Racism,* which first appeared in Dutch (1984) and recently in English (Hunter House,

California, 1990). *Everyday Racism* is tuned to a general public. It combines minimal theory with a maximum amount of real-life stories. Readers who are not familiar with race relations theory may want to read that book first as an introduction to the notion of everyday racism. *Understanding Everyday Racism* is for advanced readers. The project reported here is the result of five years of additional research and writing (1985-1990). *Understanding Everyday Racism* presents a theory and analysis of the concept of everyday racism.

The writing was, obviously, a solitary activity, but the project itself was very much a collective effort. The generous cooperation of Black women enabled me to obtain unusually detailed data about racism. I am profoundly grateful to the women—their names cannot be mentioned—who gave their time and reconstructed their experiences, which form the empirical basis of this study. I am sure many of them will read this study. I hope I have done them justice.

Throughout the years many people have encouraged me in my study and writing and I can here acknowledge my indebtedness to only some of them, doing so more or less chronologically. First I would like to thank Petra de Vries, who supervised my first course on women's studies many years ago at the University of Amsterdam. It dramatically changed my views of, as well as my relation to, the social sciences.

Support for the completion of this study has come from many sources in the Netherlands and in the United States. Henk Heeren encouraged me to persevere when initially it seemed almost impossible to acquire financial support for the project, given the sensitivity of the topic and the fact that racism is generally denied in the Netherlands. I am indebted to the Netherlands Organization for Scientific Research (NWO), which financed three years of the project. I deeply appreciate the financial contribution of the Mama Cash Foundation for the completion of the project in the United States. Further I am grateful for the financial support of the Ministry of Education and Science and the University of Amsterdam for allowing me to complete the analysis of some problems that emerged from the data when the project was nearly finished.

I thank the University of California, San Diego, for allowing me to use their facilities during my stay. Aaron Cicourel has been a most gentle and supportive supervisor at UCSD. I owe him many many thanks for his generous hospitality, for giving his precious time to discuss with me a range of interview techniques, and for providing me with much needed background information about the California area. I also benefited from talks with Hugh Mehan, whose questions and views about my research were very stimulating. The Association of Black Psychologists, San Diego, have been very supportive. They invited me to their meetings, discussed my work with me, and generally gave me the feeling that I was welcome.

I owe an invaluable debt to Chris Mullard. His comments on my work have been challenging and very inspiring.

Doing the interviews is always the nice part of the job; transcribing is a completely different matter. Without the help of Terry Grazier, Marlene Bailey, and Carol Bronson in the United States, I never would have managed. In the Netherlands, Deborah Fellows and Rina Simons did wonders on a few incomplete transcriptions of the U.S. interviews. I feel deep gratitude and respect for Micky Bictorina, who, on her own, did a perfect job on the transcriptions of all the Dutch interviews. Sharon Belden has been a great help in correcting my English. I am also grateful to Marguerite Niekoop, secretary at the Centre for Race and Ethnic Studies (CRES), where I did my research. She took over a great deal of the administrative work involved in the completion of this study.

I am grateful for the encouragement I received from many friends. Special thanks are due to Glenn Willemsen, who was not only a colleague but also like a brother. I have very much enjoyed our discussions about research and politics. It is a pleasure to acknowledge the contributions of the students in my courses on women and racism at CRES. Their questions and suggestions about the nature of racism in the Netherlands have made teaching a very stimulating challenge. I am also indebted to my family, in particular my parents, for equally encouraging daughters and sons when study and career were concerned. My mother, Ine Corsten, and my friend Kitty Lie have been supportive in a very special way. I have learned, and I am still learning, from their outspoken views on justice and injustice.

There are no words to express my gratitude to Teun van Dijk. I could not have been more fortunate than to have a partner who knew my work well enough to be a severe critic as well as a staunch supporter. I cannot image how I could have managed without his constant enthusiasm, his love, his solidarity, his commitment to the struggle against racism, and the numerous discussions we have had about each other's work.

Positive feedback has made the project a pleasant and inspiring one, despite the fact that it deals with a serious problem. I hope the perceptions of the Black women reported in this study are useful for all of us, Black and White, who feel responsible for creating a qualitatively better society.

Introduction

A NEW APPROACH TO THE STUDY OF RACISM

Confronted with a problem as complex as racism, we cannot afford to let ourselves be constrained by the boundaries of specific disciplines. This makes the study of racism more complicated but also more challenging. This study provides a compact integration of concepts originating from different disciplines. It presents an analysis of cross-cultural empirical data that were instrumental in the development of a theory of everyday racism. In this introductory chapter the various issues addressed are discussed briefly and informally. More detailed elaboration follows in the next chapters.

Many studies have identified the mechanisms of racism at a societal level, but few have revealed its pervasive impact on the daily experiences of Blacks. The impetus for this study emerged from the need to make visible the lived experience of racism and, more specifically, to analyze Black perceptions about racism in everyday life. This approach presupposes that Black people's knowledge about racism is socially relevant. Du Bois (1969) was among the first to point out that, over the generations, Blacks in the United States developed a "double consciousness." This idea is premised on the view that Blacks are familiar with dominant group interpretations of reality and, therefore, have knowledge of racist ideas and interpretations of reality. With their sense of history, through communication about racism within the Black community, and by testing their own experiences in daily life, Black people can develop profound and often sophisticated knowledge about the reproduction of racism. These qualities make Black definitions of racism interesting as an object for academic inquiry.

This study has also been prompted by the slow progress of the social sciences in the development of interdisciplinary studies of racism. By and large traditional boundaries between different disciplines were reproduced in studies of racism. Thus there is little connection between social psychological and sociological approaches, between theories of the cognitive and structural components of racism. Within sociology controversies between "macro" and "micro" paradigms have frustrated theories that integrate structural and interactional dimensions of racism.

Racism is defined as inherent in culture and social order. It is argued in this study that racism is more than structure and ideology. As a process it is routinely created and reinforced through everyday practices. With this view in mind I earlier introduced the concept of "everyday racism" (Essed, 1984), which connects structural forces of racism with routine situations in everyday life. It links ideological dimensions of racism with daily attitudes and interprets the reproduction of racism in terms of the experience of it in everyday life. Through a detailed theoretical analysis, this study articulates new sets of meanings in the concept of everyday racism.

It is my aim to demonstrate that the concept of everyday racism has a more general relevance in race relations theory. I will show that it can be relevantly applied to the analysis of racism both in the United States and in the Netherlands, although historical, economic, and political configurations lead to different styles of racism in these countries. It is not my intention to make systematic comparisons between the Netherlands and the United States but to use knowledge and interpretations of racism in the United States as a frame of reference for understanding the experiences of Blacks in the Netherlands, who are predominantly first-generation immigrants. The Dutch—here and in the rest of this study meaning "White" Dutch, unless indicated otherwise—do not generally see themselves as members of a racist society and tend to accuse other countries, such as the United States, of being racist. Blacks in the United States share the collective experience of everyday racism through many generations. We can benefit in the Netherlands from the insights that have emerged from this experience to understand and counter the massive denial of racism in this country. Conversely the Dutch case is also interesting for those who study racism in the United States, because it contains the contours of racism in a welfare state with more advanced ideas of "pluralistic democracy" than those of the United States.

EVERYDAY RACISM, EXPERIENCES, AND ACCOUNTS

Before we proceed to a more explicit analysis of everyday racism, it is useful to begin with a more informal characterization of this notion. The "everyday" has been addressed as a problematic, in particular in philosophy, phenomenology, ethnomethodology, and also recently in social psychology. The notion of "everyday" is often used to refer to a familiar world, a world of practical interest, a world of practices we are socialized with in order to manage in the system. In our everyday lives sociological distinctions between "institutional" and "interactional," between ideology and discourse, and between "private" and "public" spheres of life merge and form a complex of social relations and situations.

Everyday racism is racism, but not all racism is everyday racism. The concept of everyday racism counters the view, prevalent in particular in the Netherlands, that racism is an individual problem, a question of "to be or not to be a racist." The crucial criterion distinguishing racism from everyday racism is that the latter involves only systematic, recurrent, familiar practices. The fact that it concerns repetitive practices indicates that everyday racism consists of practices that can be generalized. Because everyday racism is infused into familiar practices, it involves socialized attitudes and behavior. Finally, its systematic nature indicates that everyday racism includes cumulative instantiation. These arguments make clear that the notion of everyday racism is defined in terms of practices prevalent in a given system. Note that practices are not just "acts" but also include complex relations of acts and (attributed) attitudes.

Experience is a central concept in this study. Experiences are a suitable source of information for the study of everyday racism because they include personal experiences as well as vicarious experiences of racism. In addition the notion of experience includes general knowledge of racism, which is an important source of information to qualify whether specific events can be generalized. These experiences of racism are made available for academic inquiry through accounts—that is, verbal reconstructions of experiences. I argue in this study that reconstructions of experiences in such accounts provide the best basis for the analysis of the simultaneous impact of racism in different sites and in different social relations. Accounts of racism locate the narrators as well as their experiences in the social context of their everyday lives, give specificity and detail to events, and invite the narrator to carefully qualify subtle experiences of racism.

The empirical data of this study consist of verbal accounts of racism, gathered in the period of 1985-1986 in nondirective interviews with a group of 55 Black women, all but 2 of them aged 20-45, from a few large cities in California and the Netherlands. The state of California was chosen primarily for practical reasons. It is, however, interesting to mention that both California and the Netherlands have the reputation of being racially progressive or tolerant compared with, respectively, other U.S. states and other European countries. Problems of racism in California are not necessarily exactly the same as in other parts of the United States. Therefore, the specific experiences of racism discussed in this book may differ to a certain degree from those of Black women in other parts of the United States. For the sake of comparability with Black American women, the study in the Netherlands involves in particular the experiences of immigrant women of African descent, from the (ex-)colony of Suriname. However, the reader must bear in mind that the experiences of the Afro-Surinamese cannot always be separated from racism against the Surinamese as a group, including people from African, Asian, and Native American descent. Furthermore, and I will explain this in more detail later, racism against the Surinamese is part of the broader system of racism as it operates against the various colonized and (Mediterranean) immigrant groups in the Netherlands.

The women interviewed were familiar with the idea of problematizing racism, which adds to their general understanding of the problem and their ability to assess routine situations. It will be shown, tentatively, that there are methods of inferring from the contents and structure of accounts whether the narrator has comprehension of racism. I used these methods only to assess accounts, but they are probably also useful for practical purposes, for instance, to elicit goal-directed information about racist events.

FOCUSING ON BLACK WOMEN

Some arguments are in order to defend an analysis of the general concept of racism based only on the experiences of women. The most important reason is to make more explicit a Black female point of view in the general field of race and ethnic relations. This does not mean that the study addresses only personal experiences Black women have with racism. We shall see that a substantial part of their experiences are shaped vicariously, through friends, family members, and other Blacks, through the media, and cognitively, through their general knowledge of racism in the system. Although this study is not about Black women in general, we have to take into account that the experiences of Black women are structured by converging systems of race, class, and gender oppression. Therefore, I have tried to minimize the role of class exploitation indirectly by selecting only women with higher education, namely, university students and professionals. They are a privileged group in terms of educational background and job opportunities, but the factor of class oppression nevertheless plays an indirect role in their lives. Through family relations and life in segregated areas, Black women with higher education indirectly participate in the collective experience of class-basedracism.

Individual Black women may feel that specific experiences are predominantly racial when theoretically it could be argued that there are also factors of gender involved. In some cases, such as the sexual oppression of Black women by White men, we may make an analytical distinction between the race and gender factors involved. Often, however, this is not feasible, let alone tenable from a theoretical point of view. Take, for instance, the following problem that will receive much attention in this study. Black women are systematically confronted in their aspirations with obstructions from Whites, who often attribute incompetence to them. One can place the problem of underestimation in a gender context as well as in a racial context, but it is analytically difficult to determine in detail the specific impact of either gender or race. For these and other reasons it may be assumed that many, if not the majority, of the personal experiences of racism in the lives of these Black women are forms of "gendered racism."

SOCIAL-POLITICAL CONTEXT: THE DENIAL OF RACISM

One common factor of racism in the United States and in the Netherlands is the denial of racism. Today many Whites condemn more blatant forms of racism and are often motivated to maintain nondiscriminating self-concepts. However, only a few actively challenge the current consensus on race as it is expressed in increasingly covert forms of racism merged with apparently nonracial issues. In the United States many liberals have come to share the conservative conviction that racism was dealt with sufficiently during the 1960s and that Blacks are no longer discriminated against on racial grounds. In the Netherlands the dominant opinion maintains that the Dutch are tolerant and that there never has been a problem of racism. This version of Dutch society is defended despite the fact that research shows that Blacks and other immigrants are excluded and marginalized in all sectors of society.

Nevertheless, we cannot deny that the Dutch, more so than Whites in the United States, actively pursue ideals of tolerance. Is this in contradiction to evidence of racism? To answer this question we must consider that in the Netherlands, more so than in the United States, racism operates as cultural oppression or, more specifically, as "ethnicism" (Mullard, 1986a). Ethnicism is an ideology that explicitly proclaims the existence of "multiethnic" equality but implicitly presupposes an ethnic or cultural hierarchical order.

At first sight it may seem strange that Blacks in the Netherlands are confronted with a high degree of cultural oppression, considering that the country has the historical reputation of cultural (religious) tolerance. However, the notion of tolerance, traditionally considered a positive value, is problematic when applied to relations of dominance. This study will show that Dutch racism operates through the discourse of tolerance. The dominant group assumes that Dutch norms and values are superior and not subject to change. This leads to all kinds of strategies to manage the presence of Blacks and other immigrants in society through cultural control. Thus the discourse of tolerance conceals the emptiness of the promise of cultural pluralism.

This critique of Dutch tolerance has earlier been leveled, in slightly different ways, against Dutch government policy (Mullard, Nimako, & Willemsen, 1988). The uniqueness of the concept of everyday racism is, however, that it illustrates the consistency of practices in all levels of society. That is, the tendency to control the influence of other cultures is not just a policy issue; it pervades the everyday practices by which the dominant group secures the status quo of race and ethnic relations. This exposure of hidden currents of the ideology of pluralism is not only relevant for the Dutch situation. Recent studies suggest that the idea of "cultural pluralism" is gaining in popularity in the United States as well. At the same time the concept of racism is losing ground on the U.S. national agenda.

Not only is racism denied in both countries, the current ideological climate allows the press and academics to openly attack Blacks (and Whites) who fight against racism. This legitimizes and reinforces indifference to racial oppression and tolerance for racism among the dominant group. It will be shown that Whites often identify with other perpetrators of racism rather than with Blacks, in particular when it concerns covert manifestations. Black women illustrate with many experiences how, when confronted with evidence of racism, dominant group members deny their own responsibility, claim that others probably did not mean it that way, and problematize those who refuse to accept racism: "You are exaggerating, you are oversensitive."

THEORETICAL BACKGROUND

The approach and relevance of this study cannot be fully understood without mentioning some major shortcomings of the sociology and social psychology of race and ethnic relations. Social psychological studies are useful, as we shall see, in understanding some of the cognitive mechanisms through which race conflict is maintained in everyday situations. However, racial and ethnic prejudice has been studied largely from a White point of view. Observed indications of prejudice have not often been tested against experiences of Black people and their perspectives. Generally little attention has been paid to the knowledge, beliefs, opinions, and attitudes of Blacks with respect to the meaning of racism.

There are also several limitations to the insights into racism developed in the sociology of race and ethnic relations. Many studies that implemented racial oppression as institutional discrimination are problematic because they ignored the role of ideology in the structuring of discrimination. Others denounced the concept of racism as misleading and of little theoretical use. More interesting are those studies that explicitly problematize racism. A theory of everyday racism obviously benefits from the accomplishments of structural approaches to racism. Yet most of these studies also have the usual problems of macrosociology. Manifestations of contemporary racism have not been studied in detail in a systematic, theoretical, and analytical way. Due to this prevailing macrosociological bias, micro-interactional perspectives on racism, as well as the phenomenological dimensions of racism, have been neglected.

The lack of intellectual interest in micro manifestations and experiences may also be due to intellectual bias against the "ordinary" and the underrating of the insights of "laypersons." It is not surprising that so few people have engaged in systematic analyses of how racism permeates everyday life. Such analyses demand an eye for detail and challenge the researcher to organize and understand an enormous number of divergent experiences covering macro and micro levels of racial domination. Finally, they require a truly interdisciplinary approach to the problem and creative use of concepts originating from different fields and paradigms.

Against this background there are four areas of theoretical debate in which this study of everyday racism must be placed. The first concerns structural approaches to racism and deals with questions of power and oppression. The second area of debate concerns (Black) women's studies and focuses on the impact of gender (and class) on forms and experiences of racism. The third area is sociological and deals with the meaning of social reality and relations between macro structures and micro processes. My main concern is not with metatheoretical models of social practice and the nature of social reality as such but with the applicability of some of these concepts in a theory of racism. The fourth area follows from the former and deals with questions of experience and social cognition. Defining general knowledge of racism as the link between structures and experiences of racism, this part of the theoretical framework draws on social psychology and deals with questions of the development and use of general knowledge of racism in the understanding of personal experiences of racism.

PLAN OF THE STUDY

In the first chapter we will look at the idea of "experiences of everyday racism" within the general field of race relations theory. Like everyday racism the experience of everyday racism is a cumulative process. New experiences are interpreted and evaluated against the background of earlier personal experiences, vicarious experiences, and general knowledge of racism in society. The more experience one has in dealing with racism, the more elaborate and organized one's knowledge becomes about the nature of racism in the system, and the more efficiently one can use general knowledge of racism to understand its specific manifestations in everyday life.

Chapter 2 deals with the methodology of this study. We shall see that this research features a methodology within a methodology; that is, comparisons are made between academic heuristics of understanding and reconstructions of real-life experiences. It is assumed that the way social scientists organize, present, and reproduce knowledge of a certain problematic is more explicit and systematically structured but in essence not different than the general knowledge and stories Black women reconstruct about racism in everyday life.

Social scientists have seldom studied the structure and content of (Black people's) knowledge of racism. Where does this knowledge come from and how is it used to comprehend racist events? These questions are central in Chapters 3 and 4, in which I shall also argue that knowledge of racism must be defined as a special form of political knowledge. To gain more insight into the relevance and use of knowledge of racism in understanding personal experiences, I reconstruct how Black women acquired knowledge about racism. Neither in the United States nor in the Netherlands had Black women had the opportunity to acquire knowledge of racism through the channels of formal education, where the problem of racism is largely ignored. Most women in the United States were socialized at home, with the relevant historical and actual knowledge, to understand and to deal with racism in everyday life. In the United States, as well as in the Netherlands, higher education provided Black women with the conceptual tools to question and analyze their own experiences as Blacks in society and to search for alternative literature and other information to compensate for the lack of study materials relevant to their point of view.

Questions of knowledge and understanding are elaborated in more detail in Chapter 4, where I discuss the structure and analysis of accounts. The analysis is based on concepts from narrative theory and social cognition theory. I will show that accounts of racism are not ad hoc stories. They have a specific structure that reflects various knowledge systems. These include general and specific knowledge of racism and general knowledge of norms, by which I mean (sub)culturally determined and situationally negotiable (implicit) agreements about social behavior (Turner, 1987, p. 181). Further these knowledge systems include general and specific knowledge of rules of acceptable (i.e., nondiscriminatory) behavior. Finally, accounts of racism reflect the rational use of heuristics of comparison to assess one's personal experience in relation to the experiences of others.

The central part of this study consists of Chapters 5 and 6, in which the structure of everyday racism is outlined and substantiated in detail. The identification and subsequent categorization of all the concrete examples of racism mentioned in the interview materials, totaling over 2,000, provide a reliable quantitative base from which to draw conclusions about the main forms of racism structuring Black women's everyday experiences of racism. Conflict is the main theme running through Black women's everyday lives. For the Black women who speak in this study, everyday life in a White-dominated society involves a continual battle against the denial of racism, against Whitecentrism, against automatic in-group preference among Whites, against constant impediments to their aspirations, against humiliations, against petty harassment, and against denigration of their cultures. The women persistently contest group conflict over fundamental norms and values, over access to resources, and over definitions of reality. The study shows that racial and ethnic conflict are maintained through three main processes: (a) marginalization (a form of oppression), (b) containment (a form of repression), and (c) problematization (ideological constructions legitimizing exclusion and repression of opposition). Although these major forms of racism are ideologically structured, their specific manifestations are situationally construed.

Once we recognize that racial oppression is inherent in the nature of the social order, it becomes clear that the real racial drama is not racism but the fact that racism is an everyday problem. When, as we shall see, racism is transmitted in routine practices that seem "normal," at least for the dominant group, this can only mean that racism is often not recognized, not acknowledged—let alone problematized—by the dominant group. To expose racism in the system we must analyze ambiguous meanings, expose hidden currents, and generally question what seems normal or acceptable. The reader is requested to keep this in mind when, in the course of the analysis, practices that may seem mundane and trivial are unfolded, reinterpreted, and reevaluated as instantiations of everyday racism.

1

Toward an Integration of Macro and Micro Dimensions of Racism

RACISM TODAY:
THE SOCIAL-POLITICAL CONTEXT

Contemporary racism is rooted in centuries of oppression and struggle that formed the bedrock of relations between Blacks and Whites, Third World and First World. These historical realities have been documented extensively (e.g., Aptheker, 1964; Berry & Blassingname, 1982; Franklin, 1952; Genovese, 1984; Gutman, 1976; Litwack, 1979; Rose, 1976; Stampp, 1956). Some authors have pointed out that prejudice against Blacks was already present in the sixteenth century, when Europeans began to remove millions of youth and young adults from the African work force (Dabydeen, 1987; Jordan, 1968). Others maintain that race ideology and White domination could only blossom through the European expansion, the development of capitalism, the colonization of the New World, and the race consciousness that emerged from biological and anthropological theories (Chase, 1980; Du Bois, 1964; Gossett, 1963; Horsman, 1981; Reynolds, 1985). Rather than race exploitation causing race prejudice or the other way round, they seem to have continually appeared together and reinforced each other over time (Lauren, 1988). Indeed racism extends beyond the mere facts of imperialism. It forms part of a much more profound problem, namely, the tendency of European civilization not to homogenize but to exaggerate and to exploit regional, subcultural, and dialectical differences as "ethnic" and "racial" ones (Nederveen Pieterse, 1989; Robinson, 1983). Racism is always historically specific (Hall, 1978, 1980). This is not to say that racism is a "natural" and permanent feature of European history; it is created and reproduced out of a complex set of conditions. Even when it draws on cultural and ideological remnants of previous historical processes, the specific forms racism takes are determined by the economic, political, social, and organizational conditions of society. Further, one must also take into account the impact of oppositional groups. In Europe as well as in the United States, there have always been groups fighting for their oppositional views and for racial justice.

Blacks in the United States tried virtually everything in their struggle for liberation—revolt, petitions, armed attacks, economic boycott, demonstrations, riots, court action, the vote, alliances, Black nationalism (Aptheker, 1966; Bennett, 1965; Bontemps, 1961; Commager, 1967; Eissien-Udom, 1962; Franklin, 1984; Grant, 1968; Hercules, 1972; Killian & Grigg, 1964; Lomax, 1962; Marable, 1980, 1984; Marx, 1967; Morris, 1984; Page, 1987; Reid, 1972; Skolnick, 1969; Stuckey, 1987; Tuttle, 1984). Due to, among other things, continuous protest and the demands of market economy, social and political conditions have changed, but the legacy of discrimination and legal segregation (Williamson, 1984; Woodward, 1957) has continued to affect race relations in the United States (Newman et al., 1978). As we move into the 1990s, segregation is still widespread, in particular in housing, and there is a tendency for desegregated schools to resegregate in the classroom (Epstein, 1985; Harris & Wilkins, 1988; Jaynes & Williams, 1989; Tobin, 1987). Indeed desegregation in schools did not sufficiently improve the quality of race relations (Adair, 1984; Hanna, 1988; Patchen, 1982). More generally economic and ideological forces operate to impede progress and to keep the majority of Blacks in exploited conditions (Glasgow, 1980; Pinkney, 1984). It has been argued that the condition of Blacks cannot be explained by the factor of race alone (Wilson, 1978, 1987). One cannot deny that class position is of crucial importance (Auletta, 1982; Polenberg, 1980; Sennett & Cobb, 1972). There is, however, abundant evidence to show that racism continues to be a major determining factor in the lives of Blacks (Bell, Parker, & Guy-Sheftall, 1979; Blauner, 1989; Boston, 1988; Duster, 1981; Hill et al., 1989; James, Mccummings, & Tynan, 1984; Katz & Taylor, 1988; Ladner & Stafford, 1981; Omi & Winant, 1986; Wellman, 1977). Its forms and manifestations, however, seem to be in a phase of transition during the postwar period. This holds true for U.S. as well as for European race and ethnic relations.

Various developments since World War II have contributed to changes in the ideological basis of racism and its manifestations. Changes in the capitalist mode of production led to large-scale labor migration from Third World to First World and from southern to northern Europe. The postwar period witnessed decolonization processes and the rise of nationalism throughout the world. The old colonial model of "race" exploitation and cultural oppression rationalized with pseudoscientific "race" theories is loosing ground. In this process the cultural elements of racism become more prominent. At the same time "ethnic" forms of oppression have emerged that are fed by strong (nationalistic) identification with the cultural heritage of the group. These "ethnic"-directed forms of oppression are an inherent part of the cultural pluralism model. The concept of pluralism was introduced by Furnivall (1948) as a description of the colonial society in which different peoples seek their own ends without developing feelings of loyalty to the whole society. Today the notion of cultural pluralism is also frequently used to describe European and U.S. society as consisting of different groups that are culturally distinctive and separate. Cultural pluralists believe in the primacy of culture and traditions as determinants of group membership, and they are positively committed to the preservation of these distinctive elements. I am not concerned here with models of pluralism in themselves (Bullivant, 1983; Mullard, et al., 1988) but with implications of the application of cultural pluralism as everyday practice and social discourse in relations of racial and ethnic dominance. Cultural pluralism interferes with and changes, to a certain extent, traditional rationalizations of racism. These processes of change occur in the United States as well as in the Netherlands but at a different pace and under different social, economic, and political conditions.

In the United States blatant notions of "racial" inferiority have become less acceptable among the dominant group and are being replaced by a much more subtle ideology, built on the bedrock of cultural inferiority (Cruse, 1987; Steinberg, 1981). Notions of cultural determinism, though not necessarily formulated in value-laden terms such as *superiority* and *inferiority,* are thoroughly integrated into White perceptions of Blacks, as may be inferred from empirical data (Wellman, 1977). Cultural determinism was not a new phenomenon in the 1970s. Earlier, authors such as Glazer and Moynihan (1963/1968, p. 310) argued that "ethnicity is . . . the source of events." Cultural arguments are used more and more to blame Blacks themselves for the situation of poverty and their slow rise in the system compared with White immigrants and Asians. Feelings of cultural superiority are not expressed alone in the blaming of Blacks for failing to develop White middle-class values and aspirations (Sowell, 1981). Underlying this discourse is the implication that Euro-American cultural standards are uncritically accepted as the norm and positive standard. The traditional idea of genetic inferiority is still important in the fabric of racism (Duster, 1990), but the discourse of Black inferiority is increasingly reformulated as cultural deficiency, social inadequacy, and technological underdevelopment (Rodney, 1982). The increasing influence of cultural determinism, or the *culturalization* of racism, is inherent in the ideological climate of pluralistic views of society, which have gained increasing importance in the United States since the 1960s (Steinberg, 1981). In conclusion these arguments suggest that the Black Diaspora in United States, from slavery onward, has begun to witness declining racism but also increasingly cultural and covert racism.

The Black Diaspora in Europe is a different story, one of colonialism rather than slavery, even as European colonialists had their own slavery systems and kept Blacks in bondage as long as the Europeans in the United States did. Unlike that of the United States, however, the racism in Europe is "new" in the sense that it is racism "in the mother country" as opposed to the traditional racism in the colonies in the "high" colonial period (Solomos, Findlay, Jones, & Gilroy, 1982). For over two decades after World War II, antiracism was quite popular and crude race theories were discredited (e.g., Montagu, 1972, 1974). With the economic crisis of the 1970s, however, the Black Diaspora in Europe began to witness a resurgence of racism and they are increasingly brutalized by racism—in countries such as France, Belgium, and the United Kingdom more violently than in the Netherlands (European Parliament, 1985, 1986, 1990; SIM, 1988). The situation may deteriorate even faster with the unification of Europe, and pogroms and violence against Jews, the Sinti, and Roma, Vietnamese workers, and African students recently having intensified in various Eastern European countries. European politicians act ambivalently. To use the words of Bhikhu Parekh, previous deputy chairman of the U.K. Commission of Racial Equality: "No European government has hitherto dared to follow wholly racist policies; none has dared to tackle racism head on either" (Parekh, 1988, p. 10).

Like various other European peoples, the Dutch have a history of exploitation of Africans in the Caribbean and in South Africa. Contemporary Dutch racism against Blacks is a complex combination of remnants of colonial paternalism, structural marginalization, and cultural assimilation under conditions of advancing pluralism. The Dutch ideology of pluralism is rooted in the previous century and has accompanied the institutionalization of religious diversity in society (Cherribi, Fuhr, & Niedekker, 1989, pp. 13-19). Because ethnic pluralism is almost invariably associated only with differences in life-style, it has the function of obscuring socioeconomic and political power conflicts (Bullivant, 1983; Mullard, 1986a). Indeed the key notions in Dutch discourse about race and ethnic relations are "culture" (Penninx, 1988, p. 32), "ethnicity" (Hoppe, 1987; Vermeulen, 1984), and "multiethnic" (WRR, 1989, p. 24) rather than "race," "power," and "cultural oppression." Arguably "ethnic group" is a problematic concept (Miles, 1982), which has been defined on the basis of diverse criteria such as interest (Glazer & Moynihan, 1963/1968, p. 17), identification with a specific culture (Smith, 1981, p. 13), or a mixture of race, religion, and national background (Gordon, 1978, pp. 106-113). Here the notion of "ethnic" or, more specifically, "ethnic diversity" is relevant not so much for its intrinsic meaning but for the political meaning it acquires in a conceptual framework of pluralism. In that context "ethnic groups" are usually seen as "culturally distinct groups within a state, that retain their cultural identity while accepting and operating within the political, institutional framework of the state. . . . The future of such groups is in constant negotiation with other groups within the overall political arena of the state" (Clay, 1989, p. 224). In this construction power differences between different groups are ignored, and it is assumed that societal stability results from acceptance of the supposedly neutral authority of the state on political issues (Mullard, 1982, p. 129).

The ideological form of racism that is used to rationalize pluralization, called "ethnicism," proclaims the end of class and race groups, thereby delegitimizing resistance against racism and denying fundamental group conflict (Mullard, 1985a, 1986a). I do not intend to elaborate upon the race-class discussion, as I shall explain in more detail later. Nevertheless it is relevant to point out that ethnicism, which is inherently part of the processes of cultural or ethnic differentiation within a pluralistic model, represents a shift from "race" hierarchies to "ethnic" hierarchies and from race and class exploitation to ethnic marginalization through social, economic, and political disempowerment. We shall see that Black women are confronted both with racism based in the colonial model and with ethnicism based in the cultural pluralism model. Because "racial" and "ethnic" criteria overlap, in particular in the social representations of Blacks, and because racism as well as ethnicism involve cultural inferiorization, we get a picture of mixed coherence. This hybrid coherence makes it difficult to distinguish in detail racism from ethnicism in the experiences of Black women. Therefore, this study maintains the concept of racism for descriptive, explanatory, and analytical purposes, and I shall return to the concept later.

In this chapter the experiences of Black women are placed in a theoretical framework. For that purpose, four areas of social scientific debate are important. First a macrosociological outline of racism is given. Second the impact of racism on the lives of Black women is discussed. The third part presents a working definition of racism. In this way macrosociological conceptions of racism are reformulated as microsociological concepts. The fourth part makes operational the notion of everyday racism as a concept that integrates, by definition, macro- and microsociological dimensions of racism.

Before proceeding it is, however, relevant to make clear the different contexts of racism toward Black women in the Netherlands and in the United States. Therefore, a brief discussion is needed concerning race and ethnic relations in both countries. We have already seen that racism is getting more covert in the United States but more brutal in Europe. Indeed U.S. and European racism are trends toward the universalization of the Black experience (Mazrui, 1986). Because there are many studies of racism in the United States and very few (in English) of racism in the Netherlands, relatively more attention is paid to developments in the latter country.

THE NETHERLANDS

Dutch racism is similar to and different than racism in the United States. The differences have to do not only with Dutch history and with economic and political conditions of the migration of Blacks to the Netherlands but also with the ideological climate. With respect to the ideologies in which Dutch racism is embedded, it is relevant to distinguish between two systems of ideas. The first is a paternalistic remnant of colonialism and may be characterized as the ideology of the "Dutch burden." This paternalism is motivated by "good intentions" to "help" Blacks cope with "modern" Dutch society. By the end of the 1980s the ideology of the "Dutch burden" decreased in influence. During the 1980s unemployment among Blacks increased dramatically, despite the efforts the Dutch felt they had made to encourage integration. To mitigate evidence of large-scale discrimination in the Dutch labor market, government advisers claimed that the government had "pampered" the minorities, who, according to this view, had become unwilling to take a job or to adapt to Dutch society at all. This sentiment is voiced in working-class neighborhoods (Bovenkerk, Bruin, Brunt, & Wouters, 1985, pp. 317-318) as well as in policymaking circles and by representatives of the intellectual "elite" (Brunt, Grijpma, & Harten, 1989). This introduces another, related ideological strand.

The second ideology is of increasing significance and concerns cultural pluralism. It has its basis in the rejection of biological determinism, the explicit norm of equality within cultural diversity, and the norm of tolerance. The idea of "egalitarianism" has, in common usage, become associated with "democracy." Implicitly, however, the ideology of pluralism assumes a hierarchical order of cultures. This can be inferred from the very notion of tolerance. "Tolerance for" is fundamentally different than "having respect for." The idea of tolerance only makes sense when it becomes clear that the current discourse of cultural pluralism is founded in the presupposition that pluralism is only possible if Blacks and other immigrants accept and internalize the fundamental norms and values of the dominant group. This is clearly implied in the government view that "cultural pluralism" should be possible and immigrants must be allowed to "keep their own cultural identity" *as long as they obey* the Dutch "legal order" (WRR, 1989, p. 24). Furthermore, those who pursue tolerance assume, by definition, that it is legitimate to limit the extent to which difference can be tolerated (Tennekes, 1985). The compatibility of cultural assimilationist practices and cultural pluralistic discourse is not surprising when one considers that those who desire to achieve in society usually have to pay the price of first adapting to and accepting the dominant culture. In the course of this book I portray and analyze the complex combinations of paternalistic, assimilationalist, and pluralistic forces structuring the experience of Blacks in the Netherlands.

Historical Overview

Because the race and ethnic relations of the Netherlands are largely unknown in other countries, a brief introduction is in order. The Netherlands has a population of 14 million, about 5% of whom are Blacks from the (ex)colonies and Mediterranean immigrant workers. Contemporary race and ethnic relations in the Netherlands must be placed in the context of colonization and decolonization of the Dutch overseas territories and the European south-north labor migration in the period after World War II. After the independence of Indonesia in 1949, about 280,000 Dutch passport-holders of European-Indonesian background were forced to immigrate to the Netherlands (Ellemers & Vaillant, 1985, pp. 34-42). A second group, about 12,500 Moluccans, most of them soldiers who had fought in the Dutch army against the Indonesian nationalists, were also forced to leave, with their families, after the independence of Indonesia (Schumacher, 1987, p. 17). The current number of Moluccans in the Netherlands is about 40,000 (WRR, 1989, p. 67). In many Dutch as well as English-language publications, the integration of Euro-Indonesians is usually praised as a perfect model of "tolerance" and harmonious acceptance of a group that was largely racially mixed (Bagley, 1973; Bovenkerk, 1978; Entzinger, 1984, p. 75; Simpson & Yinger, 1972, p. 6). Recent reinterpretations of the immigration of Euro-Indonesians, however, reveal that they were no less exposed to daily racism than later immigrants (Cottaar & Willems, 1984). Their integration into Holland was structured by factors of class, gender, and race. Euro-Indonesians with high-status backgrounds did not experience many problems entering the Netherlands, but they had to accept lower positions (Ellemers & Vaillant, 1985, p. 99). The Dutch government made attempts, though without success, to stop the large group of low-status Euro-Indonesians from immigrating to Holland, using among other things the argument that the "inherent nature" of these people would make them unsuited to living in the Netherlands (Mullard et al., 1988, pp. 15-16). The Euro-Indonesians arrived in a social context in which racism against East Asians was not a new phenomenon. Studies about Chinese immigrant workers in the cities of Amsterdam and Rotterdam in the beginning of this century make mention of police and state racism and xenophobia, culminating in racist *razzias* and forced deportation of Chinese workers in the years of the Great Depression (Wubben, 1986; Zeven, 1987). The Dutch government reacted to the immigration of Euro-Indonesians with forceful assimilation policies (Mullard et al., 1988, pp. 14-20). Perceived as culturally primitive, they were pressured to accept paternalistic guidance to imitate the Dutch way of life (Cottaar & Willems, 1984). This included the acceptance of specific Dutch gender role differentiations. Thus the women had to take courses in hygiene, housecleaning, and Dutch cooking, while the men had to participate in retraining courses.

As in other "highly developed" capitalistic nations in Europe, the migration to the Netherlands of workers from the Mediterranean countries took place in the context of the economic boom of the 1960s. Initially the Dutch recruited cheap labor from Italy, Spain, and Greece, but, with the rise of living standards in those countries, they recruited new labor in Turkey and Morocco. Together with their families, these laborers number about 320,000 (WRR, 1989, p. 66). Their structural position in the Netherlands is different than that of the immigrants from the colonies (Bel Ghazi, 1982). The large majority are workers who need a work permit to stay in the Netherlands. This makes their legal position fundamentally different than most immigrants from the colonies. The economic exploitation of immigrant workers is rationalized with a specific ideological form of racism based upon language, religion, nationality, and cultural divisions.

Among the immigrants from the Caribbean (ex-)colonies, the Surinamese, about 210,000, are the largest group (WRR, 1989, p. 68). They immigrated to the Netherlands because the Dutch colonizers had been in Suriname for four centuries, exploited its population, depleted its resources, and made its people structurally dependent on developments in the Netherlands. Small-scale migration from the Surinamese middle class and temporary migration of students had already started in the 1920s, followed by labor recruitment in the 1960s (Budike, 1982). The fast decline of the Surinamese economy, after a few years of growth around 1960, prompted many Surinamese to move to the Netherlands. In the 1970s, when large-scale migration from Suriname took place, the Dutch economy was declining and immigrants from Suriname, representing a large labor class and a small middle class, were, from the very beginning, excluded and marginalized in the Dutch labor market.

Like the Euro-Indonesians in the 1950s, the Surinamese were confronted with labor market discrimination combined with assimilation policies, in particular in housing and education (Ferrier, 1985; Mullard et al., 1988, p. 27). Note that, compared with race relations in the United States, there has been little social segregation of the Surinamese in the Netherlands because they have not been exclusively treated and defined in Dutch society as "workers" of another "race." However, increasing marginalization and developing Black consciousness among the youth may cause changes in this respect (Sanzone, 1990).

Summary of Research on Racism in the Netherlands

A more detailed conceptual discussion of the notion of racism will come later. Here a brief summary of research on racism in the Netherlands is provided. Racism as an ideology was probably latent in the Netherlands and only activated among the public when, with the immigration of "non-Whites," "race" became a topic of social discourse (Harmsen, van Leeuwen, & van Rijen, 1988; Kagie, 1989; Anne Frank Stichting, 1987). In the Netherlands early ideological traces of racism circulated predominantly among the elite, for instance, among clergymen, scholars, lawyers, doctors, traders, and representatives of Dutch parliament, who, in the mid-nineteenth century, discussed African slavery and the politics of abolition in the Dutch West Indian colonies (Reinsma, 1963). With the development of the school system for mass education in the late nineteenth century, notions of Black inferiority were also expressed in literature such as children's books (Redmond, 1980).

When large groups from Suriname migrated to the Netherlands, previously existing anti-Black notions were tested against new experiences and adapted to the new situation, in which Black groups were now within the Netherlands instead of only in the overseas colonies. In that process highly stereotypical, biologically defined prejudices against Blacks were activated and reformulated as culturally defined prejudices (Essed, 1986). Thus racial stereotypes of Blacks as inherently uncivilized, ugly, barbarian, dirty, aggressive, and stupid (Redmond, 1980, pp. 32-57) are partly replaced by cultural beliefs portraying Blacks as aggressive, lazy, and loud and as people who refuse to adapt to Dutch culture while abusing the benefits of the Dutch welfare system (van Dijk, 1984, p. 101, 1987a, p. 59). Some publications overemphasize the situation of Black "single" mothers, which may pathologize the Black family (e.g., Lenders & Rhoer, 1983). Others criminalize Black males with stereotypical studies of the so-called "hustler" culture (e.g., Buiks, 1983). The most persistent racist stereotype is that Blacks are less intelligent and less competent than Whites. We shall see this expressed in continuous underestimation of Black students in Dutch schools and in discrimination in the labor market.

The reproduction of Dutch racism in ideology and social discourse has been studied systematically in research involving newspapers (van Dijk, 1983, 1988, 1991), ordinary conversations (van Dijk, 1984, 1987a), and textbooks (Berg & Reinsch, 1983; Mok & Reinsch, 1988; van Dijk, 1987b). The general conclusions of the studies on textbooks are that examples of blatant racism are uncommon. More subtle forms prevail in which Black cultures are portrayed as deviant and backward. More specifically van Dijk's findings, in his study of social science textbooks for high school students, show that the issue of racism in the Netherlands is almost completely ignored (van Dijk, 1987b, pp. 89-90). When authors introduce the problem of racism at all, it is often explained as a race problem of "Negroes" in South Africa or in the United States (van Dijk, 1987b, p. 90). It is also relevant that, in the Dutch language, the common term for Blacks of African descent is still *neger* (Negro) and that, in contemporary comic strips and children's books, the "broad-lipped-wild-Negro-cannibal" image of the early nineteenth century has remained popular even into the 1980s (Brok, 1987; Redmond, 1980; Anne Frank Stichting, 1987).

The racist representations of Blacks in textbooks are similar to those communicated by the Dutch press. Blacks are predominantly represented in the context of problems they are assumed to create for Dutch people. They are portrayed as criminals, as people who complain too much, as violent, as a nuisance for Dutch society; in addition, it is assumed that the Dutch government pays too much attention to them (van Dijk, 1983, p. 58). This picture is supported by the fact that, if the press reports cases of racism at all, the newspapers routinely write the word *racism* between quotation marks. This is one of the strategic ways to question the experiences of Blacks, who encounter racism every day, and to mitigate the accounts and findings of Blacks and Whites involved in antiracist struggle.

These arguments indicate that since World War II, it has become taboo in the Netherlands to describe persons in terms of their "race" and to point out problems of racism. Whereas in publications just after the war, authors openly discussed problems of racial miscegenation, in particular in relation to Indonesians (Cottaar & Willems, 1984; Haas, 1987), which would be almost unthinkable today. This rejection of the term *race* does not mean that racial categorization is absent in Dutch thinking. However, it is as yet hard to assess precisely which elements of the "old" ideology have lost meaning, how surviving elements are represented in the new ideology, and which constellations of traditional and contemporary conceptions of race are used as organizing principles in commonsense notions. This taboo on explicit racial differentiations has often been mistaken for an absence of discrimination based on skin color, but recent research shows that "race" is still a determining factor in Dutch cognition and social action (see below).

Racist ideology is a social product, which has real effects only through regular patterns of action generating and articulating the ideology in, for instance, governmental policy, hiring patterns, education, service organizations, or the formulation of academic theories. This is indeed the case in the Netherlands. Despite the objections of the representatives of dominant social science in the Netherlands against the qualification of Dutch society as racist (Essed, 1987), one cannot disconnect racist ideas from the structural exclusion and marginalization of Blacks (and other immigrants) in the various sectors of society. Here I can touch only briefly on research findings about racial and ethnic discrimination.

The conditions of Blacks in housing, education, and the labor market are important indications of the degree of racial and ethnic injustice in society. In the area of housing the idea that Blacks and other immigrants do not belong in the Netherlands and that they may become a threat to Dutch national culture permeates dominant thinking from policymakers down to neighborhood dwellers. This is expressed through mechanisms of exclusion and through the requirement that Blacks adopt the Dutch way of living. A good example is the municipal assimilation policy of dispersing Blacks throughout the country. These policies were "successful," from the point of view of the government, in the case of the immigration of Euro-Indonesians in the 1950s, but they caused protest when applied to the Surinamese two decades later (Mullard et al., 1988, p. 27). Most Blacks and other immigrants live in the large cities, where some neighborhoods have become so-called concentration areas (Shadid & Kornalijnslijper, 1985, p. 11; Shadid, Kornalijnslijper, & Maan, 1985, pp. 97-100; Smit, 1985, p. 33). Despite objections against dispersion, these practices have not been abandoned (WRR, 1989, p. 188). The issue is still present, as demonstrated by protests frequently heard from the Dutch against Blacks in their neighborhoods (Shadid et al., 1985, p. 82). Dispersion may be rationalized with the argument that it prevents ghetto formation, but the real political implications are different. While there are good reasons to avoid overrepresentation of Blacks in areas with the worst housing conditions, the prevention of "concentration" also has other implications. Dispersion is a way to undermine resistance to racial oppression.

There is also direct discrimination against Blacks in housing. To obtain housing Blacks are predominantly dependent on municipalities and housing corporations, but they are frequently refused as tenants

(Kornalijnslijper, 1988, pp. 72-77). Research shows that some housing corporations favor Blacks who have acculturated in terms of language and life-style (Smit, 1985, p. 32). But even Blacks who, knowing about discrimination by private corporations, apply for municipal services are not protected against discrimination. Although the municipality intermediates between house owners and tenants, they do not take action against house owners who refuse to accept tenants on racial or ethnic grounds (Catau, 1988, p. 8). Finally, within the neighborhoods Blacks are often met with hostility and criticized for their different life-styles. From time to time they are confronted with anonymous racist slurs and threats, and some neighborhoods have even organized to keep the area "Dutch" (Affra-Meldkamer, 1986; Buis, 1988).

In education the same mechanisms of racism operate: exclusion and problematization of ethnic difference. In the cities school segregation caused by "White flight" has become a serious problem (Willemsen & van Oudenhoven, 1989, p. 14). Dutch parents complain that the school is not "Dutch" anymore (Dors, 1988, p. 47). Nevertheless the number of Black teachers in regular education is disproportionately low. This is even the case in schools with many Black pupils (Dors, 1988, p. 45). Black teachers are often only contracted for ethnically specific tasks. We shall see later in more detail that this "ethnization" of functions is an inherent product of the ideology of ethnic pluralism. It is also indicative of the structural marginalization of Blacks and of the institutionalization of the ethnic hierarchy in education. Compared with 44% of Dutch children, 62% of Surinamese children and 70% of Turkish and Moroccan children are tracked into the lowest levels of the education system (WRR, 1989, p. 142). Policymakers and teachers alike tend to see this situation as resulting from sociocultural deficiency (Dors, 1988, p. 43). Despite evidence that racism rather than cultural difference forms the major obstacle, little attention is paid to the Whitecentric nature of education, the racist views implied in many school textbooks, and the fact that White teachers continuously undervalue Black and other immigrant students (Dors, 1988; Essed, 1984; van Dijk, 1987b; Zee, 1988).

With 40%-45% unemployment, compared with the average unemployment rate of 14%, the situation of Blacks in the labor market is extremely problematic (Willemsen, 1988, p. 51). The factor of education can only partly account for high unemployment. Surveys show that even among Antillians, a group with a proportionally higher representation of college-educated members than the Dutch, there is over

40% unemployment (Emancipatieraad, 1988, p. 23). This suggests that unemployment among Blacks is largely due to racism (Choenni & Zwan, 1987a, p. 6, 1989, pp. 5-7; Willemsen, 1988, p. 59). The same mechanisms of racism discussed in the context of education occur with labor. Blacks are excluded and underestimated at all levels: from employers and employment agencies to managers and colleagues. Thus studies of labor market politics revealed an explicit preference among Dutch managers for employees with White skin color (Reubsaet & Kropman, 1985). Employment agencies routinely accept and process employers' requests to seek only White Dutch applicants (Uyl, Choenni, & Bovenkerk, 1986, see below). Recent surveys have shown that 53% of Dutch personnel managers, questioned about what decision they would make if they had to choose between equally qualified White and Black or migrant applicants, stated a preference for employees with White skin color (Willemsen, 1988, pp. 61-62). In addition the use of culturally biased psychology tests adds further to the exclusion and marginalization of Blacks in the labor market (Choenni & Zwan, 1987b).

Blacks and other immigrants who manage to get jobs are systematically excluded from representative functions. Many experience discrimination from colleagues as well as from supervisors (Bouw & Nelissen, 1986; KMAN, 1985; Sikking & Brassé, 1987). In interaction with colleagues Blacks are often harassed with racist jokes and other irritations. They are patronized and bullied by supervisors. This is particularly problematic considering that the role of supervisors is a crucial determinant of the racial climate. It is much more difficult to deal with racism from supervisors, because they are in a position of authority. However, their attitude can reinforce racism among others. Conversely racism on the job decreases when supervisors are motivated to prevent prejudice and discrimination in the department (Brassé & Sikking, 1988, p. 22). Racial discrimination on the job is reinforced at the level of labor organizations. An inquiry into one of the Dutch unions showed that White union members reject union support for racial and ethnic equality claims, for instance, in the form of specific measures. In general they feel that the "foreigners" should adapt to the Dutch standard (Jongh, Laan, & Rath, 1984, pp. 231-232).

Racism in housing, education, and the labor market is reinforced at other levels of society, such as discrimination by the police and in the courtroom. At the police station complaints about racism are not taken seriously. Police officers may refuse to take down the complaint altogether and accuse Blacks of exaggerating (Biegel, Böcker, & Tjoen-Tak-Sen, 1988). Other research also points to racial prejudice among the police (Aalberts & Kamminga, 1983; Luning, 1976). In the street Blacks are frequently subjected to police harassment, such as unwarranted searches (Affra-Meldkamer, 1986, pp. 14-17). In addition they serve longer sentences than Dutch convicted for similar crimes (Beer, 1988, p. 20).

The criminalization of Blacks also characterizes their experiences in other spheres of everyday life. In shops, citizens who look "un-Dutch" are more likely to be accused of theft, followed by the security officer, or treated rudely (Essed, 1984, pp. 136-146). Security officers for public transportation repeatedly harass Black passengers (Affra-Meldkamer, 1986, pp. 10-13). Insurance companies feel Blacks and other immigrants are more likely to commit fraud. Some refuse to accept people on racial or ethnic grounds; others charge too much money or give insufficient information (Pattipawae, 1986, pp. 10-11; Pattipawae & Burght, 1988).

These examples and much other evidence of discrimination, as regularly reported in the Bulletin of the National Bureau to Combat Racism (LBR), indicate that racism is a structural problem in the Netherlands. Nevertheless representatives of dominant social science consistently object to the interpretation of discrimination against Blacks as indications of racism (Essed, 1987). This attitude obstructs the need to take structural action against processes of racial and ethnic marginalization.

To summarize: Racism is part of social practice at many levels of Dutch society. It is a complex phenomenon because it involves ideological notions rooted in different historical processes, such as colonialism, European labor migration, and the management of economic crisis. The ideological form of racism that justified slavery and colonization attributes to Blacks biological and cultural characteristics perceived as inferior. The ideological form of racism that justifies immigrant labor exploitation and is used to regulate the position of immigrant workers asserts the idea of "natural hostility" against "foreigners" and the incompatibility of different cultures (Barker, 1981). These different ideological and structural processes combine in the current pluralization process that regulates the position of the Dutch dominant group vis-à-vis ethnic groups.

The situation of Surinamese Blacks, the group to which the women I interviewed in the Netherlands belong, is characterized by structural disempowerment and pressures to assimilate culturally under the veneer of "integration with the retention of cultural identity" (Entzinger, 1984, p. 88). These forces of oppression can best be qualified as a situation of "pluralistic assimilation" (Mullard et al., 1988, pp. 46, 51), which means the use of pluralistic strategies with the aim of assimilation. This view needs some moderation. The denial of the Surinamese cultures—a heritage of Dutch colonialism—conflicts, to a certain degree, with cultural pluralism. We shall see that the tension between the denial of culture, on the one hand, and the tendency to overemphasize cultural difference to control the process of "integration," on the other hand, has a great impact on the experiences of Black women in the Netherlands.

SOME NOTES ON CONTEMPORARY RACISM IN THE UNITED STATES

The period after World War II has been characterized by economic fluctuation. When industrial production was gradually replaced by technological production, many working-class Blacks lost their jobs. The economic position of Blacks has deteriorated during the structural crisis of U.S. and world capitalism in the past two decades (Marable, 1985). This holds even for the Black middle class, part of which has origins in the period before the war (Frazier, 1957/1962; Marable, 1983; Muraskin, 1975) and part of which emerged in the context of an expanding economy in the 1960s and early 1970s (Landry, 1987). Affirmative action programs contributed to the growth of Black professionals (Marable, 1984; Pinkney, 1984). In statistical terms there has been substantial progress in Black educational attainment. The proportion of Blacks completing high school increased from 33% in 1960 to 79% in 1982. However, the proportion of Blacks with a college degree is still 13%, compared with 25% for White college graduates (Blackwell, 1988, p. 7). Except for a short period of progress at the heyday of affirmative action, the recruitment of Black faculty members has decreased in the 1980s. In other words, there has been some progress but at the same time the basic power relations remained the same. Employment processes continue to result in racial inequality (Braddock & McPartland, 1987; Katz & Prohansky, 1987). Racism is often even more subtle and difficult to combat. On the one hand, the discourse of racism changed to meet the new norms that reject overt expressions of bigotry. At the same time, as various critics point out, the Reagan administration made forms of bigotry look "respectable" (Blackwell, 1988, p. 11). Desegregation has remained a problematic process (Pettigrew, 1971, 1986). Consequently contact theory continues to be the object of numerous studies and experiments (Miller & Brewer, 1984; Miller, Brewer, & Edwards, 1985; Slavin, 1985). It has been argued that desegregation in schools has positive long-term effects, such as better access of Black students to social networks relevant for their careers (Braddock & McPartland, 1987), but these gains must be weighed against the many ceilings still prevalent in Black career mobility (Fullbright, 1986). In the absence of comprehensive programs against racism at all levels of society, the outcomes of school desegregation also have had controversial sides. Black cultural values are repressed in White institutions. This problem is addressed later in the stories of Black women. Black professionals lost the (managing and directing) jobs they used to have in Black institutions, and in White institutions they constantly have to fight the everyday inequities impeding their careers (Pettigrew & Martin, 1987). There has also been little progress in terms of residential segregation (Bobo, 1988). Whites keep avoiding voluntary contact with Blacks. During the past 15 years overall segregation has even increased. As Smith (1988, p. 9) put it, "Racial insularity [is] still at the core" of contemporary racism.

Various social scientists, in particular social psychologists, have studied the specific nature of racism in the 1970s and 1980s. As a result new concepts were introduced, compared, and criticized (Pettigrew, 1985; Sniderman & Tetlock, 1986; Weigel & Howes, 1985). Interesting in various of these studies is their concern with the way new norms about racism pertain to the persistence of prejudice and discrimination. Gaertner and Dovidio (1986) studied the conflict between egalitarian beliefs of liberal Whites and unacknowledged negative feelings and beliefs about Blacks. In maintaining nondiscriminating self-concepts, these negative feelings lead to avoidance of Blacks. Gaertner and Dovidio called this particular kind of ambivalence "aversive racism," a concept originally introduced by Kovel (1970/1984). Sears and Kinder (1971) introduced the term *symbolic racism* to explain how individuals might hold relatively progressive racial attitudes as a matter of principle yet disapprove of the policy implications to bring about racial equality (Kinder, 1986; Sears, 1988). The idea of "modern racism" (McConahay, 1986) summarizes the main tenets of prevalent neoconservative attitudes about racial issues as follows: (a) The gains of the civil rights movement have made discrimination a thing of the past, (b) therefore, Blacks should not push so hard, (c) their tactics and demands are undemocratic and unfair, (d) therefore, Blacks are getting more attention from the institutions of society than they deserve. Today more and more liberals appear to be joining with the conservatives in adopting these tenets of "modern racism." This retreat from the pursuit of equality between Blacks and Whites began with a sophisticated attack on affirmative action in higher education, because in this sector Blacks gained most from equal opportunity policies. These different approaches to the changing nature of racism have in common a focus on contradictory attitudes: the real or token acknowledgment of the norm of equality in a "democratic" society and (un)acknowledged reluctance in accepting the policy and personal consequences of the idea of racial equality (Schuman, Steeh, & Bobo, 1985). This suggests that the norm of equality is a key concept in the dominant ideology and that this interferes with existing racist beliefs and practices.

To understand the specific nature of contemporary racism, it is necessary to proceed from the level of individual attitudes to the larger economic, political, and ideological processes in society. The terms *aversive, symbolic,* and *modern* racism do not completely explain what must, in fact, be seen as the culturalization of racism. This process is inherent in the redefinition of society as ethnically pluralist. Ideals of the "melting pot" and "integration" are being replaced by the ideology of cultural pluralism. Glazer and Moynihan (1963/1968, p. 17) presented the idea of ethnic groups as interest groups in their attempt to reach beyond the melting pot. Since then the concept of ethnic diversity or, more specifically, ethnic pluralism has been adopted by various others (Glazer & Young, 1983; Light, 1972; Sowell, 1981). The political practice of pluralism holds that all groups are defined as "equal" within ethnic diversity. This view can be used by individual members of the dominant group to claim reverse discrimination when programs are launched to compensate for past discrimination against those who were unjustly denied positions they deserved (Goldman, 1979). Indeed the substitution of "ethnicity" for "race" as a basis of categorization is accompanied by increasing unwillingness among the dominant group to accept responsibility for problems of racism. Furthermore, the redefinition of Blacks as an "ethnic minority" group provides a basis for the state to use the emphasis on ethnic identity as an instrument of control (Mullard, 1986b). They may shift support from one "minority" group to another, favoring above Blacks other "minority" groups who are perceived as less threatening or as "model minorities." These "divide and rule" practices are further supported by the increasing resistance among White Americans to affirmative action (Glazer, 1975).

Another problem with the concept of pluralism and the idea that all groups are or have been immigrants and "minorities" is that it denies the unique position of Blacks in American history:

> In a significant way, European immigrants over the past century and Blacks face opposite cultural problems. The new Europeans were seen as not "American" enough; the dominant pressure on them was to give up their strange and threatening ways and to assimilate. Blacks were Americans of a lower caste; the pressure on them was to "stay in their place" and not attempt assimilation into the mainstream culture of the privileged. (Pettigrew, 1988, p. 24)

In other words the concepts of assimilation and pluralism that were introduced for other ethnic groups were not meant for Blacks. From the beginning it was never imagined that America would mean opportunity and dreams coming true for Africans (Huggins, 1977, p. 84). The (sub)cultures of all immigrant ethnic groups were recognized. They were criticized for being "different" because it was expected that they would assimilate. The Black experience has been completely different. They were never meant to assimilate. Their history is characterized by segregation. Their cultural heritage has never positively been recognized as distinct, original, and valuable in the struggle for survival (Marable, 1980). Social scientists even denigrated the survival strategies and values Blacks developed under conditions of oppression. This and other critiques have been leveled by various critical scholars who point out that, since Moynihan (1965) popularized ethnicity as an explanatory concept in the sociology of U.S. race relations, Black cultural "deficiency" has been used widely as an argument to blame Blacks themselves for impeding their own progress (Chesler, 1976; Rainwater & Yancey, 1967). As Lawrence (1982a) argues, in many of these studies, Black culture is not treated as an original and historical experience inherently related to specific material and political conditions but is reduced to one construct: the "pathological" Black household.

To summarize: Anti-Black racism in the United States is still characterized by overall segregation, in particular in residential areas. On

an ideological level, however, there is a shift from biological to social
and cultural rationalizations for discrimination. Normative changes
(rejection of blatant racism) combine with an increasing reluctance to
see race as a fundamental determinant of White privilege and Black
poverty. What others have called "new" forms of racism are, in fact,
indicative of the "culturalization" of racism, accompanying the reformulation of society as "multiethnic."

WOMEN AND RACISM

Twice in U.S. history the Black liberation struggle gave birth to a
feminist movement. In the abolition movement of the nineteenth century and the civil rights movement of the 1960s, Black women gained
strength and power in their struggle for rights for women and rights
for Blacks (Braden, 1977; Davis, 1981; Evans, 1977, 1979;
Loewenberg & Bogin, 1976; Sterling, 1984). In both centuries, however, Black women have been confronted with racism in the feminist
movement (Essed, 1982, 1989; Hooks, 1981; Rich, 1979; Terborg-
Penn, 1978) and sexism in their relation to Black men (Hernton,
1990; Wallace, 1978). Their critiques about these problems have had
a certain impact. Many now recognize that the simultaneous impact
of race, gender, and class oppression leads to forms of racism that are
unique to the experiences of Black women, but, in their manifestations, overlap some forms of sexism against White women and racism
experienced by Black men (Ramazanoglu, 1989; Smith & Stewart,
1983). Black women claim their own place in theory and history (Aldridge, 1989; Braxton & McLaughlin, 1990; Collins, 1990; Dill,
1987; Hull, Scott, & Smith, 1982; Smith, 1977). Over the past two decades there has been an explosion of literature exposing us to the
struggle of Black women through Black women as writers as well as
through writings about Black women (Baraka & Baraka, 1983; Bell
et al., 1979; Brittan & Maynard, 1984; Cade, 1970; Evans, 1983;
Hemmons, 1973; Hull, 1984; Lorde, 1984, 1988; Shockley, 1989;
Simms & Malveaux, 1986; Smith, 1983; Sterling, 1979).

Many of these publications testify that racism not only operates as
a distinct ideology and structure, it also interacts with other ideologies and structures of domination (Brandt, 1986; Hooks, 1984, 1989).
Some authors have explicitly criticized rigid economic reductionism
and argued that Black women in White-dominated societies often

experience economic exploitation through race (Bourne, 1983; Bryan, Dazie, & Scafe, 1985; Davis, 1989; Joseph, 1981). The same may be said of gender oppression. In a summary article on Black feminism, Stasiulis (1987, p. 5) stresses that, in relation to White society, Black feminists "have reached near unanimity in agreeing that race, rather than gender, has been the primary source of oppression." Indeed various authors contend that Black women experience sexism in society at large through racist and ethnicist constructions of gender (Jones, 1985; Ladner, 1972; Parmar, 1982; Spelman, 1988; Steady, 1985; Wallace, 1978). Are we stuck with a dilemma here? In discussing the experiences of Black women, is it sexism or is it racism? These two concepts narrowly intertwine and combine under certain conditions into one, hybrid phenomenon. Therefore, it is useful to speak of *gendered racism* to refer to the racial oppression of Black women as structured by racist and ethnicist perceptions of gender roles (Carby, 1982, p. 214; Parmar, 1982, p. 237). Note that not only Black women but also Black men are confronted with racism structured by racist constructions of gender role, notable examples being the absent father stereotype or the myth of the Black rapist (Duster, 1970; Hernton, 1965). Further elaboration upon this issue, however, goes beyond the immediate goals of this study (see, for further discussion Wilkinson & Taylor, 1977). The applicability of the notion of gendered racism may be demonstrated with illustrations of White perceptions of Black women.

There are virtually no studies about Dutch perceptions of Black women. White images of Black women in the Netherlands probably include general notions of cultural inferiority because it is usually believed that people from the colonies are backward and that the "mother country" is better than anything they have known before (Memmi, 1965). There are some indications that Black women are perceived as sexually exotic and permissive (Essed, 1984; Lima, 1988; Pheterson, 1986). Also there are problems of paternalism rationalized by the assumption that Black women are lagging behind in their emancipation, as women, compared with White women (Essed, 1982, 1989; Loewenthal, 1984). It is likely that Dutch images of Black women are also strongly influenced by U.S. culture, in particular through literature, television series, and movies. It is, therefore, relevant to elaborate more specifically the dominant representations of Black women in the United States.

There is increasing documentation on the image of Black women in U.S. literature and culture (Gilman, 1985; Robinson, 1978). These images are rooted in the exploitation of Blacks as slaves, workers, and, with respect to Black women, in particular as domestic workers (Dill, 1980; Rollins, 1985). Note that the sexual and economic exploitation of female slaves in the Dutch colonies was essentially the same as in the United States. This may be inferred from various publications (e.g., H. Essed, 1984; Hoogbergen & de Theye, 1987; Oomens, 1987). Racially specific gender ideologies rationalized the suitability of Black women for jobs in the lowest stratum of the labor market already segmented along gender lines. Black women's work was restricted almost exclusively to manual labor. The nature of their work crossed gender lines. During slavery Black women were exploited sexually as women and had to do work defined as typically female work, but at the same time they were also forced to do the same arduous work as men (Aptheker, 1982; Davis, 1971; Fox-Genovese, 1988; Lerner, 1972; White, 1985). After the abolition of slavery, Black women had to take the worst-paying jobs in both "male" and "female" sectors of work. Black women have had to wash trains, have been employed as lumberyard workers, as brickyard workers, and have done other heavy work White women did not do (Jones, 1985). At the same time the majority of Black women could only find work as domestics in White households, due to blatant discrimination that limited the number of Blacks in semiskilled and skilled jobs (Hine, 1989). Only in the mid-1960s, when federal legislation forced by the civil rights movement launched an attack on racial discrimination, could Black women gain entrance to the traditional (White) female occupations, especially clerical work that had so long been denied to them (Jones, 1985). Black women were tracked into the worst paying semiskilled and skilled jobs defined as (White) woman's work. These gendered and classed forms of racism were rationalized by ideological constructions of racially specific femininity and sexuality, representing the opposite models of White (middle-class) womanhood. Also the standard of female beauty represents a White standard (Lakoff & Scherr, 1984; Reid, 1988). Contrary to the patriarchal image of White, middle-class women as weak, dependent, passive, and monogamous, Black women were thought of as hardworking, strong, dominant, and sexually promiscuous (Davis, 1981; Hooks, 1981). The "Aunt Jemima" image epitomized the sexist/racist/classist stereotype of Black women. Black women were supposed to be subservient and willing to nurture White children at the cost of their own children. These images of Black women rationalized the violation of the role of Black women as mothers and the control of Black women through rape and sexual exploitation (Davis, 1978, 1981; Hooks, 1981).

The economic recession after World War II and the change from industrial to technological production made many unskilled Black workers redundant. The deteriorated economic conditions of the majority of the Black population and mass unemployment led to an increase of families headed by Black women (McAdoo, 1986; Simms, 1986). Within this context the image of the Black matriarch was revived (Moynihan, 1965). This stereotype combines sexist, racist, and classist images of Black women, thereby reinforcing gender polarization in the Black community. After ignoring the economic necessity for Black women to work outside the home, many have accused them of taking jobs away from Black men and alienating Black men from their role as head of the family. These blaming the victim arguments have been criticized many times (Rainwater & Yancey, 1967; Rodgers-Rose, 1980; Ryan, 1971; Staples, 1970, 1973). Recently, however, conservative views are again being used to reinforce cultural determinist explanations of Black poverty.

Black women have a stronger tradition of autonomy and independence. It has been claimed that Black women are more assertive and nonconforming than White women in sex role ideology because of their longer experience as paid workers and their continuous challenge of racism and sexism (Adams, 1983; Malson, 1983). Although some find that the self-sufficiency-independence thesis has been overstated (Ransford & Miller, 1983), the stereotype of the Black matriarch remains operative and must, therefore, also be understood in terms of its sexist implications. Morrison (1989, p. 48) put it nicely when she stated: "I don't think a female running a house is a problem. . . . It's perceived as one because of the notion that a head is a man." Whereas aggressiveness and dominance are considered positive (White male) characteristics in a highly competitive capitalistic society, the same characteristics become negative when attributed to Black women. These negative images of Black women are currently reinforced through literature and the media (Joseph & Lewis, 1981) and affect all Black women, regardless of their class background. They rationalize forces in society to keep Black women in the lower strata. Thus they can be used flexibly, to rationalize the exploitation of Black women as workers as well as the range of discriminatory practices that impede Black women with higher education in their efforts to achieve their goals.

BLACK WOMEN WITH HIGHER EDUCATION

If we want to gain more insight into the racial aspects of the oppression of Black women, the factor of race has to be isolated from the oppressive social and economic conditions associated with low education and economic exploitation. To avoid problems related to the assessment of the class position of Black women, I have used an indirect indicator of class, namely, level of education. Thus I focus on Black women with a higher education. For the study of racism this is a particularly interesting group because, traditionally, Black women consider personal achievement through education a key element, if not the most important opportunity, in advancing in society (Giddings, 1988; Perkins, 1983; Smith, 1982; Wilkerson, 1986). While class oppression limits the economic resources and educational opportunities of the majority of Black women, race-gender discrimination on the labor market undercuts the middle-class benefits of education (Burlew, 1982; Jones, 1986; Malveaux, 1986, 1987; Wallace, 1980). Black women consistently have a higher rate of unemployment and lower incomes than Black men (Fernandez, 1981, p. 73). These and other forms of (gendered) racism that impede Black women with higher education in their careers are briefly summarized. Due to the virtual absence of information about Black women in higher education in the Netherlands, the following is based predominantly on data from the United States.

There are a number of structural problems Black women face in higher education and in obtaining and keeping jobs. First, the lack of role models puts them in a disadvantaged position compared with White women. Black women attending predominantly White universities also feel isolated from other Black women because there are few Black women in positions to support them in academic institutions (Carroll, 1982). Second, they are routinely underestimated. This is particularly problematic when it comes from individuals in position of authority, as was found by Fullbright (1986), who studied the career development of Black female managers. Those who had used guidance counseling services in high school reported that counselors had low expectations of them. They were always guided to traditionally female occupations and low-status schools. The tendency to underestimate Black women stands in sharp contrast to their usually high ambitions. The same forces operating against equal participation of Black women in education continue to be present on the labor market. Comparing the job opportunities for highly educated Black women with those of Black men, it appears that Black women usually get the worst paying jobs. Black women have always been a minority among Black physicians, principals, architects, attorneys, and other professionals (Carroll, 1982; Epstein, 1973; Giddings, 1986).

Third, Fullbright found that Black women do not get the same promotions as White women. They are confronted with artificial ceilings created by individuals in corporations who have control over the distribution of work and promotions and who regularly review the performance of the women (Fullbright, 1986). Black women have to meet higher demands than any other group. Compared with Black and White men, they have to be better qualified, more articulate, and more aggressive, and they need more stamina to face inevitable setbacks and fewer opportunities for promotion. Yet they have to conform to the ideal of White femininity, which means that they cannot afford to appear threatening. In addition, Black women must also be better than White women (Carroll, 1982).

Fourth, Black women in the higher skilled jobs are often pushed into "ethnic" work. In one of the few studies of this problem conducted in the Netherlands, indications were found of a decline of job opportunities for Black women (with higher education) in "general" sectors and a move toward work in the "ethnic sector" (Kempadoo, 1988). For some women who had been working in jobs that were not previously ethnically earmarked, this could imply a gradual "ethnization" of their tasks. Although Kempadoo's sample was too small to draw general conclusions, her findings are consistent with developments in the United Kingdom. Mullard (1986b) pointed out that state control operates through the appointment of accommodating "ethnic" agents for work in the "ethnic" sectors. Kempadoo's findings are highly significant in the Dutch context, because she tentatively sketched the contours of structural marginalization of Black women through policies based on ethnic diversity. They are appointed, usually on contract basis, to work with "ethnic groups." At the same time it is expected that they will conform, in their interactions with colleagues and supervisors, to Dutch norms and rules of behavior. Thus it was found that employers often use acculturation as a criterion for hiring Black women (Kempadoo, 1988).

From this discussion it may be concluded that on a macro-societal level, (gendered) racism operates through various mechanisms. Black women are (a) marginalized, (b) culturally problematized, and (c) impeded in social mobility. They encounter paternalism, they are underestimated, their work is ethnicized, and they generally have fewer career opportunities than men and White women, respectively. These mechanisms operate simultaneously and probably stimulate each other.

Given the fact that race is an actively structuring principle, it is relevant to identify in detail how racism is projected in the experiences of Black women. To understand the impact of racism in the everyday lives of Black women, one needs to go beyond issues of career problems to include racial experiences in all other spheres of life, which comprise personal experiences with racism in shops, in the street, at the university or in the workplace as well as racism experienced through friends and family, racist practices in children's schools, and other confrontations with racism such as in literature or the media. At the same time we should analyze how processes of racism that occur in different social contexts relate to each other. To study everyday racism it is, therefore, necessary to analyze it as a process manifesting itself in multiple relations and situations in everyday life.

CONCEPTUALIZING RACISM AS A PROCESS

The Fallacies of "Institutional" and "Individual" Racism

My approach to racism draws on structural theories of racism. I have, however, tried to overcome some of the shortcomings of earlier studies. One major problem was the distinction between institutional and individual racism. It places the individual outside the institutional, thereby severing rules, regulations, and procedures from the people who make and enact them, as if it concerned qualitatively different racism rather than different positions and relations through which racism operates.

The notion of "institutional racism" is a central concept in many structural approaches. Whereas Carmichael and Hamilton (1967), Knowles and Prewitt (1969), and others rightly went beyond Myrdal's definition of racism as a moral dilemma (Myrdal, 1944/1972), and beyond the Kerner Report's list of conditions of Black riots (Kerner Commission, 1968/1988), the distinction between so-called individual racism and institutional racism is not unproblematic. The notion of the "institutional" is notoriously difficult in sociology because it has been given various meanings. Some researchers use the terms *institu-*

tion and *institutional* to identify structuring relations of the ruling apparatus organized around different functions. This definition of *institutional* has been used in various European studies to narrow the problem of racism down to "institutional discrimination." Usually these approaches have a pragmatic orientation that underrates the power of ideology in the structuring of racism in society (e.g., Daniel, 1968/1971; Smith, 1977).

The term *individual racism* is a contradiction in itself because racism is by definition the expression or activation of group power. Some authors tried to find alternative solutions to set apart "institutional racism" against "other racism." Brandt (1986, p. 101) distinguishes between interactional racism and institutional racism, but he does not make clear why this is an improvement over the usual distinction between "individual" and "institutional" racism. However, he introduces another interesting concept, namely, "systemic racism." The systemic realization of institutional racism he refers to in terms of "day-to-day interactions" within institutions (Brandt, 1986, p. 102). In an excellent article Rowe (1977, p. 1) speaks in this context of "micro-inequities," which she defines as "destructive, but practicably-speaking non-actionable, aspects of the environment." Systemic racism "marks the meeting point between structural and interactional forms of racism and exists within the specificity of the 'ethos' or sociocultural environment of the organization" (p. 102). Brandt (1986, p. 102) contends that the systemic is also structural. However, he does not further work out his idea of systemic racism, which, therefore, remains rather vague. He also insists on defining systemic racism in terms of "institutional racism." Compared with many other studies, this notion probably comes closest to the meaning of everyday racism, which is the interweaving of racism in the fabric of the social system. Still the notion of everyday racism transcends the traditional distinctions between institutional and individual racism.

Everyday racism has two obvious constituent elements. One part pertains to the notion of racism and the other to the notion of "everyday." To understand Black women's experiences of everyday racism, the following concepts must be implemented: (a) the notion of racism, (b) the notion of everyday, (c) the notion of everyday racism, (d) the idea of experience, and (e) the notion of accounts of racism. The notions of racism, everyday, and everyday racism are discussed first. The meaning and methodological implications of the use of experiences and accounts are discussed later (see Chapter 2).

RACISM: A WORKING DEFINITION

My critique of structural studies of racism has already suggested that a working definition of racism must acknowledge the macro (structural-cultural) properties of racism as well as the micro inequities perpetuating the system. It must take into account the constraining impact of entrenched ideas and practices on human agency, but it must also acknowledge that the system is continually construed in everyday life and that, under certain conditions, individuals resist pressures to conform to the needs of the system. Traditional sociological approaches have defined macro structures as more or less independent of the practices in daily life. Moreover macrosociologists usually consider institutions and structures as somehow above the mundane level of practice and experience. My intention to go beyond macro social facts in addressing practice and the social reality of racism has been inspired, initially, by phenomenology, symbolic interactionism, ethnomethodology, and cognitive sociology. These interpretative and micro orientations emphasize from various points of view the active nature of human conduct and try to understand its meaning, reasons, and experience (Berger & Luckmann, 1966; Blumer, 1969; Brittan, 1973; Cicourel, 1973; Douglas, 1970/1974; Garfinkel, 1967; Goffman, 1959, 1961, 1967, 1969, 1974; Helle & Eisenstadt, 1985; Leiter, 1980; Luckmann, 1978; Mehan & Wood, 1975; Rogers, 1983; Schutz, 1970). More significant to my approach have become, however, recent developments in social theory that try to overcome the rigorous distinction between micro and macro approaches (Alexander et al., 1987; Collins, 1981a, 1983; Fielding, 1988; Giddens, 1984; Knorr-Cetina & Cicourel, 1981). This is not, of course, to imply any necessary agreement among these authors. A problem with most of the work mentioned is, however, that it is useful in theorization but lacks adequate implementation, especially when applied to the area of racism.

Despite these limitations two major attempts to integrate macro and micro dimensions of the system are particularly important for my purposes. The aggregation hypothesis advanced by Collins (1981b) contends that macrosociological reality is composed of aggregates of micro situations. The representation hypothesis (Cicourel, 1981), which comes close to the aggregation hypothesis, argues that macro social facts, or structures, are produced in interactions. These theoretical frameworks emphasize the role of routine and repetitive practices in the making of social structures. We shall see that routine and repetition play an important role in my theory of everyday racism. However, I depart to a certain degree from these approaches by giving greater weight to the mutual interdependence of macro and micro dimensions of racism. From a macro point of view, racism is a system of structural inequalities and a historical process, both created and re-created through routine practices. *System* means reproduced social relations between individuals and groups organized as regular social practices (Giddens, 1981). From a micro point of view, specific practices, whether their consequences are intentional or unintentional, can be evaluated in terms of racism only when they are consistent with (our knowledge of) existing macro structures of racial inequality in the system. In other words, structures of racism do not exist external to agents—they are made by agents—but specific practices are by definition racist only when they activate existing structural racial inequality in the system.

Racism as Power

Racism then is defined in terms of cognitions, actions, and procedures that contribute to the development and perpetuation of a system in which Whites dominate Blacks. Note that racial domination, as I pointed out earlier, interacts with dynamic forces of gender and class domination. The general issue of gender and class (Barrett, 1980) is not my major concern here. Neither is of concern the general issue of race and class. While many writers have shown particular interest in race-class debates (see Harris, 1987; Solomos, 1986, for an overview), a pure class perspective of racism is adequate to account neither for the distinctly racial experiences of Black women (Omi & Winant, 1986; Solomos, 1989; West, 1987) nor for the experience of gender oppression through race (Carby, 1982; Parmar, 1982). The need for an alternative approach is also supported by the experienced reality. We shall see later that Black women with higher education present their stories about everyday racism predominantly in terms of race or in terms of race-gender but not frequently in terms of class. When I state that it is relevant in this study to isolate conceptually (gendered) racism from class oppression, this does not mean that the conceptualization of everyday racism cannot benefit from major insights developed in a class perspective of domination.

Domination constitutes a special case of power. To conceptualize how racism, as a complex system of power, shapes the ways in which social relations and practices are actually experienced by Black women, I draw on major insights of some people who have worked on the notion of power. However, I do not necessarily adopt the whole conceptual framework of these works. The concept of power I use is based on two different meanings derived from Arendt (1970) and Lukes (1974). The combination of their perceptions of power is useful to integrate macro and micro dimensions of racism. Arendt (1970) argues that power is never the property of an individual. It belongs to a group as long as the group stays together. Therefore, power pertains to the human ability not only to act but to act in concert. This view of power is relevant to the study of racism for the following reasons: It enables us to conceptualize relations between White and Black individuals in terms of power relations, for they are representatives of groups with relatively more and relatively less power. This implies that the consciously or unconsciously felt security of belonging to the group in power, plus the expectation that other group members will give (passive) consent, empowers individual members of the dominant group in their acts or beliefs against the dominated group.

The extent to which the expectation of group consensus is a relevant source of empowerment is understood better when we take the following concrete example. The current norm that racism is "wrong" has a certain disempowering impact on individual members of the dominant group. Today the almost universal rejection of racism is often experienced by Whites as a restriction. They feel that they can no longer express what they feel about Blacks because others will accuse them of racism. This is experienced as an unfair situation. Various representatives of the Dutch intellectual establishment complain about what they call the "taboo" against expressing negative opinions about Blacks and other immigrants (Köbben, 1985, p. 55; Vuijsje, 1986, p. 21). They feel that the norm against racism has made them prisoners of their own "tolerance." At the same time anti-antiracist sentiments among other scholars, journalists, or policymakers have an empowering effect. These opinions are expressed in the media and are part of the intellectual attack on antiracism. Various intellectuals are overcoming the taboo against expressing racist views. Opponents of racism are accused of exaggerating and of denying "benevolent" Whites the "right" to give a "healthy" critique on Blacks who they feel are unwilling to progress and to integrate themselves into the system (e.g., Brunt et al., 1989). The attack on antiracism is also a prominent topic in the conservative British press (Murray, 1986; van Dijk,

1991). As Solomos (1989, p. 137) puts it, "Today, the most strident voices in the mass media and in academic discourse are raised not against racism but against . . . antiracism." The experiences of Black women will testify to the implied indifference among Whites to racism.

Group power exists as long as the group stays together against the "others." This introduces the second characteristic of power as a quality of the group. Arendt's view of power provides a basis for understanding the crucial role of racist ideologies, not only as rationalization of existing inequalities but also as determinants of future uniformity of action. This means that ideology is the binding element between practices involving different actors and situations. To keep the group intact it is necessary to cultivate ideologies supporting the idea of innate group differences based on "race" or ethnicity. Group power can only empower individuals when they have a sense of group membership. Therefore, it is necessary to keep alive a permanent sense of "us" (dominant group) as opposed to "them" (dominated groups). This point is elaborated at length in Memmi (1983) and Barker (1981). Here Lukes would speak of exercising influence to achieve and to maintain consensus (Lukes, 1974, p. 3). When dominant group members implicitly or explicitly rely on group consensus in support of anti-Black actions, they make use of an important power resource.

It is difficult to define where the determinism of group power ends and the exercise of power by individuals begins. From a macro point of view racism only exists as a specific variant of group power. From a micro point of view racism as group power only exists because it was created and is maintained through individuals. Because racism is a form of power, it must be assumed that it involves conflict of interests between two parties. At this point Lukes's notion of power is important (Lukes, 1974).

Lukes's notion of power is particularly useful in understanding situations where conflict between groups is not openly acknowledged as such. He sees as the central quality of power the attempt to successfully secure people's compliance by overcoming or averting their opposition. Exercising power over other people affects them, through action or inaction, in a manner contrary to their interests, whether or not those who exercise power are aware of the success or consequences of their practices and whether or not the other party is aware of the power being exercised over him or her. We will see later that dominant group members often control without there being any overt, actual disagreement. In turn Black women develop their own strategies for exposing, understanding, and opposing the fact that their interests are systematically undermined.

The domination of Blacks may be described as "systemic domination" (Fay, 1987, p. 123), which means that it is through the pattern of organization of the system as a whole that dominance is reproduced. Thus Whites can dominate Blacks without the former necessarily being aware of the ways in which the system is so structured that it is their interests rather than those of Blacks that are met. Lukes relates the exercise of power to responsibility when (a) such an exercise involves the assumption that the exerciser(s) could have acted differently (b) where, if unaware of the consequences of their action or inaction, they could have found out about them (Lukes, 1974, pp. 55-56). This point, the attribution of responsibility not only for action but also for inaction, is very important in the analysis of contemporary racism. A main problem today is inaction among the dominant group (detachment from racial issues and from Blacks) and, more specifically, passive tolerance of racism.

Although a working definition of racism must include the structuring role of ideology in coordinating uniformity of action, individual or group differences may also be important. It may be assumed that individuals are involved differently in the (re)production of everyday racism through their gender- and class-determined functions and positions in society. These differences are largely determined by the location of power in structural relations and in specific situations. The degree of power is determined by, among other things, the number of people affected by its exercise (Goldman, 1972, pp. 191-192). The racist practices of those who have power of position (authority) and power of property, as compared with those who do not have such power, are similar in nature but different in impact. Conversely research suggests that alternative arrangements, or antiracist strategies, are more successful when sanctioned by relevant authorities in the situation (Jones, 1988, p. 127). This does not mean that people with power that "rightfully belongs to the incumbent of any social role or organizational office possessing authority" (Lenski, 1966, p. 250) practice racism independently of those who do not have such power. Racism practiced by authorities is substantially supported by the fact that other members of the dominant racial group are more likely to tolerate than to challenge negative beliefs and practices against dominated groups. Alternatively authorities who choose to take responsibility for racism can use the power of their position to influence the views of others and to resist protest from subordinates in the implementation of alternative arrangements. Furthermore others can choose to challenge authorities who use power of position to practice racism. Hence a working definition of racism must be able to account for the dynamics of tolerance of racism and challenge to racism. In view of these arguments it can be concluded that, the more access to power in the system, the more consequences racist practices of agents have. The more access agents have to knowledge about the nature of domination, the more responsible they are for the outcome of their practices.

Apart from factors structuring the impact of racism and the question of responsibility, it is also necessary to make a clear distinction between the structural beneficiaries of racism and the actual agents of racism in everyday situations. That is, the dominant group structurally benefits from racism. This holds true for all its members, whether or not they willingly accept this. Of course there may be different interests at stake along class and gender lines. Nevertheless it must not be assumed that all Whites are agents of racism and all Blacks only the victims. Such a rigid definition of the problem ignores the psychology of being oppressed (Fanon, 1967; Meulenbelt, 1985) as well as the role of Blacks who work for what Mullard (1986b) calls the institution of ethnic exchange and those who may be involved in the formulation and enactment of racist policies. Conversely it is also relevant to take into account the many dominant group members who incidentally or frequently oppose racism, whether in small or in significant ways (Mullard, 1984; Terry, 1975). Dominant group members who take a clear stand against racism, or who otherwise identify with the Black cause, may under certain circumstances become substitute targets of racism. This problem obviously deserves more attention, but that is beyond the purpose of this study.

Given these arguments, and keeping in mind that "race" is an ideological construction with structural expressions (racialized or "ethnicized" structures of power), racism must be understood as ideology, structure, and process in which inequalities inherent in the wider social structure are related, in a deterministic way, to biological and cultural factors attributed to those who are seen as a different "race" or "ethnic" group. "Race" is called an *ideological construction,* and not just a social construction, because the idea of "race" has never existed outside of a framework of group interest. As a nineteenth-century pseudoscientific theory, as well as in contemporary "popular" thinking, the notion of "race" is inherently part of a "model" of asymmetrically organized "races" in which Whites rank higher than "non-Whites." Furthermore racism is a *structure* because racial and ethnic dominance exists in and is reproduced by the system through the formulation and application of rules, laws, and regulations and through access to and the allocation of resources. Finally racism is a *process* because structures and ideologies do not exist outside the everyday practices through which they are created and confirmed. These practices both adapt to and themselves contribute to changing social, economic, and political conditions in society. Because the role of ideology in the structuring of racism in society is powerful, it is useful to expand briefly on the meaning of racism as ideology and to relate ideology to prejudice and discourse.

Ideologically Saturated Prejudice

The concept of ideology is used here in a Gramscian sense to include philosophically elaborated thought as well as its reformulation in social representations, a substratum of ideologies (Gramsci, 1971; Hall, Lumlay, & McLennan, 1977). *Substratum* means the sedimentation of notions in belief systems and attitudes of the dominant group that serve their interests vis-à-vis other racial and ethnic groups. Racism is a conception of the world that is implicit in the manifestations of life that touch upon racial issues either directly, through inclusion, or indirectly, through exclusion, of the issue of "race." In that sense, there are two levels at which racism as ideology operates: at the level of daily actions and their interpretation and at another level in the refusal to acknowledge racism or to take responsibility for it (Ben-Tovim, Grabriel, Law, & Stredder, 1986). Racism as ideology is present in everyday activities and serves to cement and to unify, to preserve the ideological unity of the White group. It includes the whole range of concepts, ideas, images, and intuitions that provide the framework of interpretation and meaning for racial thought in society, whether systematically organized in academic discourse or in casual, everyday, contradictory, ambivalent, commonsense thinking (Hall, 1986).

Racism is a social process. This implies that structures and ideologies of racism are recurrently reinforced and reproduced through a complex of attitudes (prejudice) and actions (discrimination). *Prejudice* has been defined as "an antipathy based on faulty and inflexible generalizations. It may be felt or expressed. It may be directed toward a group as a whole, or toward an individual because he is a member of that group" (Allport,

1958, p. 9). However, prejudice as the cognitive component of racism is not just antipathy. It is a social representation compounded of in- and out-group differentiations. The basic tenets of prejudice are (a) a feeling of superiority, (b) perception of the subordinate race as intrinsically different and alien, (c) a feeling of propriety claim to certain areas of privilege and advantage, and (d) fear and suspicion that the subordinate race wants the prerogatives of the dominant race (Blumer, 1958). Social representation is a general term for a socially shared structure of cognitions, such as beliefs, knowledge, opinions, attitudes, purposes, and emotions. Therefore, racial or ethnic beliefs or opinions expressed by individual dominant group members are not relevant as personal opinions but as reflections of socially shared representations of racial and ethnic groups. Thus van Dijk (1987a) represents racial or ethnic prejudice as a schema of negative evaluations and characteristics attributed to groups perceived as racially or culturally different. Targets of prejudice are one or more groups assumed to be different. The assumed differences are evaluated as negative in relation to in-group norms, values, traditions, or goals and subsequently attributed to racial or ethnic characteristics of the out-group. These negative evaluations are generalizations based on insufficient or biased representations that are constituent elements of an ideology rationalizing and reinforcing existing systems of racial and ethnic inequality. Finally, the acquisition, use, and transformation of ethnic prejudice is a social process in which in-group preference is confirmed discursively. However, because racial or ethnic prejudice is morally rejected by the dominant group, the reproduction of prejudice requires flexible use of rational arguments in defense of particular attitudes about an out-group, such as "I am not prejudiced, but . . ." (van Dijk, 1987a, p. 388).

Because prejudice is embedded in an ideological structure, it relates to a structure of social practices. Because racism is by definition a social problem, the idea of discrimination is only meaningful when it is defined as actions that tacitly or explicitly confirm or create racial or ethnic inequality in the existing framework of racial and ethnic domination. Racial discrimination includes all acts—verbal, nonverbal, and paraverbal—with intended or unintended negative or unfavorable consequences for racially or ethnically dominated groups. It is important to see that intentionality is not a necessary component of racism (Essed, 1986; Jenkins, 1986). It is not the nature of specific acts or beliefs that determines whether these are mechanisms of racism but the context in which these beliefs and acts operate. Actors do not always have knowledge about, much less do they intend all of, the consequences of their actions. Further, racism often operates through seemingly nonracial practices. Various authors make a distinction between direct and indirect discrimination (Malone, 1980). Because direct discrimination is usually associated with interaction, and indirect discrimination with institutional arrangements, this distinction is, however, not useful for the purpose of this study, for the reasons I have mentioned earlier. Rather it is useful to make a distinction between overt and covert racism (Brandt, 1986; Essed, 1984). Discrimination as a form of overt racism refers to acts that openly express negative intentions toward Blacks. In covert expressions of racism, negative intentions cannot be inferred from the acts themselves. In these cases the definition of the situation seems negotiable and is integrated into the conflict situation. Elsewhere (Essed, 1987) I took the issue even further and demonstrated that, to understand contemporary racism, the definition of the situation must be recognized as a major source of conflict. This shall be addressed in more detail in the course of this study.

In conclusion I emphasize that one cannot grasp the true nature of discrimination without situating it within its larger sociopolitical context. That is, the relation between racist ideology and racist practices is determined by the historical, material, and political context and by the degree to which ideologies are saturated in the cognitions of agents. When agents are socialized with and systematically exposed to representations that justify White dominance, and when these notions are (unwittingly) accepted as "normal," agents will act in concert, thereby creating and reproducing similar forms of racism adapted to the specific needs or interests and situations. This view of the relation between ideology and cognitions and between structures and agents acknowledges, on the one hand, structural constraints on human agency and, on the other hand, that within specific boundaries individuals can make their own choices. They choose how they act. They either uncritically accept a dominant representation of reality or seek alternative views. Even when racism operates in such a way that the dominant group is often not prepared to believe the experiences of Black people and to take responsibility for the problem of racism (Bhavnani & Bhavnani, 1985), individuals can choose to take responsibility and to initiate change once they understand the processes of domination. This approach departs from the quasi-determinism of critical theory by emphasizing that there are "resisters" who produce alternative perspectives of society and that there are alternative, nonracist ways to use power with the purpose of change.

THE NOTION OF EVERYDAY RACISM

Theories about the meaning of "the everyday" have been developed in the fields of philosophy, phenomenology, social psychology, symbolic interactionism, and ethnomethodology, where it has often been referred to intuitively as a "known in common world" (Zimmerman & Pollner, 1970, p. 85), a "familiar world, a world taken for granted" (Luckmann, 1970/1978, p. 275). The tendency to use metaphors and other associations instead of more precise descriptions or definitions when talking about the everyday is amazing considering, for instance, that everyday explanations have been quite a popular topic of recent publications in the area of social cognition theory (e.g., Antaki, 1981, 1988a; Semin & Gergen, 1990). In the social psychology of everyday explanations, the idea of "everyday" is often associated with vague notions such as the "ordinary" (Antaki, 1988b, p. 1) or "common sense" (Furnham, 1990). Others write about everyday cognitions without giving any further explanation or just broadly characterize the concept as the opposite of the "scientific" (Carugati, 1990; Groeben, 1990; Semin, 1990) or as the opposite of the philosophical world, in which philosophy belongs to the "highest spheres of culture," and everyday life stands for the "most trivial and commonplace sphere" (Lefebvre, 1971, p. 116). Intuitive associations like these represent specific characteristics of "the everyday," but they cannot be used as a basis for a theory of everyday racism.

I do not intend to conceptualize the notion of "the everyday" in terms of a philosophy of everyday life (Heller, 1984)—a study in itself—but in terms of the categories and social relations operative in everyday life (Smith, 1987) and in terms of the characteristics of everyday life (Heller, 1984). Such a qualification of the everyday is sufficient for the purposes of this study, namely, to distinguish between "everyday racism" and "experiences of everyday racism." With these arguments in mind the following tentative proposals for the analysis of "everyday life" are relevant in understanding racism as a process operative in everyday life.

Meaning and Characteristics of Everyday Life

Everyday life always takes place in and relates to the immediate environment of a person. It is a world in which we are located physically and socially. The content and structure of everyday life are not necessarily the same for all individuals in society. It can also be different in different periods of a person's life. Obviously everyday life for a university professor who is also the mother of three children has similarities, but also differences, when compared with the life of a university professor without children or that of a mother who has a job as a bank teller. Everyday life is the direct reproduction of the person embedded in social relations. This assumption is included in Heller's (1984, p. 3) definition of "everyday life" as "the aggregate of those individual reproduction factors which . . . make social reproduction possible." Everyday life is not only reproductive of persons but also of the positions of persons in social relations and of social relations themselves.

The everyday world is a world in which one must learn to maneuver and a world that one must learn to handle. Without a minimum knowledge of how to cope in everyday life, one cannot handle living in society. This at least includes knowledge of language, norms, customs and rules, and knowledge to use the means and resources that make living possible (or successful) in a given environment, determined by factors of class, gender, profession, and so on (Heller, 1984). This knowledge includes expectations and "scripts" (Schank & Abelson, 1977) of everyday situations.

The fundamental stock of knowledge needed to cope in everyday life is transmitted by each generation to its successors. Knowledge used in everyday life is not restricted to knowledge that can be derived directly from the everyday environment. Knowledge used in everyday life can also include scientific knowledge communicated by the mass media or through education. In other words, the system is internalized in everyday life through socialization processes. The everyday is based on expectations and conditions that are taken for granted. Without these expectations the everyday cannot be managed. Garfinkel's experiments showed that the undermining, by others, of taken-for-granted conditions in everyday life is upsetting and unbearable for individuals subjected to these experiments (Garfinkel, 1967). Conversely individuals who are seen as unable to cope with "the everyday" are stigmatized as "mentally ill." These arguments do not mean to suggest that the everyday is static. It remains possible for individuals to transcend the limits of the everyday. People who reject what is seen as "normal" often become agents of change. Given these considerations the notion of "the everyday" can be tentatively defined as *socialized meanings making practices immediately definable and uncontested so that, in principle, these practices can be managed according to (sub)cultural norms and expectations.* These practices and meanings belong to our familiar world and usually involve routine or repetitive practices. Therefore, they can be expected and generalized for specific relations and situations. This addition is important in distinguishing the everyday from the noneveryday—that is, the incidental, unfamiliar, that is neither generalizable nor taken for granted.

The Structure of Everyday Life

The structure of everyday life is determined by the fact that everyday life is heterogeneous (Heller, 1984). In everyday life heterogeneous forms of activity have to be coordinated and performed, but the content of these forms of activity varies according to different classes and positions in society. At the same time structures and social relations cannot be reproduced without uniformity of practice within the heterogeneity of relations and situations (see the aggregation hypothesis). Smith (1987) has implemented the idea of the "everyday world" as located in social relations in a way that is relevant to this study. She contends that the everyday world must be seen as being organized by multiple social relations not observable within it. Development of systematic knowledge about the social relations of society is a means to disclose the social relations determining one's everyday life. Social relations in this sense are not static but form actual processes. Smith (1987, p. 134) puts it this way:

> It takes only a little imagination to see that all such relations are present in and reproduced in the organization of activities at the everyday level, as well as entering the everyday into relations that pass beyond the control of individual subjects.

If the everyday is located in multiple relations, the structure of the everyday world can be represented as a matrix of social relations present in and reproduced by everyday practices. Everyday practices are present in and reproduced by everyday situations. The situations of the everyday world are substructured by relations of race, ethnicity, class, and gender. This introduces, finally, the notion of everyday racism.

Characteristics and Structure of Everyday Racism

Given these arguments the structure of everyday racism must be seen as a complex of practices made operative in race and ethnic relations.

Race relations in this sense are a process present in and activated at the everyday level as well as prestructured in a way that transcends the control of individual subjects. Everyday racism is the integration of racism into everyday situations through practices (cognitive and behavioral, see below) that activate underlying power relations. This process must be seen as a continuum through which the integration of racism into everyday practices becomes part of the expected, of the unquestionable, and of what is seen as normal by the dominant group. When racist notions and actions infiltrate everyday life and become part of the reproduction of the system, the system reproduces everyday racism.

Earlier I made an analytical distinction between cognitive (prejudice) and behavioral (discrimination) components of racism. In everyday life, however, the cognitive and behavioral aspects of racism are mixed and operate synchronically as part of the same process. This is consistent with the view, also expressed by others, that everyday thinking is inseparable from everyday behavior (e.g., Heller, 1984, p. 200). Given these arguments it is useful not to make an ontological distinction between cognitive and behavioral components of racist practices. This can also be explained as follows: The structural exclusion, marginalization, and repression of Blacks is consistent with and rationalized by existing ideologies problematizing and inferiorizing Blacks. If the macro is created and reproduced on a micro level, this can only mean that discrimination and prejudice are inherently related, even when it may not be necessarily so that one specific act is causally related to one specific cognition or motivation coming from the same actor. Because discrimination and prejudice are fused in the notion of racist practices, there are no grounds, as I mentioned earlier, to identify intentionality as a necessary component of the definition of racism.

Analogous to everyday life, everyday racism is heterogeneous in its manifestations but at the same time structured by forces toward uniformity. Everyday racism is a complex of practices operative through heterogeneous (class and gender) relations, present in and producing race and ethnic relations. Such relations are activated and reproduced as practices. Everyday racism is locked into the underlying dynamics of relations and forces of racial and ethnic domination and governed by the powers to which they give rise. For the purpose of this study, racial and ethnic domination can be implemented as interlocking forces of oppression and repression coordinated and unified by ideological constructions. These interlocking forces represent at the same time micro and macro dimensions of racism. From a micro point of view oppression can be implemented as creating structures of racial and ethnic inequality through situated practices (oppression). Racial inequality can only be maintained when other forces operate to secure compliance and to prevent, manage, or break opposition (repression). Seen from this point of view the macro structures of domination are already contextualized in racial ideologies implicitly or explicitly familiar to the subjects who reinforce racial inequality through repression. Uniformity of oppressive and repressive practices is coordinated ideologically through socialization and the constant actualization, through the media and other channels of communication, of images, opinions, and versions of reality legitimizing the status quo.

The firm interlocking of forces of domination operates in a way that makes it hard to escape its impact on everyday life. Although individual Black women may work out strategies to break away from particular oppressive relations or situations, and frequently oppose racism, as members of an oppressed group, they remain locked into the forces of the system, unless enough counterpressure develops to unlock these forces and to transform the machinery of the system that produces racial and ethnic inequality. This explains, as will be shown later in more detail, why everyday racism cannot be reduced to incidents or to specific events. Everyday racism is the process of the system working through multiple relations and situations. Once we understand that in a racist society, race and ethnicity can operate through any social relation, when we recognize the racial or ethnic dimensions in particular relationships, it becomes possible to speak of everyday racism as the situational activation of racial or ethnic dimensions in particular relations in a way that reinforces racial or ethnic inequality and contributes to new forms of racial and ethnic inequality. This view is parallel to Omi and Winant's (1986, pp. 61-62) theory of racial formation—the process

> by which social, economic, and political forces determine the content and importance of racial categories, and by which they are in turn shaped by racial meanings. Crucial to this formulation is the treatment of race as a central axis of social relations which cannot be subsumed or reduced to some broader category of conception.

They argue, however, that racial dimensions of a particular relationship or social practice are never given automatically, whereas in my view this dimension is always present when racial meaning can be given to previously nonracial relationships. Of course the particular content of systems of racial meanings can change historically, but the presence of a system of racial meanings is a permanent feature of European culture that has been consistently activated throughout the United States in the past few centuries and in the Netherlands in more recent times. Social relations are racialized (or ethnicized) when they represent racially or ethnically identified differences in position and power. Because "race" is an organizing principle of many social relations, the fundamental social relations of society are racialized relations. However, it is only when these racial or ethnic dimensions of social relations are called upon or activated through practice that racial and ethnic relations are created, reinforced, or reproduced. In other words, even when specific relations are racialized and when these relations underlie and structure social situations, racism does not necessarily have to occur in a specific time or place.

Everyday racism does not exist in the singular but only as a complex—as interrelated instantiations of racism. Each instantiation of everyday racism has meaning only in relation to the whole complex of relations and practices. Thus expressions of racism in one particular social relation are related to all other racist practices and can be reduced to the fundamental structuring forces of everyday racism: oppression, repression, and legitimation.

Given these arguments, everyday racism can be defined as *a process in which (a) socialized racist notions are integrated into meanings that make practices immediately definable and manageable, (b) practices with racist implications become in themselves familiar and repetitive, and (c) underlying racial and ethnic relations are actualized and reinforced through these routine or familiar practices in everyday situations.*

This discussion implies that people are involved differently in the process of everyday racism according to gender, class, status, and other factors determining the content and structure of their everyday lives. It also must be emphasized that the process of everyday racism operates not only through direct interaction with Blacks but also through indirect contact. This becomes clear when we consider the role of, for instance, policymakers or journalists in the process of everyday racism. In the immediate practice of their everyday lives, policymakers formulate and enact rules and conditions that reinforce existing racial injustice, even when they do not directly interact with

Blacks in making these policies. Similarly racist newspaper articles are part of the process of everyday racism, whether or not based on direct interaction with Blacks. Finally it should be stressed that not all racism is everyday racism. The concept of everyday racism distinguishes the reproduction of racism through routine and familiar practices from incidental and uncommon expressions of racism. Of course the content of everyday racism is not static. It changes with the changing relations and practices through which the system is reproduced as a racist system. This will be illustrated later in the discussion of differences in the experience of everyday racism in the United States and in the Netherlands.

Specific agents can be involved in different ways, through different situations, in the reproduction of racism in everyday life. Given the ubiquity of sites and relations through which racism operates, it would hardly be possible to monitor the process of racism in a systematic way with traditional methods involving surveys or observation. In the experiences of Black women, everyday racism does not exist in the singular but only in the plural form. It is a coherent complex of oppression continuously present and systematically activated personally through encounters, vicariously through the experiences of other Blacks, through the media, and through the daily awareness of racial injustice in society. An experiential point of view, therefore, enables us to examine the simultaneous manifestations of racism reproduced in multiple situations. This introduces the methodology of this study that will be addressed in the following chapter.

2

Methodological Questions

In this study methodological questions acquire a broader meaning than just "methods" of research. They have to do with the logic used to validate the relevance of the concept of everyday racism and cannot be separated from my theoretical presuppositions about the concept of everyday racism. The analysis of everyday racism draws on concepts from structural sociology, phenomenology, formal sociology, and social cognition theory. This theoretical pluralism reflects the premise that structural sociology is not necessarily incompatible with inductive theory building. The first part of this chapter discusses and schematizes the methodology applied, which structures the way this study is organized and conducted.

The second part of this chapter addresses methods and techniques of data collection. In this study interpretations of racism are reconstructed through the analysis of accounts gathered in nondirective interviews. Accounts have been used as a basis for analysis by various researchers (e.g., Harré & Secord, 1972; Lyman & Scott, 1970). However, this study must not be placed in the tradition of the specific methods of analysis employed by these authors.[9] Accounts of racism are more than just personal stories: Racism is a social problem, and, therefore, such accounts represent social experiences. Accounts of racism should be seen not only as descriptions, opinions, images, or attitudes about race relations but also as "systems of knowledge" and "systems of values" in their own right, used for the discovery and organization of reality (Jaspars & Fraser, 1984, p. 102). The quality, validity, and usefulness of these empirical data depend on the way the accounts were gathered, the social background of the interviewees in the Netherlands and in the United States, the interview context, and the method of interviewing. After I have explained these and other characteristics of the research methods and techniques to elicit from Black women the relevant information, a summary is given of the method of analysis employed.

As a primary source of information for data gathering, the insights of two comparable groups of women, American and Surinamese of African descent, are used. These women are articulate, understand the issue of racism, have practical experience with the problem, are able to discuss different sides of the problem, and are able to give detailed descriptions of manifestations of racism.[*] Real-life experiences are a rich source of information and provide insights into everyday racism that cannot be obtained in other ways.[*] However, the reality constructions of Black women are checked for consistency with the structural properties of racism in the system.[*] Further, by using experiences of women in two countries, the study transcends local particularities, thus illustrating the general applicability of the concept of everyday racism as a means of qualifying processes of racism in different systems. The study is exploratory. Therefore, it was not designed to meet the requirements of statistical representativeness.

METHODOLOGY WITHIN METHODOLOGY

Because racism is an evaluative concept, it is necessary to justify the specific perspective on everyday racism developed in this study. The implications of an experiential view of racism are discussed below. Let us assume here that experiences are indeed a useful source for the study of everyday racism.[*] Briefly stated then this study is about the understanding of everyday racism through examination of Black women's understanding of racism in everyday life.[*] The term *understanding* has a double meaning. In a sociological sense *Understanding* (with a capital letter) is a process whereby researchers, after grasping the meaning of specific data, translate this information into a form that can serve their research. The other sense of *understanding* (lower case) is broader and can be used to mean any type of comprehension (Polkinghorne, 1983, p. 217). To prevent confusion, Black women's understanding of racism will be referred to as comprehension of racism (see Chapter 3), while my analytical translation of Black women's comprehension will be referred to as *Understanding* (with or without a capital letter, see Chapter 4).

These double layers of meaning given to the reality of racism indicate that the study holds a methodology within a methodology. To conceptualize Black women's comprehension of racism, an analogy is used with social scientific heuristics of understanding. For both the women's knowledge and the scientifically derived knowledge, the following rule applies: It is in the degree that this knowledge corresponds with the world that one can speak of "correct" knowledge (Gergen & Semin, 1990). In the theoretical framework proposed in the previous chapter, racism was defined as a structure and ideology, and it was postulated that everyday racism is a process. This framework, which is in fact a social scientific "social representation" of generalized knowledge of racism, structures the processing and interpretation of the empirical data. It may be assumed that Black women's comprehension of racism in everyday life works, broadly speaking, in the same way. The meaning they attach to specific events can only have significance in terms of racism within a framework of their general knowledge of racism. This general knowledge framework is inductively inferred from the data. The relation between the methodology and structure of the study is schematized in Table 2.1 and will be explained in the course of this chapter.

Experiences of Racism in a Structural Framework

This study deals with subjective reality constructions as a base for theoretical analysis (Bertaux, 1981; Plummer, 1983). There are two reasons the concept of everyday racism is developed from reconstructions of experiences of racism. The first and main reason has to do with the characteristics of everyday racism. It has been postulated that everyday racism is a multidimensional phenomenon and that it is reproduced through multiple relations and situations. Therefore, in the study of everyday racism, concepts must be used that enable us to relate macro and micro dimensions of the social world. In addition concepts must be used that enable us to relate to each other manifestations of racism in one situation and expressions of racism in other situations. Because of its structure the concept of experience is suitable for these purposes.

The emphasis on experiences and interpretation should be understood against the background of interpretive sociology, in particular phenomenology, symbolic interactionism, and ethnomethodology (Douglas, 1970/1974; Rogers, 1983; Thomas, 1928). A problem with these approaches is, however, that the definition of the situation is developed by reference to a culturally homogeneous consensus model of society (e.g., Garfinkel, 1967; Goffman, 1963/1979). Work with a consensus model of society creates complex problems when analyzing

Table 2.1 Methodology and Structure of the Study

Structure	Methodology	Method	Chapter
1. Theory	Macro and micro dimensions of racism related by viewing racism as a process		1
2. Problem	Racism as a process conceptualized as everyday racism		1
3. Implementation	Everyday racism studied by using as data experiences of racism in everyday life	Accounting	2
4. Analysis			
a. Induction	Reconstruction of social and historical context of general knowledge of racism	Processing of biographical data	3
	Construction of framework of general knowledge about racism	Classification of generalized statements about race relations and racism	3
	Construction of intersubjective schema for analysis of accounts	Classification of underlying categories and heuristics of reconstructions of racist events	4
	Reconstruction of everyday racism over time and across situations	Inventory of events in individual case story (Rosa N.) + intra-subjective comparison for consistency	5
b. Reliability	Construction of structure of everyday racism	Inventory of general and specific events + intersubjective comparisons for consistency	5/6
c. Validity	Description and analysis of range of experiences	Evaluation of experiences in terms of racism as ideology and structure	5/6

experiences of Black women. On the one hand my theoretical framework is premised on the view of race relations as conflicting. At the same time it presupposes the existence of dominant group consensus on race as part of the problem of racism. In addition, while employing a conflict model of society structured by factors of race, ethnicity, class, and gender, it must be acknowledged that, to a certain degree, people across race, class, and gender groups share, or are aware of, generally accepted or dominant views of rules and norms concerning acceptable behavior. This view, that under certain conditions structural conflict and cultural consensus are compatible, leaves open the possibility that structural conflict (racism) is managed by the dominant group on a cultural or ideological level (overall denial and mitigation of racism).

The notion of experience is multidimensional. Although the concept of "experience" is often used to refer only to "personal" experiences (e.g., Larsen, 1988), experience has a broader meaning in this study. Experiences include specific (micro) events, but experience can also be seen as the impact of knowledge of general (structural) phenomena on one's definition of reality. In this view general knowledge represents the connecting element between the individual and social structure (Cicourel, 1981). Experiences include not only witnessed events but also reported events. Experiences are inseparable from the concept of memory (Pivcevic, 1986). Everything we experience is stored in memory. Furthermore experiences involve the retrieval from memory of situationally relevant knowledge and its application in interpreting new events. Given these properties of the notion of experience, it is useful in a discussion of experiences of racism to distinguish between (a) personal experiences (racism directed against oneself, usually witnessed, sometimes reported), (b) vicarious experiences (racism directed against other identified Blacks, which may be witnessed as well as reported), (c) mediated experiences (racist events directed against or affecting a larger [sub]group of Blacks, often communicated through the mass media), and (d) cognitive experiences (the impact of knowledge of racism upon one's perception of reality). It should be emphasized that experiences of racism in everyday life cannot be seen as merely individual experiences. Because everyday racism involves the integration of racism into everyday situations throughout the system, experiences of everyday racism include racism originally practiced in one situation (e.g., racist news reporting) that is mediated and subsequently experienced in another situation (being confronted with racist views when reading the newspaper).

The second reason experiences of Blacks are a relevant source of information is that racism is often expressed in covert ways and is denied and mitigated by the dominant group. The notion of covert discrimination implies that this type of racism will be hard to "prove" when taking as a criterion the actor's definition of the situation. The pressures of the moral rejection of racism and the encouragement of equality values have made an impact to the extent that individuals may have become blind to the racist implications of their communications and interactions with Black people (Karp, 1981; Manning & Ohri, 1982; Milner, 1981). Furthermore Whites are generally motivated to present themselves to others as non-prejudiced. This has been illustrated with social psychological experiments (Dutton & Lake, 1973; Dutton & Lennox, 1974; Weitz, 1972) as well as through discourse analysis (van Dijk, 1984, 1987a).

Individuals who engage in behaviors they believe others consider morally blameworthy are likely to experience such situations as predicaments. Furthermore it has become clear from other studies that justification strategies and other kinds of impression management tactics are most likely to be used by individuals who face social predicaments (Tedeshi & Reiss, 1981). It may be assumed that this is the case for individuals who try to keep up a nondiscriminating self-image.

These reasons suggest that we may expect Black women to provide us with information about dominant group members that would probably not be obtained by using dominant group members themselves as informants. Moreover, by concentrating on Black women as active constructors and (critical) reporters (Harré & Secord, 1972) of the way dominant group members participate in the reproduction of racial and ethnic dominance, the critique of Black women can be contextualized in a framework of knowledge of racism generated over time and transmitted among Blacks from one generation to the next. Only by taking subjective experiences of racism seriously can we study how Black women in their daily lives strategically use beliefs, opinions, acquired knowledge about racism, and other heuristics of interpretation to account for their experiences. Insight into these interpretation processes is imperative for understanding experiences of racism as an intrinsic part of everyday life. It is important and inevitable that we rely on subjective reality constructions because the complexity, depth, and multitude of experiences cannot simply be observed by, for example, a participant investigator.

A relevant question concerns the reliability of subjective experiences and the validity of the methodology. Reliability is a function of the consistency between data provided by different informants, independent of each other. To transcend individual perceptions I look for shared interpretations, assessed by intersubjective comparisons. Intersubjectivity of interpretation is based on comparative analysis of interpretation procedures made operational by studying questions such as these: Are similar acts in similar situations interpreted in the same way? Do women use similar arguments? Do they refer to similar sources to support or to verify their interpretations and evaluations? These organizing categories underlying shared interpretations are discussed, elaborated, and schematized against the background of cognitive stability theories, in particular pertaining to new developments in attribution theory. This new direction moves away from highly controlled, firmly laboratory-based research toward an approach that is more sensitive to "what goes on" in the everyday lives of the "subjects" involved (Wilkinson, 1981, p. 207). Thereby attributions are placed in a broader framework of interpretive and evaluative processes. The resulting schema for the analysis of events and accounts can be seen as tentative preparation for a formal theory of rules and heuristics for exposing covert racism in specific situations.

The construction of validity involves relating Black women's shared interpretations to the overall theoretical structure to determine whether their constructions of reality are, in fact, related to the concepts and theoretical assumptions that are employed. This means that micro events must be translated back into macro-level ("structural") concepts. This translation takes place in two steps: first, by analyzing how Black women apply general perceptions of race relations to the explanation of personal experiences, and, second, by comparing Black women's interpretations to my theoretical framework for consistency. In other words, to illustrate the validity of the methodology, it is useful to make a distinction between interpretations of reality and evaluative conclusions that the experienced reality is indicative of racism. The interpretations that are used to reconstruct reality are those of Black women. Whether or not we must evaluate specific events as racist is determined by assessing Black women's descriptions of events against the working definition of racism. Questions of interpretation and evaluation are discussed more extensively below (see Chapters 3 and 4).

ACCOUNTS

Theoretically speaking one could consider (combinations of) the following methods of research useful to study experiences of racism in everyday life: (a) experimental testing or controlled observations, (b) participant observations, and (c) interviewing. There are various reasons that nondirective interviewing is the best method for the purpose of this study. Let me first summarize briefly some of the problems attached to the other methods.

Experimental testing of human behavior originates in psychology, but sociologists have developed similar methods for situations outside the laboratory context. Researchers such as Bolle, van Dijk, and Heterbrij (1978), Daniel (1968/1971), Smith (1977), Bovenkerk (1978), and Uyl et al. (1986) tested the reactions of White landlords, employers, or employment agencies to Black and White subjects, respectively, applying for rooms and jobs. The individuals and agencies who were tested did not know that they were the object of a research project. Different treatment of Black and White applicants was interpreted as discrimination. This method is useful for studying controlled situations. Indeed employment agencies that routinely accept racist demands, such as a preference for White employees, are caught off guard by (fake) employers. Through systematic testing the researcher gets insight into the frequency with which this type of discrimination occurs (Uyl et al., 1986).

These controlled observations have only limited value in the study of everyday racism because occurrences of racism in everyday life can be unpredictable and hard to control in planned settings. The variety of events, situations, and settings in everyday life, the relations between different events at different moments of the day, and the contextualized interpretations of daily experiences cannot be reduced to predefined settings to be observed by the researcher.

There are also ethical problems with experiments that induce discrimination for the purpose of observation. I find it objectionable that, for the sake of an empiricist understanding of "valid evidence," individual Blacks have to go through experimentally induced racism on top of the racism they already experience in their everyday lives. Even when it can be rationalized that it is "just an experiment," the racism against the test persons is real and not different than their experiences in ordinary life. They add to and reconfirm all other situations of daily life in which Blacks have to resist humiliation and degradation. Such methods are even more questionable in light of the fact that the social sciences have largely ignored the body of knowledge and experiences Blacks already have with racism. In this sense my methodology aims to define the meaning, function, and political implications (Hooks, 1989) of the acknowledgment of the Black experience in academia.

Participant observation would broaden the range of situations in which occurrences of racism could be witnessed. One could consider following a group of Black women and registering all the situations they engage in during a given period. However, that would be very time-consuming and the mere presence of the researcher would influence the situation. The women would have to accept being under the nonstop surveillance of the researcher. The researcher would probably become a nuisance for the women involved, and the study of everyday racism would largely be reduced to the observation of direct expressions of racism in a limited number of face-to-face interactions. This would produce only a fraction of the possible information about everyday racism. The relevant point is not only what happens but how these practices are interpreted and evaluated in terms of the history the women (or other Blacks) have in relation to that particular context and/or the particular actors.

Finally, one can use interviews with Black women as a source of information. Interviews are useful because the beliefs, knowledge, and expectations that influence Black women's experiences of the situation and direct them in detecting subtle and nonracially expressed indications of racism cannot be observed by a researcher. However, they can be elicited by interviewing. This does not mean that every method of interviewing would be useful. Research such as that of Reubsaet, Kropman, and Mulier (1982), based on questionnaires, showed that those experiences with racism that were difficult to define exactly or were open to different interpretations had to be excluded from the research because the subjects felt they could not "prove" the racism they had experienced. It appeared that more vague descriptions and elaborate stories about racism could not be studied with the method of highly structured interviews. In particular, when a delicate and serious problem is involved, such as experiences with racism, it is important to give interviewees enough space to qualify their statements and to be elaborate in their explanations.

It follows that the most useful methods are those that (a) illuminate aspects of social life that cannot be shaped into preprogrammed settings or answers and (b) stimulate the narration of experiences that would remain unexpressed within the format of a questionnaire (Graham, 1984). Nondirective interviewing—that is, simulating a "natural" conversation—has been successful before as an instrument to conceptualize experiences (Finch, 1984; Reinharz, 1983). The nondirective interviewer serves primarily as a catalyst for comprehensive expression of the subject's feelings and beliefs and of the frame of reference in which the

subject's experiences take on personal significance (Selltiz, Wrightsman, & Cook, 1976, p. 321). This method allows Black women to
optimally verbalize their feelings, opinions, and experiences in a relatively free and detailed way, as it tries to reveal, rather than to im-
pose, interpretations. Similar objectives have been identified as part
of ethogenic methodology (Harré, 1980). I did, however, not adapt
this method. The richness of personal accounts invites an impressive
degree of attention to detail. It allows insights into the details of processes of understanding and into the coherence of subjective interpretations and their relation to other experiences.

Special attention must be paid to what Black women actually say
and how they can be stimulated to explore the ways in which their insights can be fully utilized (Canter & Brown, 1981). Earlier Cicourel
(1973), as one of the first sociologists, showed how, from recorded
interview materials, not only conceptions of meanings and practices
but also the precise nature of interpretation processes can be reconstructed. The method is suitable to expose covert racism and to stimulate Black women to also verbalize those interpretations dominant
group members would or did stigmatize as evidence of "exaggeration" or being "oversensitive." To put it differently, the method was
chosen so that Black women feel free to make sociologically relevant
the seemingly "small" or "trivial," but stressful or humiliating, events
of everyday life. The women could verbalize intuitively felt racism
that they might find hard to pinpoint accurately. Eliciting accounts is
also favorable in that notions and cues that support thorough memory
search by the informant can be used effectively. I emphasize that the
study is not concerned with original interpretation processes in social
situations but with their current verbal reconstruction and representation. It may be assumed, however, that the reconstruction of experiences in the interview relies upon the same interpretation strategies as
those used in the original situation (Marsh, Rosser, & Harré, 1978).

In view of these arguments some comments are in order about the
role of memory. It has been argued that memory is not always a reliable source for the purpose of reconstructing events (Loftus, 1979).
While acknowledging this problem in general, I have mentioned before that, in this study, shared rather than individual interpretations of
social reality are the primary concern. This is also reflected in my conceptualization of experiences as more than just personal experiences.
Specific events will be presented in a framework of Black women's
general knowledge of racism. Thus reconstructions of experiences

serve the purpose of addressing structural features of racism. This will be explained later in more detail, and I shall also illustrate then how shared interpretations of reality are reconstructed from the data. Here it must be emphasized that individual idiosyncrasies in terms of exactly how specific events happened are not the issue.

Because verbal accounts are the sole empirical data, they had to be registered accurately (Have & Komter, 1982). The women were asked for permission to record the interviews on audiotape, to which all of them agreed. The women were interviewed alone, usually at their homes. A few interviews took place on the job, either in the women's offices or in mine. To reduce the constraints interviewees usually feel about the use of a tape recorder, I used a small one. In addition, during the interview, I tried to maximize eye contact with the women, which most of the time helped to keep them from speaking (in)to the tape recorder. Using a tape recorder allowed me to concentrate better on the content of the interview, so that I was able to react adequately to the conversation. This advantage of a tape recorder outweighs the disadvantage that some women may have withheld certain information because of its presence. Verbatim transcripts were made for each conversation. However, because I paid only limited attention to conversational features as such (turn taking, pauses, and so on), the transcription did not follow methods used in conversation analysis (Sacks, Schegloff, & Jefferson, 1974; Schenkhein, 1978). Due to the time-consuming nature of making literal transcripts, relatively few women could be interviewed.

These arguments make clear that, in exploratory research, ingenuity and flexible use of the method chosen inevitably play a part in determining its productiveness. This introduces the question of the validity of the method of nondirective interviews. Conversations are locally produced and, therefore, always unique up to a certain point (Polanyi, 1981). The reader will get an impression of the kind of data gathered through nondirective interviewing through the story of Rosa N. (see Chapter 5). Obviously it is possible to talk about the same experiences twice and to make the same points, but it is probably impossible to use exactly the same words or exactly the same details to describe specific events because of the necessity in nondirective interviews to fit the circumstances of the interview situation. In other words, nondirective interviews can never be repeated in exactly the same way because the interview is determined partly by the particular associations the interviewee has in reconstructing her experiences and the specifics of the interview context. Nevertheless the fact that the same project was conducted twice, once in the United States and once in the Netherlands, and in both countries the method gave consistent results—namely, comparable verbal reconstructions of experiences of racism in similar situations of everyday life—indicates that the method was reliable.

THE INTERVIEWEES

Let us now turn to the social background of both interview groups, as these eventually determine the picture of everyday racism presented in this study. Two similar groups of women were interviewed; 27 in the United States and 28 in the Netherlands. The selection was based on three criteria, of which the first mentioned was used most frequently: (a) references by interviewees, (b) references through my personal contacts, and (c) references through my professional contacts. Thus diversity was obtained in different ways. Interviewees were requested to refer to other Black women between 20 and 45. The women were usually very helpful in suggesting other candidates. This did not mean that they primarily recommended women who were like themselves. About one third of each group are students and the rest are professionals. The level of education of the Black U.S. professionals is from M.A.s to Ph.D.s. Compared with the United States there are few women with Ph.D.s. in the Netherlands. This is even worse for Black women. Unfortunately these few Black women with Ph.D.s or those in exceptional positions, by Dutch standards, such as directors or university teachers, had to be excluded from the research because their anonymity could not be guaranteed. As a result the level of education of the interviewed professionals in the Netherlands is slightly lower than that of the Americans; their degrees are comparable to B.A.s and M.A.s (Hoge School and Universiteit).

The selected groups confirm existing gender differentiation in higher education and professions. There is an overrepresentation of women with backgrounds in the humanities and the social sciences. In the selection a preference was given to employed women so that I could elicit accounts about recent experiences on the job. Some women have children, some are single, some live with a partner. There is a striking difference in this respect between women in the United States and those in the Netherlands. The impact of a high degree of social segregation between Blacks and Whites is visible in interpersonal relations. As compared with only one of the U.S. women, about a third of the interviewees in the Netherlands have a White partner. According to a recent survey this number is representative (Praag, 1989, p. 30). The large majority of both groups come from a medium-large city (about 750,000 citizens) in California and in the Netherlands. In both cities Blacks represent almost 10% of the population. The living conditions of the women are also marked by structural differences in the nature of racism in the systems of both countries. Many U.S. interviewees live in Black areas, while those in the Netherlands live in neighborhoods with a White majority.

The biographical background of the women has an impact on their general knowledge of racism. In this respect two important factors differentiate many U.S. interviewees from the Dutch: the southern experience and the civil rights movement. The professionals interviewed in the United States were in their teens or early twenties during the second half of the 1960s, when in the United States a system of legal segregation was replaced by a system of (formal) equal civil rights. Therefore, they were old enough to be aware of the social changes of the 1960s and 1970s. On average the students are younger and know about the civil rights movement by hearsay only. Some of the U.S. interviewees had lived all their lives in California. However, the majority had moved to California as a child or after finishing their studies. They came from many other parts of the Unites States: the South and Southeast, such as Texas, Alabama, North Carolina, Arkansas; the Midwest, such as Nebraska or Kansas; and the large cities and states of the North and Northeast, such as Michigan, Illinois, New York, and Washington, DC. Various interviewees discussed the impact of their regional family background on their understanding of racial issues and on their (early) experiences with racism (see Chapter 3). Some suggested that Black women from the South are better able to understand the mechanisms of everyday racism than those from other states. It is true that Black women from the South had gone through more blatant experiences of racism, but I did not find clear indications that they are more "knowledgeable" about contemporary racism in the California context. However, it would be far beyond the scope of this research to develop a method to measure subtle differences in the knowledge of women from different states.

Among Black women in the Netherlands, the main criterion of distinction is the time of their arrival in the Netherlands. The majority of the group migrated between 1967 and 1975, with their parents or independently as students. The data do not suggest that women who were born and/or raised in the Netherlands were more aware of racism than women who came later. This implies that awareness of personally experienced racism is also determined by factors other than the time of arrival. Of particular importance are the political situation in the beginning of the 1980s (when a racist party was voted into parliament), widely reported cases of violence against individual Blacks, and the impact of government policies defining Blacks and other immigrants as problems for Dutch society.

The women belong to a relatively small minority of outstanding Black women. To avoid identification their names are coded (c) for (California) U.S. women and (s) for (Surinamese) women in the Netherlands, and they are never identified by the places they live or have lived.

INTERVIEWING

Most investigations in social science tend to "study down" rather than to "study up" (Lofland & Lofland, 1984, pp. 17-18). Doing research among equals has been strongly encouraged by feminist social scientists. In certain respects this research represents the "ideal" conditions for a nonhierarchical relationship between the researcher and the informants: shared experiences, social equality, and natural involvement with the problem. This ideal is shared by many feminist researchers who reject detachment from the "research objects" (Mies, 1983). It has been shown repeatedly that Black informants are reticent about discussing their experiences of White racism with a White interviewer (Hyman, 1975, p. 159; Stephan, 1977, p. 264). Only a few White social scientists have been able to gain enough confidence so that Black informants have discussed with them their critique of White society (e.g., Dummett, 1973).

My position as an investigator had to be one of conscious subjectivity (Klein, 1983, p. 94). Of course this does not mean that I uncritically accepted all the statements of the informants. It was of crucial importance, however, that I fully respected their points of view. Unlike many (White) social scientists, I took their accounts of racism seriously and showed genuine interest in the "ordinary" events of everyday life. This attitude allowed me to ask the interviewees to qualify specific statements and to go into details without inducing defensive reactions from their side. In other words, being an insider provided a rich base for tentative probing, which is valuable in exploratory research. Therefore, I do not agree with the traditional point of view that detachment is always a better condition for doing research than close involvement (Schwartz & Jacobs, 1979, pp. 48-49). Many other factors may have an impact on the interview situation and hence on the information presented in that context (Cicourel, 1964). However, I did not use the interview situation as part of the empirical data, the reason being that few of these factors could be controlled.

One peculiar problem surfaced in the interviews in the Netherlands. Because it is a small country, various Black women knew about my earlier publications on racism. This probably influenced their opinions about me. However, it is not likely that this had a serious impact on the interviews. Due to the relative equality between myself and the interviewees, they usually did not try to avoid critical standpoints about my work or about my role as an interviewer. When women referred to my work to give more credibility to their own stories about racism, I made it a point to find out whether these were also the interviewee's own opinions and experiences.

In nondirective interviewing the function of the interviewer is to encourage the interviewee to talk about a given topic with a minimum of direct questioning or guidance. This does not mean that I did not have any control at all over the general structure of the interview. To guarantee comparison between statements of different women, I used a minimal global interview schema,[1] the use of which was adapted to the specific style and personality of the interviewee. The interview schedule was based on the main clusters of information I wished to study: (a) general perceptions of race relations and racism, (b) perceptions of racial issues and racism in relation to socialization, (c) personal and vicarious experiences of racism, (d) perceptions of self in relation to other Blacks, and (e) perceptions of self in relation to (Black) femininity.

The interviews lasted two to two and a half hours. One would probably get more data from additional (or longer) interviews. But it would not have been feasible to process so much information in this project. Apart from that, even a long series of interviews would not produce a complete reconstruction of the reality of everyday racism in the life of an individual Black woman in our society. Another advantage of only one interview per interviewee is that I could avoid the usual variations in the stories and unnecessary repetition. The aim was rather to elicit "spontaneous" accounts.

METHOD OF ANALYSIS

The analysis of the data makes explicit the implicitly used concepts, notions, and categories in the interview materials. Everyday racism occurs in a particular context, is aimed at particular goals, and involves particular actors, rules, or particular social conditions. Analyzing experiences of racism is putting systematic links between interpretations of experiences and organization of categories concerning racism, on the one hand, and verbal representations of these experiences, on the other hand. This means that characteristics of the interviews are seen as (preliminary) indications of the definition and attributive explanations of everyday racism. There is no normative model that describes the ideal steps involved in analyzing the sort of data about racism I gathered in nondirective interviews.

The purpose of the analysis was to identify the following information in the interview materials: (a) macro and micro dimensions of everyday racism, (b) racist events, and (c) use of knowledge and heuristics of comprehension. In exploratory research the analysis of empirical data is a continuous process of (sometimes intuitively) weighing the relevance of similarities and regularities in the findings, on the one hand, against the relevance of unique experiences as insight-stimulating examples, on the other hand. Further details of my analysis are given in the subsequent chapters of this study. The following is a summary of the categories included in the analytic schema:

(1) *Macro and micro dimensions of racism* are identified by distinguishing, in the data, between
   (a) generalizing statements about situations, acts, attitudes, and
   (b) statements about specific events.

(2) Descriptions of *racist events* are reconstructed through
   (a) identification of social situations (setting, agents of racism, observers of racism, acts, attributed attitudes).

(3) Different *types of experiences* are identified by distinguishing between
   (a) witnessed situations and
   (b) reported events.

(4) The use of *knowledge and heuristics of comprehension* is analyzed by identifying in the text
   (a) interpretations (e.g., "I understand that," "what happened is") and

(b) evaluations and argumentation (based on general knowledge of racism, rules of inference, comparisons).

This last category, the identification of interpretive and evaluative statements in the interviews, needs further clarification. Interpretation and evaluation of specific experiences is a process of collecting and combining often diverse and complex information into a judgment. This process is more difficult in circumstances of uncertainty, such as when acts with racist implications are not presented in racial terms. Deciding what data are relevant to make a judgment about specific experiences or events is usually based on two types of judgmental heuristics: drawing on prior theories or expectations about racial issues and about racism, and comparing characteristics of the event with other relevant cases to assess the probability that a certain event is an example of racism.

For the following reasons the second heuristic—making comparisons—is relevant for my analysis. Social psychological theories of social inference suggest a few relevant heuristics, namely, the representativeness heuristic, the availability heuristic, the simulation heuristic, and the anchoring and adjustment heuristic (Fiske & Taylor, 1984, pp. 268-274). The representativeness heuristic is used to make inferences about the likelihood that one specific example is representative of attributes stereotypically associated with that category of event. The availability heuristic is used to evaluate the probability of a certain event on the basis of how quickly or of how many instances of similar events come to mind. The simulation heuristic is the construction of hypothetical alternative scenarios against which a certain event is evaluated. The anchoring heuristic uses specific reference points as a start and then adjusts them to new instances. These heuristics are too specific to be used in a general analytical schema. Therefore, I used one characteristic these four heuristics have in common, namely, the use of comparisons for consistency and consensus. This approach is inspired by Kelley's (1967) ANOVA (analysis of variance) model. Depending on the event to be explained, Black women seek consensus, consistency, or distinctiveness information but without strictly conforming to Kelley's normative covariation schema. Here I agree with Lalljee and Abelson (1983, pp. 70-71) that the process of arriving at explanations involves seeking specific information rather than a covariation process. I shall come back to this point later (in Chapter 4).

The issues discussed in this chapter indicate that (Black women's) general knowledge of racism is a key concept in the theory and methodology. Therefore, it is relevant to first reconstruct the social and historical context of Black women's general knowledge of racism. Information about the historical context can be inferred from the beginning of the interviews. The interviews with U.S. Black women began with a question about the civil rights movement in the 1960s. The purpose was to gain insight into more general perceptions of racial issues and racism. The Surinamese women were asked about their perceptions of the Dutch before their migration to gain insight into the feelings, attitudes, and opinions the women had about the Netherlands and the Dutch when they first came to the country. In the next chapter we will see how Black women acquired knowledge of racism and what the differences are in the general knowledge structure of Black women in the Netherlands and in the United States.

NOTE

1. For reasons of space the interview guide could not be included in this book. Interested readers may obtain a copy upon request.

3

Knowledge and Comprehension of Everyday Racism

The focus on general knowledge and comprehension of racism must be placed against the background of social cognition theory (Fiske & Taylor, 1984; Forgas, 1982). Social psychologists have produced a huge amount of research about the nature and function of ethnic attitudes. Many have focused on racist cognitions, but hardly any of these studies have addressed cognitions about racism. This introduces the problem of this chapter, namely, the acquisition and meaning of knowledge about racism. It may be assumed that, without general knowledge of racism, one cannot understand the reality of racism. Cognitions of racism are not only unique personal representations about the stock of racism episodes experienced within one's lifetime; representations are continually tested, adapted, and also structured by information from the social context and may, therefore, be regarded as belonging to the social domain. The aims of this chapter are (a) to explain the notion of general knowledge of racism and the comprehension of racist events, (b) to account for the acquisition of knowledge about racism in the biographies of the women, and (c) to reconstruct on the basis of the interview materials the structure of general knowledge of racism. This structure represents the cognitive framework for the explanation of personal experiences of racism.

To refer to knowledge and understanding of racism, the rather vague notion "racism awareness" has been used (va den Broek, 1987; Katz, 1978; Meulenbelt, 1985; Satow, 1982). However, this notion has not been conceptualized in detail. Further, even when acknowledging the relevance of "antiracism" as a theory and practice (Brandt,

1986; Lynch, 1986; Mullard, 1984; Troyna & Williams, 1986), which developed from a critique of multiculturalism, one cannot deny it is a problem that the increasingly popular activity of "Racism Awareness Training" is associated with a direction of antiracism that reduces racism to a psychological problem of which dominant members can be "cured" through proper information (Sivanandan, 1985). While questioning the usefulness of the notion of "racism awareness," it remains important in the study of accounts of racism to conceptualize the cognitive condition of having knowledge and a full understanding of racism. Therefore, I introduce the notion of "comprehension of racist events"—the idea of the comprehension of racist events can be conceptualized in terms of specific presuppositions and strategies of interpretation. Also it can be placed effectively in a theory of the acquisition of knowledge that structures the comprehension of specific racist events.

Before proceeding it is useful to give a preliminary explanation of what is meant by the "comprehension of racist events." Knowledge and a full understanding of racism encompass the availability in memory of the relevant cognitions to make a distinction between racist situations and nonracist situations. This means that, when racism is expressed covertly, the interpreter must be able to pose the relevant questions and to make goal-directed inferences and observations to substantiate the evaluation that racism is involved in that particular situation. It follows that the comprehension of racist events can be seen as the application of social cognitions to explain specific experiences (a) in the light of general knowledge of racism and (b) in terms of generalized episodes or scenarios of racism, which include knowledge about acceptable and unacceptable behavior in everyday situations. Let me further explain these key notions, namely, general knowledge of racism and situational representations.

GENERAL KNOWLEDGE AND SCENARIOS OF RACISM

General knowledge of racism represents a specific space in memory that is activated when the understander processes, stores, and retrieves specific experiences of racism. Knowledge of racism is not static. It is consistently adapted and modified to include new information. New experiences are tested and interpreted in terms of earlier-acquired notions of racism and add to or (partly) replace parts of previous representations of racism. In other words, knowledge of racism is a process of constant intake, testing, and interpretation of new information and remodeling of previous representations. To gain more insight into the structure and properties of general knowledge of racism, it is useful to analyze knowledge of racism as a special form of political knowledge (Fiske & Kinder, 1981).

The availability and use of political knowledge is different for individuals or (sub)groups. As with other political knowledge, the availability and use of general knowledge of racism depends on the degree of involvement and experience with the particular realm. However, the term *involvement* is ambiguous in the context of the problem of racism because it can mean being engaged in the reproduction of racism as well as being engaged in ways of dealing with the problem of racism. Therefore, in respect to racism it is best to reformulate political involvement as problematizing racism.

Through prolonged practice in dealing with racism, people become experts. This means that their general knowledge of racism becomes organized in more and more complex ways, while their interpretive strategies become more elaborate and effective. Fiske and Kinder (1981, p. 184) found that highly involved subjects follow more complicated information processing procedures. They appear to be sensitive to schema-consistent as well as schema-inconsistent data in the processing of new information, whereas low-involvement subjects are more inclined to remember only schema-consistent information. The concept of social schema is often used to refer to general expectations about a specific type of situation (Fiske & Taylor, 1984). General expectations about manifestations of racism in a specific type of situation are included in what I call *scenarios of racism* (SRs). The concept of scenario is an alternative to Schank and Abelson's concept of "script" (Schank & Abelson, 1977). It will be explained in a moment. Here it must be emphasized that people who routinely problematize racism are likely to assess new events on the basis of scenario-consistent as well as scenario-inconsistent criteria. The question of heuristics of interpretation is only touched upon here, for the sake of argument. It is further elaborated in Chapter 4.

To clarify the concept of scenarios of racism, it is useful, first, to point out some other aspects of mental representations of racism. This can best be done with a concrete example of a racist situation, an event that occurred in the Netherlands (Essed, 1984): A Black woman calls a housing agency and is invited to come over to discuss a specific apartment. Upon her arrival the agency denies having spoken to her earlier on the phone, and they insist they do not have any apartments available. The woman suspects she is rejected because she is Black. The assessment of this event is part of a complex cognitive system of information processing. In this it is relevant to have knowledge of rules and expectations about "using the services of a housing agency." In addition one may use elements such as mental representations of personal experiences with housing agencies without being discriminated against, memories of other experiences of discrimination in the same situation, or general knowledge of racism in society.

This particular episode is processed and stored in memory as a situation model (van Dijk & Kintsch, 1983). Hypothetically it can be assumed that this situation model is likely to include the following elements (van Dijk, 1987a, p. 191): (a) knowledge of the situation (who were involved and what happened?); (b) fragments of prior episodes (the other day when I went to a housing agency . . .); (c) instantiations from general expectations about that specific situation (using the services of a housing agency); (d) fragments of prior racist events (the same thing happened when I applied for a job); (e) instantiations of general expectations about discrimination by housing agencies (if you go there, they pretend that they have no apartments available); (f) instantiation from abstract knowledge of racism (many Whites are prejudiced against Blacks). The reason for this digression is not so much to use the concept of the situation model as such in my analysis but to point out the role of general knowledge in interpretation and evaluation of personal experiences. More specifically, in the processing of new events, people activate generalized episodes of that type of situation, or "scripts" (Schank & Abelson, 1977). Scripts include socially shared knowledge about event sequences and rules and conventions of acceptable behavior in specific situations. Rules and conventions for acceptable behavior are (sub)culturally defined and to a large extent structured by class- and gender-specific conditions. This has implications for a theory of knowledge and comprehension of racism. It may well be assumed that the typical infusions of racism into specific types of situations are probably represented in memory in a scenario of racism for that type of situation. Furthermore scenarios of racism include "scripts" or general expectations about the "normal" procedures in specific types of situations (e.g., visiting a housing agency). In addition, scenarios of racism include expectations of what usually goes "wrong" in these types of situations when that situation is simultaneously a racial situation (e.g., a Black woman visits a White housing agency).

Given these arguments it can be assumed that general knowledge about racism consists of two components: (a) generalizations about specific types of racist episodes (scenarios of racism) and (b) abstract cognitions about the processes and mechanisms of racism (abstract knowledge of racism). For the purpose of this study the cognitive structure of racism representations is not elaborated upon further. Here the social aspects of knowledge acquisition and application are more relevant.

COMPREHENDING RACISM

The more information about and more practice with the problem of racism one has, the more abstract, complex, and organized representations of racism become and the more sensitively this knowledge can be used in memory storage and retrieval. Conversely, however, stored information about racism as such is not always readily usable in processing new information. This means that well-developed structures of knowledge about racism must be distinguished from newly developing scenarios of racism (see also Fiske & Taylor, 1984, p. 173). The development of scenarios of racism is still unexplored in social cognition theory. Although such an attempt is not the purpose of this study, a moderate beginning may be made by acknowledging that there are different degrees of understanding that determine the development of general knowledge of racism. Hypothetically it can be assumed that general knowledge of racism presupposes insight into at least the following aspects: (a) the ability to explain individual experiences in terms of group experiences, (b) acknowledgment of the historical experience of the group, (c) explanation of (historical and contemporary) group experiences in terms of racial and ethnic domination, (d) acknowledgment of continuity in the relation between the personal experience and the group experience, and (e) personal responsibility in the process of change. In view of these aspects it can be assumed that the comprehension of racist events depends on the availability of general knowledge about racism and on the availability of notions of "unfair" treatment or discrimination but also on the availability of representations of experience and structure of a certain "maturity."

Therefore, it may be assumed that, *without general knowledge of racism, individuals cannot comprehend the meaning of racism in their lives.* The reliability of this presupposition can be tested by applying it to the real-life accounts of Black women.

SUBJECTIVE AND OBJECTIVE ASSESSMENTS OF THE COMPREHENSION OF RACIST EVENTS

How can we establish whether the accounts of racism gathered in this study derive from knowledge and comprehension of racism? Before attending to this question, we may recall that the women who participated in the research project are a select group. They all agreed to discuss their experiences of racism. Because they knew what the project was about, all the women, with a few exceptions, tried to make explicit their general knowledge of racism and felt that they knew how to recognize racism in their personal lives. Of the 55 women 2 in the U.S. sample (c18, c28, in the United States—USA) and 2 in the Dutch sample (s19, s28, in the Netherlands—NL) did not present themselves as "knowledgeable" about racism. The two U.S. women explicitly problematize their "lack" of insight into racism. They feel confused about the issue of racism and present themselves as women who have just started to learn about racism. The two Surinamese women did not problematize their "lack" of comprehension of racism. Apart from these subjective assessments, it is also possible to make objective assessments of the presence of general knowledge of racism through discourse analysis. For this purpose a schema is constructed to test accounts for comprehension of racist acts. To illustrate I use quotations from the interviews with the four women referred to above.

In Essed (1984) I found that Blacks who have never seriously thought about racism are inclined to avoid explicit use of terms such as *discrimination* or *racism*. This is also confirmed by the current data. Consider, for instance, the following quotations. (Note: The quotations marked with an "s" followed by a number stand for an interviewee in the Netherlands while the "c" followed by a number represents a Black American interviewee from California.)

> You hear *something* on the TV, on the radio, and indeed . . . especially if I have to think about South Africa, I think *it* is terrible. Or in America. . . . But to actually say that I thought about *it*, no. . . . (s28, NL)

Now and then you do notice *something,* but you don't dwell on
it. . . . (s19, NL)

I just don't look at *things.* Not unless someone directly comes up to me
and does *something.* Then I will acknowledge *it.* (c28, USA; italics
added in these quotations)

From their statements it can be inferred that the basic condition for
the comprehension of racism is missing: The women do not define
themselves as Black or are ambivalent about defining themselves as
members of a racially or ethnically dominated group. This is also evident in their use of language. Blacks are referred to as "they," and
differentiated from the self ("I") as in "I feel different [than other
Blacks]. I don't know how they feel" (c18, USA).

Differentiating themselves from other Blacks does not mean that the
women have not experienced racial discrimination in their lives. They
could all recall specific events of unfair treatment or of discrimination,
but they themselves did not categorize these experiences as racist events.
In various cases they gave enough other relevant information concerning
the situation for me to make the objective conclusion that they had been
subjected to racism even when they themselves did not see the event in
terms of racism. A relevant question here is how the accounts of these
women can be placed in a theory of everyday racism.

From a social psychological point of view, it would seem that the
best way to explain inconsistency in accounts of racism would be
within a framework of cognitive consistency theories. The reason is
that to be the object of discrimination may be a problematic experience, which may cause psychological inconsistency between previous
cognitions and the interpretation of new experiences. In sociology
this phenomenon is known as self-deception (Douglas, 1976) and in
social psychology as cognitive dissonance (Festinger, 1957/1976).
Festinger's theory has been criticized and reformulated (Bem, 1967;
Eiser, 1980; Wicklund & Frey, 1981) but his basic premises remain interesting. His theory contends that people tend to feel uncomfortable
with cognitive dissonance; therefore, they are motivated to reconstruct their perceptions in a way that reduces dissonance. People tend
to reduce dissonance in particular when situations are felt to be a
threat to their self-concept, for instance, in situations seen as negative
and inevitable at the same time (Aronson, 1980). This may well be
the case with experiences of racism in everyday life, and I shall

demonstrate some examples of this. However, the relevance of these examples, as we shall see in a moment, is not so much the response to inconsistencies but the larger social and cognitive context of these interpretations. This touches upon the problem that cognitive consistency theories do not give insight into complex interpretation processes. I shall explain this in more detail in Chapter 4. Here it is sufficient to stress that it seems more useful to concentrate not on dissonance reduction strategies but on the conditions that stimulate effective use of strategies of comprehension. Therefore, I suggest an alternative framework.

Presupposing that the comprehension of racist acts involves the systematic testing of a specific definition of the situation, the criteria of testing, interpretation, and evaluation should be made explicit. It is then possible to follow the testing procedure step by step and to see where differences occur in subjective and objective assessments of the event.

A PROCEDURE FOR THE ASSESSMENT OF RACIST EVENTS

Comprehension of racist acts was defined as the ability to explain specific experiences in terms of situational knowledge and in terms of general knowledge of racism. The comprehension of racism in everyday situations can be conceptualized as a "strategic" process following a specific sequence. The basic elements in this process are interpretation and evaluation of specific events. The sequence of interpretive steps are followed to determine whether a specific event potentially has racist implications or consequences. Evaluative steps, usually consisting of combinations of inference and argumentation, are followed to clarify why specific events have to be seen as forms of racism. Here the interpretive aspects are addressed in detail, while only general reference is made to evaluative aspects, which will be given more detailed attention in the next chapter. In the following explanation of the test sequence, situational knowledge can be presupposed but not defined. Because culture is not a static concept, the rules and conventions of acceptable behavior are subject to change. Situated acts of racism change accordingly. The test sequence is only a rough outline of the cognitive economy of the use of interpretive steps. Hypothetically it can be assumed that the interpretation of potentially racist events proceeds as follows:

Step 1: Acceptable or Not?

First, specific practices should be interpreted as acceptable or unacceptable, given the situational conditions. In general, behavior considered acceptable will not induce further questioning. However, insufficient knowledge of normal rules and conventions for acceptable behavior may cause the interpreter to accept behavior that seems normal but that is in fact not acceptable in that specific situation. This problem is particularly relevant in cases of covert racism. Reformulated in terms of acceptable and unacceptable behavior, *covert racism* in interaction situations can be seen as racism expressed in seemingly acceptable practices that are, however, not (fully) acceptable within the particular context. Conversely, if the interpreter feels the event is unacceptable when, objectively, it has to be considered acceptable, the subjective judgment must be seen as expressing insufficient situational knowledge.

Step 2: Acceptable Excuses for Unacceptable Behavior?

Unacceptable behavior (e.g., discrimination) can sometimes be excused with acceptable reasons. This is often the case when there are circumstances beyond the control of the actor. When objectively acceptable excuses are subjectively experienced as unacceptable, subjective assessments of the event as racist must be considered objectively invalid.

Step 3: Is It Because I Am Black?

If there are no acceptable excuses, it is relevant to know whether this example of discrimination (or prejudice) is directed against a Black individual because of her or his racial-ethnic background. When this is the case, and given that the actor is acting of her or his own free will, there are no reasonable excuses for discrimination.

Step 4: Is the Specific Event Excusable?

In Essed (1984, pp. 50-52) I discussed a specific misunderstanding of racism, namely, blaming other Blacks for causing discrimination. Objectively, if the interpreter finds mitigating circumstances that make the specific case of racial discrimination excusable, this judgment does not express insight into racism.

Step 5: Is the Event Socially Significant?

Not acknowledging the social relevance of racially discriminatory acts must be considered an example of insufficient comprehension of the implications of the event. That is, even if the interpreter considers specific acts to be inexcusable forms of racial discrimination, it may still be the case that feeling discriminated against is seen as a personal problem. In other words, if you do not mention it, you will not have any problems with discrimination and you will not give people any reason to discriminate against you. In Essed (1984, p. 164) I found that, by the end of the 1970s, it was a typically occurring misunderstanding of racism in the Netherlands to think that, if you were alert for discrimination, that meant you were a failure in life.

Step 6: Evaluation

Finally, the last step places the specific event in an *evaluative framework* consisting of general racism knowledge, which can be supported by other argumentation such as comparisons with the experiences of specific other Blacks. When specific behavior is interpreted as anti-Black and evaluated as (covert) racism without additional supportive argumentation, or without making reference to general knowledge of racism, the evaluation of the situation as a form of racism has to be considered objectively insufficient. The function and use of the evaluative framework is discussed in more detail in Chapter 4. This process of "strategic" testing of the situation can be summarized hypothetically in the flow diagram in Figure 3.1.

ASSESSING REAL-LIFE EXPLANATIONS OF "UNFAIR TREATMENT"

The accounts of the four women who did not present themselves as "knowledgeable" about racism (c18, c28, s19, s28) are tested on the basis of this flow diagram as follows. It can be hypothesized that their stories probably include descriptive and interpretive categories but do not include racism evaluation categories. The material to be analyzed consists of three arbitrarily selected stories the women told about experiences of unfair treatment or discrimination.

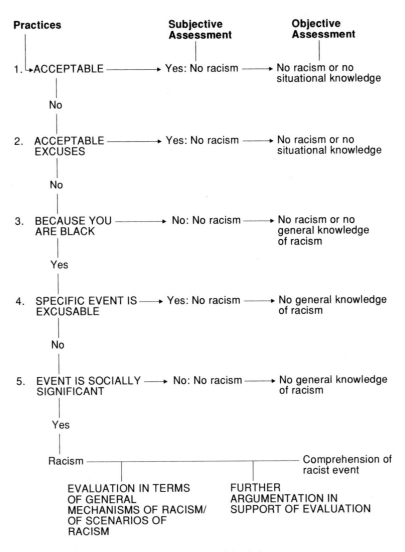

Figure 3.1. Flow diagram: Assessment of (racist) events

Example 1 (NL)

S28, aged 30, has problems finding a job with Dutch temporary employment agencies. She seems to be overqualified. She has a college degree but only ends up with secretarial job offers. Someone advises her to go to CH, an agency working explicitly (but not only) for Black clients. There she finds the sort of job she wanted. What does she think of the fact that only when she came to this agency did there appear to be vacancies the other agencies did not offer to her?

> To be honest, I've never really given it much thought. [I heard] that they do have suitable jobs. That's why I went there, not because they are CH, but because they happened to have those jobs for me. . . . I didn't worry about it. . . . But, yes, if you listen a bit to all the studies that are done in that area, then you do have to wonder why it's like that, is it really just by chance? . . . I can't tell you, look, this is how it is. I can say, look, this is what I've experienced, and you may interpret it for yourself. But I think you will still notice that often if things are difficult or seem difficult, I try to find a solution, and that I perhaps don't even think that I'm being discriminated against, whatever that may be. . . . I try to put myself in the place of the majority. . . . You know you are in a society where you are, first of all, eh, in the minority. That is, that the majority, I assume, will more often get what he or she wants. The majority will also more often have the say, . . . and you must try to find your place within this group.

With the help of the flow diagram in Figure 3.1, the interview fragment can be analyzed as follows:

(1) Acceptability?—No (hesitantly). In first instance s28 feels it is acceptable that all the other agencies did not offer her appropriate jobs ("not given it much thought"). However, in second instance she thinks maybe it is "odd" ("you do have to wonder").

(2) Acceptable excuses?—Yes, and no. Yes, the other agencies might have had good reasons. This is what s28 implicitly says. She emphasizes that she went to the CH agency not because of their positive attitude toward Black applicants but because they "happened to have" the type of jobs she wanted. However, at the same time s28 is not really sure whether it is intentional or accidental that she did not get adequate job offers elsewhere ("really just by chance?").

(3) Because you are Black?—Yes. S28 explains that the Dutch are the majority; she is a minority. These facts cannot be changed ("you must try to find your place"). This particular element in the interpretation of the event is especially interesting. What she means to say is something like this: "Yes, it is because I am Black, but I do not consider this discrimination. As a matter of fact you had better not start

worrying about discrimination, because there is nothing you can do about it." This she defends with the view that reporting about discrimination is a way to excuse oneself from trying "to find a solution" for "difficult" things. This implies that pointing out discrimination is associated with powerlessness. This belief can be explained against the background of another presupposition, that is, that discrimination is seen as a fact of life because one cannot change the majority. In the next chapters we will see that women who also see discrimination as a constant factor—not because the majority cannot change but because these women have problematized racism in society—do not view racial discrimination as a condition that cannot be changed.

(4) Specific event excusable?—Yes. Implicitly s28 indicates that the other agencies can be excused. S28 says that she understands the other agencies. She even implicitly suggests that she would have done the same in their place when she says, "I try to put myself in [their] place."

The interpretation sequence s28 follows ends with step 4.

Example 2 (USA)

C28, aged 21, has problems learning French. She is the only Black student in class. Her difficulties with the language are much increased when her French teaching assistant (TA) appears very impatient with her. The situation grows worse with each lesson, until one time c28 has become so nervous that she cannot quite understand a specific question addressed to her in French and subsequently responds quite out of line. The TA attacks her.

(1) Acceptable?—No.

One day she had me get up and do a little charade and I could not understand what she was asking me to do. I was taking certain words and thought this is what she meant and so I did that, but it wasn't it. She just stomps up to the front of the room, in front of the whole class, I was so embarrassed. She snatches the pencil out in front of me, pulls the card back, and parts it. . . . The whole class was silent, and nobody wanted to look at me 'cause they were probably embarrassed having to see the whole thing.

(2) Acceptable excuses?—No. First, there is a reference to c28's own attitude. She says that she did not cause the situation because she

"really wanted to learn." In addition c28 explains that fellow students agreed that the TA was being unreasonably harsh with her:

> I talked to one of the students, . . . she says, I never could figure out why she always would just pinpoint you and purposely embarrass you. I said I don't know, I said I thought it was in my head, I thought maybe I was imagining that she was purposely picking me out, but apparently she was.

(3) Because you are Black?—Yes (hesitantly).

> In this case, I guess that would be the only thing. . . . That's what my [Black] roommate told me too. She says . . . are you the only Black in there? And I said yeah. She says is your TA White? I said well she's French, I don't know if they consider themselves White or not, and she says well then, there you go. . . . But I don't know that, I can assume it, but I don't know.

(4) Specific event excusable?—No (see 2 above).
(5) Specific event socially relevant?—No (hesitantly). This example is interesting because it illustrates the fact that information about racism and even information about relevant questions to ask when assessing a situation for racism (see 3 above) do not necessarily lead to comprehension of the racist event. C28 is very reluctant to see the experience as a case of racism:

> I thought of it [that it was because I am Black], but I try not to think that way. I try to make that my last resort, you know. I hate using my color as an excuse. . . . And I would hate to think that that's how she was. I mean, I just hate thinking that people are really trying to discriminate against me, and I guess I'm always trying to run away from that fact. And I don't want to acknowledge it, and I guess that's something I need to deal with too, but people will definitely try to discriminate, and I can't run away from it.

Example 3 (NL)

S19, aged 43, recalls an occasion in a Dutch shop when she was being watched obtrusively by one of the saleswomen.
(1) Acceptable?—No.

> I was in some shop, and . . . immediately you have someone standing be-
> hind you, like looking to see what will happen. I found that bothersome.

The saleswoman pretended to be searching among her products for
something specific. This would be acceptable behavior in a shop situation. But the fact that s19 noticed that she was being watched from
the very minute she entered the shop means that the saleswoman's behavior was not discreet (enough). Therefore, s19 could not be fooled.

(2) Acceptable excuses?—Yes. S19 says that even though she does
not like to be considered a potential thief, the saleswoman has the
right to watch out for her products.

> It does seem a bit annoying, but on the other hand, I can understand it,
> for it's not written on my face that I'm not one of those people who steal.
> You protect your products.

Because s19 does not make a distinction between obtrusive and un-
obtrusive methods of shop protection, it seems that s19 has insufficient situational knowledge. The need to prevent shoplifting is no
excuse to make a customer feel she is picked out for special surveillance. The interpretation sequence stops here (see the flow diagram),
but admittedly the reason s19 thinks the excuses are acceptable may
give the incorrect impression we could continue to follow the flow diagram: S19 contends that the event is excusable *because she is Black.*
It may be concluded that she has neither sufficient situational knowledge nor sufficient general knowledge of racism. She accuses other
Black women of shoplifting and she excuses the saleswoman for not
knowing that she is not like the other Black women.

> I can understand it. Because it often happens that one of these Black
> women comes in and things are stolen. . . . They can't see from my face
> that I'm not one of the ones who steals.

In Essed (1984, pp. 136-146) I showed that one of the forms of everyday racism against Black women in Netherlands was that they
were often falsely accused of, or it was otherwise insinuated that they
were, shoplifting. One may infer from generalized knowledge of racist situations (in Dutch shops Blacks are often watched suspiciously)
and from general knowledge about the mechanisms of racism
(criminalization of Blacks) that the event was probably a fusion of

ordinary shop behavior (protection of products) and racism (considering Blacks more likely to steal).

After testing the structure of all the stories these four women told about "unfair treatment" or "discrimination," it appears that their stories systematically exclude the category of general knowledge of racism or other references to the shared experiences of Blacks. These arguments confirm the crucial nature of general knowledge of racism for the comprehension of personal experiences. Therefore, closer attention is paid to the acquisition and structure of Black women's general knowledge of racism.

RELATING COGNITIVE TO SOCIAL PROCESSES OF UNDERSTANDING

In this section we shift the emphasis from the cognitive orientation in the previous discussion toward a more sociological approach to the role of knowledge of racism. In the fields of social psychology and education there is an established tradition of research on racial and ethnic identity in relation to child development (e.g., Clark & Clark, 1947; Milner, 1975; Stone, 1981). There is an increasing amount of research on the ideological reproduction of racism through education (Troyna & Williams, 1986; van Dijk, 1987b), literature (Foster-Carter, 1984; Redmond, 1980; Stinton, 1979), children's socialization (Katz, 1976), and the mass media (van Dijk, 1983, 1988, 1991). After years of research on the reproduction of racism, recent publications have been concerned about the absence of well-balanced information about racism in the school system, and some authors are now contributing to filling this gap (Brandt, 1986; Dors, 1988; Mullard, 1984; van Dijk, 1987b). A few authors have emphasized the role of mothers in the communication of knowledge about racism during primary socialization (Wilson, 1987, chap. 7) and, more generally, the role of the family as a site of resistance to racism (Brittan & Maynard, 1984, p. 130). However, there is as yet no full-fledged theory of the reproduction of knowledge of racism in society in general and among Blacks in particular. While such a venture is not the purpose of this study, we can reconstruct from the interview materials how the women acquired knowledge about racism and when they began to comprehend it. Because this reconstruction depends on the memory of the women, it is beyond the scope of this project to give a complete picture of the early childhood socialization and education of the women.

Hypothetically information about racism is acquired in two different ways. Knowledge and attitudes about racism are acquired through *communication about racism* (direct mode) and through *personal experiences of racist situations* (indirect mode). Like any other form of political knowledge, information about racism is communicated through formal and informal channels. Formal channels include the mass media, the education system, and literature. Because knowledge about racism is only marginally integrated into the systems of education and mass communication (Troyna & Williams, 1986; van Dijk, 1987b), informal and alternative communication systems are very important. Informal information systems include family, friends, colleagues, and other informal networks. Alternative formal information sources include, among other things, political organizations, community organizations, and antiracist organizations.

Many factors have a potential impact on the strategies and forms of communication about racism, such as class, religious background, level of education, and racial composition of the neighborhood. These cannot possibly all be accounted for here. The comprehension of racist events as a cognitive process relates in a two-dimensional way to social conditions and processes of understanding. One dimension deals with the context in which racist events occur and the other dimension with the social base of knowledge needed to understand these events. This can be explained as follows: The context of everyday racism and the form it takes have implicit cues affecting the interpretation and representation of these situations. At the same time a theory of the use of general knowledge to explain specific events must take into account the often functional relation of knowledge structures to class, gender, and other cultural factors in addition to the personality of the individual (Forgas, 1982, p. 66). Figure 3.2 represents this dual relation between social cognition and social processes, namely, (a) the cognitive and social context of the comprehension of racism and (b) the social context of the acquisition of knowledge about racism.

ACQUISITION OF KNOWLEDGE OF RACISM

The process of political socialization starts in early childhood. Political values exist as early as elementary school (Mueller, 1973,

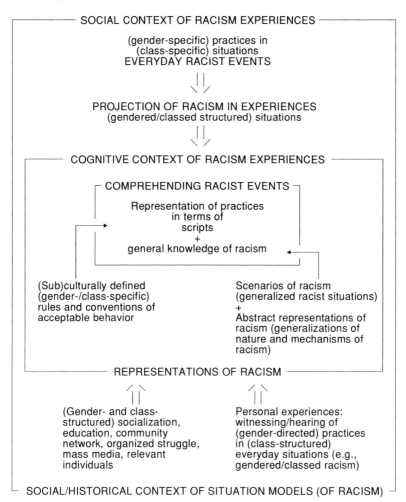

Figure 3.2. Social and cognitive context of experiences of racism

p. 67). In the first years of elementary school, children have already formed awareness of other societal groupings and definitions of self in relation to these groups. Wilson (1987, chap. 7) shows that, before children fully understand problems of racism, general orientation and values in relation to issues of race and racism, as well as the mode in which they are articulated, are substantially influenced by the socialization strategies experienced at home. As previously noted, however, this knowledge has to reach a certain "maturity" before it can be used effectively.

Indications of this were found in the stories of Black women about the first time they recalled having experienced racism. First, personal experiences with hostility, discrimination, or, more generally, negative attitudes or behavior from Whites add to the stock of knowledge about race relations, but these incidents do not mean that the women could already comprehend specific acts in terms of racism. If the women were able to recall specific experiences at all, they often explained that at that time they did not realize they were subjected to racism. In the United States being called a "nigger" was, for many women, likely to be a typical first experience with racism. Irrespective of the state or period in which the women grew up, they are likely to remember somebody calling them "nigger," even though they may not "exactly remember when and where" and "probably went and asked [their] mother, what does that mean?" (c12).

In other words, even when they could recognize racial "hostility" and "unfairness" as children, none of the women recalled being able to "fully understand what was going on" (c7) in these childhood experiences. This is consistent with other research on political cognitions. Insight into racism implies the ability to form abstract conceptions of the community. Conceptions of institutions and knowledge about the role of people representing these institutions significantly increase between the 7th and 11th grades (Becker, McCombs, & McLeod, 1975, pp. 35-36). For the purpose of this study the developmental aspects of the acquisition of knowledge are not elaborated upon further; rather attention is paid to the sites of knowledge acquisition and the communicating agents.

The historical conditions of the acquisition of knowledge about racism are different for each group of women. Black women in the United States acquired knowledge of racism against the background of the common experience of contemporary and older generations of Blacks in the United States. In other words, the historical context within the United States was a constant factor that served explicitly as a frame of reference for the comprehension of contemporary racism. Most Black women in the Netherlands acquired knowledge about racism in the Netherlands only after their immigration. Due to a colonial education only a few of them had developed critical knowledge of Dutch colonialism (see, for further discussion of the politics of colonization, Fanon, 1963/1985; Hira, 1982; Kom, 1971; Memmi, 1965). As a result of colonization and the virtual absence of well-balanced information about the relation between racism and Dutch (neo)colonialism, hardly any of the Surinamese women had relevant knowledge available to reconnect themselves, through the experience and comprehension of racism, with the history of their people.

Despite these differences in background there are also similarities in the acquisition of knowledge of racism in the United States and in the Netherlands. For the purpose of the analysis the direct and indirect sources and agents of communication of knowledge of racism in the lives of Black women are discussed separately. It must be emphasized, however, that knowledge acquisition through personal experiences of racism and through information about racism overlap and converge in real life. As indirect modes are identified, (a) life under conditions of racial segregation and (b) attending White-dominated schools. Direct information about racism is acquired through (c) the family, (d) community organizations, (e) the media, and (f) significant others. First, however, attention must be paid to the role of colonialism in impeding the acquisition of knowledge of racism.

The Denial of History: The Impact of Dutch Colonization

To understand the impact of colonization on the development of knowledge of racism, it is relevant to take into consideration at least the following factors. First, colonization is characterized by ideological domination. The colonizers present themselves as a positive identification model and ignore the relation between colonialism and racism. Second, the majority of the colonized population has little or no experience with Whites on a level of day-to-day interaction. Third, it appears that the experiences in the Netherlands, after migration, contradict previous expectations Blacks had about life in the Netherlands. Fourth, it follows from these factors that Blacks from the colonies are, initially, neither prepared to be confronted with racism when they arrive in the Netherlands nor ready to deal effectively with racist situations. With these conditions in mind the impact of colonization on the acquisition of knowledge of racism can be summarized as follows:

Of the 28 women, 20 went to school in Suriname, where the Dutch colonists represented 5% of the population. Only those women who came from the Surinamese "elite" families had developed (some) negative attitudes toward the Dutch. In Suriname they had often socialized with the Dutch, in school or in social clubs. Some women told that they resented "this whole Dutch colony . . . [because] they lived in the best houses" (s10). Those who had gone to Catholic schools in Suriname recall that the (White) nuns discriminated, for instance, by putting "black children on the right side, and on the left the girls with a bit lighter skin" (s7). At that time, however, they did not comprehend the wider implications of these experiences. Most women were aware of color discrimination. But even when, "in Suriname, it happened a lot that you were teased about being Black" (s10), none of the women was taught to understand Black-against-Black discrimination as an inherent part of the system of colonization and cultural racism.

Decolonization processes are often characterized by a radicalization against the previous colonizers. Because the majority of the Surinamese women came to the Netherlands in the 1970s, there are very few examples of the effects of independence (the period after 1975). The experiences of most of these women confirm other research on the early attitudes and expectations of people from the Caribbean who had moved to the so-called mother countries (e.g., Patterson, 1963). Initially they and their families had positive expectations about the Dutch. Most Surinamese women expected the Dutch to be friendly and rich. Many recalled the same anecdote about the first period in the Netherlands when they were surprised to find that "a White man collected the garbage" (s2). Indeed the majority of the women were largely ignorant about Dutch racism when they came to the Netherlands. In other aspects, however, they were quite well informed about life in the Netherlands. The colonial system of education was, as one woman puts it, "permeated with what they called the Dutch culture. A lot was known [about the Netherlands] from history books, geography books and reading books" (s9).

The disconnection of contemporary experiences of racism from the historical experience of Blacks under Dutch colonialism and, simultaneously, the disconnection of contemporary racism and the history of racism within the Netherlands should not be seen as a general lack of insight into racism among Black women in the Netherlands. The Surinamese women knew that "the roots [of racism] were there all along" (s7). Others agreed that "nothing has essentially changed since slavery. It's a bit more glossed over, but not really changed" (s11). However, these historical cognitions are not very complex or well organized in their stories of racism. Therefore, it can be assumed that Surinamese women's general knowledge of Dutch racism is newly developing and largely ahistorical. It is predominantly based on comprehension of racism through personal experiences in the Netherlands. In other words, initially they acquired knowledge of racism predominantly in indirect ways.

History as Experience: Growing Up Under Segregation

Among Black women in the United States, there is an explicit and immediate sense of continuity and connection with the experience of previous generations. This means that, in accounts of their own experiences of racism, the women are able to effectively use the history of Blacks in the United States as a frame of reference. One good illustration is the following story involving a young woman, aged 21. She explained that she almost exploded with anger when she was recently called a "nigger" by a "White guy." She was furious because

> I know the attitude behind that word. [It is] racist, it's a degrading term calling me worse than dirt. When I heard it, I just—I remembered everything I've ever read in my history books, everything everybody ever told me about slavery or what I've seen on TV, and I said, they can't do this to me. Not in 1985! . . . I said no, no! This is for everybody who has been called this and been hurt by it, I'm going to hurt you because of it. (c5)

For many women the immediate history, namely, the pre-1960s, forms an important frame of reference within which they place their own experiences. Therefore, it is relevant to look at the impact of the period of segregation on the acquisition of knowledge of racism.

Of the 27 U.S. Black women, 7 were born and raised under conditions of legal segregation, where "there were water fountains that said colored and white, and there were stores where you colored people went through this door and whites went through that door" (c4). For the purpose of this study the following factors are important in understanding the impact of life under segregation on the acquisition of knowledge of racism. (a) Growing up in the South meant that knowledge of racism was acquired through personal experiences; (b) there was no contradiction between the immediate experience of racism and knowledge about the system taught at home; (c) Blacks were forced to deal with overt manifestations of racism; (d) it follows from these factors that growing up in the South prepared Blacks to expect racism in society and to accept the necessity of coping with the situation. These points are discussed by women who recalled their experiences of that time.

Under segregation Blacks were confronted from an early age with the idea that they were different than Whites, that they had to live by "the rules" (c4) of a system that set them apart and denied them rights and privileges. The conditions of segregation generated comprehension of racism through the lived experience. "You know immediately where you stand because it is made very obvious from very early on" (c13). Other women agree that "having grown up in the South" means that you have seen racism, that you have "lived it" (c1). In their childhoods some women were confronted with the extreme violence of racism in segregated areas. Without immediately comprehending the wider implications of their experiences, they became, as children, part of the struggle of their parents against oppression. Thereby they began to learn how to place specific events in a general framework of race relations. The following quotation illustrates this. It is an account of a woman who, when she was 8 years old, had to flee with the family from a mob threatening to lynch her father:

> I did not understand the severity of the problem until much later when I recognized that people were upset because my father dared hit and beat up a white person. It was then that I started to understand the whole business where you have no right to hit a white person, or you can't speak back to them, or they can call you "gal" and all kinds of derogatory names. (c13)

The system of segregation operated through convergence of race, class, and gender factors. Job possibilities for Black women were almost exclusively confined to domestic work. Racism almost completely coincided with class exploitation. This is reflected in the knowledge of racism the women acquired, as can be inferred, for instance, from the memory of the daughter of a domestic. She recalls: "There were [other] ways of knowing also about racism." The fact that all her "new" clothes were the "old" ones from the family her mother worked for suggested to the young girl that "White people had all the money" (c21).

Because, under segregation, racism was an open and explicitly operating form of oppression, the facts of racial inequality were known in the families and communicated to the children. The articulation of knowledge of racism within the family depends on the mode of socialization, usually as a function of class and education (Mueller, 1973, chap. 2). A few women came from families where both parents had a college education. In these families the parents valued discussion as an important method of socializing their children. Therefore, the women recall explicit guidance and support to identify with the Black cause and to fight against the forces of racism. They were told that segregation was a system of "bad rules bound to change" (c4). Several women recall being "socialized to think in terms of race pride" (c27), to understand that "Blacks are beneficiaries of the civil rights movement" (c4), and being warned to "never accept any denigration" (c34).

The women from the South developed abstract structures of knowledge of racism and gained highly developed scenarios of racism under conditions of legal segregation. Because they were raised in a completely Black environment, women who grew up in the South usually did not have much daily experience with Whites. When they moved to other states to go to (White) colleges, in order to recognize racism they had to test and adapt their situational knowledge, namely, of the rules and conventions for acceptable and unacceptable behavior, to the White middle-class norms of the new environment. For a subtle illustration of this, an abstract is used from the interview with a lawyer (c4), 33 years old, who talks about an event in college.

Entering a wealthy college on the East Coast, this Black woman suddenly had to deal with (White) middle-class rules and conventions in daily social interaction. Being herself from a (Black) working-class background, she could not immediately identify class-specific expressions of racism in an encounter with a fellow female student from a (White) middle-class background. It may be assumed that the woman was not altogether unfamiliar with White middle-class behavior, because any American is exposed, to a certain extent, to middle-class culture through the mass media. The example is interesting because it concerns a delicate, quite uncommon situation. Therefore, it may be assumed that the woman did not have any practice with this situation in a White context. The story can be summarized as follows:

Context: The event took place on her way to the dining hall. The Black student had gained quite a bit of weight since being in college because there was so much food for free. On her way to the dining hall her pants became unzipped.

Unacceptable behavior: "One [White] girl said something like 'Oh you are gaining weight.' " The Black student answers "Yeah, I have," and continues on her way. She does not think of gaining weight as anything special. "You know, no big deal." However, when she gets back to her room, her friend, who had seen what happened, says: "She insulted you. Why didn't you realize she was catty and malicious?" It then appears that the Black student had used as a framework of interpretation another set of rules, which she realizes when she discusses the situation with her friend and says she "didn't know the rules" and "thought [the girl] was making small talk."

Her friend understands that, particularly for middle-class (White) women, "gaining weight" is a delicate issue. The norm is to be slim, and one does not comment in public on another woman who is gaining too much weight in order to save the other party from feeling embarrassed. Second, her friend also tells her that in middle-class culture one reacts very discreetly when women have an embarrassing problem with their clothing. One certainly does not make comments like that with "all those people around."

Evaluation: It is likely that the event expressed racism from the side of the White student, whether or not she intended it. From general knowledge of racism it can be inferred that Blacks are often insulted and denigrated. These are commonly occurring mechanisms of racism. Moreover dominant group members are often rude and impolite rather than sensitive to the needs and feelings of Blacks. There were no other plausible clues in the situation to explain why the White student addressed herself to the Black student in a way that would have embarrassed her on the spot, had she realized the implications of the remark. The Black student adds this new information about (White) middle-class culture—"oh, those are the rules"—to her stock of scripts and also adds the new information about the way White (middle-class) culture structures expressions of racism to her general knowledge about racism.

Reaction: The story ends with a confirmation that this new information will be used to interpret and evaluate social interaction with Whites in the future for more effective response. This event confirms the argument that the assessment of particular situations, in view of possible racism, requires at least an understanding of acceptable and unacceptable behavior given the particular circumstances. In addition comparative inference from general knowledge of racism is required.

To conclude, the experiences of women who have grown up under segregation indicate that inherent in the explicitness and overtness of racial inequality in the system of segregation is the relative absence of contradictory information about racism. The development of general representations of racism was a coherent process. The information they received at home was consistent with their personal experiences of racism. Therefore, the acquisition of knowledge of racism was probably a natural and gradual process. Because they gained insight into racism from an early age, they identified with other Blacks and with the struggle against racism. This knowledge did not remain static but continually developed and adapted itself to new circumstances. They learned how to use their comprehension of racism to survive within the system while at the same time fundamentally rejecting the system.

The Impact of Large-Scale Struggle Against Racial Inequality

Because the struggle against racism in the Netherlands is still diffuse and local, we focus in this section on developments in the United States, the impact of which cannot possibly be given due attention in this limited space (see Franklin, 1984; Marable, 1984). Here attention is paid to two sites of resistance, namely, community struggle and the campus revolts. In addition the role of the Black intelligentsia must be acknowledged (Cruse, 1967/1984) in the generation of new conceptions of racism in society and new definitions of Black identity, which could be readily used to feed resistance and demands for change. The majority of the U.S. women were in their teens and early twenties in the period of the civil rights movement, from 1960 to 1965, and the Black Power movement, from 1965 to 1970. Almost all of the women came from neighborhoods where committees organized marches, boycotts, or picket lines. There were revolts against centuries of racial inequality and conditions of extreme poverty. Some women could hear the bombings nearby. Not for all the women, however, did knowledge of community resistance contribute to comprehension of racism at that time.

Because women who grew up under segregation had learned that they should not accept racial inequality, it comes as no surprise that all of them participated in the actions, irrespective of age or class background. However, it would be incorrect to generalize the findings of this small sample. Maybe these women came from families who were more determined than others to join in resisting segregation, or maybe the women themselves were different. After all they all left the South after high school or college. Whether they were living in Alabama, Tennessee, Arkansas, or Georgia, all the women recall that "everybody around" (c13) was involved. They reported vividly on the marches, the "thousands of people in the street," and the impact this "great movement" had upon them (c4). Parents who did not allow their children to participate in the marches were likely to have supported economic boycotts of stores who refused to hire Blacks. "They would just announce it [to us children], 'There is a picket line at that store, we won't go there.' And compliance was expected at that level" (c1).

For women who were living in nonsegregated areas during the 1960s, participation in the struggle was largely a function of age, geographic background, and the family attitude toward Blacks. The women who were in their teens at that time did not participate. When there were protests going on in the neighborhood, they were kept at home. Some of the women who were in their late teens or early twenties got involved with the Black Power movement in the late 1960s. Through the movement they found a framework in which to place their experiences in relation to other Blacks, thereby enabling them to identify as students with the Black community and the common cause.

The overall aim of the civil rights organizations was equality and inclusion of Blacks in the existing society. Their strategies and goals were never revolutionary (Clark, 1966; Marable, 1984). The aims of the Black Power movement were more comprehensive. With the aim of radical change, Black students challenged society's culture and institutions. The intellectual works of Black students and scholars have greatly contributed to the dissemination of general knowledge about racism. In the period of the 1960s and 1970s academic critique of dominant society came from, among others, Cruse (1967/1984), Carmichael and Hamilton (1967), Ladner (1973), and may also be inferred from many articles in *Daedalus* ("The Negro American," 1965, 1966). Defying the idea that racism is a question of individual prejudice, Black intellectuals of the 1960s and 1970s defined racism as cultural and social domination. Others more specifically related racial domination to the economic exploitation of Blacks (see, for further discussion, Barrera, 1979; Robinson, 1983). The comprehension of racism as cultural oppression led to the massive affirmation of Black history and culture. Several women recall that they "started to really be truthful about [their] own identity" (c25). They "could talk about shared experiences, . . . about shared pain of racism" (c9). Others were "more concerned with nationalism, . . . trying to discover and recover our past and our heritage" (c19).

The Impact of Family Attitudes

Because the impact of antiracism in education and the media is still marginal, informal communication of knowledge about racism, in particular within the family, is highly relevant. The few studies available about Black girls have focused on their racial/feminine identity formation (Joseph & Lewis, 1981; Ladner, 1972), their experiences in the family, in school, in the labor market (Dex, 1983; Riley, 1985; Sharpe, 1976), and on their resistance to oppression (Amos & Parmar, 1981). However, questions of when, under what circumstances, how, and by whom in the family knowledge about racism is communicated to Black girls are largely unexplored. These questions cannot possibly all be answered here but an attempt will be made to shed some light upon the relevance of knowledge about racism in socialization at home. None of the Surinamese women were socialized at home to understand racism. The opposite appeared to be true for women who lived under segregation. This section focuses on another group of U.S. women, those who were too young at the time to witness the changes of the 1960s.

It may be assumed that family attitudes on racism largely determine the social perceptions of Black children. In a study of "mixed race" children Wilson (1987) related the mother's attitude about racism to identity formation in the child. She found that the more strongly and self-assuredly the mother would represent the injustice of systematic racial bias to her child, the less likely the child was to experience a racial identity conflict. Wilson shows that mothers who convincingly communicated to their children that the system is unfair, who gave comprehensive information about racism and explained that the success of Whites was real, yet due to racial injustice, and who also made clear that Black people are opposing this kind of injustice, made a positive impact on their children (Wilson, 1987, p. 190). Their children were motivated to gain success for their own sakes, rather than proving that they were as good as Whites, and did not have the feeling that they would forever be on the losing end. However, mothers who represented the system as fair and stressed that individual effort was the only means to success had negative results. The children in these families are more likely to experience identity conflict because their own observations contradict the idea that skin color has nothing to do with privilege and success.

For many Black women in the United States, the family played an important role in the acquisition of knowledge of racism. We shall see that, according to my findings, the communication of knowledge about racism is not a function of class. I am not sure, however, whether this may be generalized. Irrespective of whether they grew up in integrated, predominantly White neighborhoods or in Black neighborhoods, only those women who had received information about racism within the family were able to understand problems of racism in their experiences by the time of their adolescence.

Women who received comprehensive information about racism in the family were explicit about the importance of the role of their mothers in the development of knowledge and comprehension of issues of race and racism. Several women declared that their mothers had purposely prepared to compensate for the lack of information provided in school for children's understanding of race relations in the United States:

> [My mother] had all the newspaper clippings from that time [the civil rights movement], and I looked through them and I read them and she told me basically what [had happened] . . . when I was a little older. And she was telling me how things are changing and what Martin Luther King was fighting for. . . . I already had learned a little bit from school, but not so much because they don't tell you that much about things like that in school. Basically, that is how the information was transferred, and then later on I learned more in depth about it from reading books and things like that. (c5, 21 years old)

An example of the daughters whose mothers were students at the time and were politically involved is provided by a woman who remembers situations like "always [having] people at the house" because her mother was "coordinating activities and she was always going to meetings" (c14). Knowledge about the struggle against racism is not only relevant as historical information, it may motivate younger Black women to take up the challenge and to follow in the footsteps of their ancestors. The political implications of the transmission of information about racism through socialization at home can also be inferred from the fact that these daughters had a clear political advantage in comparison with their (Black) peers in school. As a result they were more likely to be involved in organizing political activities, such as a Black school paper (c5, c6), or were the ones to invite guest speakers for Black history month when "no one [else] took the initiative to put on an event" (c7).

The Impact of Education

Critical skills of reflection and communication usually increase with more and higher levels of education. This is not to say that a college degree guarantees critical knowledge or insight into racism. Education, however, is an important means of expanding one's understanding of society and of developing critical skills to interpret and evaluate the social world. Education may contribute directly or indirectly to a better understanding of racism. Through personal experiences of racism in school, Black students may develop strategies to understand and to oppose racism. This is an indirect way of knowledge acquisition. Direct ways proceed through Black or ethnic studies programs and antiracist education and teaching (Brandt, 1986; Mullard, 1984). Black studies programs have an "ethnic orientation" and are usually directed to Black students. These programs deal with the historical context of Black emancipation, problems of racism in the past and currently, the cultural context of Black identity, and radical change through the critical education of Blacks (Walton, 1969; Willie, 1981). Antiracist education rejects culturalism and transcends "ethnic" interests. The aims of antiracist education are oppositional and presuppose the experiences and the common interest of all racially (ethnically) dominated groups (Brandt, 1986, p. 125). Antiracist education is formulated for both dominant and dominated groups.

Because antiracist education is a newly developing theory and practice originating in the British critique of multicultural education in the 1980s, none of the women, in the Netherlands or the United States, had had any experience with antiracist teaching when they were in school. Some of the younger U.S. women had participated in Black studies programs. They had the advantage of a large body of relevant literature. Some women recall that they "kept reading and reading" (c6), which stimulated them to become part of the already existing structure of Black organizations in the university system through which they could further develop their comprehension of racism.

Most women, in the Netherlands as well as in the United States, also gained knowledge about racism in an indirect mode. Using the analytic skills they had achieved through college education, the young women searched for and started to develop a framework to account for their own school experiences of racism in interactions with teachers and students. Furthermore several women started to search for information about racism and alternative study programs to effectively oppose the Whitecentric nature of school textbooks and programs. The data suggest that the process in which these Black students started to understand racism through critique of their education in school proceeded along similar stages for women in both countries. These stages included the following experiences:

(1) Black students felt *excluded* as they were considered "outsiders" (c25). They "did not recognize" (s27) themselves in the subjects, because "within the course . . . attention was only given to White progress. For progress within the Black community, there was absolutely no attention" (s9).

(2) Exclusion prompted Black students to *search for recognition and confirmation of identity*. Alternative activities were organized, such as "little lectures on famous Blacks" (c6) or cultural sessions with "a guitar, a piano [where] we sang, and then it just suddenly became a party" (s25).

(3) These alternative activities were also motivated by *the need to share and discuss the common experience of racism*. One woman in the Netherlands recalls:

> There was a lot a talk about racism, discrimination, and experiences. You were sitting there in such a work group, so you heard these things flying around your ears the whole day. It was no longer book language, but actual experiences. So that was simply very credible. (s25)

(4) Growing comprehension of racism induced increasing *solidarity with Blacks* outside the school situation. Whereas, during the campus revolts in the United States of the 1960s, students went into the community to "help" and to "educate" the people, some students of a younger generation were worried that campus life would disconnect them from the Black community (c7). Others "just wanted to go work with the people" (s25).

(5) Their new insights into racism and the spirit of organizing alternative courses motivated students to start *opposition* to existing programs and to demand *change*. Black students in the United States had fought for the inclusion of Black studies programs in the 1970s. This was part of the wider organized struggle against institutional racism. Some Black women in Dutch higher education embarked on a similar struggle against the exclusion from the curriculum of issues relevant to them. They fought for their "own direction," because they wanted to include the process of finding their "own roots and own awakening within the major fields" (s25). The Dutch response to this, as various women experienced,

was motivated by the ideal of cultural pluralism. In some cases the school director agreed to offer "multicultural programs." However, this led to new forms of oppression, which induced new protest. Multicultural education tends to problematize other cultures, perceive culture as a static condition, or reduce culture to a set of traits (Alkan, Dors, Miedema, & Mullard, 1986):

> They tried to do their best, but I sometimes was really nauseated by it because it's all those stupid clichés. Like if you're visiting a Turk, you first take off your shoes and I don't know what all, and you don't say this to them and you don't say that. (s27)

To conclude, the acquisition of knowledge of racism through education proceeded for most women in indirect ways. It was basically left to the individual Black students to search for the relevant literature and to organize alternative courses in order to understand the forces of racism in school and in society at large. A few students in the United States could participate in Black studies programs, and some in the Netherlands had "multicultural" studies. In the latter case the culturally pluralistic underpinnings led to new forms of "ethnic" stigmatization and, as a reaction, to strategies to understand these culturalized forms of racism such as ethnicism.

The Impact of the Media

When occurrences of racism are considered to have news value, the media may play a direct role in the dissemination of knowledge about racism. This is usually the case when extreme forms of racism are involved and when there is an upsurge of resistance to racism. In the United States the media informed the people about the scale, spread, and forms of resistance in the 1960s. The view is commonly accepted in the United States that many Whites began to sympathize with the struggle of Blacks against segregation as a result of the media portrayals of brutal police violence against marching and protesting Blacks. Several women mentioned the huge impact on the U.S. public of television images of "police dogs attacking Black women and children" (c1). The rest of the U.S. women did not make frequent mention of positive contributions of the media in the dissemination of knowledge about racism.

The same can be said for the women in the Netherlands. The mass media covered the massive reaction against the election of a representative of a racist party in the Dutch parliament in the 1980s. Thereby they transmitted information about racism to the public. But the role of the media should be qualified. The Dutch media hardly instigate constructive discussion. In fact the press was, and still is, rather conservative on the issue of racism. They remain reluctant to report on the spread of more moderate forms of racism in the Netherlands, thereby often ignoring the views of Blacks on the problem of racism (van Dijk, 1983, pp. 138-140, 1987c, p. 117).

Conclusions

Insight into racism is determined by the acquisition of situational knowledge of acceptable behavior and general knowledge of racism. Both groups of women could explain how, and under which circumstances, they acquired knowledge that contributed to their comprehension of racism. This means that both groups of women had developed general representations of racism. My discussion of sources of knowledge acquisition is not exhaustive. Other areas to be explored concern the role of significant others, such as friends or role models. Furthermore there are few data about mediated information of racism. The most important difference between the two groups lies in knowledge of the roots of racism and the history of resistance. Black women in the Netherlands have emerging representations of the history of Dutch racism. These cognitions are probably not readily usable for interpretation of new experiences of racism in a historical framework. For the interpretation of their own experiences, U.S. Black women make more effective use of comparisons with past racism.

Table 3.1 outlines the different modes of knowledge acquisition for women in each country. It may be concluded that Black women in the United States acquired indirect as well as direct information about racism, while those in the Netherlands learned to infer general knowledge only from their own experiences. Note that direct transmission of knowledge about racism is based on relations between empirical data (contemporary racism) and models of change and order (race relations in the past and visions of the future). This suggests that direct modes of acquisition stimulate reflective modes of thinking about racism. Conversely indirect modes of knowledge acquisition probably do not lead to the development of explanatory "theories." We shall see in the next section that these differences in the mode of knowledge

Table 3.1 Modes and Sources of Acquisition of Knowledge of Racism

Modes/Sources	USA	NL
Information about racism		
1. socialization in the family	+	
2. Black studies	+	
3. large-scale struggle against racism	+	
4. the media	+	+
Practical experience with racism		
1. life under segregation	+	
2. integrated schools	+	+
Disinformation about racism		
1. cultural colonialism		−

acquisition have bearings on Black women's general knowledge of racism as well as on their views on the struggle against oppression.

RECONSTRUCTING BLACK WOMEN'S GENERAL KNOWLEDGE OF RACISM

General knowledge integrates experience and structures of domination. Black women's knowledge of racism and the (implicit) explanatory concepts underlying these shared cognitions can be reconstructed on the basis of the statements they make about racial issues. For that purpose an inventory was made of their generalizations about the nature and processes of racism and about goals and strategies to fight racism. Generalizations may be identified by pronouns such as *they* and *we* to distinguish between the dominant group and dominated groups. It may be assumed that these generalizations, when made by three or more women, reflect shared knowledge of racism. Because the method of interviewing (accounting) as well as the method of analysis (induction) are qualitative, the number of women who made specific generalizations about racism do not suggest statistical significance; it is only a rough indication of the prominence of the specific features of racism in the structures of knowledge of racism. The results must be seen as a tentative outline of the basic features of general knowledge of racism.

General knowledge of racism consists of abstract features— namely, cognitive representations about race and ethnic relations—and it programs the understanding of and reaction to personal experiences of racism in everyday life. It can be assumed that an elaborate system of general knowledge about racism probably includes shared cognitions about (some) of the following aspects of the problem: (a) Abstract notions about *the nature of contemporary racism* include information about the way racism occurs and is reproduced in society, that is, racism is a structural problem rather than an individual problem and it can be expressed covertly and overtly. (b) Knowledge about the *agents of racism* includes differentiation between Whites as primary agents and, under certain conditions, Blacks as secondary agents. (c) The general *processes* of racism are represented as generalizations about the *mechanisms* through which racism is reproduced. Blacks are subjected to marginalization rather than centralization, to cultural problematization instead of cultural acceptance, to exploitation rather than empowerment, to suppression rather than freedom and assertion. (d) Knowledge about the *structuring factors* of racism relates forms and functions of racism to class and gender relations in society. (e) The relative meaning of racism in the specific *historical and regional context* is organized in our system of knowledge through comparisons over time within or between, for instance, the Netherlands, the United States, or South Africa. (f) *Stereotypes* about Blacks represent another category of knowledge. These stereotypes can be specified according to gender. Finally, an elaborate system of knowledge about racism is likely to include (g) information about *strategies* against racism. The more general knowledge Black women have of racism, the more and the more elaborately these elements will be represented in their memories. These various dimensions of knowledge about racism will not be discussed in detail. For the purpose of this chapter primary attention is paid to knowledge about the nature and processes of racism.

The Nature and Agents of Contemporary Racism

Women in the Netherlands and in the United States generally agree that racism is inherent in the social system (11 NL, 12 USA—meaning that this idea is prominent in representations of 11 women in the Netherlands and 12 women in United States). Racism is perceived as *a given fact,* as "something that is just passed on and on" (s22). Many women agree that racism is *ubiquitous* and that it transcends other group divisions. It is "intricately woven into the fabric of everyday living" (c21) and "occurs among all classes" (s2). Several women point out that it is realistic to *expect racism* in any situation with Whites. Therefore, they develop "that kind of sixth sense that you need to suspect something, . . . to believe that whoever it is is not going to have your total welfare in mind" (c13).

Apart from the nature of contemporary racism—namely, that it is reproduced within and throughout the system—the women also make attributions about the nature of the general processes through which racism is expressed. One of the most persistent themes in the interviews is the problem of *covert* racism (14 NL, 21 USA). Racism is experienced as "intangible" (c21) and seems "very difficult to prove" (c8). Indeed all the women can testify that "no one ever said . . . you can't do that because you are Black" (c25). Unlike the U.S. women, several women in the Netherlands speak with bitterness about covert racism. They feel that "Whites are cowards, never straightforward" (s16), or, as one woman puts it: "With a smile on their face they stab you in the back" (s27). It seems as if Black women in the Netherlands are particularly upset by the hypocrisy they find in covert expressions of racism while, on the other hand, they constantly have to hear about Dutch tolerance. Their bitterness probably also suggests that they feel powerless against the practices of the dominant group. This is understandable, considering their small numbers in the Netherlands, the overall denial of racism, and in general the sophisticated forms of suppression that come with democratic pluralism. In addition Black women in the Netherlands have little experience with organized opposition to racism, while, from the side of the dominant group, there is a lack of serious sanctions against racism. This holds true even for the Dutch police and court systems (Biegel & Tjoen-Tak-Sen, 1986). In ordinary life Whites often withdraw rather than speak out against racism if they happen to witness racist events (Buis, 1988, p. 119). This is largely due to the Dutch taboo against racism, which discourages individuals from taking responsibility for the struggle against racism. In addition it seems that it is considered a greater offense against the norms to "accuse" other group members of racism than to "passively accept" ongoing racism against Blacks. Various women in the Netherlands express fear of victimization when they challenge racism and, with respect to participating in this project, worried about being identified. Indeed the strong norm against racism in the Netherlands probably prevents individuals from engaging in overt or blatant expressions of racism, but it may also incriminate individuals who expose specific practices as covertly racist. This also suggests that Blacks in the Netherlands feel exposed to a higher degree of suppression than women in the United States. Further it also explains why only the U.S. Black women state that racism is not only covert. It may also take *blatant* forms (5 USA).

Given these perceptions of racism in everyday life—namely, as ubiquitous, expected, integrated into the subtleties of interaction, and hard to deal with—it is not surprising that various women experience racism as a *forceful* and *tiring* condition of everyday life (3 NL, 5 USA). Some women feel the pressures of racism as "a brick wall that you keep running into" (c12) or as "an emotional strain that goes on all the time" (c9).

All women agree that Whites are agents of racism. However, there are differences between the women in the two groups as to the intentionality attributed to Whites. Furthermore there are differences in terms of the question of whether racism also operates through Black agents. Women in the Netherlands experience social relations with Whites as less antagonistic than women in the United States. They are also aware that racism has only recently become a topic of public discussion. These factors probably explain why various Black women in the Netherlands feel that Whites are not always aware of the racist implications of certain attitudes or behaviors. In certain respects this is consistent with my own theory about the nature and function of ideological racism. White in-group preference is usually accepted, taken for granted, hardly even questioned, and thus thoroughly integrated into dominant commonsense thinking (Essed, 1986). In a pluralistic framework, however, the idea that Whites are ignorant (6 NL) and "incapable of understanding what the problem is about" (s4) may take on another meaning. The reduction of racism to misunderstanding and lack of information fits perfectly well into the dominant group framework of cultural pluralism (Brandt, 1986, p. 121). Seen in this light it seems as if several Black women internalized the Dutch rule of the game that one has to be tolerant of deviance and even of the "error" of racism.

In contrast women in the United States take it for granted that Whites have had enough chances to get to know what racism is about and that they have become *indifferent to racism* (6 USA). Another difference between the knowledge representations of Black women in the two countries is that only the U.S. Black women point to the problem of internalized racism (1 NL, 5 USA). One explanation of this difference may be that the women are aware of the problem but are reluctant to mention it because they fear that the information will be used against Blacks.

The General Processes of Racism

For the purpose of the analysis it is relevant to make a distinction between two forms of knowledge of racism. The first category I refer to as *descriptive* knowledge, which consists of abstract representations about the nature and processes of racism. The second form of knowledge I call *explanatory,* and it consists of "theories" about the causes, history, and function of racism, about strategies against racism, and about alternative social relations. Obviously these two aspects of knowledge converge in real life. However, it is relevant here to make this distinction in order to understand the differences in the frameworks of knowledge inferred from the analysis of the U.S. and Dutch data.

It may be assumed that descriptive knowledge determines one's understanding of specific racist events but that an explanatory framework structures the long-term strategies and goals one sets in combating racism. Black women in both countries have knowledge about the nature and processes of racism. In the reconstruction of their general knowledge, as presented in Table 3.2, descriptive knowledge categories are included in columns 2 and 3. It can be inferred from their general statements about racism that Black women in both countries define racism in terms of processes of marginalization, problematization, and containment (column 3). Various explanatory knowledge categories are included in columns 1 and 4. Note that the different "theories" of racism (e.g., inequality caused by ignorance in the Netherlands and historical conflict over power in the United States—column 1) are attached to different strategies and goals in combating racism (column 4). Black women in the Netherlands emphasize the need to be alert for racism, while Black women in the United States seek to enlarge group power. I shall come back to this later.

The main purpose of the following section is to outline the framework of Black women's general knowledge. This framework is based on the inventory of general, context-free statements about racism. It must be stressed that the numbers of women represented in each category do not suggest statistical significance. They give only a general indication of the prevalence of specific processes of racism in both countries. The relations between the different dimensions and clusters

Table 3.2 Hypothetical Reconstruction of Black Women's General Knowledge of the Nature and Processes of Racism

Dimensions of Knowledge	NL	NL/USA	USA
1. Key concepts	Culture (Structure) Ethnicity (Race) Inequality Ignorance	*Racism* Ethnicism	Structure (Culture) Race (Ethnicity) Conflict Power
2. Abstract representations of processes and structuring factors	Assimilation		Segregation Gender polarization/class differentiation
3. General and specific processes of racism	Nonrecognition Undervaluation	*Marginalization* Nonacceptance Obstructing mobility/artificial ceilings	Color differentiation
Oppression	Questioning Disapproving	*Problematization* Pathologizing Criminalizing	
Suppression	Patronizing Myth of cultural tolerance	*Containment* Fragmentation Opposing assertivity Denial of racism	Aggression Violence
4. Goals and strategies in combating racism	Be watchful Do not trust Whites	Gain knowledge about racism Challenge racism Unite	Understand your history Gain power Maintain your culture and own perspective Separatism

of processes of racism will be discussed later in more detail (in Chapter 6). Similarly Black women's descriptions of the general and specific processes of racism are only briefly summarized here and substantiated in more detail with illustrations from the data later (Chapters 5 and 6).

Key concepts. Women in the Netherlands as well as in the United States define racism as racial and ethnic or cultural domination. However, the prominence of the racial and cultural component of racism is different in the cognitive representations of the women in each group. U.S. women experience racism predominantly through race (White versus Black). The underlying explanatory concepts of their knowledge structures are race *conflict* (segregation and aggression) and socioeconomic *power* (color hierarchy). In this *structural* approach racism is perceived as a primary form of oppression that operates through gender (polarization) and class (differentiation). Women in the Netherlands have a predominantly *cultural* approach to racism. The key concepts in their perception of racism are *ethnic difference* (the Dutch versus ethnic groups) and *unequal participation* (nonrecognition and underestimation). The basic explanatory concept in their knowledge structures seems to be *attitude* or *ignorance* (about racism in the Netherlands). This confirms that their explanatory knowledge of racism draws substantially on the dominant view of racism as a problem of misinformation.

The abstract representations of the general processes of racism as inferred from the data (problematization, marginalization, containment) are consistent with my theoretical framework of racism as a dynamic process of oppression and control sustained by legitimizing ideologies (see Chapter 1). These forces of racism are all represented in the knowledge structures of both groups of women. There are differences, however, in the lower-level specifications of the general processes. In Table 3.1 those processes more prominent in the perceptions of racism in the Netherlands and those more prominent in the United States are placed, respectively, on the left and on the right of the middle. The middle column includes the processes that were equally salient in the knowledge representations of both groups. Let me briefly illustrate the general and specific processes of racism as represented in Table 3.2 with examples from the interview materials.

Structuring factors and explanatory notions. With a few exceptions Black women in the Netherlands do not pay attention to class- and gender-related forms of racism. When asked to categorize themselves in terms of class structure, Surinamese women were reluctant to respond. Several women were suspicious of the question, wanted to know what could be the use of "pinning themselves down" (s4) to a specific class, or refused to answer the question altogether. I cannot fully explain their hostility toward class identification. Obviously there are problems related to the use of different criteria to categorize Black women with higher education in terms of class. Also, in comparison with the United States, class differences are less extreme in the Netherlands. However, it seems that such an explanation must also include the impact of Dutch "ethnic minority" policies and the dominant pluralistic discourse. These policies stimulate Blacks and other immigrants to identify themselves on the basis of cultural factors (ethnicity) but discourage identification on the basis of structural factors (race and class).

The different emphasis the women in the two groups put on cultural and structural aspects of racism is sharply pronounced in their perceptions of exclusion and exploitation. Unlike Black women in the Netherlands, Black women in the United States repeatedly emphasize that racism operates through the *class divisions* and that, because of their education, they are privileged in comparison with the majority of Blacks. "If you are the mother of several illegitimate children . . . they will really treat you different" (c3). More explicitly than women in the Netherlands, Black women in the United States experience that "along with being Black comes poverty" (c21). In addition most women in the United States are aware that racism is structured by *gender differentiations.* White control of the Black community works through the economic marginalization of Black men and the subsequent alienation of Black men (as fathers) from their families. For many Black men "it is becoming impossible be a family member, because they do not [have] work" (c31). Black women's knowledge of the various processes and mechanisms of racism can be summarized as follows:

Marginalization (21 NL, 14 USA). This is a process in which a sense of "otherness" is perpetuated. Blacks are denied access to positions of power within institutions, and their experiences and perspectives are considered irrelevant (Brandt, 1986, p. 104). The general processes of marginalization are specified in various related subprocesses, including *color differentiation* (3 NL, 10 USA), *nonrecognition* of Blacks (13 NL, 3 USA), *nonacceptance* (9 NL, 8 USA), *undervaluation* (12 NL, 4 USA), and the *obstruction of mobility* (12 NL, 7 USA).

It can be inferred from Table 3.2 that there are similarities and differences in the prevalence of specific processes of marginalization in the two countries. Many U.S. women not only experience racism as a power conflict between White and Black, they also agree that racism is articulated as a *color hierarchy* (10 USA). "Whites tend to be more tolerant of the Creoles" (c3) because they "feel less threatened when you are light" (c25). The color system confirms that in the United States the notion of race is used to represent a complex system of biological differentiation.

Black women in the Netherlands put more emphasis on the impact of cultural marginalization. They point out that Blacks are not taken seriously. Other women expressed this in terms of ignorance of the Dutch about colonization, life in the colonies, and the culture of Blacks from the colonies. This is not surprising considering that in school textbooks, serious information about Blacks from the colonies, let alone a critique of colonialism, are not to be found (van Dijk, 1987b). In both countries Black women agree that nonacceptance and rejection are commonly occurring mechanisms of racism (9 NL, 8 USA). However, Black women in the Netherlands stress that Whites feel that Blacks *do not belong* in the Netherlands. Black women in the United States, on the other hand, suggest that Whites *avoid social interaction.* Surinamese women, much more than Black women in the United States, stress that individual Blacks are socially accepted, to a certain degree, on a personal basis. This often implies, however, that the Dutch deny the woman's different ethnic background. Moreover Black women report that they are put under pressure to assimilate and to deny their culture, because "Dutch people never accept" (s1) the Surinamese as they are. According to the U.S. women, rejection instead takes the form of social segregation, in particular in housing and in social life.

Black women indicate that they are systematically undervalued. Artificial ceilings that impede the mobility of Black women mark, in particular, the experience of Black women in education and in the labor market. Particularly in the Netherlands Black women's general knowledge of racism in the labor market reflects the extremely high degree of exclusion. Whereas U.S. Black women (4 USA) explain that their qualities are undervalued in their work relations, Black women in the Netherlands (10 NL) see undergrading as a rationalization to exclude Black women altogether from high-status positions. Black women in the Netherlands who have succeeded in gaining higher positions find that they are consistently put down. Dominant group members "immediately assume" that Black women would "not have a college degree" (s11).

Although affirmative action programs facilitated the move into higher-status position for a small percentage of Black women in the United States, they continue to experience gender and race oppression in the labor market (Fullbright, 1986; Malveaux, 1987). However, U.S. Black women are as yet better equipped to deal with the problem (see the section on strategies below), and their cognitions about the barriers they have to overcome are more explicit:

> I am never lulled into believing that we are going to be on the same level according to their standards, because they set the standards, and any time you

think it is going to be close, they simply move the standards higher. (c13)

Problematization (14 NL, 5 USA). The main forces of racism mutually stimulate and sustain each other. In this dynamic process the role of ideology is crucial in structuring the forms of oppression and control. Knowledge of the problematization of Blacks reflects the way these ideological notions rationalize the marginalization of Black traditions and values as well as the exclusion of Blacks from access to material and nonmaterial recourse, on the one hand, and on the other hand, the suppression of Blacks in order to contain them in relations of dominance. By *questioning* the presence of Blacks in the Netherlands and *disapproving* of different cultural styles (e.g., "They consider it a nuisance when we talk loud" [s16]), an ideological climate is created that is favorable for ignoring the cultural history of the Surinamese and rejecting their identity (see the section above on marginalization). Moreover various women point out that the Dutch feel that Blacks are backward. The idea that they are "overwhelmed by the luxury of Holland and . . . look up to" (s12) Whites *pathologizes* Blacks and legitimizes their consistent underestimation (see "Marginalization" above). At the same time the cultural denigration of Blacks legitimizes the fact that they are patronized (see the next section).

Containment (7 NL, 13 USA). When the dominant group does not accept dominated groups' pursuit of equality, justice, and power, its reaction will be one of *suppression* (see Table 3.2, under 3). The women in both groups are aware of problems of fragmentation. The dominant group tries to divide and rule among the oppressed. One result of the Black struggle in the United States is that Blacks presented themselves as a force and had to be taken seriously. The women in the Netherlands feel contained in paternalistic relations. Blacks are exposed to patronizing behavior because they "do not see us as full citizens" (s12).

In the United States, because problems of racism are openly defined in terms of racial antagonism and conflict, the forms of suppression also take more openly aggressive forms. U.S. women are explicit about Whites' use of verbal *aggression* and of *violence* to contain Blacks. The first form has largely to do with the common phenomenon in the United States of calling Blacks "nigger." However, this problem seems to be disappearing, because the women refer to it in the past tense. The second form has largely to do with police aggression against the Black community, which is legitimized by criminalizing

Blacks (see "Problematization"). In both groups the women's general cognitions of the criminalization of Blacks are not very elaborate. This probably has to do with their gender and socioeconomic background. Hardly any of the women live in slums, which are often the object of police violence (Leinen, 1984). Black men are also more often than Black women the object of criminalization (Gilroy, 1982).

Suppression also refers to cognitions and practices that have the effect of obscuring the experience of racism in the lives of Blacks. Women in both countries point out that the *denial of racism* (6 NL, 5 USA) is rationalized with arguments that Blacks are "oversensitive" (c25), that they are "paranoid, putting things in racial terms [when] it is not really that way" (c31). Obviously this is another form of pathologizing Blacks (see "Problematization"). Black women in the Netherlands criticize the Dutch for making it impossible even to mention the subject of racism, because "if you say . . . this is racist, further discussion becomes absolutely impossible because they get very emotional and they become very difficult" (s4).

Unlike U.S. Black women, Black women in the Netherlands experience a specific Dutch form of ideological suppression, that is, the *myth of tolerance* (7 NL). If the reality is defined as a reality of tolerance, there is no legitimate basis for opposition to racism. The Dutch take it for granted that they are tolerant and that racism is virtually nonexistent in their country. In consequence confronting dominant group members with another view of reality, such as the infusion of racism into the routine practices of daily life, induces moral indignation. They claim that they mean well, thereby reversing the problem: How dare you make such an accusation? Various women in the Netherlands express their anger about the trap of cultural tolerance.

The discourse of cultural tolerance obscures the fact that racism is rejected, but not problematized, in Dutch dominant thinking (Essed, 1986, 1987). One woman probably summarizes the feelings of many others when she says, "Instead of acting so smug about their so-called tolerance they should admit that they discriminate and do something about it" (s5). In other words, there is lots of talk, no commitment, and little understanding of racism. As a result Surinamese women feel they have nothing to which they can cling. They object to the hypocrisy of "supposedly being so well meaning, while stabbing you in the back anyway" (s27). The myth of tolerance is a sophisticated form of suppression. "There are no sanctions, you become powerless, completely dependent on their goodwill" (s6). This introduces the question of how to deal with racism.

Dealing With Racism

The discussion of the processes of racism suggests that Black women in the Netherlands feel exposed to strong assimilative forces. Cultural differences are emphasized but not accepted in their consequences. Black women's specific history, rooted in Dutch colonization, is not recognized, and they have hardly any space for cultural expression, let alone cultural autonomy. In comparison with the women in the United States, Black women in the Netherlands feel exposed to a higher degree of cultural oppression and ideological suppression: neither their culture nor their critique of the system is acknowledged. They are rigidly excluded from decision-making positions. More so than women in the United States, women in the Netherlands experience being underestimated, not taken seriously, and being patronized. The prominence of ideological suppression suggests that it is harder for Blacks in the Netherlands to deal both with the oppressive and with the suppressive processes of racism.

Because the explanatory concepts in their knowledge of racism are not elaborate, the Surinamese women are not explicit, either, about their long-term goals as Blacks in the Netherlands. This is most likely, in part, because most of the women are first-generation Blacks in the Netherlands. They may still consider their stay in the Netherlands to be temporary.

There might, however, be another explanation. Given that their key explanatory concept implies that Whites are ignorant about racism because they keep asserting that they are tolerant, Black women in the Netherlands have been pushed onto the defensive. They are anxious to legitimize their version of the truth. Over the past years they have developed *defensive strategies* to (a) gain insight into racism (9 NL, 10 USA), (b) be watchful (12 NL, 6 USA), (c) challenge discrimination (9 NL, 10 USA), and (d) not trust Whites (8 NL, 5 USA). These defensive strategies are also common to U.S. Black women. However, their explanatory framework of racism is more elaborate and defines the situation as a power conflict. Therefore, U.S. Black women are also inclined to focus on strategies to create power as a group.

U.S. Black women are working out constructive strategies in terms of specific goals. The basic precondition is that the oppressed unite (8 NL, 13 USA). More specifically the aim of *constructive strategies* is empowerment and autonomy as a group. In short the key pillars on which their constructive strategies are based are to (a) understand the history of Black resistance in the United States (12 USA, 0 NL) and (b) create power within the system (12 USA, 1 NL) (c) while keeping and developing Black culture and perspectives (10 USA, 2 NL). Finally, several U.S. Black women see separate growth, that is, exclusive investment of energy and money in Black institutions, in the Black community, and in Black talent, as an important way to increase group power (5 USA, 0 NL).

CONCLUSIONS

Black women's descriptive knowledge of racism in the United States and in the Netherlands is to a large degree similar. These general knowledge structures of Black women also are consistent with the theoretical framework of racism presented in Chapter 1. In the United States racism works more explicitly and thoroughly through race-class convergences, whereas cultural oppression is more systematically used as a mode for Dutch racism.

However, there are important differences in Black women's "theory" of racism and resistance in the two countries. Black women in the United States have a historical orientation that Black women in the Netherlands do not have. This is not surprising considering, as was shown earlier, that U.S. Black women had acquired knowledge of racism directly, through information about the history of U.S. race relations and about racism, whereas Black women in the Netherlands acquired knowledge indirectly, that is, through their personal experiences. In addition, Surinamese women have been misinformed about the role of the Dutch in Suriname and its impact on contemporary race and ethnic relations.

These arguments suggest that probably the most destructive feature of the pluralistic context of racism in the Netherlands is the mystification of the historical basis of racism in the exploitation and colonization of Blacks. As a consequence Black women in the Netherlands define themselves as objects of racism but do not define themselves as part of the history of Black resistance. In other words, Black women in the Netherlands are debunking the myth of tolerance and have acquired elaborate descriptive knowledge about the processes of racism. However, their explanatory concepts are anchored in the dominant ideology of cultural pluralism.

In contrast the U.S. women have placed the struggle against racism in an antiracist context, in which the key concepts are history, power, and the retention of their own culture and perspective. However, their knowledge of racism is largely limited to the United States. They do not perceive the struggle against racist oppression in the wider context of international power relations between the First World and the Third World; neither do they relate their experience with the oppression of Blacks in other European-type societies. As a consequence the struggle against racism, as these U.S. Black women see it, remains a local affair. In all fairness to the women, however, I have to make the following short comment. Some women in the United States felt very much involved with the struggle against apartheid in South Africa. In the Netherlands several women expressed profound admiration for Winnie Mandela. However, in general their identification with the struggle against apartheid is a case apart that also has much to do with the massive media attention in the last few years. One of the issues I could not pay due attention to was that of Black women's terminology and conceptualization of racism in the Netherlands, which is gradually changing in the direction of a structural analysis of racism. The data show that some women have started to use the "White-Black" dichotomy as an alternative framework to express the power differences between "Whites" (the Dutch) and "Blacks" (colonial and Mediterranean immigrants). This suggests that Black women in the Netherlands, more so than Black women in the United States, are open to developing wider perceptions of racism that include the common experiences of colonial and Mediterranean immigrants. Obviously I do not mean to suggest there are no organizations with a broader base in the United States. A good example is the Rainbow Coalition. However, whereas Black women in the Netherlands made many comparisons and other references to racism against other immigrants, this hardly happened in the U.S. interviews. This broadening of their perspective of racism is consistent with the reality of racism in the Netherlands, which includes combinations of racism based in colonialism and racism against immigrant workers (see Chapter 1). These emerging cognitive changes among Black women may also facilitate the inclusion of the international context of racism and antiracism in the knowledge structures of Black women in the Netherlands.

4

Analyzing Accounts of Racism

Now that it has become clear how Black women acquire general knowledge of racism and what the key concepts are that underlie this knowledge, this chapter provides an explanation of the use of this knowledge in the comprehension of real-life experiences of racism. To prevent misunderstanding it should be stressed that general knowledge is the most important, yet not the only, condition in the comprehension of racism in everyday life. There are other factors involved, such as rational argumentation, inference, and other forms of goal-directed organization of information.

Furthermore it is assumed that there is individual variation in the problematization of racism and the processing of racist events. Therefore, it is useful to take into account two specific modes of thought characterizing different strategies of comprehension, namely, "contextualizing" and "morselizing" (Fiske & Kinder, 1981, p. 179). The first mode of thought places racist events in topical, temporal, and historical perspective, while the second mode treats racist events as isolated incidents. It may be predicted that women who are used to problematizing racism will make more sensitive use of "contextualizing" knowledge of racism in processing and memorizing racist events. Highly involved women will make more cautious inferences from covertly racist practices and will organize new information by more complex criteria. We do not have access to original interpretation processes in everyday situations, but indications of these processes can be inferred from reconstructions of racist events in accounts.

This chapter outlines the heuristics of interpretation and evaluation that structure processes of comprehension. For that purpose I present a tentative analytical framework for the use of accounts in a theory of racism. Accounts of racism consist of two components: (a) information processing and retrieval and (b) presentation. To analyze these components, social cognition theory and narrative theory are used.

Studying accounts of *covert* racism poses the problem of how Black women recognize such actions as manifestations of racism. Reformulated in social psychological terms, we may ask how judgments about racism are made under circumstances of uncertainty. This chapter tentatively explores the heuristics of observation, interpretation, and evaluation as they may be inferred from verbal accounts of racism. This venture is not only theoretically interesting in the absence of similar work but also socially relevant. In many situations Black women are the only witnesses to racism. Yet their point of view is often dismissed as "subjective" and, therefore, invalid (Elich & Maso, 1984, p. 61). Radically breaking with this perspective I will show that accounts of racism are not ad hoc stories. They have a specific structure based on rational testing and argumentation. The method proposed in this chapter has been introduced earlier (Essed, 1988, 1990a)[1] and has also been successfully applied in other research (Essed, 1990b; Louw-Potgieter, 1988, 1989). The discussion is organized as follows: First, the study of real-life accounts is placed in the context of new developments in attribution theory, emphasizing the need to transcend the restricted formula of experimental social psychology and to explore spontaneous explanations that include combinations of descriptive, logical, and motivational factors. Second, a hypothetical framework is presented of relevant reconstruction categories and interpretation heuristics in verbal accounts of racism. Third, a few examples are selected from the interviews to illustrate how such a hypothetical framework can be applied to the socially relevant analysis of real-life accounts.

To illustrate, examples are selected from accounts of job interviews because these are clear-cut situations that have rather specific rules and conventions. I am aware that there may be cultural differences in what is perceived as "proper" behavior in a job interview (Hofstede, 1980; Reynaert, 1988). However, because this project concerns Black women with higher education, it may be expected that they know dominant group conventions about application procedures. In job interviews the acting agents usually meet for the first time. Therefore, the analysis is not complicated by factors such as other experiences the participants in the situation may have had with each other or major differences of opinion about the procedures to be expected. Job applications, and especially job interviews, are hardly accessible for systematic observation with the aim of studying the impact of racism. Under certain conditions systematic discrimination can be proved with experimental methods, for instance, by comparing the success of application letters signed with "ethnic" versus those signed with "nonethnic" names (Smith, 1977). What happens in the job interview, however, remains inaccessible, known only to the personnel manager or the interviewers and the Black applicant. Accounts of Black women who experienced racism in these situations contain detailed information about subtle or not so subtle processes that result in rejection and exclusion. More specifically then the problem is how reconstructions of racist events in job interviews are verbalized and what information supports the evaluation of seemingly nonracial actions as racist because of the perceived implications or consequences.

Accounts of personal experiences in spontaneous conversation are often not as clear and comprehensible as, for instance, a properly edited autobiography. Ideas may be presented associatively, sentences may be interrupted, and arguments are sometimes not completed. Because of the exploratory nature of this chapter, extensive examples are used, namely, experiences presented as elaborate stories. The qualitative nature of the analysis does not allow a large number of illustrative cases. Therefore, the aim is not to make generalizations but to generate and discuss relevant concepts for the analysis of reconstructions of racist events.

ANALYZING ACCOUNTS OF RACISM

A verbal account is a type of discourse employed to subject an action to evaluative inquiry (Scott & Lyman, 1972, p. 405). It consists of a set of statements that reconstruct one's own behavior or the behavior of others. Accounts are not just written or spoken versions of something that has happened but are only called for when reconstructing *unanticipated behavior or unexpected acts that cause difficulties.* Obviously racist discrimination causes difficulties for Blacks. But what is "unexpected behavior" in the context of everyday racism? This question must be answered from the point of view of both macro and micro conceptions of racism. On a macro level racism is a phenomenon to be expected on a day-to-day basis. However, on a micro level it follows that, even when expected in many situations, racist actions are often not exactly predictable in terms of time, place, and participating actors. In that sense racist actions can be perceived as unanticipated behavior.

The way accounts are understood here draws largely on Scott and Lyman (1972). However, they made explanations a key element of their conceptualization of accounts, whereas I have reasons to suggest the broader notion of reconstruction. The first reason is that the notion of "reconstruction" directly reflects the fact that oral (or written) accounts are, by definition, accounts of actions in the past. The second reason is more complex. Explanation is a central concept in the social psychology of human behavior. Social psychological analyses of ordinary explanations of social behavior, in particular when studied from the point of view of the observer, are traditionally developed in the framework of attribution theory. Broadly speaking, attribution theory is concerned with the explanations and interpretations people give to actions. Therefore, it seems appealing to use concepts developed in attribution theory in the study of accounts of racism. In my view, however, the concepts developed in attribution theory are not adequate to include all the organizing categories involved in the verbalization of accounts. A brief summary of attribution theory may further clarify my argument.

Attribution theory, as first sketched by Heider (1958) and developed in greater detail by Jones and Davis (1965) and Kelley (1971), is not a *theory* in the strict sense of the word. One problem with the use of attribution theory by social psychologists lies in the research methodology. In the course of a few decades Heider's original aim of accounting for laypersons' everyday commonsense psychology of social behavior has been largely reduced to the testing of limited-range hypotheses. Recent critical developments in attribution theory, however, point to a "rediscovery" of the original ideas of Heider (Antaki, 1981; Eiser, 1983; Hewstone, 1983; Jaspars, Fincham, & Hewstone, 1983). Attribution theorists have not really studied attribution processes in all their complexities. The real nature of interpretation strategies is still largely unknown. Also few attempts have been made to analyze the contents and structures of interpretations outside the laboratory. Notable exceptions are Harré and his associates (Harré, 1980, 1981; Harré & Secord, 1972).

A second problem is that attribution theorists tend to reduce complex interpretation processes to a few attribution categories. Interpretation processes rely partly on the functional application of attributions. Attribution theorists traditionally distinguish among several types of attribution, such as personal versus situational, stable versus instable, and intentional versus nonintentional (Ickes & Kidd, 1976; Jones & Davis, 1965; Jones & Nisbett, 1972; Kelley, 1967). By predominantly using inflexible experimental designs, attribution theorists have often considered these different types of explanations to be mutually exclusive categories. However, real-life accounts include nuances in attribution categories that prestructured research designs are unable to assess. Real-life interpretations and explanations are far more complex, probably consisting of intricate combinations of different attributions.

A main critique leveled against attribution theory is its primary concern with causal explanations (Moscovici & Hewstone, 1983, p. 121; Pligt, 1981, p. 113). A good example of this is Kelley (1983, p. 343), who contends that people perceive life events as causally structured. Thereby they often make the conceptual error of treating reasons as causes (Lalljee, 1981, p. 120). The following fragment illustrates that causal explanations are not the only concern in giving meaning to perceived actions. This example also supports the previous arguments that different attributions may be applied simultaneously to explain a single event. The interviewee, a Surinamese woman in Amsterdam, aged 21, recalled an experience with a high school teacher in a gymnastics class:

Example 1

1. He roughly pushed me aside.

2. Why couldn't he say politely: "Move on, please"?

3. Just that little bit of violence. . . .

4. They think that because you are a different race, they are superior.

5. To me, they are ordinary oppressors.

6. They are trying out how far they can go with you. (Essed, 1984).

The behavior of the teacher is first interpreted as an example of White group behavior, indicated by the substitution of "they" (lines 4, 5, 6) for "he" (lines 1, 2). The explanations given for the perceived behavior of the White group member are partly causal and partly goal directed. Causal attributions are expressed in lines 4 and 5 ("they think they are superior" and "they are ordinary oppressors") and refer to attitudes and personality of the agent. The act is also interpreted in terms of its supposed goals: to find out how far he can go with the Black student (line 6).

Attribution theorists have recently started to place the concept of attribution in a broader framework of interpretive and evaluative processes (e.g., Antaki, 1988a; Wilkinson, 1981). In everyday life one does not only seek explanations. Ordinary people are also more generally concerned with giving meaning to events and with judging these events. This broad interpretation of the attribution process is supported by others as well (e.g., Antaki & Fielding, 1981; Gowler & Legge, 1981; Shotter, 1981). This also implies that there is no incompatibility between logical and motivational factors in lay-epistemic theory (Kruglanski, Baldwin, & Towson, 1983, p. 89). To know whether verbal acts are categorized as forms of racism, one needs to proceed from the level of interpretation to the notion of evaluation. To evaluate particular acts as cases of racism, one first tests the acts against *norms of acceptable behavior or acceptable reasons for unacceptable behavior* and then against notions of racial dominance in society. In the first instance this means that the observer has knowledge of the culture and of ideal behavior in particular situations. This part of the interpretation process has been discussed in Chapter 3. Second, evaluations in terms of racism are supported by critical knowledge of the social system, including notions of race relations and of racism. Let us now turn to the evaluative notions underlying comprehension of racist events.

KNOWLEDGE ABOUT RACISM AS AN EVALUATIVE CATEGORY IN VERBAL ACCOUNTS

The use of general knowledge in the comprehension of racist practices can best be illustrated by contrasting two representative accounts of discrimination in shops in the Netherlands with the earlier account given in Chapter 3. The earlier example concerned the case in which a Black woman from the Netherlands (s19) found it excusable that she was treated as a potential thief by shop attendants because she felt Black women probably steal more than Whites. None of the other interviewees in the Netherlands shares this opinion. Their typical reaction to questions about discrimination in shops is more like this:

Example 2

  1. In shops? Well, I have the stereotypical examples.

  2. If you enter the shop they immediately approach and

  3. ask what it is that you want . . . ,

  4. you know, it is like "gee a Black one, see what is happening." (s4)

Example 3

  1. V&D [department store] has gained a rather bad reputation. . . .

  2. If you hear the central information tone and the message that

  3. there is a telephone for Mrs. so and so—or some kind of code,

  4. we know [it means]: there is a Black one around.

  5. A girl who works there and who has a Surinamese boyfriend told us.

  6. We passed it along among each other. (s7)

Example 2 illustrates the use of knowledge of racism in interpretations and evaluations of personal experiences. The term *stereotypical* (line 1) implies that the interviewee assumes that the particular form of discrimination she encounters is commonly known. Example 3 indicates that racism is a topic of conversation among Black people (line 6). Both examples consist of generalized statements about racism in shops, introduced with "if you enter" and "if you hear" (in both fragments, line 2). The use of generalized statements suggest that the women present summaries of their own or of mediated experiences of this particular form of racism in shops.

HEURISTICS, INTERPRETATIONS, AND EVALUATIONS IN RECONSTRUCTIONS OF RACIST EVENTS

As one moves from the restricted and simple propositions of experimental social psychological research to real-life attributions, the complexity of the interpretation processes becomes more pronounced

(Billig, 1982, pp. 185-186). This may also be applied to the understanding of racism in everyday life. It is generally agreed among the women that "racism happens all the time . . . but [that it is something] you cannot put your finger on" (c1). Rather than engaging in a general inductive information search, women who are faced with covertly racist actions are more likely to look for specific information to test the hypothesis they have formed about the event (Lalljee, 1981, p. 138).

Given the ubiquity of racism and the often covert nature of its contemporary manifestations, the women first classify actions in terms of acceptable or unacceptable behavior in a given situation. When actions have been interpreted as unacceptable, and the implications and effects of the actions are consistent with previously existing social representations of racial issues and of racism, and if there are no acceptable excuses, the hypothesis is formed that the actions may be manifestations of racism. Then a search for supporting (or disqualifying) information is bound to follow. Thus motivated to make correct assessments of the event, Black women seek more information to make plausible, to prove, or to reject the hypothesis of racism.

In earlier research I tentatively suggested that Black women used the following, what I then called, "interpretive strategies," to recognize seemingly nonracial actions as forms of racial discrimination (Essed, 1984, pp. 167-168):

(a) Inference from social cognitions of racism, including knowledge, expectations, beliefs, and opinions about racism in general and about situated racist actions.

(b) Systematic observations of White behavior, for consistency.

(c) Opinions of others, for consistency and consensus.

(d) Comparisons with the experiences of other Blacks or with Whites, for consistency and for inconsistency.

(e) Comparisons with similar personal experiences, for consistency.

However, I used the notion of interpretative strategy rather intuitively, without explicitly defining it and without placing it in a theory of information comprehension and reproduction. No clear distinction was made between strategies of interpretation in real-life situations and strategies of interpretation and presentation in verbal accounts of real-life events, between planned and explicitly controlled cognitive strategies and strategies that are not preprogrammed or intended (van Dijk & Kintsch, 1983, pp. 70-71). For instance, one may develop a method to detect covert discrimination in real-life situations, such as making goal-directed observations (see example 2), when one suspects that an actor is indulging in racist actions. However, interpretative strategies in reconstructions of "spontaneous" accounts may be less controlled, for instance, if induced only by specific questions of the interviewer. Interpretations form a relevant category but not the only category in reconstructions of racism experiences. Cognitive strategies and other processes of comprehension and representation on which reconstructions of experiences are based are very complex and cannot be analyzed in detail in this study. Therefore, I focus on one important element of these strategies, namely, the *organizing categories* that can be inferred from reconstructions of experienced racism.

Reconstructions of experiences with racism are likely to include (some of) the following information: introductions (where did it happen, when; who were involved?), interpretations (was it acceptable or not?), explanations (why did it happen?), evaluations (was it a form of racism?), and reactions (what did I do about it?). These reconstruction categories must be placed in a wider context of methods (heuristics) of reality construction and systems of reference (beliefs, expectations, social knowledge, and other cognitions). Note that these strategies may include consensus, consistency, and distinctiveness heuristics but not in the rigidly structured way Kelley's (1971) covariation principle predicted. The intuitive "strategies" mentioned above can be reduced to a few basic methods of interpretation to make plausible seeing particular actions as manifestations of racism. These *heuristics* are

(1) inference from beliefs, expectations, and knowledge (a)
(2) comparison for (in)consistency and consensus (b, c, d, e)

In view of the arguments and findings presented above, the following *reconstruction* categories are presented as hypothetical elements of verbal accounts of racism events: context, complication, evaluation, argumentation, and decision. These categories are in part the same as narrative categories (Labov & Waletzky, 1967). Stories are distinct from other discourse genres in the way they are structured. The key elements of narrative structures are the basic categories of complication and resolution. Other constitutive elements of narrative structure are (a) setting, which features the time, location, circumstances, and major participants of the event; (b) an evaluation, in which the storyteller expresses opinions and emotions caused by the event; and (c) conclusions, linking the event to expectations, intentions, or recommendations for the future.

Stories are told because the storyteller thinks she or he has something interesting to tell. Usually what is perceived as interesting concerns events that are unexpected, "deviant," or in other ways "special." Complications usually involve the central "disruptive" actions. Although the categorical term *complication* represents a category present in any story, independent of the content, in stories about racism it acquires a literal meaning because it refers to actions of Whites that create complications for the Black woman involved.

Not all organizing categories and heuristics are included in all reconstructions of personal experiences. In the interviews, however, all personal experiences with racism include situated actions perceived as "disruptive." Therefore, the categories of context and complication are obligatory and may be seen as the core of verbal accounts of experiences with racism. The categories of context, complication, and decision are analogous to three elements of narrative structure, namely, setting, complication, and resolution. Note that these categories are all categories of a theory of account structures. However, it may be assumed that, just like narrative categories, they also have a cognitive status (van Dijk & Kintsch, 1983).

It seems useful to differentiate between "stable" and "variable" content in reconstructions of personal experiences. Stable content represents relatively fixed information, namely, the facts (what happened, where did it happen, who participated?) as perceived by the storyteller. Interpretations and evaluations of the facts do not represent fixed information, because they are subject to change. That is, if people gain more knowledge about racism, their interpretation and evaluation of the event may change. Context, complication, and decision in reconstructions feature "stable" elements in accounts of experiences. Finally, arguments that make plausible the evaluation of actions in terms of racism are variable because they are shaped by the account context in which they are presented. The reconstruction categories can be further explained as follows:

(1) Context

This category gives information about the participating actors and the time, place, and social circumstances in which racism events are situated.

(2) Complication

This complex category, which is similar to the "complication" category in stories, organizes the information about events and actions that are interpreted as disruptive or deviant from a "normal" state of affairs. On the one hand this category is descriptive in the sense that it gives an account of what the particular actions look like. On the other hand it is also a "normative" category, because it presupposes a judgment of what is "good" or acceptable and what is "bad" or unacceptable. Actions can only be perceived as unacceptable in relation to alternative actions that would have been considered acceptable in the particular situation. Therefore, this category also includes a comparative element. A problem with covert racism is that sometimes particular actions seem acceptable at first sight but, if more information is taken into account, these actions may require reinterpretation, for instance, as a result of goal-directed observations.

(3) Evaluation

This category is often explanatory, because in explanations of actions it becomes clear whether or not the actions are evaluated as indications of racism. Explanatory evaluations of particular events may be verbalized in a direct way, that is, with direct reference to the notion of racism such as "he was such a racist" or indirectly such as "they think they are superior." In many accounts of racism evaluations are not explicitly verbalized but implicitly present in the complication. For example, when a Black woman, the only Black among 300 passengers on a ferry boat from Denmark to England, says, "All passengers could leave, I was the only one who was stopped by customs," this complication needs little further explanation (Essed, 1984, p. 218). Evaluations are inferred from general knowledge of racism. This general knowledge may also include notions that link racism to class- or gender-specific oppression.

(4) Argumentation

This category includes statements in support of particular evaluations. Therefore, it cannot be separated from the evaluation category. A basic feature of argumentation is that it always concerns opinions, ideas, or perceptions that seem challengeable, at least in theory (Eemeren, Grootendorst, & Kruiger, 1981, p. 12). However, the argumentation category does not include any argument used in verbal accounts of racism, only those statements made to support particular evaluations. In the context of covert racism, argumentation is the most interesting category because it deals with the question: "Why did you think what happened was discrimination?" This category makes plausible, defensible, or acceptable the hypothetical evaluation that particular actions are manifestations of racism, even when at face value they appear nonracial. The category of argumentation includes interpretive and evaluative elements. The basic heuristics structuring the elements in this category are *social comparisons for (in)consistency and social comparisons for consensus*. The point of supporting argumentation is not to seek causality but to test the hypothesis of racism. Because racism is a group phenomenon, it is interesting to determine not only whether actions of the same actor are consistent over time or in other situations but also whether these actions are consistent with experiences in relation to other Whites. By the same token it is interesting to see whether actions of one actor are consistent with experiences of other Blacks in relation to the same actor or to other Whites. There is consensus when there is agreement about the assessment of the events, that is, when statements of others confirm the hypothesis of racism. In addition *inference* from beliefs, expectations, and knowledge about racial issues and racism may also be used as a supporting heuristic.

(a) The heuristic of comparison for consistency or consensus. This method of understanding aims at finding supporting evidence for the hypothesis that the particular complications are consistent over time, situations, or for the same actor. Comparing for consistency with actions of the actor vis-à-vis other Blacks is sometimes also a means of seeking consensus in evaluations and interpretations made by other Blacks. Supporting argumentation is likely to include references to one or more of the following sources of information:

(1) experiences of other Blacks: in similar situations/with the same agent of racism (consistency)

(2) other personal experiences: in similar situations/with the same White agent (consistency)

(3) similarity to actions of other Whites: in the same or other situation (consistency)

(4) confirming statements of the White agent (consensus)

(5) confirming statements about the event made by others (consensus)

(6) dissimilarity of perceived or expected actions by the same or other Whites to actions of Whites in similar situations (inconsistency)

(7) beliefs, expectations, knowledge, and other social cognitions about racism: in general or in specific (similar) context/with the same White person

The fourth source of information, representing the point of view of the actor, needs some clarification. First, it must be emphasized that intentionality of the actor is only one interpretive category among other sources of information. Second, in the accounts of Black women it appeared that, when confronted with the suggestion that their actions have racist implications, Whites were inclined to take offense and/or to give nonracial interpretations of the event. In theory, however—and this has happened in exceptional cases—the White actor may not take a defensive attitude when confronted with the racist implications of particular actions but apologize instead or try to find ways to compensate for the damage. The sixth source of information represents generalized formulations about racism. It reflects general or specific beliefs, expectations, knowledge, and other social cognitions about racism. Subsequent evaluation of specific events as forms of racism results from inference from general principles as in the following example: At Schiphol airport Black travelers are more likely than Whites to be searched by the customs officers. Social cognitions about racism are used in the reconstruction of personal experiences, with racism as an indicator of the discursive circulation of notions about racism in the Black community or in society as a whole. Hypothetically I suggest that the more often inference from social cognitions about racism occurs in reconstructions of personal experiences, the more likely it is that these cognitions represent socially shared representations of racism.

(b) Social comparisons for inconsistency. Comparisons with perceived or expected practices in nonracial situations—that is, situations with only White participants—represent another source of information. Inconsistency with (expected) behavior in these situations supports the hypothesis that particular actions are indications of

racism. The same can be said for comparisons that illustrate that actions of Whites are different than those one would expect when a Black, instead of a White actor, is involved, such as in this example: I'd rather go to the Black teaching assistant because she really tries to help me out, whereas with White TAs. . . .

(5) Decision

This category includes plans, expectations, and actions induced by racist events. Because this category concerns plans, whether executed or not, as well as acts and nonacts induced by the event, it would in principle not be correct to call this category a response category. However, it may often include information about specific actions or about purposeful nonaction.

The hypothetical reconstruction categories—namely, context, complication, evaluation, argumentation, and decision—as well as the structuring heuristics and evaluative references can be organized as in the framework in Table 4.1. Because the framework is only a hypothetical representation of elementary categories, heuristics, and sources of references included in reconstructions of racism experiences, it is obviously possible to make refinements and extensions by way of subclassifications. However, this is beyond the scope of this study. It has already been argued that not all spontaneous accounts in real life include all these categories. Most accounts are likely to include the context, complication, and decision categories. How explicit the evaluation category is and how elaborate the argumentation category will be depend on the account situation. Although the method is based on rational inference and argumentation, it does not mean to exclude the possibility of occasional irrational evaluation of specific situations. On the contrary, if one suspects irrationality, the heuristics can be used to evaluate reconstructions of racist events on criteria of rationality. The categories of interpretation provide a rational basis to systematically examine why a specific event is perceived as racism. In other words, the model can be used not only to analyze accounts; used as a framework for posing the relevant questions, this model can also serve to elicit elaborate accounts effectively.

I shall now apply this framework in the analysis of a few selected real-life accounts of racism. For practical reasons examples are taken from experiences of Black women in job interviews. In the analysis

Table 4.1 Reconstruction Categories and Heuristics of Accounts

Type of Category	Content of Category	Form of Heuristic	Supporting References
1. Context	Description of time, place, actors, situation	—	—
2. Complication	Description and interpretation of actions	Comparison	Norms, values about acceptable/non-acceptable behavior
3. Evaluation	Significance or value of actions	Inference	(Class-/gender-structured) beliefs, expectations, social knowledge about racial issues
4. Argumentation	Statements in support of evaluation	Inference	and about racism (gender/class domination)
		Comparison for consistency	Experiences of other Blacks Experiences with other Whites Other actions of same actor
		Comparison for consensus	Interpretations/ evaluations from others Interpretations/ evaluations from the actor
		Comparison for inconsistency	Experiences of Whites Experiences with Black actors
5. Decision	Intentions and/or actions		Expectations about the goals of particular response

the reconstruction categories are numbered as in Table 4.1. However, in real situations, such as the interview situation, stories are not told in the same order.

RACIST COMPLICATIONS IN JOB APPLICATIONS

The question: "Have you ever experienced discrimination when you applied for a job?" was met with various answers, some focusing on the structural exclusion of Black women from leading positions, others on the creation of ethnic sectors of work and the marginalization of that type of work. Some answers were presented in the form of stories about specific cases. Stories about personal experiences with racism when applying for a job are reconstructions of the actions and events that occurred at a particular time, a particular place, involving a White personnel manager or interviewer, and the Black woman herself.

Actions do not only consist of things people do, verbally or non-verbally, but also of things people do *not* do. Not doing something one would normally expect in a situation is an important mechanism of racism, called "passive racism" (Essed, 1982, p. 14). Examples include a situation in which White passengers on a bus pretend not to notice when a Black passenger is subjected to abusive language or when a student supervisor neglects her Black female apprentice by not giving the relevant information she needs to function properly in the specific context. Examples such as these have frequently occurred in the experiences of Black women in the Netherlands and in the United States (Essed, 1984). Neglect as a form of racism is particularly important in contexts where Whites are motivated to maintain a non-discriminating self-concept and, therefore, try to avoid Blacks and, more generally, racial issues altogether. The underlying thought is that, if one does not "do" anything, one cannot be accused of having "done" anything discriminatory.

For further analysis two stories about job interviews have been selected from the data. To guarantee their anonymity some changes were made in the background information; to make the stories more real I have used fake names instead of the usual codes of "c" and "s." The first story is rather complex because in it the woman, an African-American student, compares her experiences in two job interviews. The first half of the story concentrates on the initial procedures of stating interest in one particular job, and the second half looks at complications while being interviewed for another job. The second story, from a Black professional in the Netherlands, is a reconstruction of one job interview.

Job applications have a fixed organizational structure, including specific procedures for stating one's interest in the job offered, for conducting job interviews, and for accepting or declining the candidate. These procedures are basically the same in the Netherlands and in the United States. Therefore, it is legitimate to apply theories about job interviews developed on the basis of research in the United States as a basis for similar study in the Netherlands (Komter, 1987). The same argument justifies the use of examples taken from both U.S. and Dutch contexts. It is beyond the scope of this chapter to elaborate on the specific codes, guidelines, and expectations the applicant and personnel manager or interviewer take into consideration vis-à-vis each other (Komter, 1987). However, one particular aspect should be emphasized, that is, the form of power a White interviewer has over a Black applicant. One form of power is a *racial* form of power, based on the structures of racial dominance. In a racist society White group membership conditions what I have elsewhere called "consensus power" (Essed, 1986, p. 25; see also Chapter 1), the unquestioned acceptance of White dominance. In addition there is a form of *situational* power shaped by the context of the job interview. The personnel manager or the interviewer basically has power over the interviewee. The power attached to the interviewer is perhaps more crucial in that she or he has the legitimate responsibility for deciding who is invited for an interview and then for asking questions designed to elicit responses by which the interviewee will be evaluated (Akinnaso & Ajirotutu, 1982, p. 121). When a White job interviewer abuses her or his power over the applicant, and thereby confirms and reinforces the existing structures of White dominance, the job interview is considered a racist event. For practical reasons (of space and translation) I do not present the complete texts of the interviews but have tried to create summaries in my own words with quotations from the text (translated into English).

WHAT HAPPENED?
EXAMPLES OF REAL-LIFE ACCOUNTS

Stories are told because the storyteller believes she experienced something "special." This may be inferred from the event itself, but sometimes the storyteller herself explains why the event made an impact. This is the case in the presentation of both reconstructions. In story 1 an African-American computer science student, aged 21, discusses two cases of applying for jobs on campus and ends her story with this: "I remember those two so well 'cause I really wanted those two jobs and that happened."

In Story 2 a 33-year-old Black linguist, who applied for a job teaching Dutch, evaluates the event as "extremely embarrassing" and "therefore," she concludes, "it is printed in my memory." These evaluative and conclusive statements are also functional for the listener. It is a way of indicating that the story as it was told was "really the truth" and at the same time worth telling in the first place.

Story 1 (c6, 4-5, 9-12)

Case 1

(1) Context. Micky T. applied for a job at the campus accounting office. The personnel manager said she was very busy and asked her to return on Monday, which was fine with Micky T. On Monday Micky T. called first to see whether the lady she wanted to see was in.

(2a) Complication (at face value). "Her secretary answered the phone and said she had gone on vacation. And the job had been filled."

This category, in which the disruptive or unacceptable actions are described, does not in itself justify the perception that these actions are disruptive. By suggesting an alternative scenario consisting of actions that would have been acceptable in the context of the specific situation, the woman emphasizes that she is aware of the cultural rules of acceptable and unacceptable behavior and, therefore, legitimately defines the perceived actions as unacceptable.

This interpretation strategy is basic to all accounts of racism experiences. In some accounts, such as in the story of Micky T., comparative considerations are explicitly verbalized: "She could have told me that for one she wasn't interviewing any more and she had made up her mind that the position was filled, and that would have been that."

(2b) Complication (after reinterpretation). Because of the indirect and covert nature of contemporary racism, it often happens that actions that seemed OK become problematic when one learns more about the situation. At first sight it was perfectly acceptable to Micky T. that she was asked to come back at a time that would be more convenient for the personnel manager. She said, "Sure, I'll come back on Monday." She had no reason to question this request, until she found out that the personnel manager wouldn't be there, and she subsequently

infers from that information that the manager probably never intended to accept her application. Now it appears that the real complication did not concern the phone call with the secretary (above) but the request to return at another time: "The lady said she was real busy so could I come back Monday."

The "new" complication is also further clarified, this time by making explicit the contradiction between the request and its effect: "She knew she was going on vacation Monday, so why did she tell me to come back Monday when she knew she wasn't going to be there?"

(3) Evaluation. The above examples of unacceptable behavior are explained and evaluated in terms of racism: "Reason why I may not get the job is not because I don't have the skills but because of my color." This explanation is specified by the following arguments:

(4) Argumentation.

(a) Comparison with other situations for consistency. "I've seen that [discrimination because of color] a lot."

(b) Inference from information believed to be true from generalized beliefs. "It happens a lot here on campus [you would] be surprised."

(b) Inference from information believed to be true from socialized beliefs. In her conversation with me Micky T. had introduced the topic of racism by telling that her father had recently started to talk to her about racism when he had realized that, in order to go to college, she seriously planned to move from the Black community to a predominantly White area. He told her "how not to expect this and not to expect that and that things will be different."

He warned her to be "prepared" for all kinds of complications. Then, she says, he also warned her that she would be called names, which, she says, indeed happened. The experiences with job applications are subsequently introduced by the question: "Are there other examples illustrating that what your father had told you about racism was true?" The woman answered as follows: "Uhm, about job interviews and things. Reason why I may not get the job is not because I don't have the skills, but because of my color."

Mickey T. used that knowledge (you may not get a job because of your color) to explain her experience with the personnel manager (above).

(c) Comparison with other personal experiences for consistency. "I'm used to that kind of stuff in job interviews." "And uhm, what was another one? I went for a job interview over here at uh Jefferson Hall as a uhm computer technician. . . ."

Here reference is made to generalized experiences ("I'm used to that") and to a specific experience with racism ("what was the other one? I went," and so on), thereby introducing the second part of the story. Before elaborating on the second part, Micky T.'s reaction to the situation should be mentioned.

(5) Decision. Because it had seemed reasonable to move the application interview to another time, the final realization that she was deprived of the opportunity to apply for a job she really wanted comes quite unexpectedly: "I was like oh, OK, thank you, 'bye. And I just let it go."

Case 2

(1) Context. Micky T. goes to interview for another job on campus as a computer technician. She arrives early, waits until the interview with an earlier applicant, a White male student, is finished, and is then asked to come in. The interviewer is a man. Therefore, theoretically, the event is also structured by gender aspects and should be seen as a form of gendered racism. The interviewer starts with a description of the job requirements, and Micky T. affirms that she was familiar with all the tasks mentioned.

(2) Complication. "By the way [he said], do you have a resumé?"

(5) Decision. "I was like no, you didn't ask for one on the application."

(2') Clarification of the complication. Micky T. clarifies why she does not have a resumé and why this request is unacceptable in the particular situation: "If they want you to have a resumé prepared they'll tell you, have a resumé prepared."

(3) Evaluation. It was shown above that both job interviews were evaluated in terms of racism.

(4) Argumentation.

(a) Comparison with White person for inconsistency. Comparing the request for a resumé with the conversation she overheard with the candidate before her, Micky T. says: "He was interviewing this other guy and I was sitting down 'cause I had come early, and in the course of their discussion I didn't hear him ask the guy for a resumé. . . . I was like hum, OK, so why does he ask me for a resumé and he didn't ask the other guy for a resumé."

Immediately recognizing the request for a resumé as disruptive, Micky T. reacts. However, each new answer induces more disruptive requests.

(2a, 5a, 5b, 5c) Complication-decision-complication-complication. "He said oh well, you have to have a resumé, I said, OK, no problem.

And he was like what year are you, [you act] like a junior. Well, you have to have the resumé back to me by the end of the day."

(5c') Clarification of complication. ". . . and it was 3 o'clock, you know, so . . ."

(5d, 2b) Decision-complication. "I'm like hum OK, and he was like, but I may have filled the position by then."

(2-2b) Summary of complications. "He was taking me through all these changes, telling me can I get this kind of reference from this certain professor and from places where I worked at and all this kind of stuff. . . . And he was just going through all kinds of stuff."

(3b) Evaluation. ". . . [I thought] I see where this is leading to. . . . He was going all around corners trying to, you know, make me change my mind about the job."

(5e) Decision. "I let that one go."

Evaluation: Case 1 and Case 2

"So, I've run into a lot of incidents here on campus as far as job offers." The hypothetical categories not only demonstrate how reconstructions are made, they also demonstrate what they show about the problem of racism. From the category consisting of context descriptions, other information can be inferred. For instance, descriptions of gender background indicate whether actions should be seen as gendered racism. The categories of supporting references include the constituent elements of social representations of, on the one hand, norms of acceptable behavior and, on the other hand, notions of racial issues and of racism. Finally, the question concerning what forms and mechanisms of racism Micky T. encountered in job applications can be answered by looking at the statements categorized as complications. The mechanisms of racism Micky T. encountered were

processes of exclusion
    (a) by means of deception
        "The uh lady said she was real busy so could I come back Monday."
    (b) by means of introducing additional conditions
        "He said, oh well, you have to have a resumé."
    (c) by making unrealistic demands
        "He was like well, you have to have the resumé back to me by the end of the day . . . but I may have filled the position by then."

assertion of assumed superiority
   (d) by making a discouraging remark
       "He was like, what year are you, [you act] like a junior."

Story 2 (s11, 8-13)

This example is selected from an interview with a Black woman in the Netherlands.

(1) Context. Florence V. applies for a job at the ministry of Foreign Affairs to teach Dutch at a Finnish University for a period of 18 months. They stated a preference for a linguist with a background of English. Florence V. fits the description and likes the challenge of new experiences. Her written application is accepted and she is invited for an interview. The interviewer happens to be a woman.

(2) Complication. "I entered the room and there is this lady, who looks at me, stunned, and she says: 'Are *you* the one?'"

(3) Evaluation. "Well I don't think that needs any further explanation!" However, when I explicitly ask Florence V. to verbalize what she thinks the personnel manager tried to say to her, she indirectly evaluates the way she was "welcomed" by the interviewer as racism: "I think it was something like: a Black woman, that was not what I had expected."

(2') Clarification of complication. "She did not even say 'good morning,' but just: so is it you?"

(3') Clarification of evaluation. "You know, it wasn't like I wasn't dressed for the occasion. . . . "

In the course of the interview, Florence V. is faced with more disruptive actions:

(2a) Complication. "The conversation we had was not businesslike at all, it was about discos and how to spend leisure, and she said things like: well they do not have any discos over there and I am sure you love dancing."

(2a') Clarification of complication. "It was real strange."

(5) Decision. Florence V. thinks it better not to react immediately. "What good would it do to tell her that I had not been to a disco since I was sixteen and that I'd rather read books the whole evening than hang around discos?"

(2b) Complication. "Then she told me that my credentials were fine, but she still had to do an interview with another applicant."

(5b) Decision. Given the unacceptable topics the interviewer wanted to discuss, Florence V. gets the feeling that the personnel

manager is lying about the other interview. Therefore, a few days later, she calls a friend whom she remembers works at the Foreign Affairs office: "I felt something was wrong, but I only wanted to make sure. It was like I already knew what was going on, yet, I wanted to see it, in black and white."

(2a'') Confirmation of complication. The friend checks things out, and it appears that the candidate who was second on the list was only invited for an interview after the interview with Florence V. had taken place.

(3'') Confirmation of evaluation. "So what I suspected was confirmed, they did not want a Black woman in that position." Florence V. feels she "already knew" what was happening; the following argumentation illustrates why.

(4) Argumentation.

(a) Inference from beliefs about differences between racial and nonracial discrimination. It was mentioned before that, if complications are evaluated as indications of racism, it means that acceptable excuses for these actions are not available. This implies that one should be aware of what are to be considered acceptable excuses. A brief digression will clarify the point I want to make. In her account Florence V. gives an example of another application for the position of teacher at a Christian college. She was turned down. In that particular case the interviewers also thought her credentials were fine, but Florence V. did not perceive the event as racism: "My view of life did not correspond with theirs. They questioned me about it, and I honestly told them that I did not intend to read the Bible with the students every morning before class."

With this digression Florence V. illustrates that she is perfectly aware of nonracial discrimination in the Dutch system, implying that she knows how to distinguish racism from discrimination for other reasons. The data show that other Black women also made references in their accounts to other, nonracial, actions they had found disturbing but not racist, as if to anticipate counterarguments that they were overly sensitive to discrimination.

(b) Comparison with personal experiences for consistency. "It was like the experience I had when I was 8, you know, the one I told you about, in the street, when they used to call me 'pretty little brownie.' "

(c) Inference from beliefs and knowledge. Indicating that she knows racist discrimination in job applications to be often the rule

rather than the exception, Florence V. says that she has only been "lucky" in comparison with other Blacks, except for the occasion discussed above. However, she verbalized this belief quite implicitly by way of introducing that particular event: "When I hear other stories, or when I read about it [discrimination against Black applicants], I realize that I have been very lucky, which does not mean that particular elements or facts are not there. . . . Before I got the job I have now, I had some very painful experiences."

The statements classified under the categories of complication show that the mechanisms of racism in the job interview with Florence V. include processes of exclusion, by rejection and rudeness (see 2); by not taking the applicant seriously, which is in fact also a way of inferiorizing the candidate (see 2a); and finally by deception (see 2b). In summary, after her initial obvious astonishment, the interviewer displays avoiding behavior (ignoring topics that would induce relevant statements from the applicant), while trying to offer nonracial arguments (no discos, another applicant) that will justify the later rejection of the applicant. In that sense the complications include culturalized expressions of racism (reference to disco and dancing). However, these were generated on the basis of racial categorization: Only when Florence V. entered did it become apparent that she was Black.

CONCLUSIONS

In this chapter I have tried to present a tentative framework for the use of ordinary accounts in a theory of racism. Accounts are reconstructions of personal experiences with racism when (a) they tell about personal confrontations with unacceptable situated actions, (b) these unacceptable actions are evaluated as racism, and (c) plausible alternative explanations are not available. I have tried to show that evaluations of particular events as cases of racism are based on knowledge about (a) rules and norms of behavior, (b) acceptable reasons for unacceptable behavior, and (c) the structures and processes of racial dominance in society.

The core of accounts of personal experiences with racism consist of the context and complications. In accounts of racism, particularly in reconstructions of covert racist discrimination, additional argumentation is presented in support of the hypothesis (evaluation) of racism.

The category of decision, although not prominent in this chapter, gives insight into the effectiveness of particular (individual) actions against racism in everyday life. In reconstructions of experiences with covert discrimination, processes of interpretation and evaluation are structured by specific heuristics. Heuristics of comparison seek consistency and/or consensus information, and heuristics of inference aim at supporting evidence based on general beliefs, expectations, and knowledge about racism.

The hypothetical reconstruction categories of context, complication, evaluation, argumentation, and decision proved relevant for both examples I have analyzed. The categories of complication and evaluation allowed for some elaboration in further clarifications or confirmations. Not all argumentation subcategories were applicable to reconstructions of job interviews. This is probably also true for accounts of racism. The degree of elaboration depends on many factors (e.g., personal as well as interview situational) that could not be controlled in the project. With these restrictions in mind, let us now turn to accounts of the sites and situations where racism occurs and to the way racism permeates situations in the life of one woman.

NOTE

1. This chapter is a revised and extended version of "Understanding Verbal Accounts of Racism: Politics and Heuristics of Reality Constructions" (*Text, 8,* 1988, pp. 5-40). Used by permission of Mouton de Gruyter and the editor.

5

The Integration of Racism Into Everyday Life: The Story of Rosa N.

In discussing the method of understanding accounts of racism, it was shown how Black women expose clues and hidden messages enclosed in situations. Overemphasis on situational evidence, however, and insufficient inference from knowledge of the general processes of racism may depoliticize evidence of racism (Essed, 1990a, 1990b). The reader must bear in mind that reconstructions of events are always embedded in more complex and elaborate clusters of knowledge and social processes. The processes involved in the experience of everyday racism are further addressed in this chapter. For that purpose the focus of analysis moves from heuristics of understanding to understanding as experience and from events to interrelated experiences.

To conceptualize and to analyze racism as a process, it is relevant to look at the different dimensions of experience. In real life personal confrontations with racism merge with the experiences with racism of Black friends and family and others who are not even personally known. Furthermore racism operating in interactions with colleagues, supervisors, fellow students, or shop attendants overlaps and reinforces other experiences with racism, such as viewing negative portrayals of Blacks in the media or large-scale discrimination on the labor market. Racism experienced today reminds one of similar past experiences and influences one's expectations about tomorrow. If one unravels complex processes involving different situations and agents, as well as both personal and vicarious experiences, a coherence between practices and experiences can be revealed. This may be done in two ways, namely, through intersubjective and intrasubjective comparisons. Intersubjective comparisons give insight into uniformity of practices and experiences of women in various social relations and situations. These are discussed in detail later. First, intrasubjective comparisons are made to give insight into simultaneous and sequential instances of racism in personal biographies. Obviously it would be too time-consuming to analyze in detail the infusion of racism into the everyday experiences of each woman. Therefore, one detailed example is given, based on the accounts of one woman, Rosa N., from the Netherlands.

Rosa N. is a geriatrician in training, the only Black in her group. In some respects her story is typically Dutch. As noted before (see Chapter 3), Black women in the Netherlands are subjected to strong pressure to assimilate culturally. They also sketch a more elaborate system of ideological repression, in which dominant consensus operates not only to impede equal participation but also to suppress protest against racism. We will see later that the story of Rosa N. is consistent with those of other Black women. Thus the experience of Rosa N. forms a microcosm of everyday racism. I shall demonstrate that these situations are everyday situations and that each experience acquires meaning relative to other experiences.

To examine whether the reported experiences represent everyday racism, they must be tested against the definition and main features of everyday racism. To recapitulate everyday racism has been defined as a process in which socialized racist notions are integrated into everyday practices and thereby actualize and reinforce underlying racial and ethnic relations. Furthermore racist practices in themselves become familiar, repetitive, and part of the "normal" routine in everyday life. With these presuppositions in mind, let us now turn to the story of Rosa N.

A FRAGMENTARY REPRESENTATION OF EVERYDAY RACISM

Rosa N. was born in Suriname in 1951. She lost both of her parents before she was 10 years old. Her mother's sister adopted her, and Rosa N. was raised with four other children, all girls. After finishing high school in Suriname, she got a scholarship to study medicine in the Netherlands. After graduation she further specialized in geriatrics. In the period when she was interviewed, she was doing her internship at a modern complex for medical research. Four years earlier she had married a Dutchman, Rob, an architect. The following account, recorded in 1986, represents a moment of reflection upon some of her experiences of racism as a Black woman, trainee, and young doctor. The presentation of the story of Rosa N. is largely faithful to the order in which it was told. This may give us an impression of the way experiences of racism in different contexts and situations are associated and related to each other in accounts of racism in everyday life.

Why tell the story of Rosa N.? In many respects this reconstruction of everyday racism challenges (Dutch) commonsense notions of racism (see also Essed, 1987). Rosa N. has never been physically molested, her life has not been threatened. She hardly has to deal with blatant "bigots." She has not been fired. She has been called a Black "whore" only once. She is gifted, she has a job, and she is pursuing a promising career. She is a "successful Black." So one might ask: What is the problem? The problem is exactly that which is at the heart of everyday racism: the invisibility of oppression and the imperceptibility of Rosa N.'s extraordinary perseverance, despite multiple forms of oppression. Rejection, exclusion, problematization, underestimation, and other inequities and impediments are regularly infused into "normal" life, so that they appear unquestionable. This is a story of oppression in the fabric of everyday life. Some of her experiences are obvious indications of racism. Many others are concealed and subtle. Their understanding requires a certain degree of general knowledge of racism. To prevent any misinterpretations, I will clarify in detail why specific seemingly nonracial experiences can only be explained as forms of racism.

A relevant question concerns why we should believe Rosa N. The idea that Blacks are "too sensitive" is popular enough. Therefore, it may be expected that some readers think she just has a "chip on her shoulder" and that she is just as prejudiced against the Dutch as she thinks the Dutch are against Blacks. Suppose that she perceives racism where it is not present. Theoretically this may be the case, which would imply that Rosa N. has little knowledge of racism. This would mean that she is only expressing her common sense about race to account for a range of negative experiences. These crucial questions must be attended to carefully.

"Common sense" is a problematic notion. However, for my purposes the Gramscian (Gramsci, 1971) interpretation, as applied by Lawrence (1982b) in race relations theory, is relevant. Lawrence (1982b, p. 89) discusses common sense in relation to racist ideologies, which he argues have been elaborated from "taken-for-granted" assumptions. Here my concern is not with "racist ideas" but with "ideas about racism." More specifically it must be emphasized that Black women's notions about racism cannot be seen as "common sense" about racism. These notions are not based in taken-for-granted assumptions but, as I demonstrated earlier (see Chapter 3), comprehension of racism is acquired through deliberate problematization of social reality. Lawrence (1982b, pp. 48-50) argues that common sense is basically unsystematic, inconsistent, and contradictory and that it consists of notions that are taken for granted. In other words, common sense lacks reflective underpinning.

How do these characteristics apply to the story of Rosa N.? The accounts of Rosa N. cannot be seen as unreflective. We shall see that her evaluations are underpinned by years of deliberate questioning of her life in the Netherlands and searching for more information about the Dutch and about racism. Moreover Rosa N. has had many opportunities to systematically test her real experiences against her beliefs about racism. In addition, being a solo Black working in an all-White environment, she has had to strategize and assess possible risks attached to specific reactions to racism. Rosa N. finds that "if you want to say something about racism, you've got to state your case very well . . . otherwise they tackle you . . . and they make you ridiculous."

Further proof that she is careful and knowledgeable may be derived from the consistency of evidence. If Rosa N. has recollected just any negative experience to present as racism, we shall not be able to find consistency and coherence in her story. As noted before everyday racism does not exist in the singular but only in the plural form, as a complex of mutually related, cumulative practices, and situations. Some events may seem trivial but, as I stated before, the precise details of specific experiences are not my main concern. It is much more important to see that each event activates the whole pattern of injustice of which it is part. If, therefore, the experiences fit into a coherent system of oppression, control, and legitimation, there are grounds for belief that racism permeates Rosa N.'s everyday life in a systematic and cumulative way.

Finally, the Rosa N. story is also consistent in another sense, as may be inferred by the absence of the ultimate attribution error (Pettigrew, 1979). Unlike prejudiced interpreters Rosa N. does not dismiss evidence of positive behavior by dominant group members as a means of sustaining previous expectations about racism. This will be illustrated shortly.

In the following reconstruction the experiences of Rosa N. are categorized according to everyday situations, agents of racism, and the complications or disturbing factors that transform these situations into racist situations. Names and some background information have been changed. Even then, however, small (and, for the purpose of this study, irrelevant) details of the situation may betray the identity of the people involved. This is a real problem in a small community like the Netherlands. Therefore, I have substituted for two examples of situated racism in this story similar ones in the experience of two other Black women in the Netherlands. Exchanging the experiences does not affect the reliability of the data and of the analysis of everyday racism because it is consistent with my presupposition that, in essence, experiences of everyday racism are repetitive and shared rather than unique.

To understand the analysis of Rosa N.'s case, the reader is strongly advised to first read the "The Story of Rosa N." For the sake of readability an edited version of this story is presented below. Because of space limitations I could not include the precise categorization and analysis of Rosa N.'s experiences in this book[1] (the reader may request a copy of the complete story). Rosa N. discusses an average number of experiences of racism. The average number of experiences of racism presented by women with exactly the same interview time as Rosa N. (2.5 hours) is 46. Rosa N. reports 49 examples. She is the only representative in the category of 46-50 examples. Others are in the categories either above 50 or below 42.

The Story of Rosa N.

I came to Holland in 1969. My life was hard: work, study. My main friends were Dutch, the typical medical students. I had a time when I started to notice more things, such as, I have no home here, but a Dutch person does. I always had a very close friend—Ida, my father's younger sister. She was able to keep me from feeling lonely, from being homesick for Suriname. We gave each other a lot of support without ever consciously knocking the Dutch. That never entered your mind.

Even when Rosa N. did not explicitly feel different than the Dutch, fellow students reminded her that she was not like the Dutch.

I can remember once making a phone call in a dorm when a Dutch boy said: "There's Rosa with that laugh of hers." And I thought: What does he mean? Strange! Because I was laughing very loud. But that doesn't happen anymore, only when I'm with Rob. [I felt like] I had to get rid of a lot of the Suriname in me. Not consciously. Not at all. I certainly had to lose a lot of my spontaneity. I think too I might have done it because I was always getting it thrown in my face, like with the boy who said, "Why are you laughing like that?" I must say, I've got some of that back now. I'm rediscovering my own culture. That's fantastic.

As for many other Black women in the Netherlands, the 1980s represents a period in which Rosa N. developed a deeper understanding of racism in her daily experiences (see also Chapter 3). Vague feelings of oppression, of Eurocentrism, and cultural deprivation make way for a focused understanding of related practices of racism. Rosa N. preludes her accounts of a range of situated practices of racism by remembering: "How I loathed the Dutch. I saw all those depressed Moroccans, depressed Turks. And I saw all kinds of discrimination and racism. How people reacted, how people treated you." She continues with some examples:

We were in a surgery class. It was taught by a plastic surgeon whose name I've forgotten. If it were now, I'd certainly report that man. I was really angry. [He told us about an industrial accident] in a food processing plant where a Turk working on a cutting machine had sliced open his hand. And he even started the story with: "the stupid Turk." Yeah, that's how he started, "the stupid Turk. His hand is not a can!" He said I didn't really have much confidence, but still, I wanted to save the man's hand, because, he said, you know what it costs the Dutch government if that man loses his hand! He gets social security. So, he had to save the man's hand. He showed us another series of slides [about] how he'd operated on the hand. It looked really weird, but he must and he would save that hand, for it would cost the government too much. But eventually, the hand started to die anyway. It looked really terrible. The surgeon left the hand alone until it was completely black, like a hand of coal. His hand was amputated, after all. And then he showed the next picture. Someone's heel gone, that's another stupid foreigner in a factory, he says then. He talks about there being so many accidents. Only with foreigners. And he doesn't understand it, that's just how he tells the class the story. But he [doesn't add] that it's foreigners who do this kind of work and that they are the highest risk group for having an accident. The students thought it was real funny. They don't really give it much thought, because it arouses a kind of hilarity when it's told that way. Then everyone laughs about it. But I find such humor out of place, actually.

I waited until the man was finished. The lights went on, I told him he shouldn't make remarks like that again because they are offensive, and I chose that attitude because I thought: I must not become uncontrolled, agitated, or aggressive.

Implicitly Rosa N.'s reaction indicates that taking an explicit stand against acts considered racist may incriminate not the agent of racism but the one who objects to the racism. Anticipating problems if she is not careful ("you are too emotional, too aggressive"), she speaks with utter self-control. The reason Rosa N. is careful about pointing out the racism of the professor can be explained by her expectation that, apart from one other woman she knew she could trust, she would have the whole group, including the professor, against her. In addition she had already had another problematic experience in a similar situation. She explains:

And then one time in a general health class, this extremely stupid civil servant blamed the foreigners for overpopulation. I said something about that then, but what struck me was that someone said: oh, there's Rosa with that racism again. And I thought: what a prick! I thought: I'll turn in a complaint. But—and that really disappointed me—when I asked a few people I got on well with if they would testify, the one said, like no, because I have a child and a job I don't want to lose. One girl said she would testify. Then I spoke with my adviser, and he gave me some literature which showed that it has never been demonstrated that foreigners cause overpopulation. I very politely sent the man a letter. He sent such a nasty letter back. It was a totally degrading letter that said more about him than me, because he attacked me on personal points: that I had used my boss's FAX number—while my boss had even approved my letter. That I had not written "personal" on the letter and the secretary and other people had read it.

All these experiences took place when Rosa N. was doing her internship. This is a special situation in which study and work overlap. Thus people who are fellow students in one situation are her colleagues in other situations. Therefore, the distinction between the context of education and work is made only for the purpose of the analysis.

Now at my work, they find me oversensitive, probably because I just can't let certain things pass. And I can absolutely not do that. I do not want to and I will not. So I always respond [against racism], because now I just can't keep quiet. Here's another example. A student [presented] a patient—and I'm the only Surinamese present as doctor. He [introduced the patient with] she is from Suriname. He looked at me and said: sorry. I thought, what's all this? Why in god's name does he say "sorry"?! But to make things worse, when in my confusion I did this [very astonished face], another person started patting me on the back. Then I was completely at a loss.

The patient [being presented] had herpes genitalis. And the student said, oh, yeah, women in Suriname do have more than one man. Then I jumped in immediately with, then everyone in Suriname must have herpes!

Afterward, I asked him why he had said "sorry." Then he went like this [disdainful motion] with his hand. Like: That's how Surinamese are. Then I thought, yes, I've always thought that's what you people think of us, but I never thought you would express it that way, would make it that obvious.

[Because of all that] I left the demonstration, and when I came back in the afternoon, the boss came up and said: you reacted in a way in which you did not want to react. That was true enough. I really hadn't wanted to react in that way. But afterward, what surprised me was [that] he said it's because I'm Surinamese that I react like that. Everyone puts it all down to my being a Surinamese. Anything at all can happen, and I'm reacting as a Surinamese.

You know, I've got some really great colleagues too, but still, you notice there's a part of your daily reality you can't let them see. They really don't want to see it; they don't know how to deal with painful things. I told them once what I had experienced in hotels. Now, one of them reacted with: how strange, there must be something behind it. The rest kept quiet.

Rosa N. recalls about the hotel:

This was when we went to Paris. We had just arrived—it was late afternoon. Rob and I get to our hotel, and the man gives us a very strange look, momentarily a rather dubious attitude. It must have been in a fraction of a second that I discovered confusion in his eyes. We had booked a room for one night, but something told me: something's wrong. And my feeling never betrays me. I don't know just what it was, because you come into this hotel dressed very properly—it was an expensive hotel. But he really didn't have room for us. There had just been a few bombings, while we were in Paris, too. If you see such a reaction, the first thing that occurs to you is: this man thinks, like, these Blacks can set off a bomb, but it can also be that the man really didn't have a room for us because it was so crowded in Paris. We went to another hotel. [In the other hotel] we got a room next to a toilet with a dripping faucet. They didn't have anything else. The next day, I saw a lot of people leaving, then I said: do you perhaps have a different room for us, because I hear the toilet being flushed the whole night and the faucet dripping. [It was] and if you don't want it, then go away and blahblahblahblah and where is your husband? I think: are you crazy?! I thought: well, dirty boor, I thought right away, you're attacking me because I'm Black, not for anything else.

It was not the first time hotel personnel reacted strongly to Rosa N.'s skin color:

We were in London, this happened the other month. Rob had been invited to the inauguration of an important project he had worked on. We were really in the most expensive hotel, you know, where only Rolls Royces roll up. We had gone out in the evening. At two in the morning, we came back. And we come in and the man says, "You're not allowed to take a girl to your room, Sir." Talk about stereotypes! The next morning, we asked to speak with the manager, and I told him what had happened, and then we got a bouquet of flowers and oh so sorry that it happened in their hotel and most regrettable and unforgivable and so on. Speaking of preconceptions, for me, that was really the top!

And then, just a few years ago, I was with Rob in Portugal. I know Portuguese, so I asked for a hotel. They didn't take us. They sent us to a red light hotel.

She did not relate all these experiences to her colleagues, because she seemed to embarrass them with her stories about racism. Other examples also contribute to Rosa N.'s feeling that her colleagues feel uneasy about the fact that she has a different experience with and a different relation to society:

Certain examples [of racism] are so minuscule that I can't put them into words. It's difficult. Like, we were having lunch in the hospital restaurant and they were talking about the new film with Don Johnson, but I said Don Johnson ["ô" more or less like in "boy," which is a very common Dutch (mis)pronunciation of the phonetic "ä" like in "John" in English]. Someone corrected me. You must say "Don Johnson" [Dän Jähnson]. I came back with, why can't I say "[Dôn Jôhnson]"? And after lunch, one of the girls came up to me with: yes, people always have to be so careful when they talk with you. I said, it is the opinion of this group of doctors that they have to be careful what they say to me. On the one hand, I think it's great that they are so careful with what they say, on the other hand, I'm being pigeonholed: Rosa is sensitive, you mustn't say anything discriminating. You know what I mean by them pigeonholing me? That I am the one who is oversensitive? One of them even had the nerve to say: she withdraws so much, while I choose to, I just don't care to always come to the restaurant and sit and gossip while eating.

You see, I'm not interested in always listening to their stories. For example, I'd also like to tell what I do, what I did in the weekend . . . or, uh, sometimes to say what I find nice, pretty or whatever, but they never really go into this. They don't know about that, the life that I've led. Then they close up. They do go into each other's stories, for that's something they know.

Rosa N. wonders whether her colleagues even have the slightest idea what it means to be Black in this society:

One of the doctors, a woman who has a disabled son, said one time—and she really shocked herself—being disabled was something like being Black.

I find her extremely racist. And I've told her she does things that cannot be pointed out explicitly, which can be compared to racism. You can never get a grip on racism. And you know, she went to my boss and said I'd accused her of racism.

Her personal experiences are confirmed through the experiences of other people from the (ex-)colonies:

I heard an Indonesian writer on the radio. She said: I've learned to show the Dutch my Dutch side and the Indonesians my Indonesian side. I think it will eventually come to that: What I would like, to show both sides, that can't be. They won't accept that. What you want doesn't happen.

I can't accept in my heart that I cannot show my Surinamese background, for example, they showed a Surinamese patient on the video. The man was as Surinamese as you please—in his manic behavior, too. And I told them that. My words weren't listened to, because they didn't know what to do with them. I told them this was something typical of the Surinamese or Caribbean society—but [to them] I was probably overdoing it. It was put aside. Someone else was asked for an opinion, with: You've been in Suriname? And I thought: What's all this? What's going on? And I got really mad.

[According to them] I was too emotional. I spoke with too much feeling about that man. The swing of the Surinamese was what he had, and I didn't find him all that disturbed.

Recently there was another patient who [had responded unexpectedly well to treatment, after we had almost given up on her]. So I wanted to show that to one of the bosses. I said: come here, you've gotta see this. That's my enthusiasm. I saw him whispering with the others, then I thought, he's talking about me because I said, come look. That's how I always react, and when he recognized that from the video as Caribbean behavior, now, that wasn't allowed. The idea of: you're too emotionally involved, they don't like that, you have to be detached when making a report. That is the general trend in Holland. By not one analysis may one show emotion.

Rosa N. mentions that she has been confronted with racism from patients, but, because the patients are ill or demented, she is less worried about this than when it comes from her colleagues:

A patient, a woman told me afterward that during a psychosis, she had thought I was a whore. Then I think once more, yeah, a Black is a whore. . . . You know, this reminds me of one of the first times that I came into the hospital, I was with [a] demented woman. I gave her my hand. "I don't want the hand of a foreign worker, I don't want that hand." She went on [with] a heap of racist language.

I take a lot of time for things [because] I have the idea that I must work very scrupulously, must not fail. It's the same with everyone, so this isn't so exceptional, but with me there's another dimension. I may not make as many mistakes as the others. I must not do things wrong when with the Dutch. Absolutely not, I don't want to be their lesser. You've got to be better.

In this respect Rosa N. feels that the stress to prove herself as a Black woman is, in fact, the continuation of her past. In comparison with her cousins—the four daughters of her mother's sister—she was darker. She always felt treated as the "nigger" of the family:

I have the feeling that I must prove myself, that's for sure. A part of this has to do with that never taking the position of a Negro. Negro in the sense of lesser and then from Suriname. Hey, I'll show you that's not what I am, and the fight goes on. And I find I'm fighting until I'm ill. In Holland, it's: I'll show you that I'm not dumb.

Outside of the hospital the same patterns of discrimination occur, adapted to the specific characteristics of the situation:

In shops they address someone much younger than me as "Ma'am" and use the familiar "jij" with me. And I can't get it out of my head that they don't do that because I'm young, but because I'm Black. To a fat, Black woman, they say "jij," but to a "proper" lady who is much younger, they use the formal "U." They continue invariably to say that here in Holland. At my work too.

A man came in to clean the room. I was with a patient, a man of about 60 or 70, and I was busy writing. What does the bastard do? He opens the door, looks at the old man: "When can I clean your room? Or you've got a new cleaner." And [then] he gives me this really cheeky look when I say: "Hey, would you close the door," because he's not aware that I'm the doctor there.

Then the shock that people show when I say I'm a doctor. To me, it's just one more proof that the Dutch have a certain image of the Surinamese, and I've got to take that into account, so that it won't surprise *me.*

You can see all too clearly that a Surinamese cleaner is treated differently here, by the same man, the head custodian. I'm a doctor. You see that. Good day, good day, good day. Friendly nods. But to the others: "I told you to do that!" [raised voice]. Or they're treated like an infant, but still uncivilly. I think it's terrible. And my reaction is to be consistently friendly to them. This isn't out of pity; you feel that they're doing it to you if they treat a cleaner like that. And I don't mind him being proud that I'm a doctor. It doesn't happen that consciously, but in this way, I'm making my contribution.

Reviewing her life at the hospital, Rosa N. says:

I'm not safe at G. [name of hospital]. Like, I can never in my life bring up the subject of racism. That just can't be, because they'll only trip me up.

If you want to say anything about racism, you've got to state your case very well. Otherwise . . . they tackle you and lay down a thousand pieces of evidence to prove the opposite, and they make you ridiculous.

Because I'm Black, I'm more vulnerable [as a woman]. I always have the idea, if men see a Black woman . . . then they've got a good chance. You also see this on television. Then there's this stupid commercial where a White man wants a Black [woman], and he plays with her, and suddenly he reaches under her skirt. And then it seems something or the other comes out. I've forgotten what.

The above summary of racism in everyday situations portrays a story in which the woman is constantly fighting against racist oppression—a lonely struggle to keep breathing in a racist climate with an almost overwhelming degree of suppression. In this respect the story of Rosa N. is representative for the story of many other women in the Netherlands. In the previous chapter I mentioned that Black women in the Netherlands seem to be at a turning point in which their orientation is changing from mere defense toward a search for the power to act and to build. This accompanies a broadening of the perspective in which to deal with problems of racism. This is also evident from the story of Rosa N. Thus she concludes the interview with the following statement:

I used to think, when I am a doctor, this will be in the past, then I'll have proved myself, but no such thing. Then the long, hard road begins. Then you start to notice that you aren't there yet, that the fight has just begun. I would really like for it to be over, because I'd like to just be able to live. I'd find it wonderful if I could just feel good with my job and not have a third-rate position in the job. If you spend all your time competing, then it never stops. I participate in this consciously and take care that I don't backslide. I think: just keep it up.

I read at lot more about discrimination now—but then, not so much about Holland, because you don't get any further if you keep on thinking only about they do that and they do that and they do that. Now I would like to know much more about how I can deal with it. My first 10 years in Holland, I found it much too painful to see what was going on in South Africa. The slaughter there. It also has to do with being ready to let that penetrate. I find that positive. I think too that Rob has certainly learned from me. He has learned to look; he gives me support, accepts criticism, while he used to go into a discussion about it.

THE PROCESS OF EVERYDAY RACISM
IN THE EXPERIENCE OF ROSA N.

The reader must bear in mind that the story of Rosa N. is not a representation of the whole interview with Rosa N., of which the transcript has 54 pages, but only a compilation of experiences she presented as illustrations of racism. Therefore, one must not see this summary as a general bias against the Dutch, as an indication that she only has negative experiences with the Dutch, or as evidence that she does not know how to distinguish between racism and injustice for other reasons. Space limitations prevent detailed analysis of the experiences not included here, but it may be useful to give a brief impression. On various occasions Rosa N. distinguishes positive aspects of Dutch individuals from practices of racism. To give a few examples: She feels culturally oppressed from the very beginning of her stay in the Netherlands. Yet she has quite positive memories of the group of (Dutch male) friends she spent time with early on. They were "real old fashioned, even brazen in a certain way, but they were also quite straightforward," which is what she "really liked about them." At work she experiences racism from her supervisor in some situations, yet she otherwise appreciates that he is often "very perceptive" about her needs as a trainee. Her comprehension of racism—that is, the fact that she qualifies practices, rather than individuals, as racist—is particularly important.

Note that earlier I criticized the frequently occurring misunderstanding among the Dutch that the attitudes of someone who makes blatantly prejudiced remarks about Blacks cannot be seen as racist if, in another situation, the same person is quite nice toward a specific Black. This presupposition simplifies racism. In reality individuals may have internalized some racist notions although they have not internalized other racist notions. The nature and degree of saturation of racist ideologies in individual attitudes are influenced by historical, social, economic, political, and personality factors. However, we still have little insight into the precise nature of the processes that determine differences in racial and ethnic prejudice of individuals with similar social backgrounds. Neither do we know precisely the conditions that determine the unique structure and content of racial attitudes of individuals.

In other situations Rosa N. distinguishes class bias from racism. For instance, in a discussion about the pros and cons of a new type of medicine, she criticizes fellow students for giving Peter, a fellow student, undue credit in comparison with her. They feel he "knows best because his father is a cardiologist." Rosa N., who has a working-class background, replies, "So what about his father? I am not impressed. Is there anything Peter knows by himself?" Rosa N. is also self-critical, as she realizes that on some occasions, in the first period of her stay, she was wrong about the Dutch because she "did not know" enough about their cultural styles and about the way they "socialized among themselves." In other words, Rosa N. realized there were certain gaps in her understanding of Dutch culture that made it difficult to make reliable interpretations of her own experiences with the Dutch. This is consistent with my theory that comprehension of racist events requires knowledge of dominant or subcultural codes of behavior. The consequence is that examples in which Rosa N. was not sure herself whether she was confronted with racism are either excluded or presented with due reservation. Finally, some comments are in order about the criteria against which are assessed the accounts of Rosa N. Her experiences are examples of everyday racism if they are consistent with the definition of (experiences of) everyday racism presented in Chapter 1. Thus it may be assumed that the experiences of Rosa N. represent everyday racism if they are consistent with the following presuppositions:

(1) Everyday racism is reflected in different types of experiences.
(2) Everyday racism presupposes everyday situations.
(3) Everyday racism involves repetitive practices.
(4) Experiences of everyday racism are heterogeneous.
(5) Everyday racism involves specifications of general processes of racism.

Different Types of Experiences

The story of Rosa N. shows a relatively high frequency of direct experiences of racism. She connects her personal experiences with those of other Blacks and of other oppressed groups such as Turks and Moroccans. Personal and vicarious experiences of racism are embedded in the overall experience of Whitecentrism and pressures to assimilate. Because Rosa N. gives very few examples of mediated racism, these are not discussed here. It is best to start the discussion of the story of Rosa N. with these generalized experiences of cultural oppression.

Cognitive experiences. What you feel, know, or believe is happening continuously, or what you expect may happen any day, constitute permanently felt pressures lingering beneath the surface of social reality. Some of these pressures have been activated so many times they are presented as generalized experiences in memory. In the experiences of Rosa N. one of these forms of permanently felt racism is the pressure to *assimilate culturally* under conditions of *Eurocentrism.* Apparently she has been harassed or criticized so many times that she has gotten "rid of a lot of the Suriname" in her. Because the Dutch explicitly adhere to the norm of tolerance, pressures on Blacks to assimilate often operate covertly (Jong, 1989). This probably explains why Rosa N. was "not" even "conscious" herself that she was losing much of her genuine cultural identity.

We shall see that Eurocentrism has multiple manifestations in everyday life. Yet it is not easy to define this complex phenomenon precisely. Eurocentrism is definitely not the same as ethnocentrism—an in-group orientation that inhibits the ability to understand other cultures on their own terms. Eurocentrism has an explicitly normative basis in the belief that the Westernization of the world is the best recipe for non-European cultures. The underlying assumption is that the West European culture and its capitalist economy

> is not only the world of material wealth and power, . . . it is also the site of the triumph of the scientific spirit, rationality, and practical efficiency, just as it is the world of tolerance, . . . respect for human rights and democracy, concern for equality . . . and social justice. It is the best of the worlds that have been known up until this time. (Amin, 1988, p. 107)

In his critique of Eurocentrism, Amin (1988) points out that Eurocentrism makes it impossible to see other cultures in any other way than as less progressive than the superior European model. Eurocentrism forms the ideological essence of the culturalization of racism. The concept of "Western" refers to the status quo of certain cultural, economic, political, and technological characteristics as opposed to biological characteristics. Therefore, it is not recognized as the cultural expression of racism to see European culture as indisputably superior and to use that view to defend Amer-European control over oppressed non-European countries. Thus Dutch policymakers state blatantly that fundamental norms and values of Dutch culture *should be* the standard for *allochtonen* (or non-native people) in the Netherlands and that adaption to the Dutch way is the only way forward to achieve integration (WRR, 1989).

Part of the Eurocentric construction is the belief that White views of race and ethnic relations are considered more reliable than those of Blacks. Eurocentrism breeds indifference and cognitive detachment from Blacks because their norms and values, as well as their perspectives, are considered "inferior." Obviously Eurocentrism or the pursuit of the Westernization of the world is also at the heart of U.S. culture, economy, and politics. However, in the context of Black and White relations in the United States, it may be in a sense appropriate to speak of "Whitecentrism." Therefore, I shall use the term *Eurocentrism* interchangeably with *Whitecentrism* when referring to the U.S. situation.

Underestimation is another constant form of racism that must have been activated so many times that Rosa N. feels she cannot afford to be less than perfect. It is interesting to note that Rosa N. is perfectly well aware that all her colleagues work under pressure to perform ("I must not fail. It's the same with everyone, so that is not so exceptional, but with me there is another dimension"). In other words, she is not trying to hide any personal incompetence behind the explanation of racism. She only makes a qualitative difference when she suggests that, if she fails, it will not be seen as personal failure but as failure of a Black woman. In fact Rosa N. points here to a general problem that has been confirmed in many experiments in intergroup attribution (e.g., Hewstone, 1989). I shall return to the behavioral implications of this important aspect when I discuss dominant group actions against Black women who aspire to achieve and who are competent in their fields.

These three forces of racism experienced by Rosa N. symbolize the framework in which all her other experiences may be placed: (a) *Eurocentrism*; (b) the dominant group impeding the efforts of Blacks to achieve (which is rationalized with, among other things, *attribution of incompetence*); and (c) Whites exercising covert pressure with the aim of enforcing cultural *assimilation*. Eurocentrism marginalizes Blacks; low expectations legitimize marginalization; and pressure to assimilate is a form of control. Assimilation is not just a question of state policy, which is how this is usually identified. This "need for control" (Dijker, 1989, p. 87) expressed by individual members of the dominant group, who demand that Blacks adapt to Dutch ways of living, is a dominant feature of Dutch racism. The story of Rosa N., and as we shall see the stories of other women as well, demonstrate that assimilative forces work through everyday situations and practices. These forms of racism all presuppose that difference is organized hierarchically, whether it concerns culture or structure.

Vicarious experiences. Among the most characteristic differences between the experiences of Black women in the United States and those in the Netherlands are those associated with identification with other groups who are targets of racism. The tendency among Black women in the Netherlands to transcend the boundaries of ethnicity when antiracism is concerned is remarkable in light of the prevailing forces on the side of the dominant group to generate and maintain rigid ethnic differentiation in the context of a pluralist model of society. Black women in the Netherlands commonly identify with other colonized immigrants (whether Surinamese, Aruban, or Moluccan) and with migrant workers (in particular Turks and Moroccans) who are subjected to racism (ethnicism). This can also be inferred from Rosa N., who says about the period when she became "aware" of racism that she "loathed the Dutch" because of the depressed conditions of Turks and Moroccans and all of the kinds of racism she began to recognize. Black women with higher education also experience racism vicariously in its class-related forms. Due to the close relations between race oppression and class exploitation, Black women with higher education have historically always directly or indirectly been involved in a struggle for basic issues, such as better housing and education, for the majority of the Black group. This is not meant to suggest, however, that Black women with higher education have always been able to adhere to the real class-related needs of the majority of Black women (Davis, 1981). A form of commitment is Rosa N.'s protest against the lectures of a plastic surgeon who jokes about the medical experiment he did on a Turkish worker.

Rosa N. says that no matter how polite specific Whites may be to her because she is a doctor, when they intimidate another Black because he is "just" a worker, "they are doing it to you" too. Rosa N. does not only identify with other targets of racism because she feels a commitment to challenge racism. If this were the case, any active opponent of racism, including Whites, would vicariously experience racism through knowledge of the oppression of Blacks. Individual Blacks also experience racism through the experiences of others because of the very nature of racism. It is not directed against any one person but against every Black. For these reasons vicarious experiences represent a major component of the experience of everyday racism. The notion of vicarious racism underscores the fact that, in the reproduction of racism, agents and subjects are of secondary importance. Whether or not agents indulge in racist practices depends on many factors, among others the degree of saturation of racist ideologies in the individual's social cognitions, the interests involved, the personality of the agent, and expectations about reactions of Blacks or White group members. However, the characteristics of the situation determine the specific forms racism takes. To give an example, the professor abuses the authority attached to his profession by infusing his teaching with racist statements after he had used the power attached to the medical profession to physically abuse a Turkish patient. Another teacher may do the same in a teaching situation, as can be inferred from the experiences of Rosa N. The content of the racist statements that are made may be determined by other factors, such as the role of the speakers in other situations (the surgeon makes racist remarks related to surgery, and the guest speaker comes with racist ideas developed in the context of his work at the Ministry of Public Health). To avoid misunderstanding the primacy of situation over agents and subject does not mean that racism is just situationally construed. It will be shown in the course of this study that the major forms racism takes are ideologically structured; the specific manifestations of these forms, however, are situationally created.

Comparisons between the direct and the vicarious experiences of Rosa N. show that there are similarities in the forms racism takes. Here particular attention is paid to the pathologizing of Blacks. Various studies have focused on the process by which racist notions of difference translate the behavior of Blacks into "maladjusted" behavior while "maladjusted" behavior becomes subsequently "pathological" behavior (Baratz & Baratz, 1972/1977; Lawrence, 1982a). These notions constitute part of commonsense thinking (Lawrence, 1982b).

Pathologizing is in many respects worse than inferiorizing because pathological behavior needs to be cured for one to become "normal" again. Furthermore it is relevant to make a distinction between ideas of cultural pathology and attribution to Blacks of pathological personalities. The first form represents cultural deterministic explanations of "social disadvantage." The second form perceives reactions of Blacks to oppression in general or to racism in particular as pathological. This line of thinking is important in the story of Rosa N. as it draws upon the idea that, due to "social deprivation," Blacks develop damaged personalities with symptoms such as "oversensitive" and "overemotional" reactions to their social surroundings.

Rosa N. is repeatedly confronted with Whites who think that her perceptions of racism are pathological. This ideological form of racism structures direct and vicarious experiences and is expressed in specific situations according to the characteristics of the situation and the interests involved. In this process both Black professionals and patients are subjected to the same process of pathologizing so that it becomes legitimate to disqualify Rosa N. as a doctor. The story of Rosa N. holds good illustrations of the intricate relation between acts of racism directed against Rosa N. herself and racism embedded in the way doctors discuss their Black patients in the presence of Rosa N. Let us look at the following example:

(1) One colleague, who later appears to feel utter disdain for the Surinamese, presents the case of a Surinamese patient.

(2) Because he feels contempt for the Surinamese in general, there is conflict between his general attitude toward the Surinamese and his attitude toward his Surinamese colleague (Rosa N.), an equal because of her position as a doctor. This probably explains why the colleague apologizes to "colleague" Rosa N. for referring to the "Surinamese" in Rosa N. when he announces his Surinamese patient. In other words, he is the one who introduces the "ethnic" background of Rosa N. as an explicit factor in the situation. This takes Rosa N. by surprise.

(3) This is not so for her other White colleagues. Apparently they immediately understand and support the ethnic background of Rosa N. as a relevant factor in the situation. They all feel sorry for her that she is Surinamese and start patting her on the back. This makes it even worse because, in the reverse situation, it would not be expected that Rosa N. would feel sorry for her Dutch colleagues and start patting them on the back when they discuss the case of a Dutch patient.

(4) Angry about the whole situation Rosa N. becomes cynical when the first colleague starts to pathologize Surinamese culture (making denigrating generalizations about sexual behavior in Suriname) with the aim of explaining a particular sexual disease.

(5) Apparently reacting in a cynical way is not quite Rosa N.'s usual way of communicating with her colleagues. This is noticed by her supervisor. However, instead of acknowledging that the other colleagues could have acted otherwise so that Rosa N. would have acted otherwise, he also starts to pathologize Surinamese culture. His explanation is that Rosa N. was guided by the Surinamese in her when she reacted in a cynical way.

Schematically organized, the degradation of Rosa N. from "respectable" (as a specialist) via "ethnic" to "pathological" is outlined in Figure 5.1, in which the changing definitions of the direct (II, III) and indirect (I) participants in the situation proceed from step 1 to step 5.

Equating Rosa N. with Surinamese patients is even more direct in the situation, where a Surinamese man is presented as mentally disturbed because of his extroverted behavior. Rosa N. does not think the man is very disturbed. Soon after that event, when Rosa N. herself shows obvious enthusiasm when discussing a case with her supervisor, she can almost feel the supervisor comparing her with the "swinging" Surinamese patient he had watched on the video presentation the other day. This, Rosa N. infers from the sudden whispering

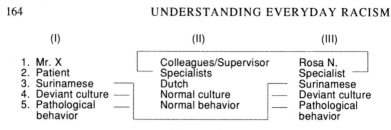

Figure 5.1. Redefinition of Rosa N. from competent to pathological

among the supervisor and other colleagues, suggests that she does not behave like a "proper" doctor. Clearly in this situation difference can only become a problem because it is related to an established White-male-middle-class norm of "healthy" behavior that reflects existing power relations of race and gender in society at large and in health care in particular (Pearson, 1986, p. 110).

Everyday Racism Presupposes Everyday Situations

The story of Rosa N. does not deal with racist ideologies of organized racist or fascist movements. She is just reporting about her day-to-day experiences in routine situations involving "normal" people. Due to her profession a proportionally high number of dominant group members with whom she has to deal in daily interactions belong to the Dutch-educated "elite." Relations between Rosa N. and dominant group members are racialized because they are structured by the wider stratifications in society. However, this racialized dimension, which Rosa N. described so well when she referred to "another dimension" compelling her to pursue perfection, is not constantly activated. Dominant group members may relate to her in a nonracist way in some situations but not in others. The racial dimension of the relationship is activated when racist practices are integrated into the situation. All of the situations in which Rosa N. experiences racism directly constitute routine situations in everyday life. To illustrate I summarize the situations of racism on the job. On the job racism permeates routine situations, formal and informal, through which the institution of a hospital is reproduced:

(1) discussing patients with colleagues
(2) small talk in the corridors

(3) having informal conversation with colleagues

(4) having lunch with colleagues

(5) discussing patients with the supervisor

(6) working with a patient

(7) giving a paper in a seminar

(8) being disturbed in one's work by the cleaner

(9) overhearing the head custodian and the cleaner

Similarly the agents of racism in these situations are part of the natural human fabric of the specific workplace, a medical complex:

(1) colleagues: doctors

(2) supervisor: doctor

(3) patient

(4) cleaner

(5) head custodian

Recurrent Practices and Heterogeneity of Experiences

Repetition is an indication of the degree of uniformity of practice. This question is discussed more extensively later when the story of Rosa N. is compared with the experiences of other Black women. In the biography of Rosa N. herself, there is also similarity in the forms of racism she encounters: (a) The same complications arise in similar situations. For instance, in various hotels she is treated as a prostitute. Also there is repetition of (b) similar forms of racism in different situations. She is not only treated as a prostitute in hotels but also called that by one of her patients. Another example concerns the rejection of Surinamese styles of communication by a fellow student in one situation and by Rosa N.'s supervisor in another situation. (c) Similar agents may be involved in similar or in different racist practices. The same colleagues who tolerate racist remarks from the professor during class patronize and pathologize Rosa N. or other Blacks in other situations.

The interview materials do not provide sufficient data to analyze in detail the impact of manifestations occurring in one context on those in other contexts. It may be assumed, however, that racism in one situation may support or legitimize practices in other situations. For instance, consider the situation where Rosa N.'s colleagues tolerate denigrating comments from one of them about Black women. Toleration of such comments creates a fertile climate for the subsequent pathologization of Rosa N. Similarly the implicit consent the students give to the professor by not supporting Rosa N. in her objections to his racist comments justify his behavior and support his subsequent denial of racism and attempts to further humiliate Rosa N. when she pursues the case. It is also highly probable that the integration of racism into teaching programs implicitly prepares and legitimizes students (young doctors) themselves to reproduce racism in their own short lectures, that is, the presentation of patient cases. This introduces the most important feature of everyday racism. Racist practices integrated into everyday situations are specifications of general processes.

Everyday Racism as Specifications of General Processes of Racism

For practices to occur systematically, there must be certain ideological conditions that both stimulate and legitimize these practices. As stated before, this is not meant to imply that relations between prejudice and discrimination are simple or straightforward. However, the saturation of cognitions with shared notions or consensus on race allows certain practices to happen routinely. This may also be inferred from the experiences of Rosa N. It is explicitly assumed that practices are allowed, rather than that agents always consciously perform racist practices or that others explicitly agree with these practices. Indeed Rosa N. says she also has (situational) allies, among others her husband and a female colleague who she thinks supports her even when she does not take any explicit initiatives against racism. Her boss supported her letter of protest to the representative of the ministry. The tolerance of racism that many other dominant group members display may be a question of indifference, of ignorance, or of mere behavioral conformity (Pettigrew, 1958). In particular in the Netherlands the tradition of establishing harmony through consensus may inhibit individuals from confronting other group members, irrespective of the problem at hand. Whatever the reasons individuals may have, the rule applies that, the more saturated social cognitions are with racist ideological notions, the more likely it becomes that racist cognitions encourage or rationalize specific actions and the more oppressive tolerance of racism becomes. For these reasons it is relevant to reconstruct from the story of Rosa N. the main ideological concepts under-lying the racism she experiences.

Problematization. Earlier I mentioned that racism is grounded in the exaggeration and hierarchical organization of difference in (but not only in) European civilization. These principles are made opera-tive through various processes, as can also be inferred from the story of Rosa N. On the highest level of abstraction two structuring con-cepts underlie ideological racism as reconstructed by Rosa N.: real or imaginary *differences* attributed to Blacks and the subsequent *hierar-chical ordering* of difference. Not only is difference organized hi-erarchically, it is common in—although not only typical of—European thinking for the "superior" to control the "inferior" (Hodge et al., 1975). The concepts of race and ethnicity are cultivated by overemphasis on (attributed) difference. As a result difference can be problematized and conceptually organized according to biological, cultural, or value hierarchies. Indications of these ideological forces are implied in many accounts of Rosa N.

Overemphasis on ethnic difference is inherent in various comments and criticisms dominant group members make about (what they pre-sume to be) Surinamese culture. One pertinent example of the fact that difference is inherently perceived in hierarchical terms concerns the situation in which a colleague introduces a patient with "she is from Suriname," after which he immediately looks at Rosa N. and says "sorry." Later the colleague confesses that he apologized because he felt it might have been offensive to his Black colleague to be re-minded that she is from the same "inferior background" as the patient.

The most penetrating process Rosa N. describes pertains to the con-tinual *problematization* of (attributed) difference. Problematization in this sense is the ideological management of pluralization. This pro-cess takes place through the dynamic interplay of two clusters of ideas. It is assumed that Blacks *have problems* (biological and cultural constraints), for this will account for the attribution that they *create problems* (society "cannot" cater to certain cultural traits and tradi-tions). Problematization of Blacks is made increasingly operative through conceptions of culture. This is consistent with my earlier statements about the culturalization of racism. However, there are still remnants of biological determinism. More specifically Rosa N. is confronted with sexual racism (Stember, 1976), ideologically founded in the idea of Black sexuality being *sexual aberration.* This takes the particular gendered form of repeated insinuations that she is a prostitute. These perceptions of Black women are indicative of the different definitions of Black and White womanhood in dominant ideology. Black womanhood is perceived predominantly in biological terms, while White womanhood is seen in biological and social terms, thereby placing Black women closer to nature and White women closer to culture. Obviously this issue is more complex than can be dealt with here, because the convergence of racism and sexism on notions of nature and sexuality has further ramifications (Carby, 1987; Gilman, 1985; Hoch, 1979; Seidel, 1988).

Allied with the aim of control over nature is the idea that human beings should control passions and emotions (Hodge, 1975b). The idea that the Dutch have better control over biological drives probably accounts for the accusation expressed by a guest lecturer that "foreigners," which in Dutch popular language is almost exclusively used for "non-Western" citizens, "cause overpopulation" in the Netherlands. This residue of eugenic thinking pertains to cultural factors that also appear in the general myth that the Third World causes overpopulation due to traditional values about the use of contraceptives. This line of thinking problematizes so-called non-Western cultures for holding on to traditional views about the use of contraceptives. They are accused of impeding their own progress and endangering the future of the human race because of their high birthrates (see, for further discussion, Greer, 1984). Given the fact that the Dutch population, like that of various other northern European countries, is aging, the problematization of the birth rate of "foreigners" is even more dubious.

Another source of problematization Rosa N. experiences derives from the underestimation of Blacks. The idea that Black people are incapable of intellectual advancement probably combines remnants of racist notions of biological determinism (Blacks as genetically less intelligent) and forms of cultural determinism (attributed low drive to achieve). Furthermore it is likely that gender- and race-based ideologies converge in the practice of underrating Black women (Hall, 1982; Piliawsky, 1982; Tomlinson, 1983). The least harmful example Rosa N. mentions is almost too stereotypical to be true: The cleaner comes in and takes the old White male patient for a doctor and the Black young doctor for the patient.

The more penetrating and serious implications of low expectations about Black women are induced by colleagues and supervisors, and these can be inferred indirectly from Rosa N.'s firm belief that she has to be a better performer than Whites. This is not only due to the negative effects of her "solo status." Low expectations about Blacks are created and sustained through conflict-maintaining causal attributions for explaining either their success or failure (Hewstone, 1989; Pettigrew & Martin, 1989). Success is likely to be attributed to situational circumstances (e.g., as proof that there is no discrimination rather than as a sign of the Black individual's exceptional ability to surmount problems of racism). Failure is likely to be attributed to dispositional factors (e.g., proof that Blacks are incompetent). Other research shows that this problem is even worse for Blacks who, like Rosa N., aspire to careers that are nontraditional for Blacks. In that case Black and White expectations are polarized. The history of the struggle shows that Black women have always placed a high value on the acquisition of learning and training (Davis, 1981; Dill, 1980; Tomlinson, 1983). In particular Black women who aspire to nontraditional careers have not only high aspirations but, in comparison with other groups, also high self-estimates of ability and performance (Bailey & Mednick, 1988). Therefore, it is less likely that they will internalize the idea that Blacks are low performers. Instead they may be more likely to engage in (collective) opposition to discrimination (Gilkes, 1982).

Rosa N. depicts an atmosphere in which difference is exaggerated, reduced to ethnicity, and subsequently *pathologized,* the prevailing assumption being that Blacks are "emotional." A very good example of this is the reaction of her supervisor when Rosa N. reacts with sarcasm, and then leaves the session, after blatantly offensive remarks one colleague makes about Black female sexuality. First, the supervisor pathologizes her reaction by suggesting that she probably "did not want to react" in that way. And he adds that she "reacted like that because [she] is a Surinamese." Rosa N. is confronted with various other attempts to pathologize Blackness. Being Black in one situation is interpreted as a "disability," in another as an indication of mental instability ("too emotional"), or in another as a condition to be pitied ("another person started patting me on the back"). The pathologization of Blackness can only partly be explained by the environment in which Rosa N. works. However, it is relevant to briefly consider further ramifications of the attribution to Blacks of emotional instability by (mental) health care professionals.

In addition to general knowledge about racism against Black women in society at large, it is relevant to consider general information about racism (class and gender bias) in (mental) health care (Littlewood & Lipsedge, 1982; Miller & Rose, 1986). The overemphasis on differences functions to reduce ethnic behavior to individual traits to justify psychiatric intervention (Mercer, 1986). The case of the "swinging" Surinamese, who, according to Rosa N., should probably not have been hospitalized at all, is an example of this. Racism nurtures the stereotype of Afro-Caribbean (men) as deviant, aggressive, and "dangerous" and as a group that potentially undermines the existing order. The "swinging" style of the patient fits the dominant model of deviant (Black male) behavior. It is behavior that mocks "bourgeois" norms and values. This suggests that the Black man is pathologized and admitted as a patient not on medical grounds but because of potential "dangerousness." Therefore, pathologizing must also be seen in its function to control opposition to the existing order. I shall come back to containment of opposition in a moment.

When difference is construed so that it is inherently problematized and used to denigrate Blacks biologically, culturally, and in terms of individuality, one does not need too much imagination to understand that these cognitive constructions constitute an ideological climate that will allow rejection, exclusion, rudeness, ridicule, humiliation, and a general sense of detachment concerning racism. These and other forms of injustice nurture, in turn, the consensus in which racial and ethnic difference is construed in hierarchical order.

Marginalization. If Rosa N. had been a cleaner rather than a doctor in the hospital, her story would have been one of racism structured by class exploitation and of class oppression permeated by racism. Indirectly she is confronted with the impact of class oppression in everyday racism. The head custodian bullies the Black cleaner, but he would never be anything but polite with Dr. N. Her own struggle, as it relates to the structural position of Black women with higher education, is directed more exclusively toward racial and ethnic marginalization. She experiences outright *rejection* by a patient who refuses to shake hands with "a foreign worker" and she is *refused entrance* to a hotel twice. She can only guess as to why there are suddenly no vacancies given that she had made reservations beforehand. On another occasion there is no need for guessing: the night porter addresses her husband with, "You are not allowed to take a girl to your room, Sir." On the job she experiences other, more subtle, marginalization. Colleagues express *indifference* rather than polite, let alone cordial, interest when she engages in casual conversation with them ("I'd also like . . . to say what I find nice, pretty or whatever, but they never really go into this").

Often Whites *passively tolerate* and probably hardly even notice *racism*. Let me illustrate: When colleagues insult Rosa N. by considering her *incompetent* to judge a Surinamese patient, none of the participants challenges the insult. It is taken for granted that a White male colleague who has been in Suriname once is more competent. It is probably not even noticed that this perpetuates the usual positive discrimination toward White males. They argue that Rosa N. is unfit to give a reliable medical opinion on culturally deterministic grounds ("too much feeling, because it concerns a Surinamese patient"), yet nobody seems to discredit the Dutch cultural background of the colleague (probably too little feeling for a Black patient and certainly too little knowledge of Surinamese culture). This difference in the application of cultural determinism is not an ad hoc phenomenon. It is highly functional in the culturalization of racism. To proceed from "race" to "culture" as the key organizing concept of oppression, the "other" must be culturalized. In that process the concept of "culture" is reduced to (perceptions of) tradition as cultural constraints. Cultural hierarchies are constructed and sustained, but the dominant culture is never made explicit. Instead dominant group members appeal to the higher order of "ethos" and "knowledgeability" to assert that their version of reality is superior because it is not affected by any cultural constraints, such as cultural bias. This introduces the third major force of racism in the experience of Rosa N.: The denial of racism.

Containment. Rosa N. is not just a "powerless victim" of racism; neither are agents of racism simply maliciously abusing power. It can be inferred from the story of Rosa N. that power is centrally involved in interracial (ethnic) situations. But power can be used, created, and deconstructed. Power in this sense is not an act but a transformative capacity instantiated in action as a regular and routine phenomenon (Giddens, 1979). In the story of Rosa N. it is relevant to bear in mind that agents of racism wield power because they could have acted otherwise. The notion of power has no inherent connection with "will," motivation, or desire (Giddens, 1979). Although all action is intentional, the implications and consequences of these acts, and the realization that one could have acted otherwise, are not inherently explicit for the actor(s) involved. Neither is it inherently explicit to agents of racism that (group) interests are involved in the reinforcement of racial (ethnic) domination through the exercise of power. In other words, there is no conspiracy against Rosa N. The ideological climate fosters oppression of the elements that are seen as different and legitimizes practices that sustain hierarchical ordering of difference. However, oppression inherently fosters opposition.

It is beyond the purpose of this study to elaborate on the conditions under which opposition takes place and on the forms it takes. Here, however, it is relevant to see that opposition is an expression of commitment to achieve change. Rosa N. is permanently involved in direct or indirect opposition to racism. Indirectly she tries to compensate for detrimental effects of racism by showing solidarity with other Blacks. It "does not happen consciously" but she feels she is "making [her] contribution" in that way. She also confronts racism directly, various examples of which are discussed. The more reluctant the dominant group members to allow or to accept change, the more motivated they will be to prevent protest and to suppress existing opposition. It is important to see that control of opposition works not only directly (retaliation) but also indirectly (intimidation, inferiorization, and denial of conflict) with the aim of discouraging opposition. Intimidation often involves physical and verbal violence. The function of inferiorizing is to instill emotional insecurity among the oppressed. The denial of conflict delegitimizes resistance. It is often difficult to deal with, because denial is implicit in the consensus on race. Therefore, the implicit must be made explicit first in trying to establish alternative definitions of reality.

Almost half of Rosa N.'s experiences concern processes of containment. This suggests that she encounters a relatively high degree of reluctance to change. The message implied in the *humiliation* of the Black cleaner is that he should accept an inferior position. Other experiences of disrespect or contempt occurred when her colleagues started to make derogatory comments about the Surinamese and when Rosa N. finds that shop assistants do not address her with the formal form "U" but with the informal "jij." I speak of *intimidation* when lecturers use racist examples in front of Black students because this situation activates group power. In the act of underrating Rosa N. dominant group members confirm racial consensus that allows these things to be said without sanctions being applied. This is even worse when racist statements are used to induce laughter, which is an explicit way to create approval and tolerance of racism. I fully agree with Lawrence's (1982b, p. 73) statement: "It is difficult to know how racist [and sexist] jokes can be funny unless, you share the underlying assumptions." Other forms of intimidation that Rosa N. discusses include the *rudeness* she experiences from a hotel clerk.

The function of intimidation is to "keep Blacks in their place." Later I will return to this important function of containment as it presupposes approval for existing relations between "superior" and "inferior" groups. Many forms of *rejection of ethnically specific behavior* operate in the same way. Stigmatizing the way you laugh or your enthusiasm about your work is giving the message that different behavior is not appreciated. One could argue that these are trivialities not even worth mentioning. Indeed these are trivialities. That is exactly the problem. We can also look at it in this way: Apparently the dominant group refuses to accept even the most trivial manifestations of difference, because they do not want to deal with them. This confirms my earlier stated presupposition that racism penetrates otherwise insignificant situations in everyday life. This introduces another subtle form of suppression, namely, the act of *patronizing*. In this context Rosa N. recalls how her colleagues made it a point to correct her when they detected a Dutch accent in her pronunciation of a U.S. name.

This last type of suppression, patronizing, is a typical example of an episode that is in itself incredibly trifling. But again its triviality is precisely an indication of an extremely high degree of control: even the slightest mistakes in her use of language induce disapproving comments. However, let us first presume that these comments do not pertain to the racial dimension of the relation between Rosa N. and her White colleagues. When she says that they are overdoing it, making a fuss about her pronunciation, her colleagues themselves activate the underlying race relations of the situation. They accuse Rosa N. of oversensitivity because she did not react as they had hoped or expected, which is consistent with findings of attribution research. Dominant group members ignore situational attributions in favor of dispositional attributions to account for unexpected behavior from a member of the dominated group (Hewstone, 1989). Allegedly Rosa N. reacts as she does because she is oversensitive. Because these colleagues generally agree that Rosa N. is "too emotional" and "oversensitive about racism" anyway, they now implicitly reproach her when she victimizes them with her "accusations" of racism. This emotional reaction of the colleagues is understandable. Racism is publicly and explicitly judged. Emotions associated with ethnic prejudice are often regulated by reversing the situation: The colleagues are benevolent, and Rosa N. is ungrateful. Elsewhere I noted that this reaction may well be seen as characteristic of the ideological climate in the Netherlands of the 1980s (Essed, 1987). These and other strategies to regulate ethnic prejudice are discussed at length in van Dijk (1989). This question remains, however: Why do her colleagues introduce the factor of race and racism in the first place, when Rosa N. only tells them to "shut up" about their unwarranted concern that she pronounce the name of Don Johnson in 100% correct English? Does this not suggest that they themselves are unable to communicate with Rosa N. without overemphasizing the racial dimension implicit in their relation?

I do not intend these arguments to suggest that only Blacks are patronized. As such patronizing, underestimation, or the extreme act of murder are social acts, which may happen to other people in other situations and for other reasons. However, the implications and consequences, and the systematic nature of specific processes, are specific forms of racism. Therefore, specific experiences of racism only have meaning when they are contextualized in terms of other experiences of everyday racism. In theory this includes all other experiences discussed in the interview. It is sufficient, however, to look at the experiences Rosa N. has with fellow students and colleagues: negative comments on the way she laughs, pathologizing Surinamese behavior, equating Rosa N. with Surinamese patients, ridiculing her attempts to challenge racism, patting her on the back because they think she is pitiful, being indifferent, not taking her seriously, jeering at her, ignoring her medical opinion, and the like. Against this background, it seems that the patronizing language correction, and certainly the subsequent pathologizing of Rosa N.'s reaction, are consistent with the colleagues' usual attitudes and behavior toward Rosa N. and other Blacks.

Rosa N.'s colleagues apparently do not place that particular event in the context of their behavior with her in other situations. As the context for understanding Rosa N.'s irritation about the language correction, therefore, they have only the particular lunch situation and the presupposition that Rosa N. is too sensitive anyway. However, Rosa N. in turn contextualizes accusations of oversensitivity in the framework of the overall *denial of racism* in the Netherlands.

If dominant group members are tolerant of racism in many other situations, it is not surprising that Rosa N.'s refusal to tolerate racism induces new forms of control. The final step in the process of denial is the incrimination of Blacks (or others) who make a point of opposing racism. Rosa N. is accused of "malice." A colleague who had first compared Blackness to being "disabled" wants the supervisor to do something about Rosa N.'s. "accusing others of racism." Elsewhere I have discussed the problem of denial more extensively (Essed, 1986,

1987). Here it is relevant to note that the denial of racism is already programmed into the dominant Dutch definition of racism. If only overt and blatantly social Darwinist ideas of race are considered forms of racism, the logical conclusion is that there is no racism. It is highly functional to restrict the definition of racism to blatant ideas of White supremacy. These traditional ideas of race are rare in the Netherlands, which supports the belief that Dutch society does not have any problem with racism.

These indications of pathologizing and denial also confirm that Rosa N.'s position is marginal. She is not (considered) part of the in-group, and racism operates to sustain racialized dimensions of social relations. Rosa N. is tolerated as a student and colleague, but she must not expect her colleagues to be sensitive or feel responsible for problems of racism, for they do not acknowledge it to be a problem. The analysis of everyday racism in the life of Rosa N. is not complete. Many other factors may be looked at, such as the specific consequences of racism from people in positions of authority, gender differences in expressions of racism, and conditions for change.

Another relevant question pertains to reliability. Therefore, we must proceed from intrasubjective to intersubjective comparisons for consistency between the accounts of Rosa N. and the experiences of other Black women. I have summarized and categorized for all women (a) the situations in which they experience racism and (b) the specific mechanisms of racism they reported. These are briefly discussed. Then the experiences of Rosa N. are assessed against these shared experiences of racism.

THE MACRO CONTEXT OF EXPERIENCES OF RACISM

Like Rosa N. all other Black women experience racism in multiple situations. To give an idea of the relative frequency and heterogeneity of racism, Tables 5.1 and 5.2 contain a summary of over 2,000 different situations in which the women had direct, vicarious, or mediated experiences of racism. Here only abstract (macro) representations of social situations are mentioned. The table gives only a rough indication of the distribution of racism in the lives of Black women. In reality each of these abstract dimensions of the social system stands for clusters of relations and practices. Each woman reported more than

Table 5.1 Distribution of Racism in Everyday Life in the United States[a]

Black Women in the United States (N = 27)[b]

Codes (read vertically): c01 c02 c03 c04 c05 c06 c07 c08 c09 c12 c13 c14 c15 c18 c19 c20 c21 c22 c24 c25 c26 c27 c28 c31 c32 c33 c34

Macro Situations	c01	c02	c03	c04	c05	c06	c07	c08	c09	c12	c13	c14	c15	c18	c19	c20	c21	c22	c24	c25	c26	c27	c28	c31	c32	c33	c34	Total
1. Symbolic language	x	x	x	x	x	x	x			x	x								x							x		11
culture[c]									x									x										2
science				x														x							x			3
religion									x																			1
2. Media		x			x		x	x												x		x						6
3. Politics		x				x		x								x	x			x			x	x				8
4. Education	x	x	x	x	x	x	x		x	x	x	x	x	x	x	x	x	x	x		x		x	x	x			23
5. Work	x	x	x	x		x	x	x	x	x	x	x		x	x	x	x	x	x	x	x	x	x	x	x	x		23
6. Housing	x		x					x		x		x	x				x				x			x				9
7. Neighborhood	x		x		x	x	x		x	x	x	x		x		x		x								x		13
8. Family	x	x	x				x	x	x		x		x	x	x	x	x	x	x	x			x		x			17
9. Friends		x					x		x										x	x		x						6
10. Shopping	x	x	x		x	x		x	x	x	x	x		x	x	x		x	x		x	x	x		x			19
11. Restaurants	x			x	x	x		x							x		x	x						x				9
12. Street		x																										1
13. Hotel																												0
14. Organizations						x	x	x																				3
15. Services	x						x										x			x								4
	0	0	1	0	0	0	0	0	1	0	0	0	0	0	0	0	0	0	0	0	0	0	0	0	0	0	0	
	8	7	0	3	5	6	8	3	3	7	7	3	6	3	4	4	6	5	5	9	5	3	4	6	4	6	8	158

a. For reasons of space, the codes of the interviewees are written vertically instead of horizontally. For women in the United States, codes are "c" followed by a number and, for women in the Netherlands, "s" followed by a number.

b. Numbering is according to chronological order of the interviews. The numbering exceeds the total of 27 interviewees. Interviews not included here concern those with informants who do not fit the selection criteria.

c. For practical reasons I used the term *culture* to refer to racism mediated through specific rituals or traditions.

one experience of racism per situation; the length of the list is confined, however, by the length of the interview. In other words, these tables *do not represent the total number of racism experiences in the lives of the women but only the total number of experiences 55 women discussed within the time span of about two hours.* The categories included in Tables 5.1 and 5.2 are not necessarily mutually exclusive. In the United States the number of macro situations discussed by each woman varied between 3 and 13, with an average of about 6 per

Table 5.2 Distribution of Racism in Everyday Life in the Netherlands

Macro Situations	Black Women in the Netherlands (N = 28)																												Total
	S001	S002	S003	S004	S005	S006	S007	S008	S009	S010	S011	S012	S013	S014	S015	S016	S017	S018	S019	S020	S021	S022	S023	S024	S025	S026	S027	S028	
1. Symbolic language	x									x					x	x		x					x		x				7
culture	x	x			x		x																	x		x			6
science	x				x											x								x					4
religion					x	x																x							3
2. Media	x	x		x	x	x				x	x	x	x	x		x		x	x		x	x		x	x	x		x	19
3. Politics					x	x	x										x												4
4. Education	x	x	x	x	x	x	x	x	x	x	x		x	x			x				x	x	x	x	x		x		20
5. Work	x	x	x	x	x	x	x	x	x	x	x	x	x	x	x	x	x		x	x	x	x	x		x	x		x	25
6. Housing					x									x						x						x			4
7. Neighborhood	x	x		x	x		x	x	x				x	x	x		x	x		x		x		x	x		x		17
8. Family	x		x			x	x	x				x			x	x	x		x		x	x	x		x	x	x	x	17
9. Friends	x				x								x	x		x		x	x		x	x							9
10. Shopping	x	x	x	x	x	x	x	x		x	x	x	x	x	x	x	x	x	x					x	x	x	x	x	23
11. Restaurants							x							x															2
12. Street	x	x		x	x	x	x		x				x	x	x		x	x	x		x	x	x	x	x			x	19
13. Hotel	x													x		x													3
14. Organizations			x			x	x		x		x													x					6
15. Services	x					x	x	x	x							x					x	x	x	x		x	x		12
	1	0	0	0	0	1	1	0	0	0	0	0	0	0	0	0	0	0	0	0	0	0	0	0	0	0	0	0	
	1	8	6	4	7	6	1	6	8	6	5	6	9	7	9	6	7	8	3	7	8	8	5	8	6	4	7	4	200

interview, and in the Netherlands between three and 16, with an average of 7. Finally, I emphasize that these tables do not represent a complete overview of the occurrence of racism in everyday life; neither do the numbers suggest statistical significance.

The overall picture in Tables 5.1 and 5.2 confirms that everyday racism operates in different situations throughout the social structure. In both countries there is a high concentration of direct and vicarious experiences of racism in the areas of work, education, and shopping. These spheres of everyday life represent, more than others, sites of intensive and/or frequent interaction with dominant group members. Both groups of women experience vicariously a relatively high amount of racism through (friends and) family members. Racism experiences related to the family concern, in the majority of the cases, vicarious experiences of racism. Other examples concern cases of White friends or White family members who engaged in racist practices (NL) and color discrimination among Black friends and family members (USA).

These differences in my findings are consistent with my theoretical framework as well as with the general knowledge framework of the women, in which social segregation and biological racism are more prominent in the United States than in the Netherlands. The overview may suggest that women in the Netherlands experience more racism than women in the United States. However, such a conclusion would be unfounded. On average the interviews in the Netherlands lasted somewhat longer than those in the United States. An average interview in the United States lasted two hours and in the Netherlands two and a half hours. Furthermore the interviews in the Netherlands took place after those in the United States. Therefore, the project in the Netherlands might have benefited from information gathered in the United States and from additional situations of importance suggested by Black women in the Netherlands, such as travel and vacation (see the "Hotels" category in Tables 5.1 and 5.2). The marked presence of neighborhood racism in the Netherlands may be due to the fact that Black women live in White-dominated neighborhoods. This is the case for only part of the U.S. group. Women in the Netherlands are more frequently confronted with racism when riding the bus or streetcar (see category 12). Public transportation in large Dutch cities is organized quite efficiently, and most women in the Netherlands make use of it frequently, unlike the women in California, who traveled by car. Another remarkable difference has to do with mediated racism, in particular the role of the mass media. Nineteen women in the Netherlands criticized the mass media for perpetuating racism. Only six women in the United States brought up this subject. This may suggest that Black women in the Netherlands are more sensitive to ideological racism or that media representations of race issues are more problematic in the Netherlands than in the United States. Obviously this problem needs further investigation. These and other factors suggest that the numbers presented in Tables 5.1 and 5.2 may not be generalized.

CONCLUSIONS: ROSA N. AND THE SHARED EXPERIENCE OF RACISM

To examine whether the experiences of Rosa N. are consistent with those of other Black women, it is useful first to reiterate some of the earlier findings about the general processes of racism (see Chapter 3). Earlier I provided a reconstruction of the main descriptive and explanatory concepts included in Black women's general knowledge of racism. This reconstruction reflects highly abstract knowledge and is based empirically in the categorization of statements about the general nature of racism. The structure of Black women's general knowledge of racism reflects the fact that racism consists of general processes (marginalization, problematization, containment) and various subprocesses (e.g., nonacceptance, pathologizing, patronizing). The specific (micro) expressions of the general mechanisms of racism are locally structured and projected in the experiences of Black women. This is expressed in Table 5.3, in which all reported specific experiences of racism are summarized. Table 5.3 is in fact a more detailed version of Tables 5.1 and 5.2, the latter representing experiences according to the situations in which they occurred and the former according to the forms of racism implied.

Table 5.3 reads as follows: For each specific mechanism of racism I have indicated per country (a) the number of women who experienced this form of racism and (b) the total number of experiences that were reported. Most women reported more than one example of the various specific mechanisms. This accounts for the relatively high number of experiences for the number of women. It must be emphasized that the number of experiences reported is probably conservative. These are mostly experiences the women brought up voluntarily. I stated before that longer interviews and more systematic probing of memory would induce a higher number of accounts.

The women's descriptions of racism can be considered experiences of everyday racism only if they are consistent with their own framework of general knowledge of racism (see Chapter 3, Table 3.2) and with my working definition of racism (Chapter 1). It was already concluded that these Black women's descriptive knowledge of racism is consistent with my theoretical framework. Therefore, it is sufficient here to assess the situated experiences only against the women's own framework of general knowledge. Obviously it is not feasible to make detailed comparisons, because the summary of situated experiences in Table 5.3 is much more detailed than the summary of the context-free descriptions of general processes of racism in Table 3.2.

At the highest level of abstraction, there is consistency. The concepts underlying the statements on both general and situated racism can be identified as indicative of marginalization, problematization,

Table 5.3 Frequencies of the Forms of Everyday Racism

	The Netherlands (N = 28)	United States (N = 27)	Experience (N = 2074)
Marginalization			
cognitive detachment			
withdrawing altogether	4	0	5
lack of responsibility for race relations	5	6	22
ignoring the problem of racism	5	4	13
Eurocentrism/Whitecentrism			
Whites as the normative group	23	25	121
passive tolerance	18	19	77
tokenism	7	9	21
to define one Black as the good exception	6	3	13
obstacles impeding equal participation			
barring	18	21	86
avoiding or withdrawing from social contact	20	14	78
ignoring	6	15	35
failing to facilitate Black participation	11	3	19
discouragement	5	15	33
not acknowledging contribution/qualification	19	21	119
inflexibility/additional requirements	14	22	95
to give less/secondary facilities	8	13	25
excluding from positions of authority	15	21	71
reserving menial work for Blacks	3	4	12
to lower the standards	4	2	11
to withhold relevant information	2	1	5
deception	6	9	20
to fire	3	3	7
Problematization			
denigration of perspective/personality			
to attribute unreliability	12	8	35
attributing oversensitivity	4	2	9
to pathologize	4	0	18
cultural denigration			
to define as uncivilized	15	2	37
to define or treat as backward	8	4	15
to attribute happy-go-lucky mentality	7	1	10
to attribute language deficiency	13	4	25
to attribute laziness	5	3	11
to attribute insensitivity	2	4	7
biological/cultural denigration			
criminalization	22	11	78
underestimation	18	13	72
to define as overly fertile	2	0	2

Table 5.3 Continued.

	The Netherlands (N = 28)	United States (N = 27)	Experience (N = 2074)
biological denigration			
race purism	4	19	56
to attribute sexual pathology	7	9	24
Containment			
denial of racism			
failing to take a stand against racism	12	10	36
reluctance to deal with racism	10	5	26
refusing to admit racism	5	8	19
anger against Blacks who point out racism	7	2	10
overfriendliness	0	3	4
claiming to mean well	2	0	3
self-pity/backlash	2	7	9
overemphasizing Black against Black conflict	1	1	3
acknowledging only extreme racism	0	1	1
management of ethnic difference			
overemphasis on difference	20	12	85
majority rule	3	1	5
ethnization of jobs/tasks	12	5	34
cultural nonrecognition	10	12	38
rejection of "ethnic" behavior	9	5	25
mistrusting/unity among Blacks	7	6	16
fragmentation	5	1	10
ethnic registration	2	0	3
pacification			
patronizing	17	5	32
expecting gratitude	5	2	8
to keep close control	1	6	7
to give pity/charity	3	2	5
creating/reinforcing dependence	5	3	14
denial of dignity			
humiliation	17	17	86
belittlement	2	8	9
intimidation			
physical violence	7	11	40
sexual harassment	3	5	11
petty harassment	1	9	22
rudeness	12	18	53
ridicule/jokes/racist talk	12	5	24
name calling and verbal threats	16	20	78
authoritarian behavior	0	2	1
retaliation			
resentment	4	6	11
opposing/punishing assertiveness	11	12	44
other			15

and containment processes. In addition the global differences between general knowledge categories of Dutch and U.S. racism are confirmed at the level of situated experiences. Dutch racism problematizes Blacks more strongly through cultural determinism. In Table 5.3 this can be inferred from the overrepresentation of women who report the various forms of cultural and moral denigration of Blacks in the Netherlands. In the United States, more than in the Netherlands, racism operates through race, which was indicated by general statements of Black women on color hierarchy in Table 3.1. This feature of U.S. racism is, as we can see, also projected on a local level. In everyday situations many more Black women in the United States (70%) than in the Netherlands (14%) are more frequently confronted with the attribution of superiority on the basis of White skin color (see Table 5.3, "Problematization"). Note that Black women's general knowledge, as well as their situated experiences, indicate that Dutch racism is legitimized more strongly than in the United States through the underestimation of Blacks. Concrete examples of this are mentioned by more than 70% of the women in the Netherlands and 48% of Black women in the United States.

In both countries mechanisms operate to impede Black mobility. Marginalization in the Netherlands, however, operates more thoroughly through rigid exclusion. Earlier I mentioned the devastating impact of racism on the position of Blacks in the labor market. The Dutch government passively tolerates racism from employers. They do not sanction employers who refuse to take Black workers (see also WRR, 1989). It is significant in this respect that 39% of women in the Netherlands and only 11% of the women in the United States report a chronic lack of initiative to facilitate the participation of Blacks in various institutions. Tolerance of racism is not only a policy question; it is, as we will see later in more detail, endemic to Dutch society. An indication of the severity of the problem can be inferred from the fact that 35% of the women in the Netherlands reported that Whites are reluctant to deal with the topic of racism. The corresponding number for the United States is 18%. Further, 25% of the women in the Netherlands report that dominant group members get furious in situations where Blacks object to racism. Only 7% of U.S. women brought up the same problem. These figures must not be read as an indication that racism is sufficiently dealt with in the United States; rather they indicate that racism is not taken seriously at all in Dutch society.

Finally, Black women's situated experiences confirm their general knowledge about containment processes. In the United States more

Table 5.4 Experiences of Racism Reported by Rosa N.

biological denigration	denial of conflict
overvaluation of White skin color	reluctance to deal with racism
to attribute sexual permissiveness[a]	anger against Blacks who point out
biological/cultural denigration	racism[c]
to define as overly fertile	management of ethnic difference
underestimation	failing to take a stand against racism
cultural denigration	overemphasizing difference
to pathologize[b]	cultural nonrecognition
personality denigration	rejection of "ethnic" behavior
attributing oversensitivity	pacification
cognitive detachment	patronizing behavior
neglect/indifference about race relations	denial of dignity
tolerating without accepting	humiliation/disrespect
Euro-/Whitecentrism	intimidation
obstacles impeding equal participation	disregard for feelings (racist talk)
barring	rudeness
avoiding or withdrawing from social	physical violence
contact	sexual harassment
not acknowledging	
contribution/qualification	

a. Includes insinuations about prostitution.
b. Includes the pathologizing of culture and personality Rosa N. discusses.
c. Includes counteractions Rosa N. discusses such as incrimination and other retaliation against Blacks who oppose racism.

women report verbal and physical aggression and violence "to keep Blacks down." In the Netherlands more women report that the Dutch attempt to intimidate Blacks through ridicule and other "nonaggressive" methods. Whereas Black women in the United States report that Blacks are often the object of retaliation, the Dutch patronize them more frequently. Also the Dutch situation is fundamentally characterized by assimilation. Blacks are pressured to reject their own culture.

Let us now return to the experiences of Rosa N, which are summarized in Table 5.4. If we compare Table 5.4 with the overview of all other reported experiences (Table 5.3), the result is overall similarity and consistency between the experiences of Rosa N. and those of other Black women. The general and subprocesses of racism as inferred from the story of Rosa N. are the same as those reported by other Black women. Therefore, the story of Rosa N. is, though unique in its biographical detail, inherently reflects experience shared by other

Black women. This introduces the next chapter, the purpose of which
is to conceptualize the structure of these shared experiences.

NOTE

1. To give the reader an impression of the categorization system, here is an example
of the systematic analysis of the first two paragraphs of the story of Rosa N.(pp.
151-152):

Fragmentary representation of everyday racism in a given period in the life of
Rosa N.

    (1) Context: college life
    Situation: generalized experiences over a time
    Complication: *Whitecentrism*
        Lines 1-7: I came to Holland in 1969 . . . That never entered . . . your mind
    (2) Context: neighborhood (dormitory)
    Situation: making a phone call in the lobby
    Agents: students
    Complication: *Overemphasizing (rejecting) culturally different behavior*
        Lines 0-11: I can remember once making a phone call . . . not happen
        anymore, only when I'm with Rob.
    (3) Context: generalized experience of culture
    Complication: *Enforced assimilation*
        Lines 11-16: I had to get rid of a lot of the Suriname in me . . . rediscovering
        my own culture.

6

The Structure of Everyday Racism

RACISM AS CONFLICT-MAINTAINING PROCESS

How does racism pervade the life of Black women? This chapter answers this question by analyzing and conceptualizing relations between oppressive, repressive, and legitimizing forces of everyday racism. Grounded in the analysis of the accounts of Black women, it examines how processes of marginalization, problematization, and containment are made operative in their everyday lives. This analysis is descriptive as well as explanatory. It is relevant not only to identify in detail the elements of domination but also to examine how these operate under specific historical, socioeconomic, and political conditions to maintain racial and ethnic conflict in both countries. For the purpose of this study three areas of conflict are important: (a) The first domain of conflict between the dominant and the dominated group is cultural and concerns *norms and values*. (b) The second area of conflict is structural and concerns society's material and nonmaterial *resources*. (c) The third source of conflict is also cultural but operates on a metalevel; it concerns *definitions of social reality*.

Racial conflict is pervasive in Black women's everyday lives. We have seen this in the story of Rosa N. Her experiences are a clear illustration of the continuous and simultaneous battle over cultural meanings and structural resources. She persistently contests the hidden norms and values of dominant culture, in which ethnic difference can only be conceptualized in hierarchical terms. At the same time Rosa N. fights against all kinds of informal obstacles during her training. Colleagues and supervisors systematically undermine the authority attached to her profession by referring to her Surinamese background, which they associate with pathological behavior. Finally, she challenges dominant ideas to assert and to act upon her version of reality, in which racism is real and persistent. In the course of this chapter we shall see that the schematic representation of the experiences of Rosa N. presented in the previous chapter constitutes a microcosm of the way racism structures the life of other Black women.

The chapter is divided into three large sections. This first section deals with the culturalization of racism. More specifically it addresses *hidden agendas* of cultural diversity. Black women's experiences expose some of the underlying currents of the dominant culture that inherently reproduce inequality. It demonstrates that the superior status of the dominant culture is taken for granted whereas "other" cultures are problematized. This does not mean to suggest that culture is a static concept. It contains a complex of experiences passed on from generation to generation and includes changing (perceptions of) language, religious ideals, habits of thinking, behavior, and social relationships. Culture is "interwoven with all social practices" (Hall, 1981, p. 25). It represents meanings and values that are inherent in the social practices through which existing race, gender, and class relations are reproduced. For the purpose of this study culture as a terrain of struggle is relevant when referring to real or attributed distinctions in meanings, values, and lived traditions between Whites and Blacks given the historical context of their relationship. This means that cultural racism cannot be perceived outside structural racism and vice versa.

Given these arguments it is obvious that the second section, which addresses structural racism, presupposes (knowledge of) the workings of culturalized racism. The experiences discussed in this section address what I call *the basic agenda* of racism. Whether the discursive expressions of oppression are organized around notions of "race" (in the United States) or "ethnicity" (in the Netherlands), Black women in both countries are repeatedly frustrated in their pursuit of fair access to and use of resources. This is rationalized with ideological constructions in which the intelligence and competence of Black women are problematized. Black women do not accept these situations and engage continuously in oppositional practice. However, a range of mechanisms operate to discourage and to counter everyday opposition. The third section expands on the two preceding sections in which Black women describe the reality of racism in their lives. This is not, however, how social reality is usually seen by the dominant group. Ideological conflict over perspectives is crucial, as it deals with *the agenda of the agenda* of racial and ethnic domination. At this level of struggle the dominant group exercises control through the manufacture of illusions about race and ethnic relations. From their side Black women defy the dominant view with their own knowledge and comprehension of racism. Thereby they challenge Whites not only for denying racism but for conditioning an ideological atmosphere that is tolerant of everyday racism. Finally, the findings of these three sections are organized in a schema that shows how racism is structured in everyday life (p. 285).

Before proceeding a few comments are needed to place the accounts of Black women in the right perspective. The cognitive processes involved in Black women's comprehension of racism, which I showed in Chapters 3 and 4, will not be discussed in detail here. Unless important for other reasons, only those clusters of experiences that are shared by at least one fourth (seven or eight women) of the U.S. or Dutch group are included in the analysis. This will rule out the possibility of similarity by chance. Note, however, that the women mention similar problems independently of each other and that they usually initiated discussion of these problems themselves. Thus coincidence is not even the case when three or four women in each group come up with similar experiences. In the analysis the codes used in the text correspond with those in Table 5.3 (Chapter 5) and indicate the (minimum) number of women who volunteered to discuss this particular mechanism of racism. There is no space to discuss in detail all the interviews I conducted. Yet I shall give many illustrations when, in the following sections, I gradually unfold the process and dynamics of race and ethnic conflict as they are experienced in real life.

The illustrations of everyday racism included in this chapter may cause the skeptical reader to question whether the women have been accurate in their interpretations. They are, after all, aware of dimensions of everyday life Whites normally would not notice or would not see as racism. Because Black women portray a reality that is completely different than the dominant view of race and ethnic relations, why would we see their representations as judgments and not as prejudice?

These questions call for a reiteration of the main points of Chapters 3 and 4 about the heuristics of interpretation. It was demonstrated that Black women do not tend to use other sources primarily as strategic confirmation or justification of their own opinions. Their interpretations and evaluations are tested against a framework of general knowledge of racism and general knowledge of normal or acceptable procedures. This knowledge can be reassessed every day in direct and indirect experiences with many different agents. Moreover this knowledge is likely to become more and more sophisticated because it is challenged every day by the dominant media and by others who provide counterarguments that problematize Blacks. Such counterarguments attempt to mitigate rather than acknowledge racism. This massive reproduction of counterviews and the general denial of racism probably motivate Black women to assess their experiences even more carefully. Many feel they have to be "sure" that their observations are accurate because, as one woman puts it, "they are waiting to see" that "we" make a misjudgment so that "they can say that we are oversensitive" (s18). Through various comparisons they test the hypothesis of racism against hypothesis-consistent and hypothesis-inconsistent interpretations. Last but not least Black women have reasons not to perceive situations as racist because it is troublesome and the struggle against racism drains their energy. These and other reasons suggest that the illustrations of racism in this chapter are probably only the tip of the iceberg.

The reader must also bear in mind that everyday racism is a process of (relative) uniformity of practice in daily situations. I mentioned earlier that there is never absolute consensus or uniformity because there is variation in the nature and degree of involvement in the reproduction of racism. I can imagine that, in the course of the analysis, readers may think of examples in which Black women have not experienced discrimination. Of course this is also part of the reality, as much as there are Whites who are critical of oppressive elements of the dominant culture. When relevant I shall note this. Furthermore it must be noted that the majority of the examples discussed are probably also part of the experience of Black men. Therefore, when I speak of Black women I do not necessarily imply that these forms of racism are directed against them alone. When relevant gender- (and class-) related differences in the experience of racism shall be noted.

HIDDEN AGENDAS: THE DOMINANCE OF EURO-AMERICAN VALUES

It may be useful first to recapitulate the main arguments put forward in Chapter 1 about the culturalization of racism. The advance of "democracy" in the Euro-American tradition involved normative changes in the conceptualization of "race." While blatant racism based on skin color has become objectionable, the problem of cultural ethos is becoming a major site of racial and ethnic conflict. During this transition biological racism is still an active component, in the United States more so than in the Netherlands, but even in the United States conceptions of ethnic diversity gradually permeate dominant discourse. I do not intend to discuss the idea of ethnic diversity as such. It is more important to address some of the hidden agendas of the ideology of diversity.

Normative values inherent in Euro-American culture ensure that cultural difference is overemphasized and conceptualized in hierarchical ordering. Culture, in this sense, must not be seen as an entity but as structures of changing meanings including traces of history and seeds of change in the future. I must also emphasize that neither the dominant culture nor the dominant ideology are homogeneous structures. Hidden under the surface of diversity, there is a strong tendency among Whites, in the United States as well as in the Netherlands, to assume the superiority of Euro-American values. Hidden also is the expectation that, in due time, Blacks must accept that the norms and values of the Euro-American tradition are superior and that adaptation is the only way to progress in society. For the purpose of this study it is particularly relevant to point to the notion, inherent in Euro-American culture, that human progress demands increasing control over "nature," that "reason" is a value superior to "emotion," and that so-called non-Western peoples must be subjected to Western dominance to "free" themselves from the constraints of "nature."

The concrete experiences of Black women must be placed within the following macro framework of culturalized racism. One process underlying cultural expressions of racism is the *objectification* of the "other." Objectification symbolizes that "the other" is not seen as a legitimate part of the situation. Many women in both countries attest to this, but significantly more women in the Netherlands do so. Objectification is the bedrock of various strategies to control ethnic difference in society. For the purpose of this study two seemingly contradictory repressive processes are important: the enforcement of *cultural assimilation,* on the one hand, and *ethnization* of roles and functions, on the other. *Ethnization* is the activation of the ideal of tolerance, which involves the redefinition of specific areas of the system on the basis of "ethnic" criteria (e.g., ethnic policy, ethnic business, ethnic jobs, ethnic experiences) and the concomitant creation of specific functions to control these "ethnic" niches (Kempadoo, 1988; Mullard, 1986b).

Objectification: Overemphasis on Difference (20 NL, 12 USA)

If there is one experience any Black in the Netherlands can tell you about, it is probably described by this simple statement: "The first question was always: 'Where do you come from?' The second question: 'When are you going back?' " (s24).

Who are you? Why are you here? Negative undertones predominate in these messages communicated to Black women when they are "being looked at and checked out" (c1). The idea that Black women "do not belong" cannot only be seen as cultural racism. Obviously the primary categorization is racial: They look "different" because they are Black. Furthermore all other forms of racism presuppose exaggeration of difference. However, salience of difference implies that there is a norm or standard compared to which the "other" is different. This standard is culturally defined. More specifically, Whites question the presence of Black women when their situation script does not include Black women. For instance, it may well be that the Black cleaners hired by the university are not objectified in the same way as the few Black professors employed by the same institution. The first are likely to be included in dominant representations of "cleaners," while Blacks are often not included in dominant representations of university professors.

The question of belonging or not is experienced differently in both countries. The strong impact of class factors on racism in the United States and the remnants of formal segregation lead to specific ways of objectification that are less common in the Netherlands. Because it is taken for granted that Blacks belong, but in segregated areas and at the bottom of society (Pettigrew, 1988), many U.S. black women will probably recognize the situation in which you enter a White-dominated setting and "they stare at you like you have mud all over you. They will sit back and look [as if] saying: Who are you?" (c13). In the Netherlands, a similar situation would probably not have denigrating and hateful undertones but a touch of hostility, like "entering a burger bar and they are staring at me from behind their beers" (s18).

Unlike Blacks in the United States, Blacks in the Netherlands are "voluntary" immigrants. However, this must be qualified. One can hardly speak of "free will" when people from much exploited colonies flee to the idealized "mother country." In the Netherlands they face charges of being "un-Dutch" and not belonging. This explains why many more Black women in the Netherlands than Black women in the United States feel they are put on the spot. Blatant situations such as the following one used to happen frequently: "A mother enters with her daughter who says: 'Look, a Black one' " (s4), when she sees the Black shop assistant. They are decreasing but women are still often questioned about when they are "going back" to Suriname (s7). It is generally felt that they always have to "account for being different" (s6). The data suggest that Whites in the Netherlands are often rude in the way they react to "difference." For instance, women report that their children were "troubled a lot with questions about where they came from" (s6) because fellow students could not place them. The underlying tone in these situations is negative, as can be inferred from the use of the word *troubled*. Another woman had a teacher who made it a habit to "stare right into [her] face" (s21). It is further assumed that Black women take from the Netherlands what is not rightfully theirs. The following quotation describes an ordinary Dutch way of indicating that Blacks do not really belong (see also van Dijk, 1984, 1987a). It includes a mixture of superiority feelings (the Netherlands is a highly civilized country and the Surinamese are from a poor [ex-]colony) and priority claim to the country (reproach that people from the colonies profit from the Dutch):

> It was not always very nice to be the only colored person. Most people wanted to know why I was here, whether I was pitiful, if I wanted to go back. Always the same questions. Always assuming that it was good in the Netherlands, and that *they* would never immigrate to another country. . . . Underneath these questions seemed to be the assumption that it had been foolish of me to come here or that I had another, probably, economic reason to come, not just to study. It was like suggesting that I had come to live off the country. (s18)

Even though White Dutch often openly question Black women about being different, the most typical way to overemphasize difference in both countries is through nonverbal communication. Various women report about situations where people "always stare" because there are "very few dark people" (s14). Singling out Black women is communicating that they are not considered to be normally part of that situation. This is structured by the rules of the situation and by the function and interest of the people involved. Whether in the United States or in the Netherlands, Black women know what it means when "for them we were the 'Blacks' of the neighborhood" and "the

'Blacks' of the school" (s14). In situations where they have to perform, such as in class or on the job, there is a "solo effect," which is,
as we have seen in the case of Rosa N., usually mixed with low expectations about Blacks. Students notice "hyperalertness" when "a
Black student would say something" (c1). Black women professionals
report similar situations when a Black woman may "quiet a whole
room, particularly White people, they become wide-eyed" (c12) when
she starts talking. Indeed women in both countries notice that dominant group members overemphasize "difference" when they "do"
something, like entering a bar, making a statement, or greeting their
students at the entrance of the building, and you find that they "are so
busy staring at you that they even forget how to say good morning or
good afternoon" (s27). The common feature in all these situations is
that the salience of difference increases because the presence of
Black women is not taken for granted.

The experiences of Black women in the Netherlands completely
contradict the Dutch self-perception of being a people with a high degree of cultural tolerance, implying that they respect others and "let
them be." Rather the data suggest that White Dutch have problems
with what they see as "ethnic difference." To understand the nature of
this Dutch reaction, a few comments are needed about the function of
overemphasis on difference in relation to control of the Blacks. I shall
come back to this problem later, but here it must be noted that Dutch
policies as well as Dutch common sense (van Dijk, 1987a) express
the belief that the "ethnic problem" is largely a problem of unwillingness to adapt to Dutch culture. In other words, from state policies
down to the population, White Dutch do not seem prepared to respect
the consequences of cultural difference. Therefore, it may well be
that the Dutch overemphasis on difference prepares for other, more
sophisticated mechanisms of control over other cultures.

Despite certain differences between the two countries, it may be
concluded that the way respective dominant groups react is a question
of strategy under specific economic and political conditions. However, both countries are on the same wavelength in their belief in the
superiority of Euro-American values. This ideal is made operative
through Eurocentrism, another aspect of cultural racism. When
Blacks constantly receive the message that they do not belong at all
(in the Netherlands) or only at the bottom of society (in the United
States), it is not surprising that Black women almost unanimously object to being immersed in Euro(White)centrality.

Eurocentrism

"I cannot expect to turn on the television and see some recognition of us, or some obvious value for us, or something that shows us in a good light" (c9). This statement suggests that Blacks do not count. This does not contradict the overemphasis on race or ethnic difference discussed above. Racial or ethnic difference is made salient when associated with negative traits and overlooked otherwise. Indeed what this woman misses is "some obvious value" and to be shown "in a good light." Whether it concerns the media, the lack of "books and toys for my child to identify with" (s3), or that "colors in the cloth stores are all focused on these very White housewives" (s1), the message that society is culturally tuned to the interests and needs of the White (middle-class) group constantly penetrates the lives of Black women. Eurocentrism is a feature of society as a whole, but it is felt acutely in situations in which Black women represent a small minority among a large majority of Whites. For most women this applies to their experiences at the university and on the job. All of these Black women, in the Netherlands as well as in the United States, have gone to universities with "hardly any Black students" (c1). And most women can talk about being "the only Black" (s18) in the department, in the workshop, in the meeting, at the conference, or in many other situations that make up the life of a Black female professional. In the Netherlands Black women in solo positions are sometimes treated "as a curiosity" (s4). In the United States some women had similar experiences at "liberal" universities in the beginning of the 1970s, when the first Blacks enrolled in White institutions and teachers wanted to know "everything" about the "poor family background" (c4) of these Black students. However, even the exceptional situation, in which Whites perceive the Black participant as a novelty, assumes that Blacks are explicitly defined as outsiders.

Whitecentrism is a problem of who is central and who is marginal. This is expressed by one woman in the United States when she says: "I was at a predominantly White institution, and we were really not accepted as a whole. We were tolerated, I think. That was the general setting" (c13). The distinction she makes between acceptance and toleration summarizes the basis of Euro(White)centrism as it is also experienced by most other women in the United States and in the Netherlands. The ideal and practice whereby interests and perspectives of the White group are used as the norm is an enduring and inescapable feature of the experiences of Blacks. Eurocentrism is interwoven in social relationships, in the language, in habits of thinking, in institutional regulations, and more generally in the conditions under which individuals or groups gain access to resources. Eurocentrism is so much ingrained in the social cognitions of the dominant group that Whites are often incapable of understanding the world from the point of view of Blacks. They "bring in a pure White point of view" (s4), Black women find, whether it concerns the media, literature, lectures, or argumentation in a meeting.

As a consequence of Eurocentrism Black women, willingly or not, become familiar with dominant culture through constant exposure in everyday interactions, through the media, or through school textbooks. They learn how Whites think, learn to distinguish between (sub)cultures and how they behave. They learn how Whites think about Blacks. They develop, in Du Bois's words, a "double consciousness" (Du Bois, 1969). In Chapter 3, is was argued that knowledge of the dominant culture enables Black women to distinguish between acceptable and unacceptable practices. Whitecentrism prevents Whites, in everyday life, from being systematically confronted with the way Blacks perceive reality, with what they feel, and with what their purposes in life are. As a result Black women feel a cognitive barrier between themselves and the dominant group when they want to get across what they have to say. Many tell the same story about "always having to repeat things all the time" (s10). Indeed they are speaking from a background to which the dominant group has not been exposed with the same intensity. Later I will return to this cognitive detachment from Blacks. The question of *how* Euro(White)centrism permeates everyday situations calls for attention to the following factors: (a) Whites are taken as the norm group while (b) Blacks are passively tolerated.

Whites as the norm (23 NL, 25 USA). Centralization of Whites is perpetuated through the standards that determine the conditions of access to resources. Institutionalized conditions basically reflect the dominant group's not considering specific needs, interests, and values based in the Black experience to be of any importance. As a result issues relevant to Blacks are rarely included. This is particularly problematic when cultural domination works to exclude Blacks from opportunities. It is not surprising then that Black women feel the problem most severely in education and at work. Isolated and marginalized, Black women never become part of the established clique. About half the women in each group describe cultural domination at school and at work, so that "Blacks could not come into their own" (s1), that "you get books, and you don't recognize yourself in them" (s7) because it has a "pure White orientation" (s22), and "social activities on campus included only things interesting to Whites" (c6).

In the labor market formal and informal patterns counteract explicit rules, such as those requiring that appointments and promotions be based on competence rather than cultural or racial favoritism. Discrimination against Black applicants is a major form of racism in the U.S. and the Dutch systems. In both systems cultural determinism plays a role in the exclusion of Blacks. However, cultural rationalizations are more complex in the Netherlands than in the United States because "ethnic differentiation" interferes with traditional religious differentiation. Ethnic discrimination is morally rejected, but discrimination against non-Christians is allowed under certain conditions. Christians have the legal "right" to discriminate against non-Christians in appointments in Christian institutions. This historical feature of religious pluralism is a major obstacle to progress in Dutch antidiscrimination legislation. An example of this was discussed earlier by Florence V. (see Chapter 4). When cultural elements, in this case religion, are considered acceptable reasons to exclude members of specific backgrounds, one does not need too much imagination to understand that it seems reasonable to exclude a Surinamese woman on the ground that she does not fit into the (European) culture of the organization. In the Netherlands White-oriented psychological tests are still commonly used (Choenni & van der Zwan, 1987b). Although this problem has not been emphasized sufficiently in the interviews with Black women in the Netherlands, the women reported about various cases. In the story of Florence V. the interviewer attributed "frivolity" to Black women and used that as an argument to consider Florence V. culturally unfit for the job offered. Other women were told that "clients will have problems" (s1) because they are not used to dealing with a Black woman. This rejection is a more general statement that a Black woman does not fit the racial and cultural profile. However, the Dutch norm may also be specified in trivial details. A clear illustration of this concerns a Black student who applies at the same time as a White student at an employment agency for temporary work. They favor candidates who speak foreign languages. The White girl gets the job, but she speaks only English in addition to Dutch. The Black student, who speaks English, German, and French, as well as Dutch, and who even has better credentials, is never called for a job. She does not fit the cultural profile because, as they told her, she should be wearing as makeup the "pastel colors" that look good on White girls, even when "dark colors" look better on her (s14).

Other, less overt applications of Euro-American norms and values to Black women concern dominant perceptions of health (Pearson, 1986) and family life (Carby, 1982; Parmar, 1982). This area is particularly important for women, because they often take responsibility for the care of family members. Their role as wife and/or mother is repeatedly the focus of racist distortion (Staples, 1970, 1973). Here an additional issue needs attention pertaining to the specific role of the Black family in the protection of their children in a racist society. Against this background consider the objections of a Black social worker:

> At the shelter [for runaways girls] it was actually a fixed rule that we had no contact with the parents, and especially for the ethnic girls I found that wrong. . . . Every time we tried to bring the matter up, we were put off with [incorrect] arguments, such as there is really no difference between ethnic girls and Dutch girls. (s1)

Working within a feminist framework the staff sees the family exclusively as a site of oppression of wives and daughters (Barrett, 1980). In addition it is assumed that girls must become independent of their parents. However, for Black daughters the family is not only a site of gender oppression. I stressed earlier in the discussion of Black women's acquisition of knowledge of racism (Chapter 3) that the family is also the place where oppressed culture is reproduced and reinforced and where daughters seek protection against the racist forces of society. The application of White norms and values to Blacks contains marginalizing and repressive elements. There is only a thin line between the use of dominant norms, rejection of "ethnic" behavior, and coercion to adapt. I shall come back to coercive practices later. Here another side of the centrality of White norms and values is elaborated upon: Blacks can be tolerated as long as they remain marginal.

Passive tolerance: Lack of sympathy, support, or feedback (18 NL, 19 USA). Passive tolerance means not taking any specific action against the presence or participation of Blacks but not doing anything to support or to facilitate it either. Given the racially unequal relations in society, passive tolerance of Blacks has marginalizing effects. Many everyday situations become racist situations for Black women because their presence in the situation is considered to be of no consequence at all. This is manifested at many levels of social interaction, varying from "the administrator on the job [who is] always confusing me with the only other Black woman, because they think all Blacks look alike" (c25) to severe neglect of Black students. The situation in education seems of paramount concern, first, because students depend on positive feedback from the teacher and, second, because school performance has a bearing on future job opportunities.

Yet the many debates on multicultural education, in particular in the Netherlands but also in the United States, would make many people believe that real concern for Black students is at the heart of the school system. An explicit (and one-sided) focus on "ethnic" issues, which relates to what I call active tolerance, has other, repressive implications. These are dealt with later. Here we may observe that the experiences of Black women suggest that indifference to the progress of Black students and their intellectual contributions is endemic to the school system. Even the way the women in both countries describe these situations is remarkably similar. They feel that "White students could not care less" about them (c28). "As a Surinamese, you didn't exist" (s27). But, as one university professor notes, when you ask White students why there are not more Black students out here, "They have never really thought about it. Now that is a form of racism too, because you don't think about us. That we do not exist points to severe lack of interest from the side of students" (s27). As a result Black students are often excluded from study groups. The typical way of doing this is not by rejecting them openly, for then discrimination would be obvious. Therefore, White students often use small lies and deception. One woman describes such a situation as follows:

> I would ask other females in my section, and they weren't the least bit interested. It is like they did not want to be associated. "Oh, oh, uh, I'll call you back about that," and "Let's get together tonight and study." And you would not hear from them later. Or, you know, "Can I get into your group?" "Oh no, I don't know, we have just the right number. Let me take it to the group and I'll get back to you." But I was never in a study group. (c4)

Even more detrimental to Black students is neglect by the teachers. Women talk about teaching assistants who "give a cold feeling, so that you never want to go back" (c7) and about their children coming home to "complain that the school is not stimulating at all" (c9). Others have experienced that, when they answer questions posed in class, the teacher does not pay attention. "In the end, you don't say anything any more" (s5). Because neglect often operates nonverbally, it is difficult to handle.

Various Black students are quite perceptive about the subtle ways in which teachers communicate that they do not really care about their performance. One way, registered by various women in the United States, is that the teacher behaves "real distant. He is looking off and doing other things and he really does not listen" (c5) to what you are saying. A woman in the Netherlands is discouraged to find that the professor "repeatedly cancels his appointments, does not keep his promises, and gives me the feeling he finds it a burden to see me" (s6). Note that this behavior is similar to that of the students who use pretexts to disguise indifference. Various women who attended segregated schools agree that they did "not have the problems their children have now" (c27) because "Black teachers encouraged" (c34) them to learn. Black women in the Netherlands point to the same problem when they compare the teaching in Suriname with that in the Netherlands. A few school counselors say that Surinamese parents are often dissatisfied with the schools their children are attending because they feel the teachers "don't draw out the best in their child. The school in Suriname, there you can entrust your children to them, but here you have to be very alert" (s9). Black educators in the United States try to make up for injustice against younger students by reinforcing Black cultural values and a Black point of view. "Frankly," says one Black studies teacher,

> A lot of my Black students will tell you they are sitting here for their sanity. . . . They may be the only Black student in their classes, and they find it very reinforcing to be in Black studies class where they're getting all this information, and they have something to fall back on when they get into another class. (c27)

It is important to understand this reaction to neglect in its cultural context. It is probably because U.S. Black women see indifference in the light of Euro(White)centrism that they respond not only to the lack of concern but to the fact that it comes from a background that undervalues Black culture.

For various reasons similar reactions were not found among the women in the Netherlands. First, the protest movement of the 1960s and 1970s encouraged many U.S. Blacks to reclaim their African background. Black women in the Netherlands cannot draw on recent protest movements against cultural domination. Second, it may well be that the memory of Suriname and the cultural experience in the confinement of family and friendships keeps this first generation of immigrant women from feeling culturally deprived. However, it may also be the case that the Dutch dominant discourse of cultural toler-ance blinds Black women in the Netherlands to the lack of institu-tional support to pass Surinamese culture on to the next generation. It is this context that explains the different responses of Black women in the two countries to the education of their children.

Most U.S. black women feel they have no choice but to send their children to White-dominated schools, whereas Black women in the Netherlands are positively motivated to integrate their children into White schools. Like some U.S. women they are concerned when they find there is "no one Black or of color" (c1) in the school. However, Black women in the United States are more explicitly concerned about cultural domination of their children. "How can I have a child who does not grow up White? How can I build some kind of racial consciousness and feeling for Black community? . . . These are the concerns that most of the Black professional parents have now" (c34). For Black mothers the expectation that issues relevant to the develop-ment of their children as Blacks are not going to be included in the regular school programs is a constant problem. It means that they have to make extra efforts to compensate for the inadequacies they find in the school system or, as one woman explained: "My daughter goes to a Muslim school" (c8). In this way the mother tries to protect her child from overexposure to the dominant culture at an early age.

Legitimation: Cultural Denigration

For the dominant group to maintain cultural control, progress in the system is defined as the extent to which the value orientation of the dominant culture is adopted. In this construction "other" cultures are identified with disadvantage. In the United States popular as well as various social scientific views see this "cultural disadvantage" of Blacks as a product of slavery. In this view Black culture is not an in-digenous experience, that is, anchored in the African legacy, but a re-active experience. Cultural denigration of Blacks in the United States is substantially class related. Black culture is reduced to patterns of collective adaptations to centuries of social and economic deprivation (Jones, 1988). It is not, therefore, very prevalent in the personal experiences of Black women with higher education. In the Netherlands the situation is more complicated. It seems that dominant representations of Black culture include neither notions of the African heritage nor notions of continuity and change under cultural domination in the colony and afterward. Dutch notions about culture from Suriname are probably part of Dutch perceptions of life in the Third World. In this view Blacks are not deprived but *uncivilized* (15 NL, 2 USA) and *backward* (8 NL, 4 USA). By this is meant that they are not adapted to a high-technology capitalist system. In other words, underlying these concepts are fundamental value orientations. Surinamese culture and behavior are normatively conceptualized according to values of the dominant group, and real or attributed deviations are problematized. Here two values are discussed that have both been functional in the development of Western capitalism.

The first pertains to the concept of "time." Cultures differ significantly in the way they organize and experience time. The dominant (Western) perspective of time is organized along an ever increasing future time dimension with the view of specific goals, behaviors, and rewards (Jones, 1986). This notion of time is functional to another basic value, namely, that of human beings being able to control nature through efficient use of technology. The time experience is problematized, for instance, when a Black student is late in class and the professor says, "I am sure you never bothered about time in that bush were you came from. But here in the Netherlands we are always on time" (s23). Being late in class may or may not express fundamentally different notions about time. However, because it is a Black student who is late, the professor adheres to (presumed) fundamental conflict over values concerning time. Given the tendency to attribute to Blacks incompetence and low motivation to achieve, a Black student who is late is immediately assessed in terms of the dominant concept of time and subsequently denigrated.

Another dimension of the time concept, prevalent in the Netherlands but probably obsolete in the United States, attributes to Blacks a happy-go-lucky mentality (7 NL, 1 USA). This derogatory perception of Blacks is not surprising given that, as noted earlier, Blacks are still predominantly referred to as *negroes,* without a capital "n," in the Dutch language. Because Dutch has always been the first language in Suriname, many Surinamese have adopted the same word to refer to the Afro-Surinamese. As Robinson (1983, pp. 164, 268) argued, "Negro" is an "invention." It is not a word but a concept, a derogatory image of Blacks rooted in the slave-master relation. This image recognizes Blacks as "lazy" and "irresponsible" and denies the history of Black resistance. This traditional racist construction of "the Negro" is still prevalent in the Netherlands. Therefore, it seems acceptable for a White woman to say things like, "There goes another one of those swinging negroes" (s14) when she notices a Black young man who crosses the street carrying a huge portable stereo cassette. Other Black women confirm that the Dutch think of the Surinamese as a people who "only care about parties and good food and are less concerned with matters of the mind" (s13). This summarizes the basic ingredients of the happy-go-lucky image. This representation is consistent with the examples mentioned above, suggesting the Surinamese do not have the right mentality (yet) to participate as equally serious members of Dutch society. This introduces a second basic value in dominant culture, namely, the concept of rationality, which is considered the motor of progress and civilization.

Values associated with the idea of rationality are part of the metavalue that reason is superior to emotion. This view is probably rooted in the Calvinistic rejection of sensuous and emotional elements in culture (Trost, 1975) and supports the idea that the mind should control the body (Hodge, 1975a, 1975b). Later I will show that this value structures the denigration of Black sexuality and moral values. Here the idea of rationality is addressed in terms of cultural development and efficiency. The dominant group in the United States as well as in the Netherlands attributes to Blacks a low degree of cultural refinement, but Surinamese women are confronted with even more blatant expressions of this idea. This confirms that the Dutch, just like other European colonizers, have hardly begun to decolonize culturally (Mazrui, 1986). The Dutch ideological atmosphere allows a teacher, for instance, to say to a Black student that it is a " sign of [her] primitiveness" (s27) that she uses yellow and red in a drawing while the White students are using blue and purple. I will come back later to the ideological conditions that allow Whites to express racist views without sanctions being applied.

Another aspect of the idea that Blacks are primitive and emotional can be inferred from statements of various women who mention that the Surinamese are accused of making too much noise, of being chaotic, or unable to organize things properly. These ideas are deeply ingrained in dominant group perceptions of the Surinamese and are not considered denigrating, let alone racist in their implications. Therefore, it is not even questioned when, for instance, in a lecture hall the

professor criticizes the faculty council for functioning "like the Suriname Parliament," by which he means that it was "chaotic and bad"
(s9). On the contrary his "joke" (s9) invoked quite a bit of hilarity
among the White students. U.S. Black women reported ostentatious
denigrations only with reference to Africans, who are seen as representatives of "backward nations with no technical history and primitive characteristics" (c27) as one woman "loosely translated" the
words of a White professor.

The most commonly occurring example of cultural problematization
in the Netherlands is the idea of *language deficiency* (13 NL, 4 USA).
Together with the idea of educational deficiency, it forms the standard
rationalization for the high unemployment among Blacks (WRR, 1989).
Given the virtual lack of government action against racial discrimination
in the Dutch labor market, it is highly functional to perpetuate the idea
that Blacks do not speak proper Dutch. Irrespective of class and educational background, Black women in the Netherlands are harassed with
comments about their use of language, even on the street. "Someone has
started a conversation and cannot help exclaiming that my Dutch is so
perfect" (s1) says a woman who has lived practically all her life in the
Netherlands. She has one of the Dutch regional accents. If she had a Surinamese accent, the Dutch might have had comments on that too, as one
woman explains: "Another thing is that one of your colleagues might
come and say: 'your Dutch is different' " (s4), which is more often
meant as disapproval than as a neutral observation.

The language argument often operates to obscure underestimation
of Black women. This may be inferred from the fact that several
women have exactly the same experiences in group discussions.
"There is always one who is going to tell you that your Dutch is excellent, . . . instead of taking up the point you are making" (s9). In
these cases dominant group members marginalize the intellectual contributions of Surinamese women when they patronize them with compliments about their perfect Dutch instead of reacting to the content
of their words. Let me further explain the presuppositions of such
compliments. This is best illustrated by the following story, in which
a group of Black women, annoyed with comments on their perfect
Dutch, thought of an effective reaction. The reaction works, because
it exposes the underlying mechanisms of the situation:

> After the first session of the workshop, the teacher, a woman, came along
> with us for a drink. There were several Black women in this group. At

one point the teacher looked at us and said by way of compliment: "Your Dutch is excellent." We answered simultaneously as in a choir: "So is yours!" She was totally confused and did not know what was happening to her. So we had to explain why we reacted that way. (s6)

This event illustrates that instantiations of racism may change some of the structural properties of the situation. In their reaction the Surinamese students (pretended that they) presupposed that it was exceptional too that the teacher, native Dutch, could speak perfect Dutch. In other words, they redefined the position of the teacher in that situation from insider in Dutch language to outsider. This explains her helpless confusion. Conversely one reason for Blacks to be alert for racism and to be motivated to make correct assessments of the situation is that looking ahead or assessing the situation on a metalevel enables them to cope with situations that are restructured by instantiations of racism.

Even when teachers are aware that Surinamese have been trained in Dutch language schools, whether in Suriname or in the Netherlands, they are convinced that their Dutch can never be as good and genuine as Dutch spoken by a Dutch person. Black women in the Netherlands find again and again that Dutch language teachers give unfairly low grades to Black students. This is one of a series of impediments Black women face in the pursuit of a career, as shall be shown later in more detail.

These examples of cultural denigration illustrate that Blacks in the Netherlands are considered culturally "not yet ready" to function properly in the Dutch system. This ideological construction legitimizes persistent pressure on Blacks to assimilate culturally. This introduces the question of control of cultural difference.

Control: Management of Cultural Difference

The dominant group claims that the problem is one of cultural difference, but it is more than this. Bullivant (1983, p. 2) puts it very clearly when he states that culture embodies strategies by which one group competes with other groups to maximize its advantages. We have seen that Euro(White)centrism and indifference toward "the Black experience" frustrate institutional transmission of Black values and perceptions. This process is reinforced through either suppression or isolation of cultural expressions. For the purpose of this study only four mechanisms of this type of cultural control are addressed. It is important to demonstrate these mechanisms because they underscore

the necessary conceptualization of other cultures as inferior in dominant
ideology. The first three operate through neglect of cultural difference
when recognition is relevant for the dominated group and the fourth
through overemphasis on cultural difference to marginalize the "other."
These mechanisms of cultural control can be identified as follows:

(1) majority rule (3 NL, 3 USA), a mechanism that operates to reinforce
the dominant group consensus on race;

(2) cultural nonrecognition (10 NL, 12 USA) through denial of the historical roots (USA, NL) or through denial of cultural identity (NL);

(3) rejection of "ethnic" behavior (9 NL, 5 USA); and

(4) ethnization (11 NL, 5 USA) with the purpose of encapsulation.

Overruled by the majority. Defense of a "minority" standpoint in
work meetings, as the woman from the shelter for runaway girls already suggested, is often a losing game. Dominant values, conceptions of reality, and style habits are further reinforced through
majority rule. There is reason to believe that what Marcuse has called
the "tyranny of the majority" (Marcuse, 1969, p. 137) has specific re-
percussions for race relations. Majority rule may be experienced as
"tyranny" when the oppression of Black women is repeatedly legitimized through majority decisions in everyday situations. This is the
case when the dominant group does not problematize racism in society. Kanter (1977) has studied this problem as it applies to gender oppression as well. She identified a specific set of factors as
characteristics of what she calls "skewed groups" and "tilted" groups
(Chapter 8). Skewed groups are those in which there is an overwhelming numerical majority of one type so that "others" in the
skewed group are "tokens" or "solos." They are treated as symbols of
difference rather than as individuals. They are marginalized because
they are highly visible. Through exaggeration of contrast or through
enforced assimilation, the dominant group persistently confirms the
superiority of the dominant culture. Tilted groups have moved toward
less extreme numerical differences. The "minority" group has formed
subgroups according to roles and abilities, so that they can affect the
dominant culture to a certain degree (Balbo, 1989).

In institutional contexts, Black women in the Netherlands and in
the United States are usually in skewed group situations. Because
they do not belong, Black women find it very difficult to break
through the cultural mechanisms that perpetuate cultural and structural

exclusion. They are often in situations in which they are far out-
numbered by Whites, who control the group and its culture. Under
these conditions, plans and initiatives that do not fit the dominant culture and interests are not accepted. The next U.S. student verbalizes
the experience of many other Black women when she summarizes the
relation between not belonging and structural exclusion by saying: "If
Black students were welcome on this campus, they would have more
events that Black students need." Then she continues to describe how
this relation operates through majority rule:

> Part of my internship is to try to get resident deans to put on some
> events . . . for Black students or Latino students . . . because we are pay-
> ing our fees, too. And even when [Black student organizations] go there
> and ask for funds for an event, they say: "I don't think it represents the
> majority of the school." So, it is because Whites are the majority it is not
> a good event to put on. (c7)

As a result Black women are often pressured into acceptance. This
is particularly the case when it concerns issues relevant to Blacks that
Whites do not acknowledge as relevant to them too. This applies also
to the issue of racism. Women experience not being able to discuss
"discriminatory remarks," for instance, "in a book we read in class"
(s27), because the teacher thinks the subject is "only relevant" (s1) to
the Black student. Another woman explains, "When I write a report
with a White woman, then she has the standard version, and I have
the deviating one. . . . Then I always have to compromise" (s6). I
come back to the marginalization of Black perceptions later. Here it
may be concluded that, through majority rule, the ideas, suggestions,
critique, plans, or requests formulated from the perspective of the
dominated are shelved because it is assumed that these issues are relevant "just to" the only Black representative (s1).

Nonrecognition: Euro-American denial of the African heritage.
Two processes are central in Black women's discussion of cultural
nonrecognition. The first takes place in a Dutch assimilative framework that denies Surinamese identity. The second must be placed in a
U.S. segregative framework, where the African heritage of Euro-
American culture is denied and the transmission of African culture is
frustrated. Their specific history of cultural and structural segregation
and the role of the Black church in opposition movements suggest
that Blacks have succeeded in maintaining a certain degree of cultural

autonomy (Franklin, 1984; Wilmore, 1983). However, U.S. black women say that their use of White institutions to reinforce a sense of Black culture causes White aggression. It is relevant to give a concrete example to illustrate much of the petty harassment Black women continually experience when they assert themselves. One woman, a coworker at a Center for Women's Studies and Services, says that Glenda, the only Black project leader, is no longer with them because:

> She did bring so many Black people in there, and they just could not handle it. . . . Because they looked up and saw Black people with dread locks, Black people with naturals, with all their hair shaved off. And [they] were going like: "Oh my God what is this!" And in the weekend we would have cultural events, and they did not like us using the facilities to have Black cultural events, like Quansa, the celebration of the winter harvest in Africa we celebrate each December 26 to January 5, I think it is. And they fired Glenda because of that. (c3)

As this woman further explains, White women could use the center facilities for gatherings and events. When Black women organized something, however, there were always complaints that things were left untidy and the place was allegedly a mess, even when the Black women would leave the place cleaner than it was when they had gotten there. In this situation Blacks find strength in the reinforcement of beliefs and knowledge from their ancient past. These are still functional because they help them survive and cope with life in a White-dominated society. A sense of connection with the life and struggle of the ancestors is essential to our definition of what is valuable and worth a fight. Therefore, frustration of Black aspirations to reconnect themselves to "Africa" can only be seen as repression.

We cannot understand contemporary racism in the United States unless we see it in part as a reflection of Euro-American bias against African culture (Jordan, 1968). In the 1970s many U.S. Blacks rediscovered the African orientation as a significant part of the program of cultural survival. In the first half of this century Marcus Garvey developed a program for the return of African people to their motherland. It may be said that all subsequent Black Power movements have owed a debt to his example (Clarke & Garvey, 1974). Blacks became more aware of African values and traditions. Some changed their names and their way of dressing, thus symbolically reclaiming their African heritage. Politically Blacks were joining forces. There was a strong reaction of Whites against Black Americans' symbolic acceptance of African culture as expressed, for instance, in the reclaiming of African names. One woman who replaced her American name of "Angela" with an African name reported that Whites in her surroundings were deeply offended. They were infuriated and accused her of "disowning" her country, while others came to be "afraid of [her] just talking about social issues" (c8), only because she had decided to reidentify herself as "Assafra," a name adopted from a culture deemed inferior.

Another aspect of White rejection of the African heritage has to do with the history of European culture. Many studies have identified the roots of European culture in African civilization (Diop, 1974; Snowden, 1969; Van Sertima, 1985). Recognition of this historical connection will necessarily have implications for the status quo of the dominant culture. U.S. Black women point out that this heritage is consistently denied. This is not only a problem in religion, where, "If you see pictures of God, he is always White, like he flew right over from England" (c3). It occurs in science too, as one woman explains when she describes an astrology conference where "the first speaker said that astrology was from Europe, but it is from Egypt" (c33). There is still little motivation among Whites for official recognition of great African thinkers or leaders. In this context several Black women recalled, "They still have not used the new name: Lumumba College" (c25) given to one of the University of California colleges in the 1970s.

Denial of cultural background and identity. This form of repression is more prevalent in the Netherlands and must be considered against the background of Dutch norms and practices concerning the idea of tolerance. Black women find that Whites are often intolerant of "ethnically" different styles of behavior in daily interaction. The question of (in)tolerance is even more complex, not in the least because racism, discrimination, and tolerance are concepts placed in a moral framework to distinguish "good" from "bad" behavior toward Blacks. Because White Dutch are generally inclined to maintain a nondiscriminatory self-concept, the norm that one should be tolerant—that is, not discriminate—is often interpreted so that making a distinction is in itself "wrong," that is, discriminatory. On a deeper level the cultural tendency to order difference hierarchically also structures the mode through which nondiscriminatory self-concepts are created. This interplay of different, and on the surface even contradictory, forces may be illustrated with a concrete example: Various Black women in the Netherlands—who do not satisfy the dominant view of Black women as uneducated, unsophisticated, and living on welfare—experience Whites as only being able to accept them as equal by denying their (Surinamese) cultural background. A typical example is the following:

> [A personnel training supervisor:] It got really emotional [in the refresher course that I gave there]. One of them asked if she could talk to me sometime, with: "I absolutely do not discriminate. I don't find you at all Surinamese." I ask, "What, according to you, is Surinamese?" Well, she couldn't really define that, but what it came down to was that they are less confident and awkward. . . . They like it a lot better if you're a bit awkward, in a kind of dependent position. (s15)

This quotation exposes combinations of two essential values in dominant culture, namely, the hidden value that difference is organized hierarchically and the explicit value that one must not discriminate against Blacks. This results in mutually exclusive definitions of "ethnicity." When it concerns positive values, Blacks are considered Dutch; when it concerns negative values, Blacks are seen as completely different. The Dutch woman sees ethnic differentiation as an act of discrimination because, apparently, she conceptualizes ethnic difference in terms of (evolutionary) hierarchies based on notions of backward versus modern, underdeveloped versus civilized, dependent and helpless versus independent (Lutz, 1988). At the same time, however, it is a taboo to feel superior. This explains why the Dutch woman in the example thinks the best way to defend herself against accusations of discrimination is to pretend that she is color blind. The situation is emotionally charged. This can probably be explained by the fact that the Dutch woman tries to manage an internal conflict. She denies discrimination but (unconsciously?) feels superior. This she cannot hide: Her statement that the Surinamese is not a "real" Surinamese in her view is patronizing and offensive.

Rejection of "ethnic" behavior. One typically Dutch expression is "You mustn't think that you can behave *here* like *you people* do in Suriname" (s8). The experiences of many Black women in the Netherlands confirm the strong repressive element in pressures to adapt to the Dutch way. Rejection is most severe when Black women participate in the situation as solos or tokens. For instance, various women recall that complaints against the first and only Black news reader on television took a cultural form. The public complained that they "do not like her accent, that she cannot speak Dutch" (s17). Similarly in school, at work, or in private situations, it often happens that dominant group members will make disapproving comments when they find a Black woman is "too often in the best of spirits or laughs too much" (s14), which they find "exaggerating" (s14) or probably interpret as an indication that Blacks are unable to be serious about things.

Before proceeding let me briefly return to an earlier statement about a major implication of cultural racism, namely, that the dominant cultural status quo must remain unaffected. Containment secures this aim. Whereas voice pitch, accent, or eating habits of Blacks are matters White Dutch may get irritated about and try to suppress, attempts to induce (small) changes in the habits of the dominant group may cause enormous commotion. As an example let us consider the account of a Black woman who is an active church member. Blacks in the United States traditionally have their own churches. This is not the case for Black Christians in the Netherlands. See what happens when a small group of church members organize to bring about some minor reforms:

> We were a group of 2 Moluccan, 2 Surinamers and 2 Dutch women. We started a cooking group . . . a Dutch meal one week, the next week a Surinamese meal and then an Indonesian one. Anyone from the community can eat for fl 4.50 [U.S. $2]. It's an enormous success. But in the beginning, there was a lot of resistance, like "What do we have to do with them, all those strange people?" And you even heard people say: "As long as they don't put me next to a Turk . . . and I don't sit next to Negroes either." . . . Last year we organized a multicultural Christmas. . . . It turned out lovely, but it caused a lot of agitation among the church members. They were really angry, what nonsense, after all, it was *their* Christmas. (s22)

It remains "their" Christmas, even when the norm of tolerance wins in the end when some "ethnic" elements such as "Indonesian songs" (s22) are adopted. This introduces another form of containment through culture that is typical for the Netherlands. Unlike in the United States, where monoculturalism is the norm, advanced pluralistic democracy proclaims the ideal of multiculturalism.

Ethnization: The workings of active tolerance.

> There's a very thin line. On the one hand, they mean well. . . . They've got something like, if I know a lot about you, I'll also know how I should act towards you. Yet, I really resist that. Why must they now place such an emphasis on behavior patterns to get along with another? . . . I really feel I'm

up against the wall, because I do not understand why they have to strip me naked. . . . I don't feel good about it. (s27)

This characterization of ethnization applies to the Dutch situation where the norm of tolerance structures racism more evidently than in the United States. This woman touches on the heart of the problem when she redefines tolerance as repression. In everyday life the mirror image of the "I do not discriminate, but . . ." attitude is the "they say that they mean well, but . . ." experience in the lives of Black women in the Netherlands. The norm of cultural tolerance has two sides. The dominant group is expected to be tolerant. Therefore, the dominated must believe in the "goodwill" of the dominant group. Obviously the idea that both parties must be equally tolerant ignores the power differences involved.

"Ethnic" minority policy in a "multicultural" society, "multicultural" education, "transcultural" psychology, "ethnic" social workers, and many more variants and concepts indicate that the dominant group manages cultural difference. Multiculturalism is the application of the norm of tolerance. I stated before that tolerance presupposes that one group has the power to tolerate, and others have to wait and see whether they are going to be rejected or tolerated. Therefore, cultural tolerance is inherently a form of cultural control. The control element of tolerance is the most pervasive but least understood hidden point on the multicultural agenda. Active tolerance is hard to deal with because the agents involved are usually convinced that they are making positive contributions: They honestly believe that they are doing the right thing because they fulfill normative expectations. I do not intend to discuss all the problems related to multiculturalism (Alkan et al., 1986; Mercer, 1986; Mullard, 1982). Here we will look at its major presupposition—namely, cultural tolerance proves that "others" are treated as equals and that information about other cultures increases tolerance.

Hidden below cultural tolerance is the idea that cultural suppression will inevitably lead to emotionally charged resistance. Therefore, the dominant group is willing to accept institutional reforms to include "ethnic" issues. However, it is implicitly understood that the dominant group is in charge of the reforms and will decide on the conditions under which ethnic elements are tolerated.

Under conditions of cultural dominance, as will be illustrated in more detail later, the dominant group aims to keep control of the definition of reality. This implies that the dominant group creates and disseminates its own version of the nature and experience of "ethnic groups." Black women do not agree with this: "They get all the jobs in ethnic studies programs that we ought to have" (s7). Issues of racism are generally ignored, and the problem of multiculturalism is redefined as a problem of cultural deficiency. "They supposedly prove that ethnic minorities are stupid," (s7) says one woman. Indeed social scientists have contributed in many ways to the multicultural quest for more information about "ethnic" groups. "They are doing research about us and get their diplomas at our expense" (s6). Academic studies of ethnic problems are then applied to this reality. Several women report that their White colleagues attend "workshops about ethnic problems" (s10) organized to facilitate the work of "ethnic specialists" (s9) with their "ethnic clients."

The norm of cultural tolerance legitimizes objectification of Blacks for Whites to control the nature and extent of cultural differences. The language of tolerance expresses goodwill, while the practice of tolerance means that other cultures are scrutinized, categorized, labeled, and assessed by dominant norms and values.

> You've got to start by explaining how you are different. Where you're from and so on, and if you don't eat pork, then it's usually settled for you, oh, yes, so you are a Muslim and then comes an entire volume of what they all know about Muslims and so on and so on, you know. So, it always reverts to your being different. It's always negative, it's never nice. I think however positive they do it, it still has something negative, of not recognizing or seeing another as an equal. So, as far as that goes, for me, it is always negative [It is interesting to note that this woman is a Christian who happens to be on a special diet]. (S6)

It is Dutch government policy to decentralize public services so that "ethnic" community organizations are replaced by "ethnic" add-ons in general institutions. Women talk about phenomena such as "ethnic sports" (s7), "ethnic teaching courses" (s25) for "ethnic students" (s22) of "ethnic social work" (s7). This process will certainly be reinforced if affirmative action is endorsed in the Netherlands. Note that affirmative action in the United States aims to include race, not culture, in dominant institutions. Ethnization appeals to the Dutch sense of cultural tolerance: It is proof of flexibility and openness. On the other hand, all women who have been included in organizations as "ethnic" elements (in the Netherlands) or as tokens (in the United States) testify that they get secondary facilities and are subsequently marginalized. Let me give some examples taken from education. Black women in the Netherlands report situations in which Black students are enrolled and told, "Just say what you want to learn, while that was not asked of the other first-year students. They actually had to set up their own curriculum" (s1). Or the director who obtained government subsidies for an "ethnic program" for "ethnic" sociology students advises the (White) teachers: "Just let them talk about their own roots, and then we'll see what books we can use" (s25). As a result "no books were used and the [Black] students left the academy with a diploma in personal experience. It was something like, we'll make them happy with a diploma, then they'll keep quiet, and we just have an exótic group at the academy" (s25).

The experiences of U.S. Black women confirm the indifference and lack of responsibility dominant group members often display when the interests of Blacks are at stake. The context of the following example, taken from the U.S. data, is not multiculturalism but a credit system to stimulate high achievers among Black students. In practice, however, the results come down to the same thing for Blacks in both countries. The impression is created that a huge amount of positive attention and funding go to Black students but, in reality, they are not the ones who benefit (most). Several women knew of scandals and even court cases concerning their children's school, where it appeared that,

> that particular school had these [Black] kids on the list as if they were in the mentally gifted program, but it was only for paper purposes, so that the school could get credit. But the kids were not at all being placed in the mentally gifted classes. And when she did a little checking it was a breakdown, the kids of color were on the list, White kids were on the list, only the White kids were in the class. (c27)

Black women in the Netherlands criticize school directors for not accepting Black teachers to teach "ethnic" programs. When they talk about "ethnic studies," a recurrent theme is of the White instructors hired for "ethnic" students being "ignorant about other cultures . . . fail[ing] to stimulate the students, so that there is a high dropout rate. They underestimate the students and generally fail to give any supervision to speak of" (s3).

To conclude, active tolerance must be understood in its relation to control mechanisms in a pluralistic model of society. Racism or, more specifically, ethnicism is instrumental in the management of ethnic add-ons within existing practices and relations. If "ethnic niches" are disseminated across numerous institutions, it becomes increasingly difficult for Blacks (and migrants) to organize effectively. In the United States residential and social segregation ensure that Blacks maintain some form of togetherness, which is an important basis for empowerment. As yet the hidden agendas of domination, as manifested in the culturalization of racism, have not been fully explored. There have been studies about the cultural marginalization of Blacks, but the control implications of the culturalization of racism have as yet hardly been explored (see, e.g., Mullard, 1986a, 1986b; Mullard et al., 1988). There must be in particular more research on the role of the dominant group in controlling cultural difference in daily life. Their historical orientation gives U.S. Black women an advantage over Black women in the Netherlands in the struggle to keep their culture so that it eventually can be used in their best interests. However, the orientation on their own cultural history must be integrated with a fundamental critique of injustice as implied in values of Euro-American culture.

In the Netherlands there is also the question of numbers: Blacks and other immigrants constitute only about 5% of the population. Unless dominated groups can work in units so that they are not solos or tokens, they may not succeed in generating sufficient alliances to gain power to affect the dominant culture within a specific environment. Research on schools has shown that concentrations of 40% to 60% of Blacks and other immigrants in Dutch schools are favorable for Dutch as well as for Black students. Under these conditions there is a decrease in racism among White pupils. Kanter (1977) had similar findings in her study of conditions for the "feminization" of corporate culture. To use Kanter's concepts, detrimental effects of ethnization may be controlled when it is possible to move from skewed group to tilted group conditions (Kanter, 1977). Through informal communication with Black women in the Netherlands, it has come to my attention that their wish not to be a solo in an organization is often held against them. It seems that (small) organizations use this as an excuse not to hire any Blacks at all, saying they could financially afford only one Black, but not two (let alone more). These and other indications illustrate that, when the underlying norms and values operative in society remain unquestioned, while other cultures are problematized, ethnic "niches" do not move from margin to center.

THE BASIC AGENDA: PERPETUATION OF
EXCLUSION AND SUBORDINATION

> I was talking to a friend of mine last week who works at the City Gas
> and Electric, and she was saying, Donna, why don't you come out here
> and apply for a job. I said, well, number one it is really hard getting on at
> the CG&E if you are not White, and number two, even if I got the job
> and I was down there I would have so many parameters placed around
> me, it just would not be worth it, you know, I'd come home all stressed
> out, headaches, high blood pressure. I have friends like that. . . . They
> have developed heart conditions. . . . I just have to think of another way
> of making more money but have it in a Black environment where I can at
> least use all my talents and grow as much as I want to. (c3)

This quotation makes it remarkably clear under which conditions
many Black women with higher education work. White institutions
have not essentially changed and Blacks are forced to adapt. They get
employment under conditions formulated by the dominant group,
which means that "nothing" can be taken for granted because Black
women are not automatically included in the normal fabric of institutional life. Their aspirations are frustrated; they must be constantly
alert to fight unfair decisions at work or to see that their children are
not neglected in school. They are under constant pressure to protect
themselves against racial injustice, sometimes blatant, sometimes
subtle, that operates in many places and locations, in looks, gestures,
conversations, decisions, meetings, job applications, buses, and
streets and through all social relations that are also race relations.

Marginalized positions are created through everyday exclusion and
everyday inequities. Nonacceptance (in the Netherlands) and segregation (in the United States) represent major exclusive mechanisms, in
particular in housing, schools, and the labor market. Segregation
merges with class exploitation and is reinforced ideologically through
constructions of race purism. Segregation and the great differences in
living standards it represents are maintained substantially through intimidation. This may be inferred from the violence that permeates the
lives of Black women. When I speak of *violence* here I do not mean
violence associated with extreme exploitation, depressed hopes, and
deprived opportunities but racially motivated violence. In the Netherlands there seems to be less racial violence, but it may well be that
this nonviolent image has been created partly because the media do

not report racial attacks. Even then, however, physical violence is not as ingrained in Dutch society as it is in the United States.

Segregation (USA) and Nonacceptance (NL)

A large majority of women in both groups are regularly barred (18 NL, 21 USA) on racial grounds, and in interracial situations they find that Whites often avoid or withdraw from social contact (20 NL, 14 USA). There are no forms of exclusion that occur only in the United States or only in the Netherlands, as far as can be judged from the accounts of Black women. However, we have to take into consideration differences in the degree of exclusion and the impact of the specific social, political, and historical contexts. In the United States the recent history of segregation is important. After two decades of desegregation Blacks are represented, if often as "tokens," in most levels of society. Desegregation has been least successful in housing and in informal contacts. In schools there seem to be covert developments toward resegregation.

In the Netherlands there is relatively little concentration of Blacks in special neighborhoods. This is partly the result of Dutch housing policies that aimed to control Blacks through dispersion. Rejection of Black women must be placed into the framework of a previously all-White country, which, according to official statements, never claimed to be an immigrant country. Only in 1989 was there a change. For the first time the Dutch government acknowledged that the Netherlands has and always will have immigrants.

Segregated housing (USA). In the United States rejection is most blatantly endorsed in housing. The impact of class factors on racism is crucial in the allocation of housing. For all U.S. Black women, institutionalized housing segregation is a fact of life. "There were places where I could not buy a home" (c9). All of the U.S. women are aware of housing segregation, and some contend that "this place is more segregated than it ever was" (c34).

The direct experiences of the women show the strategies used to keep Blacks out of certain neighborhoods. Openly racist ways seem more likely to occur when organized by the neighbors themselves. In two cases, one in the United States and one in the Netherlands, the Black woman heard afterward from a neighbor who had refused to participate in these racist activities that certain neighbors had "organized a petition to keep us out" (c12) or that "they wrote a letter to the city housing distribution asking them not to send another Surinamese family" (s18). These Dutch and U.S. examples show that the same mechanisms of racism (petitioning against Black neighbors) are used in both countries. In the United States, however, organized action against Blacks who move into a White neighborhood is more common.

We see that in the United States there is rigid segregation in housing and concomitant segregation in informal networks, although there is some integration at local levels. Compared with the United States there is no housing segregation to speak of in the Netherlands. In both countries housing distribution agencies or committees often discriminate covertly. Thus it may take some time, or a pure coincidence, to discover that "the secretary did not put me on the normal list but on the special list for the housing of Blacks" (c9). In some respects discrimination against Blacks in the Dutch housing system works differently from that in the United States. Rather than aiming at total exclusion of Blacks, housing agencies often use quotas to determine a maximum percentage of Blacks to be allowed in a neighborhood. It is implicitly assumed that it is unfair to the White population to "expose" them to too many Blacks. Black women who are exposed to a large majority of Whites in the neighborhood are aware of the hostile sentiments among some neighbors, who are reluctant to accept Blacks on "their" street. Individual house owners are inclined not to give overtly racist arguments in their rejection of Black buyers. A common excuse is that "we would not mind having you but the neighbors would" (c34). I show later that, in many more situations, dominant group members hide behind the racism of others.

Neighborhood hostilities (USA, NL). When barring is not successful or no longer opportune, and Blacks move into White-dominated areas, they are often confronted with hostility. Most of the women in the Netherlands live in predominantly White neighborhoods. Some indications of anti-Black sentiments are indirect, such as reading in the newspaper that "they gave a lot of votes to the CP [a racist party that attracted people who believe that Blacks must go back]" (s22) in your neighborhood.

Hostile staring is one of the most frequently mentioned forms of rejection that Black women in the Netherlands feel in the neighborhoods. "They act strange" (s9) or "they look cross at you and start whispering among each other" (s20). One way to express discontent about Black or migrant neighbors is through gossip and other casual conversations (see also van Dijk, 1987a). Dominant group members may even complain to one Black they see as a positive exception to most Blacks. Various Black women could tell about polite conversations with a neighbor who "says to me she does not like Blacks" (s26) or "foreign neighbors" (s9). The presupposition in these situations is that the Black woman must consider it a compliment that the White person involved does not reject her. It should probably also be seen as an indication of cultural tolerance.

Most U.S. Black women live in segregated areas. The women who do live in integrated neighborhoods experience racism. Neighborhood hostility in the United States is completely different than that in the Netherlands. Living or working in a predominantly White community carries the inherent threat of racial violence in everyday life. It may happen every day that your teenage daughter walks to school and "White guys about 18, 19 [call out] "Damn niggers, give them an inch . . . them damn niggers'll take a mile" " (c27). You may rent an apartment and find "nothing but rednecks" (c13). Mothers fear for the safety of their children particularly when they find that their son or daughter is called "nigger" all the time. "I was really worried," says one woman, "because of rednecks doing a lot of crazy things. We moved because I was really concerned about that. I did not even have him go to school in that area" (c25).

Racial purity (USA). Segregated housing is an expression of combined race and class factors. In this respect it is relevant to understand that the ideology of race purism (4 NL, 19 USA) profoundly pervades U.S. society. As one woman puts it: "Color is a pervasive part" (c34) of the United States. Overvaluation of the "Caucasian race" is deeply ingrained in the United States. This of course has specific implications for Black women (Lakoff & Scherr, 1984). Practically all Black women are aware of ideological notions about race traits. "Lighter complexion" (c13) is evaluated more positively than dark complexion; "straight hair" (c31) becomes "good hair" (c33), and "blond hair" (c15) is superior. This is even endorsed in Black magazines, where often "the models are light complexioned" (c12). Black women fight the ideological indoctrination that "White is better" (c4), and various of them "admire Black women who do not press their hair, who are willing to wear African clothes" (c14). However, Blacks do not have the structural power to implement these different values. Structural reality shows that the dominant group considers "Caucasian traits" a social asset. Women with lighter skin color agree "that it would make a difference" if they were "very dark" (c15) and give examples where they "have gotten hired" because they "did not look too threatening" (c25).

This is hardly the case in the Netherlands. Despite the general agreement among Black women from Suriname that "White skin color was very superior there," this subject is not even mentioned when they discuss their experiences in the Netherlands. To avoid misunderstanding, Black women in the Netherlands are certainly discriminated against on the basis of skin color. Some women mention that they have experienced less discrimination than others because they are "light colored" (s17). As I noted earlier, however, Dutch perceptions of "race" intricately merge with perceptions of ethnicity so that "race purism" is not a major part of the dominant ideology on race. Furthermore "race" is not historically anchored in the Dutch class structure in the same way as in the United States. Indeed in the Netherlands (class-related) cultural traits are more important indications of status, whereas in the United States racial characteristics (White, blond) represent status symbols.

The area of social life that most directly reflects the fundamental basis of U.S. racism in ideas of "race purism" is *interracial dating*. The strong sentiments against racial miscegenation in the United States and the relative absence of this form of race consciousness in the Netherlands is indicative of the more general difference in the systems of racism in both countries, namely, more racial racism in the United States and more cultural racism in the Netherlands. The few U.S. Black women who used to have a White boyfriend felt the impact of the taboo against interracial dating in their everyday experiences. "He never showed any affection to me in public" (c28) says one woman. In the Netherlands, problems with interracial dating seem far less extreme and in some cases absent. More than one third of the Surinamese women interviewed had a White partner. Note, however, that this number may be different for women of working-class background. Parents-in-law may think them "strange, too loud, too much talking" (s14), but few women felt openly rejected.

The rejection of interracial dating in the United States cannot be separated from racist constructions of Black sexuality and the history of sexual racism against Black men and Black women (Davis, 1981). Racialized sexual violence against Black women is still a primary form of racism in the United States. Also commonly accepted among Whites is the racist construction of Black men as sexually dangerous. Resistance to interracial dating is openly expressed. It is considered "normal" that White families "protect" their daughters against Black boys in school or in the neighborhood. The extent to which this is an everyday problem for Black boys in so-called integrated situations can be inferred from the account of a mother (s9) who says that it was "usually" the father who dealt with her son and "asked him not to see his daughter anymore." Sometimes the parents called her to say that "Jerry is spending a lot of time at my house with my daughter." This suggests that disapproval of interracial dating is often "openly communicated" (c9). Moreover racial purity and, more generally, the status quo of existing race relations are pursued with violence.

Violence (USA). Black women are aware of the history of violence to contain Blacks in subordinate positions, and they are alert for violence every day. Consider, for instance, the following account of a student:

> I live off-campus and stayed for the weekend to catch up with some studying, and everybody else is outside partying. You are scared to walk down the hall where all those White people are drunk, because you really do not know how they are going to act when they are so drunk. It is very dangerous. Me and my friends used to get together and spend the weekend together in one house. It was almost as if we were locking ourselves in, which is really bad, scary. (c7)

Experiences like these should not be seen as isolated incidents. Racial violence against Blacks on college campuses occurs across the country and has increased in the 1980s (Reed, 1989). Local racial violence relates to the general racial politics in the country. Therefore, it is not a symbolic statement when Black women say that they fear that their children will get killed. One woman probably verbalizes the feelings of many others when she says, "I am fearful for my existence and the existence of my children and my children's children" (c9).

Although the number of Black women in the Netherlands who discussed problems of physical violence (7 NL, 11 USA) is almost as high as that for African-American women, the stories are essentially different. Black women in the Netherlands referred to everyday situations, such as watching television, in which they were indirectly confronted with violence against Blacks in other countries. A few women discussed particular events they had witnessed. "The other day," says one woman, "my neighbor was waiting for the bus, but the driver did not stop." Instead he hit the man and declared later, "That man is a dirty Moroccan who should go back to his country." Together with an antiracist organization they "are going to press charges" (s7). Violence against Blacks is not just perpetrated by citizens. It is allowed and often endorsed by the police. The police were "right there, watching the whole thing, but they did not do anything" (s7) about the bus driver. Another woman tells that she "saw policemen taking some boys from the underground and that they kicked the Black boy in the face" (s12).

Obviously physical violence against Blacks in the Netherlands occurs. But as yet the situation is not as extreme as in the United States and Great Britain, where the criminalization and violent (police) harassment of Black men is a major form of control of Blacks as a group. In the United States White aggression and violence against Blacks is a form of everyday racism. Therefore, sons are educated by their parents to deal with this problem:

> The thinking Black parents will tell their kids this is what's out there. Even though [my son] lives the integrated life-style, when he turned 16 and got his driver's license, his father sat right down at that kitchen table and told him how vulnerable he was going to be 'cause he was a Black man in a car, and that if he had a White girl in the car, they were probably going to stop him, 'cause it's true. Darryl has to understand that he could go out here today and get blown away. (c27)

The expectation that he can be violated by the police ("here today, can get blown away tomorrow") is embedded in the framework of general cognitions about police harassment of Black men ("they are probably going to stop him"). The woman indicates that the frequency of police violence against Black men makes it necessary for Black parents to integrate knowledge into the education of their sons to enable them to deal with the problem ("the thinking Black parents will tell their kids"). Other women confirm the necessity to warn their sons that "if some boys are running from a theft" and their son happens to be in the wrong place at the wrong moment "the police will aim at him" (c26). These examples suggest that violence against Blacks is (partly) structured by gender factors.

Criminalization (USA, NL). These examples demonstrate that violence against Blacks is a fact of everyday life in the United States. Anti-Black violence is legitimized through criminalization, which has gender-related forms. In particular Black men are criminalized. The function of the criminalization of Black men must be understood in historical context. It is a postslavery phenomenon. Let me explain this with a historical event. When in 1712 the French attacked the Dutch colony of Suriname, Dutch planters left their wives and children with the (male) slaves who were asked to hide them in the jungle. The planters felt the women were better off like that because they "feared that the French would rape and rob them" (H. Essed, 1984, p. 28). Many slaves used the opportunity to join the Maroons, but the White wives and children were returned safely. Likewise reconstructions of U.S. history point out that only after abolition was the myth of the Black rapist invented to legitimize new terror and violence to keep the "free" Blacks down (Davis, 1981). Criminalization (22 NL, 11 USA) of Blacks is a major instrument of repression that has different functions in the United States and in the Netherlands. In the United States criminalization reinforces class exploitation of Blacks and legitimizes the perpetuation of housing and social segregation. In the Netherlands criminalization is a part of a more general idea that Blacks profit from the Dutch social system and that they do not belong. However, it also takes specifically male-directed forms. Black men, especially the Surinamers, are often seen as drug dealers and as pimps. Despite these male-oriented prejudices in Dutch discourse (van Dijk, 1984, 1987a), Black women in the Netherlands have many personal experiences in which they are criminalized. U.S. Black women have fewer personal experiences but vicariously experience racism when their sons are criminalized. In the stories of Black women in both countries, criminalization is often related to the idea that Whites must protect their rightful property against Blacks. In the United States this prejudice denies the reality of class exploitation of Blacks, whereas in the Netherlands the same prejudice denies (neo)colonial exploitation.

Blacks are criminalized on all levels of social organization. On a political level the European and U.S. gates are closing against political refugees from the Third World. Expulsion does not directly affect African-Americans or Surinamers with a Dutch passport. Indirectly, however, policies such as the introduction of Pass Laws or the obligation to have your work permit with you criminalize all Blacks. These policies reinforce police control and legitimize the implicit accusation that any individual Black is potentially an illegal alien. State control is reinforced symbolically through the media, such as the film industry, newspapers (van Dijk, 1983, 1991), and social scientific publications (Lawrence, 1982a).

"Moroccan hits man with his car. This is how the press influences the readers. As a result, people get more suspicious about non-Dutch citizens" (s7). Various women explicitly point out the negative role of the media in preformulating and disseminating the idea that Blacks are criminal. Black women in the Netherlands criticize the newspapers in particular, while U.S. Black women pay more attention to television. This probably reflects the different prominence of these sources of information in the two countries. Another explanation may be that, in U.S. newspaper reports about criminal offenses, it is common to release the name and pictures of the accused. In the Netherlands the police are not allowed to give names but often give information about the ethnic background of the accused, thus making offenses committed by Blacks or other immigrants more salient in the press than offenses committed by White Dutch. The women suggest that overt racism in the press is decreasing. This is consistent with recent research in this area (van Dijk, 1987c, p. 94). Covert racism in the media is more difficult to fight. The perspective is White, the media are controlled by Whites, and Black actors are often forced to accept roles that criminalize Blacks as a group: "You turn on the television, and Blacks are arrested for prostitution and Blacks shot somebody else" (c9).

The media have a strong impact on the criminalization of Blacks in society. The media create, preformulate, and reinforce many stereotypes (Hartmann & Husband, 1974; van Dijk, 1983, 1991). These stereotypes are uncritically accepted and projected onto Black citizens. Blacks are accused of mugging and other illegal practices, and Whites disseminate these racist opinions in everyday conversation. Many Black women in the Netherlands report situations on the bus or streetcar, and "a few passengers start talking about a burglary and how it must have been one of those Blacks. Immediately, the [driver] joins the conversation telling that he was threatened the other day by two Negroes" (s17). This happens not only in public situations; group discussions during lunch break at school or on the job often become racist experiences: "They make remarks about those Surinamese and their gleaming cars, and my supervisor wonders how come they have such nice cars" (s3). I shall return later to the repressive function, in particular in the Netherlands, of racist talk in front of Black women.

These negative images are confirmed and acted out in other situations. Locally the same processes of criminalization that operate on a state level (Blacks profit/steal from the country's economy) and in the media (emphasis on the ethnic background of criminals) are reinforced in public situations (shopping), at school, in employee-supervisor relations, in the neighborhood, in family and other relations. All sorts of everyday practices confirm and reproduce the idea that Blacks are a danger to society, cannot be trusted, and steal from Whites. Black women experience this in the following situations, among others:

(1) shopping and being followed around (17 NL, 6 USA)
(2) TV movie with Blacks in criminal roles (1 NL, 1 USA)
(3) large headlines in newspaper about criminal offense of Black (5 NL)
(4) neighborhood living: Blacks blamed for any trouble (2 NL, 1 USA)
(5) going to Disneyland: son accused of stealing (1 USA)
(6) colleagues/students talk about "those Black criminals" (4 NL)
(7) Black students accused of cheating on the examination (1 NL, 1 USA)
(8) parents accuse Black daughter-in-law of stealing (1 NL)

The situations are heterogeneous, but the basic processes of criminalization are the same. The way Blacks are criminalized depends on the properties and constraints of the situation and the participants involved. Various women experienced personally or through their children that, if there is trouble in a situation, racialized neighborhood relations are actualized by blaming the Blacks. For instance, neighborhood vandalism becomes Black vandalism, a theft becomes a Black person stealing because

> each time there was damage done in the building they called the police and the police came to us. And it would always turn out later that we had not done anything. If there was a fight among children, the parents would always come to us to complain. (s20)

The same problem occurs in other situations. Note that in the following example there is a direct relation between race and class in the accusation against two Black students in the United States:

> We were using the computer program in the D. Building, and a lady's purse got stolen. She immediately blamed us. She said, "You are punks that are from the ghetto, anyway." What she was saying was, we had stolen because we were the only Blacks. (c25)

Even when nothing has happened, the very presence of Blacks induces Whites to insinuate that something will get damaged or stolen, such as in the streetcar when, "you take a seat next to an old lady, and with a scared look she grabs her handbag. . . . She does not say anything, just presses her bag against her chest" (s5). In shops Black women are so frequently considered potential thieves that they memorize shop events as "tracks" (Schank, 1982, p. 6), that is, possible variations of the scenario: A Black customer enters, the personnel reacts. As one woman comments: "I can give you all the stereotypical examples" (s4). This means that racialized relations between shop personnel and Black customers are actualized on a daily basis. This is a common experience for Black women in the Netherlands as well as in the United States. The following illustrations, selected from a range of experiences, substantiate that instantiations of racism are structured by the properties and constraints of the situation (e.g., whether it concerns a small or a large shop, browsing or paying at the cashier). Whites integrate racist practices by which Blacks are criminalized in any situation, from the moment you enter to the moment you leave the shop. Shop personnel pretend they are going about their usual business, but these practices show that Black customers are put under strict surveillance.

Entering a small shop, usually a clothing store. "They approach me immediately," says one woman. And "I watch to see if the same happens with a Dutch woman when she enters. If not I leave the shop. They are extremely prejudiced" (s16). In the United States shop personnel in boutiques are more likely to "just look at you and watch until you walk out of the door" (c5) because it is presumed that Black customers do not have money to spend anyway. Therefore, they are checked out but not offered any service. In the Netherlands class factors may also have an impact. Just as in the United States the woman is likely to be "ignored," and after she claims that it is her turn, race-class bias is expressed in a question such as "Do you realize that these skates are expensive?" (s18). It is more common in Dutch shops, however, that personnel want to make money on Black clients but reduce the time these clients spend in their shop. Therefore, they "approach immediately to ask" (s16) what you want. When a Black woman *enters a department store or a supermarket,* the shop personnel is alarmed: "Watch it a Black one!" (s26). *Casual browsing* becomes a nuisance when you are "being followed constantly" (s18). "I notice that they are following me because if the same person is still behind you after two rounds through the shop, you can be sure they are checking you out" (s11). And when you stop to *look at particular articles,* "They follow you. You find that they come to the place where you are standing, supposedly to rearrange the articles, or so (s5)." Meanwhile it may also happen that you *pass other customers or shop attendants* and you "overhear the shop attendant say to another client, watch your purse madam" (s3). Suspicion continues to play a part when you *pay at the cashiers.* In the Netherlands, "They used to ask you to open your bag. Now they have stopped doing that because Blacks have become more assertive and do not take that anymore" (s9). In the United States institutionalized class factors are activated when "someone will assume that you are paying cash instead of with credit cards." Black women who *pay with a credit card* often find that

> White people will write checks in the line and just give their check and go through. I write a check, they get out the IBM sheets and they look for my name down the sheet. They get out the book and they look for my driver's license number through the book. Now all the people that wrote checks before me, nobody checked them, but I'm suspicious just because I'm Black. (c9)

The Black women's critique is not that they should be exempted from the normal security checks in shops. However, the problem is the same as in other situations when there is real trouble: the Black participant is more likely to be accused. In shops the entrance of a Black woman is often interpreted as a prelude to trouble. In addition overattention to Black customers helps Whites who are planning to steal (Essed, 1984).

The same idea, that Blacks are more likely to be dishonest, underlies the treatment of Black customers or clients in other situations. One employee of an insurance company says, "Normally claims below 750 guilders [U.S. $400] are processed without any problems. But when they see it is a foreign name, they call in an expert, even when it costs them 150 guilders, because they always assume they are cheating on them" (s18).

Finally, when there is real evidence that one Black indeed broke the rules, it is more than likely that this criminalizes the whole group, as happened when it came out that "one of the boys" had used notes during the examination.

> After that they put all the Surinamese in the same part of the room when there were examinations, so that they could check on us more easily. . . . As a result, White students a few seats down were copying all the time while the teacher was practically sitting on my table. (s23)

These experiences illustrate that criminalization as legitimation of exclusion cannot be separated from its control function.

Overcharging and underpayment. While dominant group members accuse Black women of cheating and stealing, these labels are not called for when Black women are *underpaid* for their work and *overcharged* for services for which they apply. These practices are clear indications of the economic marginalization of Blacks. Underpayment is a problem in the United States as well as in the Netherlands, but in the United States the problem is openly acknowledged and probably more visible than in the Netherlands (Malveaux, 1987). "The boss tries to give a 2% raise when the mean is 5" (c13). "When I got hired as a professor, I had the same qualifications as my White counterparts. But when the system looks at you they will put you in at a different level" (c27). Another woman says: "Instead of bringing me in as assistant professor, step 5, like my White counterpart, I might come in at step 3" (c9). "A young White girl who was 6 years younger . . . was being paid 3 times my salary for the work I was doing" (c26), says another woman. Not only are these women underpaid, at the same time Black women in both countries find that Blacks are overcharged when they apply for the same resources and at the same facilities as Whites. Examples come primarily from experiences with banking, housing, and insurance companies. "Any 'ethnic name' caused them to raise the insurance premium" (s18) says the ex-employee of a large insurance company in the Netherlands. A U.S. project developer confirms this when she says, "Black developers get worse loan conditions than White. . . . You think you have to pay 10-15 points but the White developers don't" (c26).

School segregation. There is increasing segregation in the inner-city schools of the Netherlands. Class factors, in combination with direct and indirect discrimination, caused overrepresentation of Blacks and migrants in these areas. The number of Black and other immigrant children attending certain schools increased dramatically, and Dutch parents began to send their children to other, predominantly White schools. None of the women involved in the project mentioned this problem, and I did not raise the subject either. Maybe they do not have children attending so-called concentration schools. Another factor may be that the extent of segregation was not yet a topic of public discussion at the time the interviews in the Netherlands were conducted. There is some evidence, however, that Black children are kept out of White schools. Although few Black women's children had been refused admittance to public schools, some women found that the situation is different when private (elite) schools are concerned. Women who send their children to private schools referred directly or indirectly to discrimination. One woman said that because of the status of her husband (a national celebrity), the school "would never dare" (s15) refuse them. Another woman reported that "the school was hesitant" about accepting her son. They said her son would be "The third Black kid in class and the other parents felt they had enough Blacks already, and why couldn't he go to a neighborhood school" (s18).

Blocking participation of Black women in the labor market. A second large area where Black women face color/culture bars is the *labor market.* I have shown before that this form of racism is more acute in the Netherlands. "During those eight years that I worked there they never hired another Black employee (s18)," says an insurance broker who works for a private enterprise with 250 employees. Other women agree that the Dutch labor market excludes Black women: "Model agencies don't take Black models, or only one or two" (s22), explains a woman whose cousin started her own agency for Black women. Another woman knows that "the V&D [department store] in this town does not hire any Black women" (s7). Exclusion of Black employees not only occurs in large city department stores; recent research findings show that discrimination against Black applicants is even worse in middle- and small-scale businesses. Of the Amsterdam butchers, for instance, 90% do not want to hire anyone but White Dutch employees (Choenni & T. van der Zwan, 1989). The women hear "about so many Surinamese who cannot get a job" (s26) and "read in the newspaper about discrimination by employment agencies" (s12). Their general knowledge of racism in the labor market is consistent with their own experiences. "I mentioned my [foreign] name; the person said the job was gone" (s19), says one woman who used to be a school director in Suriname. For years she was only accepted for temporary jobs as a teacher. Finally, she took a hair dressing course and opened her own shop. Others confirm similar experiences, such as "When I arrived and she saw I was Black she did not even give me a serious job interview" (s11) or "They said the vacancy was filled" (s26).

U.S. Black women mention that they are aware of discrimination in the labor market, but none of them gives examples of cases involving other Blacks they know, and only two women say that they have recently experienced racism when applying for a job. These indications suggest that, due to affirmative action, Black women with higher education have better chances of getting a job in the United States than in the Netherlands, where discrimination on the labor market is severe and rigid.

Apart from active discrimination against Black applicants, there are also passive ways to erect color/culture bars. Black women in the Netherlands criticize Whites because they *fail to facilitate participation* of Blacks (11 NL, 3 USA). The relatively low number of U.S. women represented in this category of experiences is probably the result of improved antidiscrimination legislation and affirmative action policies. This statement needs to be qualified, however; U.S. Black women severely criticize the fact that they are included as tokens and that the lack of "multicultural" orientations (c9) indirectly keeps Blacks out. In the Netherlands, however, there are not even proper sanctions against direct racism. In other words, it is a question of "no commitment, not a single step in our direction" (s1), as one woman in the Netherlands puts it, whereas insufficient commitment to increase the number of Black women (in higher functions) in institutions characterizes the job situation in the United States.

Black women in the Netherlands present a picture of marginalization through ethnization when they note that only White experts in "ethnic" problems are hired to work with Blacks and migrants in schools, in health care, and in community organizations. "Only 3 of our team of 24 teachers are Black, while the large majority of the pupils are Black and migrant children. We have enormous problems because of this" (s9) says a school counselor. A student adds:

> Black researchers have problems in getting funding for research among their own group. But a White researcher like [name] gets funds all the time. But he also sits on an important advisory committee dealing with ethnic minority research. (s24)

This list can easily be extended. In the Netherlands the majority of the experiences deal with White control of funding and facilities made available for education and training of Blacks and other immigrants. This is part of state and council "ethnic minority" policies. Because Blacks are excluded from key positions in the formulation, organization, and execution of these special programs, they have hardly any benefit from them. White experts in ethnic minority issues get preferential treatment in the appointment of jobs while, as a result, the special programs are insufficiently tuned to the needs of Blacks and other immigrants. Similar problems are experienced in sectors where there is a majority of Blacks and other immigrants, such as in some schools and in specific neighborhoods, but where educational and community work is controlled by Whites.

About half of the professionals in the Dutch project are hired in "ethnic" positions. None of them has a permanent job. They agree unanimously that their work is marginal compared with the number of Whites hired to make government and local policies and to work in community organizations to solve "ethnic problems." I will show later that this conflict of interest—namely, control of the definition of the problem through the exclusion of Blacks with executive training—is legitimized with arguments that Blacks are not competent. In the meantime the "old-boy network" operates. The government releases funds for "ethnic" training programs, and White supervisors "look around among their friends asking who is interested" (s3) says one woman. Another woman, a student, volunteers to assist primary school students of Hindu-language background with their Dutch language lessons (the Surinamese population has over 30% descendants of immigrants from India and Pakistan). Informally she had heard from parents that the children do not get sufficient support. The director assures her that there is no reason to worry. "We have no problems," he says (s8). And otherwise "they are already taken care of" (s8). "I am trying to get a project off the ground in which Black social workers are hired to work with the Black clients we have," (s10) says a therapist, the only Black worker in a mental health organization. "All the time they keep telling me there is no money" (s10). The real reason behind the excuse of financial problems is that Blacks are low in the priority hierarchy. These situations are not surprising when even the government does not keep its promises. "They are working on legislation that the government must hire 3% minorities. I have seen none of it" (s7).

Getting a job is one problem; rejection in the workplace continues to affect the situation of Black women in exercising their professions. Various women in the social and medical professions experience White clients not wanting to depend on a Black professional. In the Netherlands this was often expressed overtly, such as in the case of Rosa N.: "Sometimes they just say they do not want any help from a Black" (s22). According to the U.S. women, overt rejection is less common. This suggests that Whites are motivated to give a nondiscriminatory self-presentation. This, however, makes it more difficult to distinguish uneasiness, or other reasons to keep distance, from rejection because of racism. It takes repeated experiences, and comparison of many situations, for Black women to view particular patterns of rejection as racism. "They are slow in committing," (c1) explains a therapist when asked how she recognizes racial problems with White patients. Another typical way for dominant group members to withdraw when they find out they have been assigned to a Black professional is to leave with strange excuses. One doctor who has often worked with children says that the children themselves never have problems. It is always the parents who cause problems, and they try to disqualify you as a doctor. "The relation with the child is fine, but then the mother says the treatment is not doing any good" (c21). Despite rejection and objections to Blacks in a position of authority, the major problems do not come from the clients, because especially in education and social work they depend on professional help or advice from Black women.

Ignoring. This occurs both in the United States and in the Netherlands. *Ignoring* (6 NL, 15 USA) Black women is more than indifference or withholding feedback, and it is less than complete rejection. Instead Whites often communicate to Black women that they should not have been in the situation and that they are going to be treated as if they were not there. This mechanism of Whitecentrism is more common in the United States than in the Netherlands and seems to combine race and class factors. In the Netherlands, but decidedly more frequently in the United States, Black women are typically overlooked in shops. "The sales girl always goes to the White person first" (c21). Repeatedly they have to say, "Excuse me I was first" (c31). Other situations, typical for the United States, where informal association between Blacks and Whites is minimal, contain class elements and remnants of segregation. Various women told the same story of being invited to a "high society" event in which they are "not introduced" (c19) to specific important guests or "the photographer taking pictures skipped our table" (c15).

Petty harassment. Various U.S. women report *petty harassment* (1 NL, 9 USA) by their colleagues. The persistence of this suggests that the offenders feel a lot of hostility or even hate Blacks. They seem quite determined to go on with this until the woman cannot stand it any longer and leaves. This emotional undertone probably explains why this form of nonacceptance occurs more often in the United States than in the Netherlands, that is, as far as interactions with middle-class (highly educated) Whites are involved. As I demonstrated above

U.S. Whites can have strong negative feelings about racially mixed settings. Petty harassment involves pestering, "picking on" (c9) Black women, "telling all kinds of lies" (c12), or "making chronic complaints" (s25) to discredit them in the eyes of authorities. Subsequent negative evaluations jeopardize a woman's career. In some situations there is clearly malice involved as a student who worked as a lab assistant on campus recalls

> everyday they [White male students] put broken glass in the wash area where I was and blamed it on me when the supervisor asked about it. They started going to the supervisor and telling her how bad I am doing. They looked at me weird and tried to make me feel uncomfortable. Constantly complaining: you forget to do this, why are you late. They were trying to be "supervisorly." Or they first told me to let those flasks sit for a week and then go: "Why didn't you pick up these flasks, can't you tell we are running out?" Then I would pick them up and wash them . . . and they go: "When are you going to bring them back here?" whereas they were supposed to come in and get them. They were picking on me to force me to quit which worked in their advantage because I did. (c6)

In situations like these the role of the supervisor is crucial. This student said that she resigned because the supervisor "was on their side" (c6). Supervisors may not always take sides explicitly. Experiences of other women suggest that the supervisor is more likely to be tolerant of petty aggression against Black coworkers. They mitigate the problem. "The head of the department acted like this is not a problem. He says: Oh everybody knows the guy is crazy" (c31), says one university professor who had a male colleague "attempting to keep me out. He even had students spying in my classes" (c31). "The department is afraid to confront him directly" (c31), she explains, because he has a strong position at the university. As a result the Black woman involved has to solve the problem on her own.

Situations like these can be handled in ways that are much more supportive of Black women. An alternative example is worth mentioning and concerns a Black female principal in the United States. She says that problems of racism have not been completely solved but are much easier to handle when you have the implicit support of colleagues and the explicit support of your boss. The (White) superintendent was serious about the goal of racial equality, and he hired "all different races" (c25). He is consistent in his rejection of racism.

Therefore, he does not accept any racist talk or racially biased complaints from parents against the Black principal. In other words, he is not going to be responsive to a parent who appeals to their common racial background. As a result these parents are discouraged from voicing racist opinions and have to accept (perhaps grudgingly) that they must address themselves to the Black principal for issues concerning their children and not to the White superintendent.

In addition to harassment there are many other obstructions in school or on the job that slow down or completely undermine Black women's careers or goals. As a result they have to spend more energy, time, and money to get even fewer rewards than Whites under similar conditions. These practices are legitimized when dominant group members attribute to Black women intellectual inferiority and general lack of competence. Let me first portray the ideological context that rationalizes the intervention of Whites into the educations and careers of Black women.

Underestimation

None of the students had a clue, except my brother Glenn, upon which the professor commented: Well, do you need someone from an underdeveloped country to tell you the right answer? (s28)

It must be really something that you have come this far, says one colleague, in other words, she means broken out of all those Black dialects. (c1)

These quotations summarize two important implications of the undervaluation of Blacks. First, according to the White norm, achieving means getting rid of all those cultural constraints of underdevelopment (in the Netherlands) and of "this depressed, deprived background" (c19) of the ghetto (in the United States). Second, one Black who succeeds becomes salient because the invisibility of the oppressed majority is not questioned. In a social system where it is explicitly claimed that "accomplishment" is the result of "individual merit," *underestimation* (18 NL, 13 USA) is a crucial legitimization of the continuing exclusion of Blacks from fair access to and use of resources. Historically the idea of White intellectual superiority has been one of the most persistent features of Euro-American ideologies on race.

When Whites began to relate color to intelligence in the eighteenth century, Blackness began to mean mental inferiority (Trost, 1975).

Today this idea is part of a cluster of ideas attributing to Blacks innate and cultural deficiencies in competing on equal terms with Whites. It is taken for granted and hardly ever questioned that the dominant group profile of a university student or a professional does not generally include Black women. It is even overtly or covertly communicated to Black women in a range of situations that they do not belong in these positions and that they should not have these high aspirations because they are going to fail anyway. Obviously both gender (Griffin, 1985; Hall, 1982) and race factors structure the idea that Black women are not competent to function on a certain level. The dominant group has a huge stake in perpetuating the idea that Blacks are less intelligent, low achievers, and generally incompetent because this forms the major legitimation of a whole range of factors operating to impede the upward mobility of Blacks.

Moreover the idea that Black women cannot perform is actively created in school. It is not surprising then that most experiences discussed by both groups of women involve school. Obstruction of Black women's aspirations in higher education institutions is even more dramatic when we realize that traditionally Blacks, in the United States as well in the ex-colony of Suriname, see higher education as the most important opportunity for social mobility. At the same time Black women's strong will to persevere, even under White(male)centric conditions induces systematic counteraction from dominant group members. As a result the women feel a permanent outer pressure. "We have to do well because they do not think we can do well. So it is a must to make sure other students are doing well at school" (c7). We have seen that Rosa N. felt the same way.

Underestimation is an attitude and can, therefore, only be inferred from behavior. Sometimes the women do not make explicit what exactly was said or done to make them feel that they were underrated. They explain that they just "know" and recognize it (10 NL, 12 USA) when Whites assume that "Blacks do not know anything" (c2), that "they think we are not intelligent" (s4), that they "have low expectations" (s14), think "a Black kid will fail," (s18) or "think we Blacks are not qualified" (c4). In many other situations the attitude can be inferred from surprised reactions (8 NL, 5 USA) when a Black student "got high grades" (s8) or "knew the answer" (c15). Women report that Whites are "shocked to hear that I had such a high education" (s14) or "for two weeks afterwards I heard 'oh, we did not know you had a master's degree' " (c12) when that was mentioned. Other women infer that Whites have low expectations when they introduce themselves (3 NL) and "people keep looking strange . . . because they think it is weird for a Black, and even more weird for a Black woman, to go college" (s5). Another scenario of underestimation is the situation of registering for a science course (1 NL, 4 USA) and, as one student recalls, the room

> was full of White males and they looked at me like, okay, the trash is right here. Everything got quiet and they would really pay attention to what I say and after I had asked enough questions it was like, oh I guess she is one of the special ones, or that is not normal for a Black student. (c7)

These and other examples suggest that the idea that Black women are incompetent is so ingrained in White ideology that it permeates a wide range of everyday practices.

Impediments to the Pursuit of Personal and Group Interests

The majority of the women involved in both countries are high achievers. This is probably one of the reasons that many women believe obstacles they face are often created intentionally: One can hardly accidentally give a C for an excellent essay, force a student to repeat a task, or discourage students from taking courses that prepare them for college. Whether or not agents are motivated by racist ideas, however, these injustices hit Black women in particular.

Of course unequal conditions and relations in school are not only reproduced through factors of race (and gender) per se but also through convergence with class factors. Most of the Afro-American women who attend(ed) college were at a disadvantage compared with many White students because of their financial situations. They studied on grants, and others came from wealthy families. They had to do all their typing themselves, while rich students had their papers typed for them. Rich students could afford to pay for additional tutoring in subjects in which they have problems, and so on.

The everyday obstacles dominant group members produce are generally the same in the Netherlands and in the United States, but U.S. Black women experience more of what they see as "vicious" (c4) attempts to stop Blacks from achieving, especially in school. This probably has to do with the fact that Whites in the United States have a long tradition of practices that keep Blacks at the bottom of society. High dropout rates, children "telling us, mama, there is a teacher up there who throws my homework away and then claims I didn't do it" (c22), and other stories show that Black women have to play watchdog all the time to see that their children are not disadvantaged by the teachers.

Despite their high motivation to achieve, a university background, and readiness to work hard, Black women generally feel that the preference among Whites for their own group turns out to be a permanent obstacle. The creation of obstacles in everyday situations always involves changes in the normal procedures. The majority of the obstacles that can be inferred from the data are those made operative in education and on the job. This is not surprising given that the level of education and vertical mobility at work are important indicators of "success" and crucial determinants of access to power in society. Black women report that dominant group members generally (a) *fail to acknowledge positive contributions* of Black women (19 NL, 21 USA) and (b) *discourage* (5 NL, 15 USA) Black women who aspire to achieve. They are (c) *inflexible* toward Black women or even *introduce additional requirements* (14 NL, 22 USA). This happened to Micky T., who applied for a job and suddenly had to produce references within a few hours, while the other (White) applicant was not asked to show his references (see Chapter 4). Due to these hindrances Black women must put in more effort and spend more energy and time than Whites in the same circumstances.

Failing to acknowledge positive contributions. Much has been published in social psychological studies of race relations about low expectations of Blacks and factors that contribute to making this a self-fulfilling prophecy (Pettigrew & Martin, 1989). The role of exaggerated expectations (unrealistically high, so that the result will be disappointing) and the ultimate attribution error (explaining away evidence of Black competence) have gained much attention in that research. Real-life accounts of Black women do not contradict these findings, but they also emphasize various other mechanisms of racism. Black women are systematically not taken seriously, and they describe in detail how this happens. Their plans or suggestions are simply not heard, not understood, and not reacted upon, and their work gets an unfairly negative evaluation.

Black women in the Netherlands report that they are *excluded from decision-making processes* in meetings. This also happens in the United States, but in the Netherlands this marginalization of Black women operates through repressive tolerance. Obviously exclusion from decision-making processes relates to the earlier mentioned problem that Whites generally fail to acknowledge Black views of reality. I shall return to this point later. Here it is relevant to see that Black women are being silenced. Note that nobody forbids them to speak. Quite the contrary, first the democratic principle of tolerance is underscored: They can say what they have to say. But then what they say is not considered to be of any consequence. As such this seems rather trivial. But one has to take into consideration that meetings in which everybody can voice an opinion are a key instrument in Dutch democracy. More than in the United States decisions at any level are made during meetings. One can even speak of a Dutch "meeting culture."

Pervasive exclusion at meetings may also be inferred from women's use of language in their accounts. Practically all the Surinamese women who described their experiences in discussion groups did not talk about particular events but presented the stories in the "generic *you*" form. This suggests that these events are represented in their memory in scenarios of racism (meeting SRs). The women experience the same situation so often that they literally know by heart the various "tracks" of how their participation in group processes is mitigated. There is a high degree of consistency, even in the description of subtle acts by which Black women's contributions are ignored. Compare, for instance, the statements in italics in the following quotations:

Situation 1: Meeting with colleagues.

In meetings with my colleagues it often happens that one *does not understand what you are saying,* being a Black person. . . . In particular this is the case when you look at things from an alternative perspective. You make your point, *they look at you weird,* they steamroll your point, or, and this is the crucial thing, *your point is not taken down in the minutes* because they do not understand what you are saying, therefore, they cannot restate it, they do not see the relevance of what you are saying. It may also be the case that they exclude your point from the minutes on purpose, because what is in the minutes counts in the process. Therefore they do not take it up. (s4)

Situation 2: Student workshop.

Another thing that happens in workshops is that you can hear *your own arguments being reformulated ten minutes later.* Somebody else takes up your point, reformulates it, and then it will be taken down in the minutes. Then the others react to the point. Another irritating thing is to discover that *you have an interpreter,* someone who always makes it a point to say things like, "What Cynthia [Black student] really wanted to say is. . . ." If you try to correct this by pointing out that that was not what you were trying to say, the person does not listen, leaves out further reference to you, and just continues now to bring in your point as if it was his point. Every time you make a proposal, it is not acknowledged as such. Therefore, your proposals never get accepted. But if someone else makes a proposal, it is taken into serious consideration. (s9)

Experiences of other women confirm that they are "not being understood" (s10): They are looked at as if they are weird, they do not "penetrate or reach" (c32) wherever the others are, and they have to repeat themselves or have "others repeating" what they were saying but in "different words" (s13). Sometimes dominant group members apparently pick up what the woman is saying but do not give any response: "They do not know what to do with it" (s9). Finally, because the points are not understood or not being responded to, they are not taken down in the minutes either. As a result Black women are systematically excluded from participating on the same level as White group members. These situations convey that their sense of reality is not the same as the shared reality of the participating Whites. In other words, Black women are treated like people who are insane: One does not take seriously what they are saying because it comes from a world that is different and "unreal." I shall come back later to the denial of Black definitions of the social world.

They have to push themselves "to the limit " (s10) to make their meanings clear. Whereas women in the Netherlands may be included explicitly (you even get an interpreter who helps you voice your opinion), U.S. women point out another mode of exclusion: You do not get the opportunity to speak at all. As a result Black women are alert and learn to register the most subtle disruptions in the ordinary course of conversation. These include nonverbal communication. "The person's body posture lets you know that they do not feel that your feedback is important. . . . All the direct attention will be focused on my colleagues, all of whom are White, and their expertise will be sought" (c13).

A second way of denying the contributions of Black women is by *not giving credit* for work they have done. Whites may fail to say "thank you" to a Black person who has voluntarily invested a lot of time and energy for their benefit, because "it is taken for granted that Blacks would go back and forth and run all these messages" (c19).

Overlooking the accomplishments of Black women not only happens when the work is associated with a servant's work. One woman who organized all the staff duties when she became chair of a university department says: "Nobody in this department remembers that I did this. I put this into place, and it has been going on ever since." Even worse somebody else may get credit for the work of Black women. "If you ask anybody who did it," the woman adds, "they will say it was always there or that Jack Collins [White, male, previous chairman] did it" (c19). Situations like these happen frequently, but it is hard to prove this unfairness unless you get a case such as this one:

> He [the professor] commented on what an excellent summary Mary [White Ph.D. student] did, and he hoped everyone got a look at it. He started to read it, and Mary said that is not mine. That is Cherry's [Black student]. The man was absolutely devastated. It was like he would not say a thing about my doing a good summary. (c24)

Even then the woman could not do anything about it, because she would risk retaliation from this professor, her Ph.D. supervisor. This introduces the most frequently mentioned situation in which Black women are not given due credit, namely, grading in school. This topic is emotionally charged for Black women in higher education, which can be inferred from the way these experiences are presented in the interview. Almost all accounts of artificial ceilings are elaborate stories, which suggests that the women are particularly motivated to expose adverse reactions to their capacity to excel. The following reasons are relevant in explaining why Black women could remember so well the situations in which they were deprived of recognition according to their merits. First, the idea of rewarding according to merits is fundamental both in the Dutch and in the U.S. culture and tradition. This is not to say that people usually live up to this norm. Neither do I suggest that people might neglect this norm for only racist reasons. Here the symbolic value of this norm is important. Traditionally Black women believe in education and qualification as an opportunity for upward mobility. Therefore, the denial of their competence deeply violates Black women's sense of fairness, especially when they excel. Second, they are indignant, and often angry, about the situation. All these situations of racism involve dominant group members who are in positions of authority, as teachers, supervisors, or as counselors. They have functional power because they are entitled to make consequential judgments about the Black women. Often the women cannot take action against the abuse of functional power for fear of retaliation. This adds to their anger about the situation. Therefore, these events are likely to be remembered with precision, and they are readily retrieved from memory.

Situations where teachers *give* Black women *unfairly low grades* are too frequent, in both countries, to all be discussed here. Many Black women feel that Whites are often deliberately obstructing Black students who perform well. Even Black women in the Netherlands, who, as I mentioned earlier, are usually more inclined to explain racism as ignorance, see intentionality in unfairly low grading. This may be inferred from various stories, such as the following case where the preconception that a good chemistry student must be a White male and certainly not a Black woman is reproduced. One student (s21) notices that the White boy next to her always needed help in setting up his experiments. "He could not even do the most simple experiments by himself," but he always ended up with an A. She did not get any help, the results of her experiments as well as her reports of the experiments were always "good," but when it came to grading she only got a C. This had gone on for two semesters when she finally went to talk to the principal about it. The teacher was reprimanded. She excused herself by saying: "I cannot keep track of the doings of all the students, therefore, it happens that I may make misjudgments." However, the student does not really believe this "nonsense" because she was the only Black student and, in addition, "it was such a small classroom that I really cannot imagine how she managed to overlook me" (s21).

Through experience, comparisons with other students or colleagues, and general information, students or professionals are usually capable of assessing their own relative intelligence and competence. "Therefore," one student of education says, when she heard about her grade on a subject she used to be quite good at, "I was sure the D I got was unfair." She objected, and the professor learned that she had already finished the teacher academy before she started a university degree. "He skimmed over the exam again and changed the D into an A. I could only conclude that he had not even looked at my exam before. He had put down a D when he saw my [Surinamese] name on the paper" (s6). Other women confirm that teachers often do not even care to assess the real level of Black students:

My son grew up in [name of town in California] and I found it much more blatantly racist than my own experience in school [on the East Coast]. When he started high school, he was immediately downgraded; his classes were downgraded. His papers from junior high school obviously [placed him on] a college track. When they saw him they made the assumption that if he was a Black child he could not handle college track. (c9)

Usually unfair grading occurs when the assessments of the student's work includes a subjective element. This is particularly the case with qualitative tests such as essays, poems, or speeches. One woman (s17) reports that "each time" she handed in an essay, "It was returned to me with a D." Even when she made "almost the same summary as another student," the other student passed and she did not. The following year she decided to give her essays "to another professor," and she passed.

There are situations in which the teacher cannot get away with giving the Black students an unfairly low grade. This is especially the case when the Black student is not only average or good but delivers excellent work. Several women tell about reactions of covert or overt aggression against them because they excelled. For the purpose of this study, three examples are discussed. The first and second cases demonstrate reactions that occurred more often. The Black student is punished for excelling by having to redo the test, and the teacher speculates she will now fail. The first case is from a professor of Black studies (c27). A Black student came to her: "She had passed the exam that the teacher had given with the highest grade in class. The teacher insisted the student must have cheated." She had to do the exam again in his office: "With him sitting there at his desk while she was taking the exam in another part of his office." She got a high grade again, and he "accused her again of cheating" (c27). In the second case the student is humiliated in front of the class when she writes an excellent essay:

We had one assignment to write an essay, and I wrote it about love. . . . She gave me my paper back and told the class that they had someone among them who was a plagiarist and . . . she went on and on about never being capable of producing anything of that quality. It really shook me, that anyone could be so evil. (c32)

It is significant that in these situations the normal procedures are completely reversed. Instead of positive feedback for good performance, these Black students are punished for good performance. This situation is even more dramatic in the following case, in which it is demonstrated that undergrading is never an isolated event. It is always part of a process. Here it involves a series of events in which different agents (the school counselor and the principal) attempt to prevent a highly gifted Black female student (c14) from trying to get a scholarship to go to college. The example is also important because it illustrates convergence of race and class oppression in school.

Situation 1: Seeking advice from the school counselor and getting discouragement instead of support.

> She told me that I really did not need to take the PSAT test because Blacks usually did not do very well on those types of test and, knowing that I came from an impoverished family, she said we could better use the $35 application fee to pay our utility bill because it was going to be cold this winter. . . . Yet, I was in all of the honor-level classes that were offered, and that particular exam that she was discouraging me from taking was the initial exam that led to the awarding of numerous scholarships that were a minimum $1,000 each. . . . It seems to me that, knowing what my folks did for a living, you would want them to take everything that they possibly could that would get them more money for me to go to college.

Situation 2: The application form arrives and the authorities keep it back for more than two weeks.

> I did not see my application and my additional forms that I needed to fill out until January 31. . . . The principal's secretary, who happened to be Black and was in his office doing something, saw my application just sitting on his desk and called me out of class and gave it to me and stressed the importance that it needed to be postmarked no later than February 1.

She managed to write her essay by staying up all night. Despite these unfair conditions, she appears to be the only Black and the only person out of that high school to receive a national merit scholarship.

Situation 3: At graduation exercise, students who won awards are honored.

> My principal chose to acknowledge all the scholarship finalists and the winners of other scholarships but did not tell anyone at graduation exercises that I had won a national merit scholarship.

These examples confirm the point I made earlier that racism is particularly consequential when people in authority are involved. A degree is at stake when the thesis supervisor keeps saying "you are going to flunk" (c24) and when the teacher says "you cannot possibly write that well" (c32). The Black student who depends on the judgment of these teachers must be strong willed, needs a lot of courage and self-confidence, and must be very good to defy the prejudice that she cannot make it. Similarly a new job or promotion is jeopardized when the personnel manager discourages the Black employee from applying, and a future is at stake when the school counselor assesses a Black student far below her capacities. Therefore, it is relevant to take a closer look at situations in which Black women are discouraged.

Discouragement (5 NL, 15 USA). Underestimation is implied in the many situations in which Black women are *discouraged* by a person in a position of authority who is supposed to give them good information but tells them to forget whatever they were planning because Blacks do not do well. It is not known how many Black students have tried to enroll in higher-level mathematics, chemistry, or physics, or high-level courses in any field, and have been told by the counselor: "You do not need to take that class, you can get into college without it. Which is true. But at what disadvantage are the students who go in without it going to be when they are competing against people who have taken those classes?" (c14). Many women can describe situations where they are discouraged from taking high-level classes. "I talked about going into graduate school while still being in the master's program, and one of the professors said to me, 'Well, we really need more people at the master's level' as if to undermine my ambition to go further" (c1). Another woman may add that the teacher "consistently communicated that I was smart by accident" (c15) or "a lot of teachers made me feel like I was a dummy" (c28). Indeed a school counselor is not unlikely to advise: "I do not think you should apply to the University of Chicago. Why don't you try one of the little junior colleges" (c34). As these examples demonstrate there are subtle and not so subtle ways to discourage Black female students. These women succeeded nevertheless. As one woman explains: "Their attempts to discourage me from going to the university became an even greater challenge for me to prove that I would make it" (s6).

Inflexibility and additional requirements (14 NL, 22 USA). Episodes like these are repeated in different situations, involving different agents and different targets, not only in education but also on the job. U.S. Black women, who were more career oriented than Black women in the Netherlands, were also more alert to obstacles frustrating their careers.

Half of the group in the Netherlands and almost every woman in the U.S. group mentioned that they are consistently confronted with additional requirements, inflexible attitudes, and problems of underpayment. Their interpretations and evaluations of their experiences are based on inferences from knowledge about normal requirements, the flexible application of rules, and acceptable salaries and prices when Whites are involved under similar circumstances. This can be inferred from their use of language. Note in the following cases that Black women talk about how things "normally" go, what the "mean" salaries are, or the "usual" procedures. They see the difference between their "White counterpart" and make other comparisons for inconsistency between their own experiences and the experiences of specific Whites.

Many women feel that Whites are generally *inflexible* toward them. This mechanism of racism is particularly consequential when supervisors are involved. The women mentioned many variations of inflexibility, including economic (salary matching), formal (rule application), career-oriented (space to grow), and task-oriented (job satisfaction) behavior. This area would require a study in itself, and all the examples cannot be included here. In school, for instance, various Black women are required to repeat certain tasks or are requested to perform additional tasks. Under similar circumstances White students can continue without these interruptions causing unnecessary delay in their programs: "I had to do an additional internship," says a woman who went back to the university, "while normally you are exempted from internship if you already have work experience. And I had worked for over 10 years" (s6). "They even did not look at my grades," (s24) says another woman who switched from the Surinamese to the Dutch teacher's academy. They "*insisted*" that she continue on a lower level, because "they felt that Surinamese students did not do well." The student says she'll "be damned" if she takes that, upon which she is allowed to continue at the level where she belongs. U.S. women expose another typical indication of inflexibility. In fact several women tell exactly the same story about teaching assistants whose "attitude was that I was lazy. That I had not done everything I was supposed to do. That he was not there to do my work for me. That he wanted to see my notes" (c14). While tutors "habitually do not ask for that information," says one student who had been a TA herself (c14).

At work women experience supervisors not allowing them to take certain responsibilities that would "normally come with the job description" while "if it had been a White girl she could take advantage of whatever was there, and . . . she would get added responsibilities, no questions asked, and she would get the promotion" (c4). Supervisors may suddenly decide to follow rules about time schedules and start asking questions about being late when, "It was agreed when I took the job that I would have great flexibility" (c33). "Problems that were ignored for years become suddenly acute when it involves a Black colleague" (c19), says a woman who temporarily took a leading position that had previously always been occupied by Whites. Then her boss complained about the administration files: "I am following the guidelines of my predecessors, and I never heard anybody talking about their files. But I had to do 100% better" (c19). The supervisor may also refuse to give a positive evaluation when the woman applies for promotion or "refuse to give permission" (c8) for her to take advanced courses. Apart from supervisors, bosses, and teachers, there are people from the administration who may get difficult, such as the budgeter. One woman, editor of a monthly paper for Black students, explains: "They may give you problems for things that need not be difficult" (c5), such as when a person starts patronizing Blacks and implicitly accuses them of irresponsible spending of money: " 'You want to buy something from the storehouse?' And she would go into depth and ask us 'Well why do you need it, did we not already have one' " (c5). This detail about the budgeter is part of a larger experience, namely, the gradual dismantling of the only Black newspaper on campus because they "have articles in there they [Whites] do not want to read about, and that we publish anyway" (c7).

Not only is there a problem of inflexibility, Black women often face *additional requirements* so "there is not anything you can do at the same level that they do and still survive as a Black person. It is almost like you have to do what they do plus a little bit more than they do " (c21). This quotation summarizes the experiences of many other women. To prevent Black women from making use of the same facilities as Whites, people in specific positions of authority introduce, each time, new demands the Black woman needs to fulfill before she can have access to particular facilities. "They set the standards, and any time you think it is going to be close, the simply move the standards higher" (c13). What is relevant here is not the specific additional requirements Black women encounter in particular cases but that, in any set of social arrangements, Black women may be discriminated against through changes in the normal procedures of the situation.

Given these impediments it is not surprising that higher professions remain largely a White privilege, while Black women are systematically *excluded from positions of authority* (15 NL, 21 USA). Various women in the Netherlands were offered "low qualification jobs only" (s7). Some U.S. women experienced the same in the southern states or, years before, in other places. It still happens, however, that they cannot get a job because they are "overqualified" (c12) and end up working "for peanuts" (c12) below their level. Related to this is the tendency to *reserve menial work for Blacks* (3 NL, 4 USA). This form of exploitation is expressed in various ways. In the Netherlands women discuss supervisors who "always" ask the Black woman on the team "to make coffee" (s25). This may also be seen as a form of sexism. However, when there is a Black woman on the team, she may be requested to do the service work before White women are asked. The idea that Black women are more suitable for service or menial jobs may affect the supervisor's decisions about task allocation. "I started working before this White girl," says one woman, "but they cut my hours and increased hers, and she did the easy work and I had to do the hard boring work like filling papers, and she did the more fun stuff like greeting people at the door" (c7).

Abuse of functional power by supervisors and others in positions of authority is hard to counter because the women who complain or refuse to submit risk retaliation. These and other mechanisms aimed at preventing or undermining opposition are discussed in the following section.

Undermining Opposition to Structural Subordination

It may be tempting to think that repression involves only actions against existing opposition. This definition of repression, however, overlooks the ways of reducing motivation to resist. For the purpose of this study, four processes that contain this everyday opposition are important. These are (a) pacification, (b) intimidation, (c) denial of dignity, and (d) retaliation. In real life, processes of containment are embedded in historical dynamics of oppression and opposition. This is illustrated by a case study of the daily struggle of an Afro-American Studies Center. This case study is relevant for two reasons. First, it is a good illustration of the battle over resources. Second, an Afro-American Studies Center is more than just an institution; it represents the struggle to assert an alternative view of race relations. However, for the purpose of the analysis, these four modes of repression are discussed first as if they were independent elements in the domination process.

Pacification: Patronizing (17 NL, 5 USA) and Expecting Gratitude (5 NL, 2 USA)

Rosa N. got annoyed when a colleague insisted that she adopt his correct pronunciation of the name of Don Johnson because she recognized the Dutch "teaching and preaching." Given their colonial history, one does not need much imagination to understand the typical forms patronizing takes in the Netherlands. There is a strong paternalistic element in these residues of colonialism. Many situations are permeated with some "teaching," "help," or other "advice" telling Black women what they need or really want.

The Surinamese are portrayed as colonial children. "News about Suriname is always presented in such a patronizing way. They always give the impression that they know what is best for us" (s12), says one woman. These attitudes recur in interactions. "I am reading the map on the bus schedule and timetable and all these people start meddling with me: Where I want to go, if I need any help, people trying to direct me" (s6). What happens in the street is reinforced in other situations. Women report that Dutch policies are also patronizing and moralizing. One woman active in Surinamese organizations explains that the city has refused to give more subsidies to the Surinamese organizations. She has heard "from reliable sources that the city wants to punish the Surinamese organizations for the past years of hostilities and fights between each other" (s7). In these situations "helping" the underdeveloped Surinamese fuses with active tolerance, a factor that was noted earlier. Dominant group members involved "will make sure that you realize that they are doing all this for you and that you must be grateful for that" (s3) because they are "doing us a favor" (c10). One woman was even told by her boss that she "must be grateful that he gave her the job" and that he saved her from "ending up just like the other [Black] junkies down the street" (s18). Because the dominant group insists upon the positive meaning of benevolence, Blacks who reject this "help" can be problematized: Why are you being so ungrateful? I will return to similar ways of repressing opposition to racism.

Another, related way to discourage opposition described by U.S. women is the tendency to *keep close control* (1 NL, 6 USA) of Black women. Various women find that supervisors want them "to explain" all the time "what [they] are doing" (c4).

Denial of Dignity

On an ordinary day, during lunch break, you overhear casual conversation among two fellow (White male) students. The one tells the other about "this accident" in the street that morning and how he went to take a look. A man was bleeding. "Oh well, it was only a Surinamese" (s17), he concludes the story. Not all the examples are as blatant as this one, but openly racist statements expressing contempt for Blacks occur regularly. Through *humiliation* and display of contempt (17 NL, 17 USA), dominant group members aim to repudiate the human dignity of Blacks, as individuals and as a people. This form of racism reinforces the subordinate positions of Blacks. As one woman puts it: "People try and either purposely insult you or not give you credit for whatever it is" (c25). Through humiliation dominant group members implicitly claim that they are superior. These practices reinforce the idea the Blacks should remain in subordinated relations. Humiliation of Blacks expresses reluctance to change. Only a few variants of the use of contempt or disrespect to express reluctance can be illustrated here.

Given the extent of culturalization of racism in the Netherlands, it is not surprising that humiliation, more than in the United States, has cultural implications. For instance, while trying on clothes in the shop, one Black woman notices a Dutch woman who tried on colors that did not match at all. When she came out to look at herself in the mirror, she cried out: "Don't I look just like a Negress now!" (s5). This statement expands not only on the historical and current exploitation of Black women but is part of ideological constructions representing Black women as ugly, primitive, without sophisticated taste or culture. Therefore, not only the particular situation of indirect insult against the Black woman who is present in the situation is relevant but also the uncritical, if not approving, reference to the oppression of Black women contained in that specific remark.

When another woman asks for a certain type of bread at the baker's and uses the Surinamese Dutch word for it, the man "first corrects" her language before he gives the loaf of bread "upon which the other customers could hardly repress their laughter" (s9). This particular situation has implications greater than just those of a person's feelings of embarrassment when laughed at in a public situation. It extends to the systematic overemphasis on ethnic difference throughout the Dutch system, to the complete lack of recognition of Surinamese Dutch in the Dutch media, literature, and school system, and to the systematic pressures on Blacks in the Netherlands to accept the Dutch way of speech and communication.

In the United States humiliation is explicitly class based with the purpose of keeping Blacks at the bottom of society. In some examples dominant group members explicitly object to and reject the economic or social progress of Blacks. One woman (c21) recalls, about her internship as a medical student, that there was "this guy," a fellow (White) student with whom she talked "from time to time." She "thought" that they were "having nice conversations." It happened that the two students, while talking, discovered they had grown up in the same town in Arkansas. Her mother was a domestic servant and his father was a medical doctor. His new clothes came from the shop, her new clothes were the "hand-me-downs" from her mother's employer. In both families the adults had encouraged the children to learn. She went to segregated schools with poor facilities, and he went to a private high school, for Whites only. He went to T. University, which does not compare with W. University where she went. And yet they were right there together doing their internship at J. hospital, which is a top hospital. The woman continues that on the day "when he was ready to leave, he said: You know what, you should go back to Arkansas and plan on being a seamstress or a maid" (c21).

A comment like this is not only bad taste or viciousness from one person to another; it symbolizes race relations and the history of racial oppression and exploitation in the United States. Though expressed against an individual Black woman, the White male student refers with consent to the system of segregation, the exploitation of Blacks, and the many hours of overwork Black parents had to go through to enable their children to go to school. This remark expresses disapproval of the institutional changes enabling more Blacks to go to college. It implicitly approves of inequality in the school system and the marginal representation of Blacks in the medical professions. Implicitly this remark expresses the hope that White dominance will be maintained.

The following examples are important because they are good illustrations of the ultimate consequence of the Whitecentrism and indifference toward Blacks that I discussed earlier. Dominant group members do not question the legitimacy of existing race relations. Let me illustrate this with the case of the university teacher who had traveler checks left over from a trip abroad with which she wanted to pay in the supermarket. As others noted earlier, in the United States the cashier will often assume that Blacks pay with cash only. As soon as the checker sees her taking some paper that does not look like cash, he says: "You can't use those here." Because she was Black the checker "assumed that they were food stamps. I wanted to strangle him. I thought here is this little checker making these kinds of assumptions" (c9).

What angers this woman "to no end" (c9) in this situation is probably not the fact that she is taken for a welfare mother. Would she care about people taking her for poor when she makes much more than the cashier is ever likely to make? Does it really matter when evidence of luxury (traveling abroad) is taken as a sign of poverty (food stamps)? It seems to me that other factors represent more plausible explanations for her outburst of anger.

Let me first point to class bias from the Black woman herself. The fact that it is this "little checker" who insults her makes it worse. This suggests that she herself uncritically accepts the reality of class exploitation, which is not untypical for middle-class Black women. Here a second factor is also important, which is the checkers's *casual* reference when noticing the piece of paper in her hand to the over-representation of Black women on welfare as if that is a *normal* condition for Black women.

The assumption that it is *normal* or *acceptable* that so many Black women remain servants, menial workers, or on welfare all their lives is the implicit message in situations where Black women are addressed as "jij" (informal "you") (s15), which in Dutch is more or less the same as being "called by your first name" (c27), as many women experience in the United States. Although the particular insults are directed against an individual Black woman, these insults express consent to the reality of White dominance in society as well as reluctance to accept the changes Blacks have fought for or to accept Black women behaving as equal to Whites.

This is further explained in the following example. The woman involved is a faculty member. This case is interesting because it brings into focus how much more effectively Black women can oppose racism when they are in a position of authority. She is referred to by her first name by the cashier at the university bookstore, a White female student. "I talked to the supervisor. And they did in fact hold a meeting and talked to the clerks about their attitude towards the Blacks on the campus." However, the student herself still "didn't know what she had done wrong, couldn't understand why I was so upset" (c27).

The student's interpretations of the situation decontextualize the event from her implicit acceptance of White superiority. She looks at it as a person-to-person issue and problematizes the Black woman: Why does somebody get so upset about a slip of the tongue? The Black woman involved recognizes the racial implications of the act and interprets it on that level. She speaks to the manager because she does not see the situation as a slip of the tongue but as symptomatic of racism. Therefore, she wants to proceed from the person-to-person level between her and the student to the general relations between White checkers and Black (faculty) customers. Further the Black faculty member recognizes in the specific event the symptom of reluctance to give up preference for an all-White university faculty. This, and not any personal satisfaction, is the point she makes, and the problem she symbolizes when she says to the cashier "I'm going to come through your line every time I come in here to get you used to calling me Dr. [name]" (c27).

Intimidation

We have seen that patronizing is a relatively mild form of racism but that Whites have less refined ways of denying dignity to Black women. The same holds true for many forms of intimidation, which is instrumental in the enforcement of compliance with the system. Here attention is paid to *sexual violence,* meaning verbal and nonverbal harassment and other sexual aggression against Black women, to *rudeness,* and to other verbal aggression, such as *threats* and *name calling.* The relatively high number of women in the Netherlands who experienced verbal aggression is somewhat misleading because more women in the Netherlands than in the United States recall name calling only from the time they were in primary school. One form of intimidation more prevalent in the Netherlands than in the United States is *ridicule, joking,* and *other* racist talk about Blacks. This seemingly nonaggressive form works through the reinforcement of consensus. We shall see that the Dutch situation is a perfect example of containment through nonaggressive repression. These practices are illustrated with examples from Black women's everyday lives.

Sexual harassment (3 NL, 5 USA) *and the myth of sexual pathology* (7 NL, 9 USA). The idea of Black sexuality as pathological is well implanted in European and U.S. consciousness. Nineteenth- and early twentieth-century attempts to prove that Blacks are inherently different than Whites rested largely on sexuality. Some authors sought psychological explanations for this obsession with Black sexuality and interpreted this phenomenon as one that articulates publicly repressed sexual fantasies (Gilman, 1985; Stember, 1976). Psychological explanations of the sexual objectification, oppression, and exploitation of Blacks are valuable but not comprehensive enough. The association of Blacks with an insatiable sexual drive is probably part of more complex processes rooted in social relations between men and women, European and "exotic" cultures, colonizers and the colonized, slaveholders and slaves.

Sexual racism is a form of gendered racism and cannot, therefore, be discussed separately from gender-specific control of Blacks. The stereotype of sexual availability is the female form of the attribution to Black men of sexual aggressiveness. Both constructions have been and still are used to rationalize the use of aggressive mechanisms of control over Blacks. In U.S. history Black men have been lynched, jailed, and murdered based on allegations of sexual harassment of White women (Davis, 1981). Black women have been assaulted and raped because they were seen as the sexual property of White men. Historical constructions of Black sexuality were reproduced and still operate today. Black women continually have to deal with the danger of sexual abuse by White men. This knowledge causes many Black women to restrict the goals they pursue and the choices they make for reasons of self-protection. Women were taught by their mothers to protect themselves against White men, and they transmit the same knowledge to their daughters. Indeed the issue of interracial dating and the racially structured sexual abuse of Black girls and women is integrated into the socialization of Black children. "I went off into the Black-White thing when she was 13," says one woman.

> As Black mother talking to Black daughter, I had to tell her what it was going to be like for her as a Black woman. . . . 'Cause I think she's too vulnerable. She's a Black woman. I had to help her understand that she was a stereotype to White guys. Because White guys are still told by their fathers, you practice on the Black woman. (c27)

Little is known about sexual racism in the Netherlands. Some research points out that its current forms are similar to those in the United

States. I stated earlier that Black women in the Netherlands are often seen as prostitutes and as sexually exotic, but as yet the precise relation between these ideological constructions and the position of Black women in the Dutch socioeconomic structure has never been studied. Hypothetically it can be argued that sexual violence against Black women in the Netherlands is not rooted in the same structural relations as in the United States. In the Netherlands sexual violence against Black women is probably more of a racialized specification of male control over women rather than a function of White control over Blacks through women. The connotations of the Dutch ideological constructions of Black female sexuality are probably more closely related to notions of "savage" or "exotic" sexuality than to the image of "the Black slave or domestic servant" whose sexuality can be owned by White males.

After this necessarily brief, and therefore incomplete, discussion of some differences in the roots and functions of sexual racism in both countries, the question is whether this is incidental or recurrent in the experience of Black women. From the data it can be inferred that for Black women, in the United States as well as in the Netherlands, sexual racism, whether verbal or physical, whether consisting of "mild" or "extreme" violations, is a daily reality. "It happens every now and then, but it is still pretty consistent" (c12).

The real extent of sexual racism against Black women cannot be inferred from the data. It is still a taboo, in the Netherlands as well as in the United States, to bring into the open experiences of rape or other sexual violations of the body. Given the fact that I only interviewed the women once, thereby remaining a relative stranger to them, I was reluctant to ask explicitly about these experiences. Nevertheless several women introduced the topic themselves. In this respect U.S. Black women seemed less inhibited than Black women in the Netherlands, which probably has to do with fear of identification, for the Netherlands is a small country.

Black women in both countries are confronted with stereotypes about Black female sexuality. It is presumed that Black women are "good at 'it' " (s20). Says one woman: "One time a guy asked me if it was true about Black women being so hot" (s10). As we have seen from the experiences of Rosa N., the dominant ideology pictures Black women as prostitutes. As a result a Black woman who is seen with a White man in an "exclusive French restaurant" or any other place where they go out may find "that the people [are] looking at me as if I had managed to pick up a White man for a night" (s11).

These ideological constructions rationalize actual harassment of Black women. Here it is relevant to consider in particular the cases where White men abuse functional authority to force women into sexual acts. Various women have been assaulted by White men in positions of authority who threatened or actually retaliated when the women resisted. These situations are particularly detrimental because a woman's education, job, or career is at stake. One woman in the Netherlands reported that she was "blackmailed" (s6), together with four other Black women in the same neighborhood, by a social welfare officer. Several U.S. women have been harassed by White professors in college. One woman says that the teacher made it a point to humiliate her in class after she had refused to meet him "in some shady corner" (c32) for a date. Other women unsuspiciously accept the professor's offer "to meet for an extra session" (c2) on a specific subject with which they have problems. He then tries to abuse them sexually: "I said 'No' and he says 'Well you know that you want me to. You want this' " (c28).

This subject deserves more attention than space allows. It is sufficient here, however, to say that, when White men in positions of authority abuse functional power to force themselves sexually upon Black women, they are likely to use the same power to retaliate when the woman refuses. When other authorities intervene this becomes more difficult, as was the case when the bank manager who "puts his hand in the blouse" (s14) of a Black secretary. She "slaps him in the face" (s14), he calls her into his office and threatens her, upon which she goes to the director, who reprimands the manager.

Rudeness (12 NL, 18 USA). "They step in front of you and never say excuse me . . . kind of stuff I used to see in the South, which is what it reminds me of. There is an attitude, like people who think they are better than anybody else, and they are going to show you that by just being plain and rude" (c13).

Rudeness can be identified as a form of racism in the Netherlands as well as in the United States, but it seems as if the threshold to behave rudely toward Black women with higher education is usually lower in the United States. Note, however, that the experiences of Black women of working-class background are probably different in this respect (Cock, 1980; Rollins, 1985). Almost all situations discussed occur in the United States and are probably a reaction to desegregation and to the increase of Blacks in middle-class positions. The situations express resentment against Black women's access to the same college or living in the same neighborhood. Many examples deal with the resentment of waiters when they have to serve Blacks. "We went to a restaurant with a whole lot of my friends," a woman recalls. "They were all White, and the waiter would not serve me. Finally he came over there and it was like 'what do you want,' with a real mean voice" (c6). There is resentment that Black women shop in the same areas as Whites. One woman finds that this involves "not necessarily the cashiers, but people who are in the grocery line. They just cut in front of you" (c13). Rudeness in these situations is intricately related to class oppression. The idea that Blacks should remain servants is clearly expressed, for instance, in the following situation in which a student who works as an administrative assistant at a university department says: "They [faculty and staff members] push their way through [when they have to pass] instead of saying excuse me. If I tell them excuse yourself, just use a little courtesy, they look at me as if I am crazy. . . . I get the treatment that I am just to cater them" (c28).

A second function of rudeness is to enforce obedience. A good illustration of this comes from a U.S. school counselor who observed that the school secretary was consistently inflexible toward Black children with problems. "A Black kid comes in, the school secretary goes: 'What do you want? Do you have a note from your teacher? Go back to your room and get it!' . . . But when a White kid comes in she goes: 'What can I do for you? Are you hurt? Are you feeling bad?' " (c12). Obviously the secretary is not only inflexible when she always enforces the rules (no requests without a teacher's note) strictly when a Black kid is involved and not (always) when a White kid comes in, but she is also rude. Situations like these occur when unexpected things arise and when Blacks make mistakes or otherwise behave differently than expected.

Unlike in the United States, where rudeness reinforces race-class relations, rudeness in the Netherlands seems to have a cultural function, that is, to force Blacks to adopt the Dutch way of life. For instance, when Blacks break a rule or deviate from expected behavior, it is a typical Dutch reaction to snap "*here* we do not do that" (s5). Similar are the cases in which rudeness seems to express that Whites feel they do not have to put up with problems of Blacks. Several women gave examples of rude behavior on the part of medical doctors. It is not surprising that they mention this group, because visiting a doctor is one of the few situations where women with higher education ask for help. In this respect the experiences of Black women of working-class background differ. They are often confronted with rudeness from Whites when they appeal for welfare money or public housing or deal with other agencies of the welfare state (see, e.g., Bryan, Dadzie, & Scafe, 1985). Doctors may become rude in situations in which the treatment of a Black woman demands specific attention, such as when the doctors do not know the specific disease. "There is nothing I can do about you dirty toe" (s23) says one doctor when a Black woman comes to see him about a tropical infection she got on vacation in Suriname. Impatience and aggression also play a part when a dentist who extracts a wisdom tooth finds it took more effort than he had expected, "He started swearing while I was sitting there with my mouth open: 'God damn it, give me the other tongs. I cannot get it out. [Angry]: With these people it always gets stuck' " (s15). Obviously both doctors are reluctant to put extra effort into the treatment of a Black patient. As yet the real extent of racism in doctors against patients is unknown in the Netherlands. However, other women, among them Rosa N., report similar cases of rudeness against Black patients.

Rudeness is also the reaction in situations in which, in the view of Whites, Blacks take liberties dominant group members may or may not be willing to accept from Whites, but certainly not from Blacks. A typical example is when children play in the street and neighbors get annoyed about the noise. A neighbor is likely to "yell only at the Black kid among them" (s16). Similarly at school, when students arrive late in class after the lunch break, the teacher may look at the only Black student among them when he "yells" (s17) at "them."

Name calling and verbal threats (10 NL, 17 USA). "Like I said, these assholes are everywhere. The other day they wrote on the wall 'death to the Blacks' " (s23).

"My sister is quite a spitfire. She really let go flying when she was called names . . . and came home with tufts out of her hair and scrapes and bruises" (s14).

There are two points I should make about verbal abuse. One regards reactions of the women themselves to this racism and the other is about the implications of verbal aggression in both countries. To start with the first, the quotes just given show that women react strongly to racial slurs. The significance of this becomes clear when we consider that Dutch culture is more Calvinistic than U.S. culture and that, therefore, there is a deeply rooted negative attitude to emotional elements, whether constructive emotion such as enthusiasm or destructive emotion such as direct, angry confrontation. Therefore, aggressive racist talk is less common. I will return to this feature of Dutch racism in a moment. Furthermore strong reactions of Black women to name calling are dealt with in a Calvinistic way too: "You are overreacting." This is an effective way to *depoliticize* racial name calling. Let me illustrate this with the following case.

One woman recalls from high school that she refused to speak to the boy in class who had called her a "roetmop" (akin to "nigger"). She pursued this decision strictly: for her he did not exist any more. She was called to see the principal, who did not agree with her reaction, thus problematizing her instead of the boy. "The principal told me it was wrong to keep on being angry with somebody for such a long time . . . because it was damaging the classroom climate" (s18). The student feels this was all caused by the boy. "*He*" started the whole thing. The principal gives her two days to think over her decision. Otherwise "one of us would have to look for another school" (s18). In this example the student does not define the situation as ordinary rudeness. The director depoliticizes the situation when he blames them equally (one of you will have to go to another school), thus forcing her to solve the problem on a personal level. Faced with this threat the Black student submits. The problem is indeed solved on a personal level because the two students remain on speaking terms for years. However, the political implication is that racism was tolerated: All the other students in class who did not reject the boy's behavior and who, like the director, felt that the Black student was just making a scene are reinforced in their belief that racial slurs are like any other slurs, except that they are racial.

U.S. women see racist slurs in a structural context. From that point of view *nigger* is not a word but a concept representing the history of oppression of Blacks. Name calling then is intimidation because Whites use, as a symbolic weapon, the body of cultural and structural oppression. This is explained by the following example in which a Black mother repoliticizes racist name calling after the teacher had depoliticized the fact that a "White girl" had called her son "a nigger." He hit her and was suspended from school. The mother went to see the principal and asked what the teacher had done with the girl: Nothing. "I said you don't think being called a nigger by a White girl a form of attack? He got back into school" (c19).

Outside the classroom, in neighborhood situations, or even outdoors on campus it is more difficult to deal with name calling or racist graffiti. This form of aggression is, like name calling, more common in the United States than in the Netherlands. The stories of the women suggest that there has been little change in this respect during the past decade, which is also an indication of the persistence of real violence against Blacks (Reed, 1989). The same "signs on our doors" (c25) meant to scare Blacks who were in college in the 1960s and 1970s reappeared on the doors of students in the 1970s and 1980s. "We could find 'niggers' written on the walls. One time we had to wash 'niggers' off the [Black student union]" (c2).

Whereas racial threats in the United States often pertain to race-class factors ("keep Blacks in their place") similar aggression against Blacks in the Netherlands pertains to cultural-nationality factors ("you do not belong"). Among the cases of overtly racial intimidation that occurred most frequently in the lives of Black women in the Netherlands are those in which they are confronted with racist conversations or verbal racist attacks in public situations where they are the only Blacks and Whites present pretend not to hear. In the Netherlands one typical public place for verbal harassment of Blacks is public transportation:

> Two drunk guys got on, and they said to me, "Stupid Black, what did you come here for? Why didn't you stay in your own country? Came here to steal our jobs, huh?" . . . I couldn't say anything, I was really dripping wet. . . . No one did anything. But they were all looking, you know. A Turkish boy got up and came to stand next to me. I found that really something. The solidarity. (s23)

Transcending sexual and ethnic differences, the Turkish boy acts in support of the Black woman because he experiences at that moment the same racism vicariously. It is significant that only the Turkish boy clearly distances himself from the racist slur. Other women agree that, in such situations, "You want to know what the Dutch do? They look out the window. They act like they don't see or hear it" (s24). This may be generalized for other cases of racist talk, jokes, and ridicule of Blacks.

Ridicule, jokes, and other racist talk (13 NL, 7 USA). Joking is expecting or hoping for consent from others by way of laughter. "Racist talk" is the ventilation of racism in the form of complaints, insinuations, and other gossip about Blacks. "Racist talk" is different than name calling or threats and usually takes place during casual conversation. In everyday life many ethnic jokes, supposedly funny comments, and forms of ridicule are integrated into casual conversation or presented as casual comments. This is illustrated by many examples in school and on the job where teachers, students, colleagues, or supervisors indulge in "racist talk." The repressive impact does not refer to racist conversations in themselves but to the situation in which these take place: in the presence of a single Black.

In the Netherlands anti-Black or anti-immigrant jokes, gossip, and other casual talk represent one of the least understood forms of racism. Yet racist talk in the presence of Blacks is an important mechanism of control. "Racist talk" and jokes often are not aimed at specific Blacks in the situation and can, therefore, not be interpreted as direct racial confrontations. The indirect nature makes them suitable for situations that are not acknowledged as situations of conflict. This probably explains why racist talk is more common in the experience of Black women in the Netherlands than in that of the U.S. women. The tendency of the Dutch to avoid direct confrontation and the expectation, among the Dutch, that Blacks will probably not indulge in direct confrontation either makes supposedly nonserious comments against Blacks a suitable strategy for expressing prejudice against Blacks. The Dutch keep their tolerant self-image because they redefine "racist talk" as joking or as "just" complaints.

It is important to understand that racist conversations in the presence of Black women are repressive because other dominant group members refrain from criticizing or otherwise rejecting what is being said. As a result group power is reinforced and displayed again and again in front of the only Black woman present. To illustrate the process of intimation I discuss the case of one woman, whose story is confirmed by the experiences of other Black women. Although the particular details of the situations are unique, it may be assumed that many Black solos or tokens in the Netherlands recognize their own experiences in this.

Jacky F., insurance broker for a multinational company, the only Black in a large department, comes into contact with a variety of people. These include clients of all backgrounds, representatives of other companies, various colleagues at different levels and departments, the director, and, last but not least, administrative and canteen personnel. She is engaged in what she feels is a loosing battle against discrimination against Black and other immigrant clients. This happens routinely, and she explains:

Situation 1: Agents on the line.

I've had agents phone to ask how can that premium be so low, it is a Brown, isn't it? There've been loads of those remarks, like we'll just nail them with a premium, after all, it is a Black.

Jacky F. feels she cannot openly contest these practices on her own. Two different forces operate to subdue protest. Colleagues try to involve her in discriminating practices. At the same time she is continually silenced through expression of White group consensus in racist talk and joking. This practice is business as usual. It seems completely acceptable for her colleagues to behave as follows.

Situation 2: Black clients on the line.

> Someone phones, and it's like, "Gerold [name of supervisor] get on the line, it's a Black." Or "Oh gee, a Black." Or "Jacky pick up the phone, it's a Black." . . . They sit there with that listening-apparatus helping each other, with "get on the phone, it's a Black."

In addition to these recurrent telephone situations with White agents and Black clients, Jacky F. faces variations of casual racist conversations that happen so often that she comments: "You know, they forgot that I was Black."

Situation 3: Casual conversation with the supervisor.

> He had a quite definite opinion against Blacks. . . . Once he'd been rolled. . . . He hadn't seen it, but it had to have been a Black, because, he said, it was black with people.

Situation 4: The director drops by.

> The director comes up with a story, "I've got that Negro," and he looks at me, I see him backing up a bit. And, there you sit. Then I say, "Go right ahead. Make yourself at home." Now, I think, what can you do? Well, he goes ahead with his story. It's lost its punch, of course, and the others realize it. They're all like that. . . . They don't think about your feelings as a Black.

Situation 5: Colleagues are taking a break; they stay around.

5a: Generalized situation

> I've had those who were really out to get me because I don't laugh [at racist jokes]. They only told Black jokes. Especially at our desk. And then I'd say, "Not today, thank you. Come back tomorrow."

5b: Specific example

And then [after the "come back tomorrow"] he stops, but then he tries the line, "I'm from Holland, you're not in the Belgian Congo," and that kind of idiocy. But under the guise of a joke that others laugh at, he insinuates, "Me better than you. I'm the White boss."

As Jacky F. says, "Every day I heard I was Black." If she did not hear it from her colleagues, then she heard it from the other personnel:
Situation 6: Coffee lady makes her round.

Always making comments like, "Ho! You're really a pesky Surinamer" and "I've never served a Black like you."

These comments, complaints, and jokes have a specific function. The Black woman is challenged ("and he looks at me," "really out to get me," "especially at my desk," "never served a Black like you"), in a situation where she is on her own against a group. Because confronting behavior is not really acceptable, prejudice is ventilated in a joking way. It is a constant battle in which she may have small victories ("it's lost its punch and the others realize it") but not enough to alter daily reinforcement of "we Whites" against "you Black" rituals ("every day I heard I was Black"). Despite the fact that some colleagues may be out to "get" her, it would be a mistake to infer from this that "the Whites" are plotting against Jacky F. Rather than a conspiracy, this indirect form of intimidation seems to be completely accepted and fluently integrated into the course of daily life at the department. Indeed, "it almost seems," says Jacky "as if they forget that I am Black."

It should be noted that in her account Jacky F. used words such as "always," "loads of those remarks," and other generalizations. This suggests she remembers these generalized experiences as general models of agents who call about Black clients, of colleagues who get Black clients on the line, and of the coffee lady who comes by to take orders (Situations 1, 2, 5a, 6). Other experiences she memorizes as specifications of the "telling racist jokes" scenario on the job (Situations 3, 4, 5b).

The accounts of Jacky F. can easily be complemented by experiences of other Black women in the Netherlands, such as "jokes about stupid Blacks in South Africa" (s23) during lunch hour or fellow colleagues in the working session who refer "giggling" to a Black patient as the one who talks like "me hurt in me tommy" (s10). The Black woman is always on her own in these situations, and she may "sweat inside" (s23) as one woman puts it but "let it go" because furious reactions may make them "laugh at you" (s23).

These situations confirm the point I made earlier about the implications of the marginal inclusion of Blacks. Whether in the name of ethnic variety (in the Netherlands) or affirmative action (in the United States), accepting Black solos or tokens leads to new forms of oppression and concomitant forms of suppressing opposition. It is interesting to note that racist talk loses its intimidating impact when there are more Blacks present in the situation.

One student recalled a geography class she took with a few other Blacks. Of course the large majority were Dutch. The professor made a pun with the name of a Surinamese town and the word *nikker* (Dutch for *nigger*), which ended with, "So it's the country of the niggers." When he said that "he looked at the Surinamese students, but we just stared back as if he were crazy. So he faintly apologized with: 'Oh well I was only joking, you know' " (s10). In this case the teacher probably succeeded in reconfirming White consensus because none of the White students challenged him. The intimidation (he looked at the Blacks while saying this) failed, however, because the Blacks students could support each other by taking a common stand against the teacher.

These examples illustrate that a solo position hardly affords opposition. This is even worse when the woman seeks to challenge the racism of authorities. This brings us back to the point that dispersal of Blacks in the name of ethnic diversification, or minimal inclusion in the name of affirmative action, lead to new forms of repression. Let us further pursue the issue of opposition, a point that, as yet, has not received much attention.

Opposition and Reactions

In rejecting the oppressive conditions of everyday life, Black women repeatedly and consistently challenge racial constraints. Everyday opposition against racism is a process that exposes and challenges practices that are often unquestioned by the dominant group but that are unacceptable because of their detrimental implications for Blacks. The specific goals Black women formulate in the struggle against racism reflect general and abstract knowledge of racism. I have noted before (see Chapter 3) that Black women in the Netherlands primarily have ahistorical descriptive knowledge of racism. They conceptualize racism as unequal participation, and their opposition is largely defensive. U.S. Black women conceptualize the problem as race conflict over power. They stress the need to pursue defensive as well as constructive opposition. This distinction between defensive and constructive confrontation is inferred from the data. However, it is analogous to some aspects of Mullard's transformative theory (Mullard, 1984). He argues that opposition develops along three stages, that is, deconstructive, constructive, and reconstructive confrontation. In this process oppressive race relations are dismantled and transformed into nonoppressive social relations within a new social order. Constructive opposition draws on the historical experience and aims to empower the group through control of resources and assertion of alternative values, namely, their own cultural identity. I shall come back to these aims later.

The more Black women internalize specific plans and goals for opposition, the more they will pursue them in everyday life. For many women opposition becomes everyday opposition as it is integrated into the critical way they perceive and experience daily life. Oppositional practices are not simply a reflection of ideas. The nature of opposition is also determined by situational circumstances. The reactions or expected reactions of dominant group members are part of these situational circumstances. Note that, under certain conditions, dominant group members become opposers themselves and may constructively become part of the struggle for a just society. For the purpose of this study two reactions are relevant. Dominant group members often retaliate, in particular when it concerns single opposition against a person with functional authority. Furthermore various forces operate to *marginalize opposition*.

Retaliation: Resentment (4 NL, 6 USA) *and opposing assertiveness* (11 NL, 12 USA). A good illustration of the dynamics of oppression, opposition, retaliation, and reinforced opposition is the following concrete example from the Netherlands about a mother, a social worker (s7), and her 14-year-old son, who challenges the racist practices of his teacher. The woman makes it a point to discuss racism with her sons to stimulate their developing critical attitudes and to give them feedback when they confront racism. This attitude is not typical for other mothers involved in the Dutch project. Earlier I pointed out that Black women in the Netherlands are still fighting the overall denial of racism in society. It may be presumed that, in the next generation, more and more women will include knowledge of racism in the socialization of Black children in the Netherlands. "I found out," she comments, "that the school regularly receives publications from the South African Embassy, very propagandistic stuff." The teacher wants her son to write an essay on "Bantus." "They gave him literature that said very derogatory things about 'Bantus.' That they are inferior and things like that." Her son is the only Black in class: "They wanted him to talk about 'Bantus' because then the South African situation would sound less threatening. That was one of those mechanisms." Her son writes a very critical piece and "for that they deducted points." He was prepared for that reaction, "but he did not care because normally he gets straight As, so that one lower mark would not hurt that much. He was just glad he had his say in his essay."

The mother realizes that, when the school accepts racist propaganda from South Africa and allows a teacher to uncritically use this material in class, there are probably other ways as well that racism is integrated into the everyday reproduction of that school system. After this affair with her son's essay, she took a look at the literature in the school's library.

> I asked my son to bring me all their books on this sort of topic. I read like mad. They had all these obsolete books, dating from even before I was born, with the most outrageous things about Blacks. About any other continent they had at least something positive to say. Not about Black Africa.

This prompts her to question the various publishing houses concerned who are apparently receptive to racist views from authors. She also places racism in that particular school in an explanatory framework. "These children are indoctrinated, they go to the university with these perceptions, and they become professors themselves. No wonder you get all this racism at the university" (s7).

The more the implications of this event are investigated, the more explicit it becomes that transmission of racism in the classroom is embedded in the many institutionalized relations of dominance through which racism operates. Meanwhile her son "constantly criticizes those teachers." They start making complaints about him but he perseveres. "You see, they get these school textbooks, and he notices [racist comments]. The kid thinks this is wrong and he is going to talk about it. But then they say he is becoming a nuisance." We will see later that Whites routinely problematize other opponents of racism as well. The mother realizes that the problem of racism cannot be solved by taking her son out of that school. There is no guarantee that he would not face similar or other forms of racism in another school. Therefore, she thinks of strategies to challenge racism on both an institutional and a political level.

These experiences suggest that everyday opposition is always multidirectional. This summary continues with the experiences of the mother herself. She has been refused jobs more than once because she is considered too assertive. In an application interview for participation in a government-funded training program on women and management, for instance, the interviewer reacts strongly when, upon being questioned, this woman said she would not work for Shell "because of their investments in South Africa." To voice antiracist ideas in such a situation is taking a risk. She has the necessary qualifications for participation in the program and is told she will hear from them "within one week." More than three weeks later, one day before the training programs starts, she finds out that the committee had called additional candidates and selected a " 'Danish woman' to fill the only 'ethnic minority' place they had reserved in the training program" (s7). Here it is relevant to note that it is official practice in the Netherlands to count only immigrants from the colonies (except Euro-Indonesians) and immigrant workers from the Mediterranean as "ethnic minorities."

Many other women talk about dominant group members who abuse functional power to threaten or to get even with opponents of racism. Various of these cases concern school situations. Taking revenge does not necessarily suggest that the perpetrator explicitly aims to defend racist practices. It is often a question of resentment because the Black woman does not accept actions she perceives as racist, whereas the agent may not even see these actions as racist. Some women report that they are threatened with counteractions when they refuse to accept discrimination by a professor. "There was nothing I could do," comments a U.S. student about a professor who systematically gives lower grades to representatives of specific groups. "He does it to women and Howard and I were the first instances of doing it to minorities" (c24). Although the evidence was blatant—he gave different grades for the same point scores—

they all said it is political; you cannot mess with him . . . because if you confront this, you are going to make things harder for yourself. You will never finish here, because there are lots of ways of making sure that you fail something else. There are ways of getting you out of school if you fight it, so let it pass. (c24)

These examples are not meant to deny that in many other, nonracial situations, authorities may abuse functional power to subdue individuals who are dependent on them. It is important to note here, however, that the situationally structured possibilities authorities possess to force others into submission may become a mode of racism.

Protest against unacceptable practices is one part of offensive confrontation; the other part consists of actions that call attention to the problem of racism. "They started calling me a radical" (s7) is a standard reaction when women openly problematize racism. Various women, mostly in the Netherlands, get furious reactions when they try to break through the taboo against discussing Dutch racism. One student who wrote a paper in which she exposed racism in school textbooks they were using that year reports that her supervisor said, "I don't like your tone. There is too much indignation, you are getting to sharp and too emotional." This pathologizing of oppositional perceptions legitimizes subsequent threats: "Either you change it or you can find yourself another supervisor" (s1). Later I will return to the pathologizing of antiracist actions.

Detailed discussion of opposition to a problem that is inherent in the system would require another study. Therefore, the next section focuses on aspects that transcend the particulars of specific situations, practices, and social relations. It deals with *power* and *responsibility*. There is no question that the struggle for justice is effective only when it is carried out as a socially shared responsibility. However, it is relevant to differentiate among various forms of responsibility according to the position of individuals and groups in different social relations. The analysis of everyday racism showed that instantiations of racism in everyday life are structured by the constraints and properties of the situation and the social relations involved. Within these relations racist practices of people in positions of authority are more consequential for Blacks as a group than practices of those who have or can use little or no functional power. Conversely people in positions of authority have access to and can use functional power to oppose and prevent racism more effectively than others.

Support from Black women in positions of authority. Opposition to racism in everyday life must not be seen in situational terms alone. Even when Black women challenge situated practices, they also have to deal implicitly with the larger processes through which specific practices are structured. This explains why various women complain that dealing with racism is tiresome. The structural and ideological relations of society are

favorably predisposed to (re)produce racism, but they form an inflexible and unfavorable climate for action against racism. One Afro-
American woman, a university lecturer, summarizes this as follows
when she discusses the struggle against racism in education:

> We not only have to spend energy to dig out of dusty corners any kind of
> information that is not in the film strips. It's not on the tapes, it's not on
> the records that are available to us. We have to go beyond that, we have
> to work harder to get that, we also don't get any particular strokes for
> that. The opposite is the case. If you come from the place that I come
> from in education, you're seen as a radical, you're seen as a rabble
> rouser, you're seen as a person causing trouble. (c9)

Situations in the educational system are helpful in examining the
role of Black women in positions of authority. As shown earlier Black
students in predominantly White universities are constantly confronted with racism. Therefore, when the word spreads among the students that they can count on the (political) support of specific Black
professors, they know how to use this support.

> I tell the students to confront as long as they have facts to do it. And it
> happens all the time, I cannot tell you the number of students that come
> here in the course of a week with crazy stuff, very disturbing stuff that's
> said right up the street, right [in] their classroom. (c27)

However, in the absence of effective institutionalized practices to
prevent and to oppose racism, the struggle against racism becomes
the sole responsibility of the Blacks involved. "So we have a tremen-
dous job to do. . . . Not only do we service those student categories
[who take Afro-American studies classes] but also the student who is
confronting racial stereotypes, myths, etc. in other classes and helping them to cope with that" (c27).

Black women professionals use the possibilities they have in their
work to oppose racist practices. Black female professors develop alternative education programs; school counselors become "watchdogs"
when it comes to the protection of Black children against racism from
school authorities. Some women choose to work in education: "As a
result of some of my own experiences, not running into counselors
who were receptive to the needs of students of color, who purposely
track students into wrong courses" (c13). However, protecting Black

students and giving the "normal" attention they are denied when working with White professors often induces counteractions from Whites. Even when you "do have a special interest in helping and working with minority students, quite unfortunately, you cannot be narrow in this area, because you end up putting yourself in a very bad predicament politically as well as professionally" (c13). This introduces the problem of repressive tolerance.

Marginalizing opposition. In a system of pluralistic "democracy," physical violence is more and more rejected by the dominant group as an acceptable instrument of repression, because "nice society" (c25), as one woman puts, it does not engage in blatant oppression. The ideology of pluralism contends that oppositional views are relevant to stabilize "democratic" societies. It is assumed that the diversity of opinions and interests has a balancing function. This understanding of "democracy" ignores power differences in the possibilities different groups have to assert their views and to pursue their interests. As a result opposition to the dominant group can be tolerated because confronting views can be managed through marginalization of views, practices, and people attacking the existing order (Marcuse, 1969). Ethnic pluralistic ideology, as noted earlier, is more developed in the Netherlands. However, in the United States similar processes are developing. One example may be found at the universities where "Black," "African-American," and other "ethnic" studies departments were set up throughout the country during the past two decades.

In rare instances the initial motivation for change can be traced to the altruism of top executives. In the United States the boycotts and demonstrations in the 1960s and 1970s impelled reluctant authorities to tolerate a degree of change. I have purposely used the notion of tolerance, because, as we have seen throughout this study, one can hardly say that the dominant group recognizes the relevance of systematic opposition to racism. Instead opposition is repressed through tolerance.

The repressive function of tolerance may be illustrated with an example from academic life, namely, the account of Lorraine H. about the struggle of the Afro-American Studies Center, of which she is the director, to assert Black culture and history despite situational and general counterpressures. Afro-American Studies Centers are a good example of combined defensive and constructive opposition to racism. Afro-American studies develop from perspectives of the oppressed and contribute to the production and use of critical knowledge to bring about social change.

This critical element in the university system is tolerated. The director's position is precarious because of the operating forces to marginalize the center. In turn her precarious position makes her and the center more vulnerable to unfair critique and attacks from others: "Afro-American Study Centers are in a very tenuous position in the universities in this country. There are lots of people who don't want them to exist."

One crucial source of empowerment is the ability to attract the personnel, researchers, and teachers whose work gives maximum support to the organization and the ideas for which it stands. Through *forced dependency* the university keeps control over the center. "We do not have our own faculty. We have been given full-time equivalents, teaching slots." The department "hires the person and makes the decision about tenure. And we have a hard time being able to input in that decision." This makes the center structurally "impotent."

Another way to decrease the influence of Afro-American studies is through *underfinancing*. "All Afro-American Studies Centers" face the same problem. The director confirms this through comparisons of funds available for Afro-American studies and those for other (nonracial) research. One of her coworkers wrote to all of the agencies that fund "ethnic research" and asked who they had funded for the last 10 years and how much money had been made available. The inquiry showed: "There is definitely a drop in the amount of funding that is available for ethnic studies research." When there is less money available to do research, the center's position at the university becomes even more tenuous. If you cannot get funding to meet your research, how can you exist? "There are those kinds of *institutional strains* on an organization like this. You are working under constraints that a number of other people don't operate under." The tenuous position of the center affects the work atmosphere, so that the director has to work under *permanent high-stress* conditions. "You can only do this job for so long." When Lorraine H. goes on to explain how much of her energy is absorbed by her job, she does not compare the amount of work she has with that of a White female or Black male director but with the reverse (and most frequently occurring) situation of the White male who is not involved in (antiestablishment) politics. Two other White people on campus, males, are heads of organized units just like her center. But "they are not politically enveloped in the same way this one is." She recently talked to one of them and "just gave him examples of some of the things we have to confront in a single day and he was just shocked 'cause he does not have to deal with all that and because they are not challenged in the same way."

There are these *"constant challenges* people make to your authority" (italics added). Black women in positions of authority are more critically observed. If they make mistakes reactions occur more quickly and are probably more severe. At the same time, even when they do not make mistakes, it is easy to unfairly accuse them of mistakes. Given the existing racial climate the public is likely to believe "any" accusation. At the time the interview took place, Lorraine H. was involved in a lawsuit by a White employee against her. This secretary "filed grievance against us" because she was disciplined. "She was asked to come on time." Such "personal challenges," says Lorraine H. "they would not make to a White male." There is a "refusal to accept authority" from Black women.

The status of academic work greatly depends on an author's access to publishing agencies, journals, or publishing houses. Afro-American studies as a field of theory and research is often *excluded.*

> As an academic there is an underlying edge of racism in what gets accepted as legitimate work in the field. There would be the belief, I think, among most Black academics that the kind of work that most of us are interested in doing is not the kind of work that is acceptable in mainstream journals.

Lorraine H. can also prove this with her personal experiences, because she publishes both about racial issues and about speech pathology, her initial specialization. She had a "couple of articles in what might be called mainstream journals," but usually she does not "even attempt" to publish in a mainstream journal. "I can publish in mainstream psychology if the emphasis is not necessarily on race."

These accounts demonstrate coherence in the constraints structuring the center and the director's position in the center. Her statements relate the following clusters of marginalization and containment mechanisms:

(1) *Rejection:* People do not accept Black women in positions of authority.

(2) *Rejection:* Lots of people do not want the center to exist.

(3) *Opposition:* The center is being challenged.

(4) *Control:* The center is politically enveloped; they cannot appoint their own faculty; the center cannot make tenure decisions.

(5) *Exclusion:* Funding agencies are spending less on ethnic issues. *Consequence:* The Afro-American Studies Center is in a tenuous position. Anxiety about getting enough funds to survive is a constant strain. Managing the center is very hectic and stressful, you cannot do it for too long a period.

(6) *Exclusion:* Ethnic issues are not always granted academic status. Publishers of high standing may be less inclined to accept a book on ethnic issues. Mainstream journals do not have much ethnic content. Papers on ethnic issues from Black academics are not readily accepted by mainstream journal editors.

Consequence: Black academics who work on ethnic issues have less chance of getting tenure because their work does not get published. The struggle for recognition is a constant battle.

These fragmented representations of opposition in everyday life are far from complete. However, it may be inferred from these experiences that this struggle is energy draining, in particular when Blacks are left with sole responsibility for solving problems of racism themselves. The struggle of the Afro-American Studies Center takes place on both cultural and structural levels. It involves the development and assertion of Afro-American values and perspectives and the structural empowerment of Afro-American influences in education. Here special attention was paid to the structural undermining of the center. Another crucial part of the conflict is ideological. The frequent rejection by mainstream journals of manuscripts developed from the perspective of Blacks is symptomatic of the larger ideological conflict over the definition of race and ethnic relations. This introduces the third section of this chapter.

THE AGENDA OF THE AGENDA: PROBLEMATIZING THOSE WHO PROBLEMATIZE RACISM

Ideology is a terrain of race struggle (Mullard, 1985b). It is relevant to give attention to the definition of reality, because it is here that the dominated contest dominant definitions of structural and cultural power relations in society. In this section I will demonstrate that three combined ideological forces operate against oppositional definitions of racial reality. First, there is an overall denial of racism. I noted earlier that pluralistic ideology and the norm of tolerance reinforce the denial of racial and ethnic conflict. One of the most problematic consequences of the ideology of tolerance is that this includes *tolerance of racism.* Given the prominence of the Dutch norm of tolerance, it is not surprising that repressive tolerance pervades the lives of

Black women in the Netherlands more thoroughly than is the case with Black women in the United States. Second, tolerance of racism is legitimized by discrediting and, more specifically, *pathologizing* those who problematize racism. Third, both these processes, denial and pathologizing, are structured by, and in turn reinforce, what I call *cognitive detachment* or ideological marginalization of Blacks, which is the failure to understand the world from the point of view of Blacks. It symbolizes indifference to oppression.

Cognitive Detachment or Failing To Take Responsibility

> I gave a paper about Black and White relations. Afterwards, I overheard a fellow student say that "it was it was just like her to talk about a subject like that." You see, then I get mean. I said sure it is always me, because you would never ever come with a subject like that. (s24)

The woman quoted here exposes an important element of tolerance. She can have her say about race relations as long as she does not expect that others problematize racism too or expect that others take responsibility. Indeed it is "just like her" to talk about race relations because it is not like "them" (White students) to get involved. This has to do not only with Eurocentrism. The dominant group believes that their version of reality and the "truth" is right and objective. As a result, "they are incapable of seeing the world from another point of view" (s4), and "they don't see the racism that is there" (c14). This blindness to racism plays a role in many situations. Therefore, dominant group members will be inclined to ignore racism (5 NL, 4 USA). Women discuss this problem in particular with reference to education. "We had one lesson about Suriname, and it was stated that Suriname is an underdeveloped country. Yet, the causes and most of all the role of the Netherlands were not mentioned" (s1). Other women report that, in textbooks and courses about "ethnic minorities," "they make all kinds of statements which imply that racism is not an important issue" (s7). Whites generally *fail to feel responsible for existing race and ethnic relations* (5 NL, 6 USA). "Like the students in multicultural class," says a lecturer from the United States, "who will say why do you have to talk about this stuff all the time. Why can't you just accept the way things are" (c9). As a result various Black women in the Netherlands feel it is "their duty" (s24) to make Whites more aware of racism. In the United States reactions to the dominant group's indifference to racial oppression are more likely to resemble that of the school counselor who feels she has to act like a "watchdog for all Black and brown kids at the school . . . so that they [the Whites] are not going to run over these kids" (c12). Indifference about Black issues is even more pronounced in the case where a Black woman is the only coworker and finds that "you are seen as the expert on Blacks" (c13) and that "everything that has to do with Blacks is shoved onto me" (s10). Clearly this must be placed against the background of ethnization processes I discussed earlier.

At first sight overemphasis on ethnic difference, which underlies ethnization, seems to contradict the dominant group's feeling indifferent or failing to take responsibility. However, there is no contradiction when we find that control, which is the implied goal of ethnization processes, is not the same as responsibility. Solo or token Blacks are tolerated in some situations because they can be controlled, but dominant group members are seldom motivated to understand the social world from the point of view of Black colleagues, clients, or other Blacks. As a result White colleagues are not interested in Black women's expertise as an opportunity to gain more critical knowledge of race relations and to make this a shared responsibility. On the contrary, when understanding of the perspectives and interests of Blacks does not increase control, the "few Black and minority faculty members are asked to serve on anything and to be everything," while dominant group members maintain a White orientation. Experiences of other women confirm that "ethnic" information is gained to increase control over Blacks and not for the benefit of Blacks. This problem is even more complicated when, in the Netherlands, dominant group members "claim to mean well" (s27).

Disqualifying Opponents of Racism

As a result of cognitive detachment, dominant group members do not understand, neither are they motivated to understand, the critique of Black women. This failure to understand and to feel responsible for racism is legitimized by *questioning the perspectives and personalities* of opponents of racism. This means that the struggle against racism is *depoliticized*. Antiracist perspectives are rejected by disqualifying not the perspective but the person who conveys these views. Thus Whites who have antiracist views are problematized in the same way (van Dijk, 1991). In dominant thinking Blacks are *unreliable* (12 NL, 8 USA) as a source of information about race relations in society. Their suggestions to improve race relations are not accepted, which is rationalized with the argument that Blacks are "partial" (s3). Of course Blacks are partial when they oppose racism. However, this argument obscures the fact that, while they question the integrity of Blacks, Whites legitimize their own ideologically saturated definitions of reality.

Several women confirm that accusations of bias are used to question their competence and integrity as professionals. This often happens as follows: When working together on projects involving Black clients, the White colleagues redefine their Black colleagues as Blacks. Subsequently Black colleagues are put on the same level as the clients. Rosa N. explained how the argument of partiality was used to prevent her from making a professional judgment about Black patients. Situations like these are repeatedly confirmed by others. An educational counselor, a solo Black hired to advise on "ethnic" aspects of education, describes how the implicit accusation of partiality operates in meetings with White colleagues and representatives of Black and other immigrant organizations. If a representative of one of the organizations, "for instance, a Moroccan" happens to make a sharp point that touches upon things the Black counselor had discussed earlier with her White colleagues, the colleagues "start looking" at her "as if [she] had been briefing the Moroccan beforehand about it" (s4).

This situation contains various forms of racism. First, it is apparently believed that a Moroccan is too stupid to think of intelligent arguments. Second, the Black woman is accused of disloyalty as a professional, while Whites do not normally question their own integrity as professionals when they work with White clients. Third, the situation is restructured through race: The Blacks are lumped together and the Black professional is redefined as a member of the opposite party in the negotiations. Conversely, when Black professionals are in the position to make judgments about Whites, the Whites may try to neutralize this functional power by accusing the Black woman of bias. Several U.S. women gave examples of this in school, as when a student may insinuate it was "because I was Black and he was White I was not signing his credential. That it was reverse racism" (c9).

The problematization of Blacks who problematize racism is even more fierce when it concerns the definition of racism. Whites accuse Blacks of *oversensitivity about racism* (4 NL, 2 USA). Obviously it is in the interest of the dominant group to mitigate racism because acknowledgment questions racial privileges and calls for responsibility to act. When dominant group members are generally not motivated to understand reality from the point of view of the oppressed, they have neither knowledge nor motivation to comprehend racism. It is not surprising, therefore, that they feel Black women are "splitting hairs" (s12), that they are "exaggerating" (s27), unfairly "jumping to conclusions" (c14), and generally being "oversensitive" (c25) about race.

Tolerance of Racism

These examples demonstrate that the dominant group feels their version of reality is superior and nonbiased and least of all biased in favor of Whites. Indeed the women encounter racism although the dominant group "does not necessarily see it that way" (c13). Most women agree that "Whites would not see the racism that is there" (c14). The reinforcement of their nondiscriminatory self-image leads to further *reluctance to deal with racism* (10 NL, 5 USA) in general *or to admit racism* (5 NL, 8 USA). Because the Dutch have strongly internalized the idea that they are a tolerant people, which they probably translate as a tendency not to discriminate, they are more reluctant than Whites in the United States to acknowledge that racism is a Dutch problem as well. They even *feel offended* (7 NL, 2 USA) when they are confronted with "their" racism. Pointing out racism is seen as an *accusation* and, therefore, as an *offense* to the other party's personality. This leads to strong emotions, which subsequently makes it almost impossible for Black women to confront perpetrators with the racist implications of their behavior.

A good illustration of this is the following fragment in which a Black woman got "real mad" and said to the other party, a Dutch woman: "That is a racist comment you just made," upon which the Dutch woman "got very emotional" because she was "not a racist" (s1). Indeed several Black women in the Netherlands feel they had better "not use the word *racism,* not even the word *discrimination*" when talking to Whites, because "it stops the discussion. You scare people off" (s4). "You end up twisting yourself into all kinds of impossible positions so that you do not step on their toes" (s9), and "How dare you call that discrimination. Don't you realize you are hurting people!" (s8). In other words, opponents of racism are accused of victimizing innocent Whites. These arguments suggest that the Dutch definition of racism as a moral issue represses opposition. The problem is reversed: Racism is not the problem; people "who go around accusing" others of racism are the problem.

The data suggest that in the United States, where the issue of racism is not taboo, reactions to Black women who point out racism are not as emotionally charged. Rather than using emotional blackmail (you are hurting me), dominant group members deny the extra knowledge and perceptiveness Black women have about racism and claim that it is the intention that counts. They either go on "denying and protesting too much" (c15), which lets you know that they refuse to admit it, or they might "look you dead in the face and say 'no, that is not what it means at all. You cannot read my action' " (c19). As I noted earlier the claim of nonracial intentions is not relevant when the implications of the actions are "telling you what they mean" (c19).

Various U.S. women point out another strategy of denial, namely, ignoring the racist dimension of the situations. "They threw the egg at me," reports the 8-year-old Black girl living in a White neighborhood where there have been a few racial encounters "because I am Black." Says the White neighbor: "No, no, no, they are just stupid kids, that's why they threw the egg" (c12). Even when Whites shout racial slurs, the racist dimension of these slurs may be ignored. A clear example is the case of two roommates who are giggling and laughing in their room; it is already late. Apparently they are waking up another student. He comes upstairs and threatens them with a bat. "Then he said something to the effect that 'you don't need to be here anyway, you need to go back where you came from.' Then we got into this real racial argument." The resident attendant (RA) who is called in ignores the racial threat and says: "You really do not have to make such a fuss about it" (s6). But the mother of one of the students backs her daughter in pressing charges. There is a court hearing on campus, and the White student is banned from student housing.

As this example shows the RA ignores the racist element of the situation and only refers to the problem of how to deal with a fight between one student who accuses other students of making too much noise. This denial of racism is exactly the reason that another student does not even try to talk to a White RA about a case of racism. This student is accused of having slammed a door, thereby allegedly scratching a White girl's record that is playing. Furiously the girl starts banging on her door, calling her a "stupid nigger who looks like an ape anyway" (c7). The Black girl involved does not want to go to her own RA, who is White and might have thought: "The main problem was the banging on my door and that she called me names, but not really think about what she called me. That is why I went to the Black RA" (c7).

How do dominant group members react when they witness racist events?

> Halloween time, we're talking four years ago, kids showed up dressed like Ku Klux Klan. . . . Complained to the principal, who could not understand why we were so upset. So we took the whole year and sensitized that fool about why we were so upset, White parents as well as Black parents, which was important. So the next year when some kids came, they handled it very differently, they called their parents and they talked about it. (c27)

Sometimes dominant group members object to everyday racism, but this is usually not the case. Note, for example, that while the previously mentioned student was threatening the two roommates with a bat, "all the other girls in the dorm, who were all White, came out of their rooms and they looked, and they all went back to their room and closed the door. Nobody called anybody for help" (c5). Other women from both countries confirm that dominant group members not only deny racism but often tolerate it when they see it. They generally *fail to take a stand against racism* (12 NL, 10 USA).

Usually the Black woman stands alone in the situation. Rosa N. showed that her colleagues are not even willing to speak out against racism when she explicitly asks for support. In this final section of the discussion on ideological conflict, situations where dominant group members remained silent about racism or mitigated the situation are looked at in more detail. Many of these situations are similar in the United States and in the Netherlands. However, different contexts and presuppositions must be considered to understand the meaning of nonaction in each country.

In the Netherlands nonaction is structured by the taboo on racism, by the reluctance to confront others in communicative situations, and by the virtual absence of sanctions against racial discrimination. Moral disapproval will usually not be expressed directly to the offender, and there are no effective antidiscrimination laws and policies. Therefore, nonaction is not necessarily a question of explicit consent to racism but (partly) due to *inhibition to confront*. The implications though are nevertheless that nonaction gives implicit approval to the situation.

In the United States nonaction is more likely to be structured by the idea that racism is an issue to be dealt with by the courts and through policies. This suggests that the idea underlying nonaction is indifference: It is *none of my business*. Note that these different attitudes are not exclusive in either of the countries.

The Dutch situation is important because it demonstrates the repressive impact of pure tolerance on Black women. That is, the norm of tolerance legitimizes nonaction against racism, even when its damaging effects on society, and in particular on Blacks, are evident. As a result of tolerance the offenders are supported in their racist practices. This is illustrated by two examples. The selected cases purposely concern blatant racism to avoid the problem of whether dominant group members did not react because they were "unaware" of the racist implications.

The first case concerns a student (s23) who tells: "When they [fellow students] talk to me I don't so much get the idea that they find Blacks inferior or anything." However, when one particular student, a South African, is among them and makes "discriminating remarks about the Brown race, they just sit there quietly nodding yes. And I get the feeling, like yeah, they play up to everyone. In such a discussion, they still feel closer to him than me, so they don't contradict him." To understand the implications of this story, it must be emphasized that in the Netherlands there is no taboo against openly rejecting apartheid. On the contrary, there is (almost) a taboo against defending apartheid. Therefore, it is unlikely that the other students really agree with the South African student. The Black woman indicates this by introducing the story by saying that normally fellow students do not treat her as if they feel superior. But when the South African student joins in and starts with racist talk, he appeals to White group membership. Whether intended or not the students consent to this appeal by refraining from confrontation. Given the norm that one has to be tolerant of different views, the students seem to feel inhibited to confront this South African student so as to avoid disharmony and fights. This explanation of nonaction is confirmed by other data. In van Dijk's (1987a, p. 344) research Whites explained that they often felt embarrassed about racism from other group members but that they were reluctant to voice their disagreement for fear of causing trouble.

This tolerance of racism is dramatized in the following situation of a Black woman who has a drink in a restaurant with (White) members of an organization against racism. The refusal of the waiter to serve the Black woman (i.e., racism operating before their very eyes) literally paralyzes the whole group. The group talks about it, that this is racism; they feel embarrassed, but nobody confronts the waiter. They all seem to wait for the Black woman herself to solve the problem. The situation is presented in detail because it demonstrates clearly how dominant group members literally fail to act against racism. Whereas the antiracist goals of the organization unite its Black and White members, underlying *racialized relations are actualized* by the waiter when "the Whites were all asked what they were having, but when he came to me, the man forgot to ask what I wanted" (s7). The Black woman thinks they may not have noticed, but,

> They said yes, he didn't ask you. And then the man came back for the orders, and he went through the whole list, and the woman next to me didn't want anything, and he asked her very explicitly, you really don't want anything? And again, he didn't see me.

The group, however, feels *inhibited from confronting.* This becomes even worse when one of them asks the Black woman: "Don't you want something to drink?" and the woman responds, "'What do you think? Of course I'd like something!' But that's as far as it went." Apparently the group does *not want to cause any trouble.* "They were really at a loss—imagine, this is a work group on racism!" The woman goes on to explain that the group *failed to take responsibility* as Whites to speak out against racism of another group member: "At the moment that the man said, 'Anything else?' one of them should have said, 'Haven't you forgotten someone?' Because he directed his words to them, not to me" (s7).

The different nature of nonaction in a racist situation in the United States was clearly expressed in the example of the two Black students who were threatened with a bat. The other students looked out and then went back into their rooms because nobody thought it was any of their business.

THE STRUCTURE OF EVERYDAY RACISM

In the course of this chapter it was shown that cultural and structural domains of conflict are related and reproduced through marginalizing, legitimizing, and containment processes. These relations are schematized in Figure 6.1. The far left column shows that the three domains

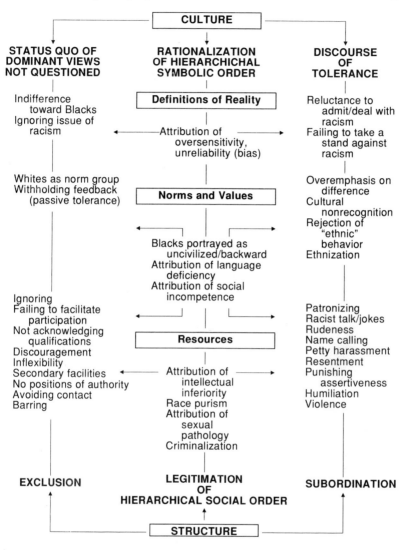

Figure 6.1. The structure of everyday racism

of racial and ethnic conflict are maintained through marginalization
of Blacks and centralization of Whites. We have seen that the major
hidden current in cultural conflict concerns the assumption that

dominant norms and values are superior and that, therefore, the dominant culture is not questioned. Dominant group members do not gain knowledge of social reality from the (critical) point of view of the dominated. They generally fail to feel responsible for existing race and ethnic relations, a condition that must be distinguished from interference in race and ethnic relations to increase the control of Blacks. Conversely Black women are submerged in White culture transmitted by the media, in education, and through personal experiences. They share with the dominant group general knowledge of norms of acceptable behavior in everyday situations (situation scripts). In addition a vital strategy of survival for Black women is to acquire metaknowledge of the dominant culture. Their knowledge system includes alternative situation scripts, or scenarios of racism, which they apply in everyday life to comprehend racial experiences.

Black women's perceptions of race and ethnic relations expose the Whitecentric nature of the dominant culture and the exclusive mechanisms that keep dominant culture central in the fabric of the system. One of these mechanisms is passive tolerance, a process based on the presupposition that cultural influences from "the other" must remain marginal. This process is reinforced by general reluctance to change. This may be inferred from the large range of obstacles Black women encounter in everyday life. These include White in-group preference in the distribution of resources, economic exploitation, petty harassment of Black women, discouragement of their aspirations, and refusal to acknowledge the positive contributions they make. The normative profile for leading positions, for students of higher education, and for functions that give access to power remains to be formulated for Black (women). So far it is still tuned to White (men).

The far right column of Figure 6.1 shows that repression of (potential) opposition is an instrument in cultural and structural areas of conflict. There is a virtual lack of institutionalized support to stimulate retention of Black culture, and assimilative pressures coerce Black women to adapt. At the same time the dominant group is reluctant to deal with racism. Racism is generally tolerated when, in the Netherlands, the norm of cultural tolerance is consciously and systematically pursued. The experiences of Black women demonstrate that tolerance is by definition repressive because people assume that basic norms and values of the dominant group must be accepted. This again links repressive forces to oppressive forces because active tolerance operates as a marginalizing mechanism through isolation of "ethnic" elements within Dutch institutions.

The U.S. variant is affirmative action. Many Black women with higher education in the United States have benefited from affirmative action policies. They agree that affirmative action is necessary to ameliorate the effects of past discrimination, because "you could be the most intelligent person, but Blacks were just not accepted. If not for affirmative action I would never have had the chance to go to a good university" (c4). One of the hidden currents of affirmative action policies, however, has been the negation of its cultural implications. Under conditions of monocultural norms and values, it is virtually impossible to preclude that Blacks are stigmatized as less qualified (Jones, 1981). When asked about tokenism, many Black women testify: "They will not hire another Black person unless they fit some criteria like affirmative action" (c21). This suggests that U.S. state management of racial difference through affirmative action reinforced the legitimacy of the dominant culture. In the United States "race" was meant to be included in public institutions when affirmative action policies were introduced. However, because Black women are often included as solos or as tokens, they can hardly exert any influence on a cultural level. In some circumstances Black cultural elements are tolerated because they can be kept structurally isolated. This was demonstrated in more detail by the case of an Afro-American Studies Center.

Pluralistic ideas and the increasing importance of tolerance as an instrument of control represent largely covert and often subtle processes of racism. The implied hierarchical order of knowledge and values is hidden behind practices that are presented as "good intentions" and explicit acknowledgment that "ethnicity" or "race" must be included. At the same time other, more blatant mechanisms, such as intimidation and retaliation, which are meant to coerce subordination, are tolerated. As a result Black women who interact with Whites on a daily basis are systematically harassed, threatened, ridiculed, insulted, and generally discouraged from moving from margin to center positions.

Finally, the middle column of Figure 6.1 forms the cement of both oppressive and repressive processes. The oppression of Blacks is legitimized by the denigration of their culture in dominant ideology. The constant creation of obstacles and subsequent marginalization of Black women throughout the system is rationalized in ideological constructions attributing to Blacks biological, social, and cultural deficiencies. In other words, Black women are considered unfit to participate "normally" in this society. The accounts demonstrate that Black women, through the development and routine application of knowledge of racism, constantly contest situations and practices that are seen as "normal" by the dominant group because of their oppressive implications. Acknowledgment of this critique can only mean that fundamental norms, values, and the existing social order must be questioned and subjected to change. The dominant group, therefore, marginalizes these oppositional views and portrays antiracist perceptions as too emotional or otherwise pathological.

This representation of relations between the various forms and dimensions of racism has implications for the struggle against racism. The structure of everyday racism shows that the main areas of racial and ethnic conflict are intricately related. Racism must be combated in all these spheres of social system. The schema of everyday racism can be used to (roughly) assess possible implications of specific modes of intervention in race and ethnic relations.

Consider, for example, the Dutch situation. Dutch dominant discourse conceptualized racial and ethnic oppression as a problem of ethnic difference. It is no wonder that interventions developed in that framework led primarily to increased control of "ethnic groups," because the system remained fundamentally Whitecentric. Not only are Blacks and other immigrants subjected to combined forces of cultural assimilation and "ethnization," the exclusive focus on the cultural domain diverts attention from basic issues, such as the virtual absence of action against massive discrimination in the labor market. I noted before that it is now a point of public discussion in the Netherlands whether the government must intervene to encourage "positive action" programs. The U.S. experience suggests that so-called positive action policies will reinforce ethnization as long as essential elements of the dominant norms and values continue to be in contradiction to the struggle of Blacks for cultural assertion and empowerment.

It also may be inferred from the U.S. example that violence and other forms of repression used to subordinate Blacks have not been addressed seriously. Recent developments have demonstrated that the dismantling of affirmative action has been reinforced by an enormous increase of racial violence in the 1980s (Reed, 1989). These and other arguments underscore that opposition to racism must be multidimensional, because successes on one front, whether small or even ambiguous, can be neutralized and countered through the continuation of racial and ethnic conflict in other domains.

7

Conclusions

The empirical data presented in this study defy those perceptions of racism that only recognize as problematic its extreme manifestations. Neither is it correct to address discrimination in specific sectors without including the whole complex of racial structures and ideologies in which they are embedded. In short if we should ignore the permeation of racism throughout the entire social system, if we should fail to perceive its integration into the routine practices of everyday life, we would miss the point, and we would leave racism intact. While this view of racism is gradually being accepted by other social scientists as well, the extent to which racism systematically marks Black women's everyday experiences has seldom been demonstrated in so much detail. With many illustrations the women have made clear that one cannot deal with everyday racism without overturning practices and situations that are too often experienced as "normal" by the dominant group.

This study is more than a Black female view of racism. I have tried to integrate theory with research and research with its political implications. The perceptions and experiences of Black women were instrumental in demonstrating that the concept of everyday racism has general relevance in race relations theory because it has wide applicability. It proved to be a useful instrument for exposing the real-life experiences of racism in both Dutch and U.S. society. By analyzing the everyday experiences of Black women, local similarities as well as structural differences in the way racism operates in the two countries were revealed. The concept of everyday racism can also be applied to the specific experiences of Black women as structured by racist and ethnicist notions of gender, namely, "gendered racism."

THE EXPERIENTIAL BASIS OF
KNOWLEDGE OF EVERYDAY RACISM

One of the most consequential conclusions of this study, both in a political and in a social scientific sense, pertains to the idea of experience.
By marrying cognitive insights with structural theories, micro experiences could be related to macro theories of racism. Moreover it has been
shown that *knowledge of everyday racism is based on the understanding
of its experience.* The notion of experience was given a broader meaning
than that of witnessed events alone. Racism is also experienced cognitively. Those who define themselves as members of a racially dominated
group are affected by the knowledge of the general features of racism and
the way processes of racism restrict the goals and opportunities of one's
group. Black women's knowledge of racism always includes comparisons with experiences of other Blacks or with the experiences of Whites.
This is not surprising because, as it was shown, everyday racism is not
limited to personal experiences. It is experienced in multidimensional
ways, in personal encounters, and vicariously through racism experienced by other Blacks. Everyday racism is also mediated by discourse
and practices affecting larger (sub)groups of Blacks.

Black women's perceptions of racism are an important contribution
to our understanding of racism. Their reconstructions of experiences
confirmed other theories of political cognition. I conceptualized
knowledge of racism as political cognition. To the accounts of these
Black women I applied the insight, gained from social cognition theory, that people who are politically involved become more knowledgeable about political issues than those who are not. After having
redefined "involvement" with racism as the "problematization" of
racism, I demonstrated that Black women who are used to problematizing racism develop a more complex understanding of racism.
Thus this study defies popular views in which Black perceptions of
racism are dismissed as just "biased." On the contrary Black women
who problematize racism, in the assessment of specific events, become more sensitive to information that may be either consistent or
inconsistent with the hypothesis that racism is involved. Among other
things this characteristic distinguishes their knowledgeable perceptions from prejudiced perceptions, which would only be receptive to
hypothesis-consistent information.

Comprehension of racism presupposes critical knowledge of the
dominant culture. Because Black women have become sensitive to the

nuances of the ways dominant group members relate to each other, as opposed to the way they often relate to Blacks, Black women recognize racism even in its covert manifestations. Conversely dominant group members usually lack sensitivity to racism in everyday life. They have little understanding of the problem because they are not confronted, on a regular basis, with critical views of race and ethnic relations, such as those shared by Black women. This is not surprising given that, in both the United States and the Netherlands, knowledge of racism is scarcely included in the formal systems of transmission of knowledge, namely, the media and education.

THE MODE OF ACQUISITION HAS AN IMPACT ON KNOWLEDGE OF RACISM

The mode of knowledge acquisition is a crucial determinant of the degree of understanding of racism. I made a distinction between direct and indirect modes of knowledge acquisition. Direct transmission—that is, communication of information about racism—relates empirical data (contemporary racism) to models of change and order (race relations in the past and visions of an alternative social order). This mode of acquisition stimulates reflective thinking about racism. Indirect modes of knowledge acquisition involve inferences from repeated personal experiences, which do not lead to the development of explanatory "theories."

It was shown that most U.S. Black women acquired knowledge of racism directly, through socialization in the family, community involvement in the civil rights movement, media reports of the Black Power movement, and, as some of the younger women reported, Black studies programs in college. In addition they learned from practical experiences with racism in integrated schools. Those who grew up in the U.S. South knew from an early age that they belonged to an oppressed group. Most Black women in the Netherlands grew up in Suriname, where, due to cultural colonialism, the Dutch and the Netherlands were idealized rather than criticized. They started to problematize racism after they had migrated to the Netherlands. Black women in the Netherlands acquired knowledge of racism by inference, from personal experiences, and through comparisons with the experiences of other Blacks. As a result they acquired predominantly descriptive knowledge of racism, whereas U.S. Black women have descriptive as well as explanatory knowledge.

Keeping in mind that this study is based on the experiences of a select group of women, the most important difference between the general knowledge systems of the women in the two countries may be summarized as follows: In the Netherlands there is a virtual lack of historical knowledge of Dutch racism and of the Black liberation struggle. This is not surprising when we consider that ethnic pluralistic thinking predominates in Dutch common sense as well as in available publications about race and ethnic relations. These pluralistic ideologies are ahistorical, idealize cultural tolerance, and generally deny the existence of racism.

It was tentatively proposed that an elaborate system of general knowledge of racism includes notions about at least the following aspects of the problem:

(1) Abstract notions about the nature of contemporary racism. Women in both countries agreed that racism is pervasive, that it is ubiquitous, and that it can be expected in all social relations that are at the same time race relations.

(2) Notions about the agents of racism. The women agreed about the decisive role of primary agents (dominant group) but many also pointed to the problem of secondary agents (members of the dominated groups).

(3) Conceptualizations of structuring forces of racism in a historical perspective. This dimension of knowledge requires explanatory knowledge. With illustrations from the data it was shown that many U.S. Black women were explicitly informed by family members that the history of race relations is marked by White aggression to "keep Blacks in their place." Compared with Black women in the Netherlands, those in the United States were more consistent in pointing out the impact of class factors on racism. Class differences are mitigated in both Dutch and U.S. dominant ideology, but the neglect of class factors by Black women in the Netherlands cannot be explained completely by differences in general knowledge of racism. Compared with that of the Netherlands, U.S. racism operates more explicitly and thoroughly through class relations. U.S. Black women were also more explicit about the way racism operates through gender. They resent police violence against Black men. As mothers, partners, and sisters they feel the threat of male-directed racial violence every day. Racial violence also occurs in the Netherlands, but it is as yet not part of the everyday experiences of this specific group of Black women.

(4) General knowledge of racism includes notions of the major "macro" mechanisms through which racism is reproduced. This

category of knowledge is largely the same in both countries. It consists predominantly of descriptive knowledge about marginalizing, problematizing, and repressive forces. The most important differences pertain to continued segregation in the United States and the prevalence of cultural assimilation in the Netherlands.

(5) Conceptions of strategies and goals in the struggle against racism reflect the differences in explanatory knowledge Black women in both countries apply. Black women in the Netherlands explain racism as Dutch ignorance about Blacks and about racism. This reflects a certain degree of internalization of the discourse of tolerance and "good intentions." However, the problem is much worse than mere ignorance. The Dutch generally refuse to listen to talk of racism because this does not fit their self-image as a tolerant people. When we consider that it is a Dutch tradition to take pride in the value of tolerance, one can imagine that there is massive resistance by the Dutch to admitting that Dutch society is permeated with racism. The denial of racism in the Netherlands is so pervasive that Black women get "stuck" in a defensive stage of opposition. They keep fighting to assert their version of the truth because, when even the very fact of racism is denied, one cannot pursue practical policies against racism. In other words, the denial of racism is an effective instrument of repression: It denies the very legitimacy of Black liberation struggles.

U.S. AND DUTCH RACISM: VARIANTS OF THE SAME PROBLEM

The results of this study oppose the Dutch myth that racism is a structural problem in the United States but not in the Netherlands. Few manifestations of racism are unique to the United States. This is consistent with the fact that anti-Black racism is ideologically rooted in the same Euro-American value system and in the same historical relations between Europeans and Africans. There are, however, some differences in the prevalence of specific manifestations of racism in the United States and in the Netherlands. Due to different historical, economic, and political developments, racism in the United States, more explicitly so than in the Netherlands, is expressed as "racial" racism. Ideologies of race purism in the United States reinforce social segregation and converge with class and gender differences in the system. In the Netherlands more advanced ideas of "pluralistic democracy" render White supremacist ideas obsolete. Although racial characteristics are still a distinct category of differentiation in Dutch ideology, "racial" racism merges with cultural racism (ethnicism). This process expresses the gradual restructuring of racism from race hierarchies to cultural hierarchies. The decreasing importance of "racial" racism is accompanied by the emergence of ideological instruments of repression, especially those resulting from the ideal of cultural tolerance.

The different nature of the ideologies and politics of racism in the two countries may also be inferred from the nature of repression. U.S. Black women experience more aggressive forms of repression (physical violence, petty harassment). Those in the Netherlands are confronted with nonaggressive forms of repression (patronizing, active tolerance, casual racist talk, and joking). The sophistication of nonaggressive instruments of repression becomes clear when we consider that the norm of nonaggression is used as a symbolic weapon against opponents of racism. The experiences of Black women in the Netherlands demonstrate that opponents of racism are accused of violating the norms of tolerance when they "harass innocent and benevolent" Whites with "accusations" of racism. In other words, repressive tolerance delegitimizes the very idea of resistance.

MAIN FEATURES OF EVERYDAY RACISM

One major thesis of this study is that the traditional distinction between institutional and individual racism is misleading and insufficient to explain the (re)production of racial inequality in society. The concept of "everyday" was introduced to cross the boundaries between structural and interactional approaches to racism and to link details of micro experiences to the structural and ideological context in which they are shaped. The analysis of these experiences has shown that everyday racism does not exist as single events but as a complex of cumulative practices. Specific instances acquire meaning only in relation to the sum total of other experiences of everyday racism. Another major feature of everyday racism is that it involves racist practices that infiltrate everyday life and become part of what is seen as "normal" by the dominant group. Analogous to everyday life, everyday racism is heterogeneous in its manifestations but at the same time unified by repetition of similar practices.

In both countries instantiations of everyday racism in the lives of Black women can be reduced to three fundamental mechanisms, the firm interlocking of which makes it hard to escape the impact of racism in everyday life. These main mechanisms of racism are (a) marginalization, that is, the perpetuation of the status quo of the dominant norms and values and the creation of artificial ceilings to the progress of Black women. These processes are rationalized by (b) the problematization of Black women's perceptions of social reality, their cultural experiences, and their social and intellectual qualifications. The dominant group considers Black women to be "incompetent" to function at the same level as Whites. Black women challenge these views, are constantly alert to racial injustice, and work out strategies to challenge and oppose racism. Opposition is frustrated by (c) containment strategies of the dominant group. Through intimidation, patronizing, pressure to assimilate, cultural isolation, and the overall denial of racism, the dominant group tries to prevent or counter opposition to racism. Because racism is inherent in the nature of the social order, Black women remain locked in oppressive relations even when, on a local level, there may be small victories in the struggle against racism.

THE STRUCTURE OF ACCOUNTS OF RACISM

Accounts proved to be very useful in conceptualizing these multiple expressions and experiences of racism. The use of accounts of racism also has other implications. Accounts are not just stories about racist events, they contain elements of knowledge about racism. Because accounts of racism are hardly ever taken seriously in the dominant social sciences, close attention has never been paid to their nature. Therefore, I developed a method to reconstruct, from accounts of racism, the underlying interpretive heuristics and knowledge categories Black women use to interpret and evaluate specific situations as racist situations. Contrary to popular beliefs that Blacks are oversensitive about racism, it was demonstrated that accounts of personal experiences of racism are not ad hoc stories. They have a specific structure based on rational inferences from knowledge about rules and norms of acceptable behavior, knowledge about acceptable reasons for unacceptable behavior, and knowledge about the structures and processes of racial and ethnic dominance in society.

The core of personal accounts of racism consists of the (a) context (setting, participants) and (b) complications (unacceptable practices). These are hypothetically (c) evaluated as forms of racism, when the implications of these practices are consistent with general knowledge of the mechanisms of racism and when plausible alternative explanations are not available. In accounts of covert racism it is likely that additional (d) argumentation is presented to support the hypothesis of racism. These supportive arguments are based on various heuristics of inference and comparison and involve, among other things, reference to general knowledge of racism, to experiences of other Blacks, to knowledge of other racist events, to "normal" procedures in nonracial situations, and to experiences with other Whites. Finally, the (e) decision category gives insight into the effectiveness of everyday strategies, reactions, and actual opposition to racism.

MICROCOSM OF EVERYDAY RACISM EMBEDDED IN PERSONAL BIOGRAPHY

In real life different dimensions of experiences of racism merge. New experiences of racism activate memories of previous experiences of racism and influence one's expectations about the future. I have demonstrated how this process operates in real life by analyzing in detail one case story, involving the only Black medical doctor affiliated with a modern Dutch hospital complex. Her account defies the view that racism comes from ignorant and frustrated Whites. Her experiences on the job are pervaded with racism from the "elite," that is, fellow doctors. The story features sharply the Dutch nature of racism. She has to resist constant assimilative pressures and a suffocating degree of ideological repression. Not only is there a virtual lack of motivation among her colleagues to give feedback when she protests against racist comments and jokes from supervisors or other colleagues, it is held against her that she refuses to accept racism. She is accused of oppressing Whites with her critical attitude.

The woman contests dominant norms and values in which ethnic difference is overemphasized and by definition conceptualized in hierarchical terms. She fights all kinds of obstacles, such as colleagues and supervisors who consistently underestimate, reject, and pathologize her while systematically undermining the professional authority that allows her to do her job adequately. Finally, the analysis of everyday racism in the life of this woman illustrates that a solo position hardly allows opposition. The political implications of this become clear when we consider that dispersal of Blacks as solos or tokens in the name of ethnic diversification (in the Netherlands) or minimal inclusion in the name of affirmative action (in the United States) reinforce repression of resistance.

RACISM IS A CONFLICT-MAINTAINING PROCESS

The general differences between racism in the two systems are created and reproduced locally and expressed in the everyday experiences of Black women. This study has shown in detail that racism operates in three domains of conflict: (a) conflict over norms and values, (b) conflict over material and nonmaterial resources, and (c) conflict over definitions of the social world. Each of these areas of conflict is maintained through marginalizing, problematizing, and containment processes, but the specific forms they take in everyday life are locally determined. The experiences of Black women in the Netherlands (and to a lesser degree those of the U.S. women) expose the hidden agendas of the discourse of ethnic difference and cultural tolerance. The study demonstrates that the ideology of cultural tolerance is by definition repressive because it presupposes that Blacks accept the basic norms and values of the dominant culture. Moreover, the discourse of tolerance is the bedrock of an ideological atmosphere that sees as a positive value individuals' toleration of each other's expressions of racism.

Tolerance is not contradictory to racism. It is in the Dutch imagination that the one excludes the other. Analysis of everyday racism in the Netherlands revealed that active tolerance complements the repressive implications of cultural pluralism in a system of dominance. The overemphasis on ethnic difference misleads Blacks into thinking that the main goal of the struggle is the preservation of "ethnic identity," which in fact reduces culture to personality features. The data from the Netherlands suggest that the reformulation, in Dutch dominant discourse, of structural oppression (marginalization) into cultural and personal goals (maintenance of ethnic identity) seems to have affected Black women's perceptions of strategies against racism. None of the women in the Netherlands appears to have a power-oriented framework of struggle. Meanwhile the degree of exclusion of Blacks from the Dutch labor market continues to be among the highest in Europe.

Whether racism is racially or culturally expressed, the basic struggle is for power and control of society's resources. In both countries Black women are repeatedly and systematically frustrated in their pursuit of fair access to resources. Nonacknowledgment of their qualifications, discouragement, pestering, unreasonably high demands, avoidance of social contact, and many other mechanisms of exclusion maintain a society that is basically Whitecentric and that only tolerates Black women in marginalized positions.

The third area of struggle takes place on a metalevel. Black women's definition of race and ethnic relations includes the knowledge that racism is real and pervasive in everyday life. This view is consistently contested by the dominant group. Black women who challenge racism are pathologized ("You are oversensitive") and their knowledge and understanding of racism are denied. They are accused of bias against Whites. In the Netherlands, where racism is defined as a moral issue, Black women are even incriminated for objecting to racism ("You are victimizing Whites with all these accusations").

In the United States as well racism is increasingly denied, but there is a tradition of opposition to racism. Because U.S. Black women conceptualize racism not as ignorance but as conflict over power, they are determined to remain connected in spirit with the history of Black struggle. Their strategies have a constructive orientation. Knowledge of the consistent denial of Black norms and values in U.S. society motivates them to reclaim and assert their culture (as distinct from identity). Recognizing that cultural conflict has structural implications, U.S. Black women plan to use their resources to increase the power of the Black group.

Black women experience racism in all spheres of social life, but racism in the areas of education and work are more pervasive and detrimental because in these areas artificial ceilings are created to impede Black women's aspirations. Many of these impediments are created by agents in positions of authority: school counselors discourage Black women from taking a college track. Instead of giving Black students feedback, teachers often punish Black students who excel. Black women get unfairly low grades, are humiliated in front of the class, or are accused of cheating. Many courses become racist events when teachers punctuate their lessons with racist comments and jokes about Blacks. More women in the Netherlands reported this form of racism than women in the United States. Apart from actively indulging in racism, school authorities also passively participate in racism.

They do not intervene when it is evident that Black students are ostracized. Often they allow Black students to be called names while they ignore the racial element in racist abusive language. On the job supervisors are inflexible toward Black women, refuse to allow them to take certain responsibilities that come with the job, underpay Black women, allow Black women to be bothered by colleagues, and, in the Netherlands, indulge in racist joking and other verbal offensive language.

SCENARIOS OF RACISM (SRs)

The women introduced what I called scenarios of racism in generic forms, such as "If you enter a shop . . . ," or generalized forms, such as "In meetings there is always going to be someone who . . ." These descriptions combine situation scripts (knowledge and expectations about "normal" procedures) with alternative group knowledge of the various complications one faces as a Black woman.

I did not systematically reconstruct the SRs of specific situations, because this requires more refined instruments of analysis. Tentatively, however, the following suggestions may be considered. The *school test* SR is likely to include notions of unfairly low grading. The *meeting* SR may include properties such as not being heard and not being addressed. The *dating a White man* SR probably includes notions about being seen as a one-night stand. Scenarios of racism may also feature alternative "tracks," that is, possible variations in manifestations of racism. This can best be illustrated with a concrete episode, for instance, searching for a room. The experiences of Black women suggest there is variation in the racism they expect in this situation. That is, this *searching for a room* SR includes the following "tracks": (a) you go to the address, and they tell you that the vacancy is gone or (b) they tell you that it is OK with them to have a Black tenant, but that the neighbors will mind.

The idea of scenarios of racism has various implications for our understanding of racism. First, it supports one major thesis of this study, namely, that we must use more effectively the critical knowledge and understanding Blacks have of racism. Second, this finding opens up a whole area of research (possibly quantitative as well) into the structures of SRs for a range of everyday situations. Third, it seems that the more frequently certain practices occur, the more likely it is that these are stored in memory, in generalized SRs, instead of in modes of personal experiences. Through memory research it can be established which forms occur most frequently or which forms have become so repetitive that they are memorized as scenarios. Last but not least knowledge of the SR of specific situations simply tells us what can go "wrong" in these situations. Conversely SRs can be used as a form of general knowledge in assessing the value of the (White) actor's point of view in the situation.

RESEARCH IMPLICATIONS

The central place of experience in my approach to racism suggests an agenda for another kind of research. More studies of racism are needed that start from real-life experiences. This study provided a methodology for just that. It has elevated experiences to the level of knowledgeability. A beginning has been made in developing a new method by which Blacks' own comprehension of their experiences of racism can be used effectively for a better sociological understanding of the problem. Obviously the proposed method for understanding accounts of racism must be tested systematically on a larger scale. Further refinement of elicitation techniques and of the proposed strategies to distinguish rational from irrational accounts may enhance the applicability of the method to practical purposes. A sophisticated and reliable method of assessing accounts may even be useful in legal action. Note that, apart from racism, the same method can be applied to assess other accounts of systematic injustice, such as gender oppression, in everyday life.

More research is required to understand the precise nature of the acquisition of knowledge of racism. The reconstructions I made must be tested on a larger group. However, these reconstructions are not a goal in themselves. We have seen that Black women had to rely on alternative modes of knowledge acquisition because of a virtual lack of sufficient information about racism through the formal channels of communication. We need to enhance our understanding of efficient modes of transmission of knowledge and of ways to efficiently use this knowledge to develop strategies for change.

The problem is not only how knowledge of racism is acquired but also what kind of knowledge is being transmitted. It was found that Black women in the Netherlands have little general knowledge of Black liberation struggles. Disconnection from their own cultural history is reinforced by pressures to assimilate. Moreover insufficient historical understanding of the struggle undermines each emancipation process. For these reasons it is urgent that the history of resistance of Blacks in the Netherlands is reconstructed, through research, with the aim of asserting their place in liberation from colonial relations and cultural oppression.

I have not been able to analyze, in all its consequences, the role of authorities in the reproduction of everyday racism. The findings suggest that more research will be especially important in this area. More specifically the women pointed out power abuse in education on a massive scale. Many women criticized the detrimental role of school counselors and teachers who consistently downgrade Black students. This was the experience of their parents, it was their own experience, and they find that little has changed for their children. Racism in education is reinforced by racism in other spheres of life. Therefore, it must be examined more generally when and how authorities abuse functional power and how this can be opposed. Conversely it is relevant to examine how people in positions of authority can use the power attached to their positions to prevent and to combat racism. Various Black women in such positions could give much needed feedback to younger Blacks. It appears, however, that the forces of racism consistently jeopardize the position of Blacks who take a stand against racism. Much more research needs to be done to expose the local dynamics of oppression, opposition, and repression.

REALITY AND STRUGGLE

Once we recognize the fact that racism is systematically integrated into meanings and routine practices by which social relations are reproduced, it follows that it is not specific agents but the very fabric of the social system that must be problematized. This requires that we reformulate the problem of racism as an everyday problem. The analysis of everyday racism makes clear that racism must be combated through culture as well as through other structural relations of the system. The domains of conflict, as well as the various mechanisms of racism, are related in complex ways. These cannot be countered by fragmented policies. One cannot pursue pluralism without addressing the hidden presupposition that the dominant culture is superior and need not be receptive to change. We have also seen that we cannot successfully counter the systematic marginalization of Black women without addressing the various processes that discourage and repress resistance.

The purpose of this study was not to develop a theory of change but to provide a description and analysis of reality based on the knowledge and experiences of Black women. We have seen that the structural and ideological relations of society are favorably predisposed to (re)produce racism; at the same time they form an inflexible and unfavorable climate for opposition to racism.

The results of this study imply that political programs should start from an understanding of the way racism is experienced. Furthermore the elements in a program to increase a critical understanding of race and ethnic relations appear to include at least more general (descriptive as well as explanatory) knowledge of racism. This requires that hidden implications of the ideal of cultural tolerance are countered, that the mechanisms of cultural racism are exposed, and that overall denial of racism is resisted by massive dissemination of oppositional views through the media and in the education system. As I stated above this does not mean that ideological solutions should be prioritized above political-structural solutions. It must be stressed though that we have to face the problem that, both in the United States and in the Netherlands, the denial of racism legitimizes increasing aggression against those who oppose racism. Thus a consensus is cultivated that may eventually allow racism to disappear from the political agenda altogether.

Last but not least the analysis of the accounts of Black women suggests that everyday racism cannot be countered without reevaluating values of the Euro-American social order that are taken for granted by the dominant group. Black women's reconstructions of everyday racism provide conceptual as well as practical tools to question the unquestioned, to reject what seems acceptable, and to start sharing responsibility in the struggle against racism.

References

Aalberts, M. M. J., & Kamminga, E. M. (1983). *Politie en allochtonen* [Police and foreigners]. s' Gravenhage, the Netherlands: Staatsuitgeverij.

Adair, A. V. (1984). *Desegregation.* New York: University Press of America.

Adams, K. (1983). Aspects of social context as determinants of Black women's resistance to challenges. *Journal of Social Issues, 39*(3), 69-78.

Affra-Meldkamer (Institution). (1986). *Klachten over racisme, discriminatie en extreem-rechtse organisaties* [Complaints against racism, discrimination, and extreme right organisations] (January 12, 1985-June 30, 1986). Amsterdam: Author.

Akinnaso, N., & Ajirotutu, C. S. (1982). Performance and ethnic style in job interviews. In J. J. Gumperz (Ed.), *Language and social identity* (pp. 119-144). Cambridge: Cambridge University Press.

Aldridge, D. P. (Ed.). (1989). The African-American woman: Complexities in the midst of a simplistic world view. *Journal of Black Studies, 20*(2), 123-223.

Alexander, J., Giesen, B., Münch, R., & Smelser, N. (Eds.). (1987). *The micro-macro link.* Berkeley: University of California Press.

Alkan, M., Dors, H., Miedema, W., & Mullard, C. (1986). *Onderwijs onderzoek in Nederland: etnicisme in de wetenschap?* [Education research in the Netherlands: Ethnicism in (social) science?] (Working paper No. 1). Amsterdam: Centre for Race and Ethnic Studies.

Allport, G. W. (1958). *The nature of prejudice.* New York: Doubleday, Anchor. (Original work published 1954)

Amin, S. (1988). *Eurocentrism.* London: Zed.

Amos, V., & Parmar, P. (1981). Resistances and responses: The experiences of Black girls in Britain. In A. McRobbie & T. McCabe (Eds.), *Feminism for girls* (pp. 129-148). London: Routledge & Kegan Paul.

Antaki, C. (Ed.). (1981). *The psychology of ordinary explanations of social behaviour.* London: Academic Press.

Antaki, C. (Ed.). (1988a). *Analysing everyday explanation.* London: Sage.

Antaki, C. (1988b). Explanations, communication and social cognition. In C. Antaki (Ed.), *Analysing everyday explanation* (pp. 1-14). London: Sage.

Antaki, C., & Fielding, G. (1981). Research on ordinary explanations. In C. Antaki (Ed.), *The psychology of ordinary explanations of social behaviour* (pp. 27-55). London: Academic Press.

Aptheker, B. (1982). *Woman's legacy: Essays on race, sex, and class in American history.* Amherst: University of Massachusetts Press.

Aptheker, H. (1964). *Essays in the history of the American Negro.* New York: International.

Aptheker, H. (1966). *Nat Turner's revolt.* New York: Grove.

Arendt, H. (1970). Communicative power. In S. Lukes (Ed.), *Power* (pp. 59-74). London: Basil Blackwell.

Aronson, E. (1980). *The social animal* (3rd ed.). San Francisco: Freeman.

Auletta, K. (1982). *The underclass.* New York: Random House.

Bagley, C. (1973). *The Dutch plural society.* London: Oxford University Press.

Bailey, C. R., & Mednick, M. T. (1988). Career aspiration in Black college women: An examination of performance and self-esteem. In E. D. Rothblum & E. Cole (Eds.), *Treating women's fear of failure* (pp. 65-75). New York: Harrington Park.

Balbo, L. (1989). *The political, institutional and social conditions for a feminist social policy: A stage of transition.* Unpublished paper, Frankfurt.

Baraka, A., & Baraka, A. (1983). *Confirmation: An anthology of African American women.* New York: Quill.

Baratz, J., & Baratz, S. (1977). Black culture on Black terms: A rejection of the social pathology model. In T. Kochman (Ed.), *Rappin' and stylin' out* (pp. 3-16). Urbana: University of Illinois Press. (Original work published 1972)

Barker, M. (1981). *The new racism.* London: Junction.

Barrera, M. (1979). *Race and class in the Southwest.* Notre Dame: University of Notre Dame Press.

Barrett, M. (1980). *Women's oppression today.* London: Verso.

Becker, L. B., McCombs, M. E., & McLeod, J. M. (1975). The development of political cognitions. In S. H. Chaffee (Ed.), *Political communication* (pp. 21-63). Beverly Hills, CA: Sage.

Beer, P. de. (1988). Nederlandse studies naar de criminaliteit van etnische minderheden [Dutch studies into the criminality of ethnic minorities]. *Migrantenstudies, 4,* 17-27.

Bel Ghazi, H. (1982). *Over twee culturen, uitbuiting and opportunisme* [About two cultures, exploitation and opportunism]. Rotterdam: Futile.

Bell, R. P., Parker, B. J., Guy-Sheftall, B. (Eds.). (1979). *Sturdy Black bridges: Visions of Black women in literature.* New York: Anchor.

Bem, D. J. (1967). Self-perception: An alternative interpretation of cognitive dissonance phenomena. *Psychological Review, 74*(3), 183-200.

Bennett, L. (1965). *Confrontation: Black and White.* Chicago: Johnson.

Ben-Tovim, G., Gabriel, J. Law, I., & Stredder, K. (1986). *The local politics of race.* London: Macmillan.

Berg, H. van den, & Reinsch, P. (1983). *Racisme in schoolboeken* [Racism in schoolbooks]. Amsterdam: SUA.

Berger, P. L., & Luckmann, T. (1966). *The social construction of reality.* Harmondsworth, England: Penguin.

Berry, M. F., & Blassingname, J. W. (1982). *Long memory.* New York: Oxford University Press.

Bertaux, D. (Ed.). (1981). *Biography and society.* Beverly Hills, CA: Sage.

Bhavnani, K., & Bhavnani, R. (1985). Racism and resistance in Britain. In D. Coates, G. Johston, & R. Bush (Eds.), *A social anatomy of Britain* (pp. 146-159). Cambridge: Polity.

Biegel, B., & Tjoen-Tak-Sen, K. (1986). *Klachten over rassendiscriminatie* [Complaints about racial discrimination]. 's Gravenhage, the Netherlands: Vuga.

Biegel, C., Böcker, A., & Tjoen-Tak-Sen, K. (1988). *Rassendiscriminatie . . . tenslotte is het verboden bij de wet* [Racial discrimination . . . after all it is against the law]. Zwolle, the Netherlands: Tjeenk Willink.

Billig, M. (1982). *Ideology and social psychology.* Oxford: Basil Blackwell.

Blackwell, J. (1988). Dynamics of minority education: An index to the status of race and ethnic relations in the United States. *Trotter Institute Review, 2*(3), 5-13.

Blauner, B. (1989). *Black lives, White lives.* Berkeley: University of California Press.

Blumer, H. (1958). Race prejudice as a sense of group position. *Pacific Sociological Review, 1,* 3-7.

Blumer, H. (1969). *Symbolic interaction.* Englewood Cliffs, NJ: Prentice-Hall.

Bobo, L. (1988). Group conflict, prejudice, and the paradox of contemporary racial attitudes. In P. Katz & D. Taylor (Eds.), *Eliminating racism* (pp. 85-114). New York: Plenum.

Bolle, W., van Dijk, H., & Hetebrij, D. (1978). Discriminatie bij het verhuren van kamers aan gastarbeiders [Discrimination in accommodation for guest workers]. In F. Bovenkerk (Ed.), *Omdat zij anders zijn* [Because they are different]. Meppel, the Netherlands: Boom.

Bontemps, A. (1961). *100 years of Negro freedom.* New York: Dodd, Mead.

Boston, T. (1988). *Race, class, and conservatism.* Boston: Unwin Hyman.

Bourne, J. (1983). Towards an anti-racist feminism. *Race and Class, 25*(1), 1-22.

Bouw, C., & Nelissen, C. (1986). *Werken en Zorgen* [To work and to care]. 's Gravenhage, the Netherlands: Ministerie van Sociale Zaken en Werkgelegenheid.

Bovenkerk, F. (1978). Rasdiskriminatie in Nederland? [Racial discrimination in the Netherlands?]. In F. Bovenkerk (Ed.), *Omdat zij anders zijn* [Because they are different] (pp. 9-30). Meppel, the Netherlands: Boom.

Bovenkerk, F., & Breuning-van Leeuwen, E. (1978). Ras-diskriminatie en rasvooroordeel op de Amsterdamse arbeidsmarkt [Racial discrimination and race prejudice on the Amsterdam labor market]. In F. Bovenkerk (Ed.), *Omdat ze anders zijn* (pp. 31-57). Meppel, the Netherlands: Boom.

Bovenkerk, F., Bruin, K., Brunt, L., & Wouters, H. (1985). *Vreemd volk, gemendge gevoelens* [Foreign people, mixed feelings]. Meppel, the Netherlands: Boom.

Braddock, J. H., & McPartland, J. M. (1987). How minorities continue to be excluded from equal employment opportunities: Research on labor market and institutional barriers. *Journal of Social Issues, 43*(1), 5-39.

Braden, A. (1977). A second letter to southern White women. *Southern Exposure, 4*(4), 50-53.

Brandt, G. L. (1986). *The realization of anti-racist teaching.* London: Falmer.

Brassé, P., & Sikking, E. (1988). Discriminatie van migranten binnen arbeidsorganisties [Discrimination against migrants in labor organizations]. *Migrantenstudies, 2,* 13-23.

Braxton, J. M., & McLaughlin, A. N. (Eds.). (1990). *Wild women in the whirlwind: Afra-American culture and the contemporary literary renaissance.* London: Serpent's Tail.

Brittan, A. (1973). *Meanings and situations.* London: Routledge & Kegan Paul.

Brittan, A., & Maynard, M. (1984). *Sexism, racism and oppression.* Oxford: Basil Blackwell.

Broek, L. van den. (1987). *Hoe zit het nou met wit?* [What about White?]. Amsterdam: An Dekker.

Brok, H. (1987). Het Sjimmie-syndroom. In Anne Frank Stichting (Ed.), *Vreemd Gespuis* (pp. 152-164). Baarn, the Netherlands: Ambo/Novib.

Brunt, E., Grijpma, P., & Harten, C. van. (1989). *Doodgeknuffeld* [Cuddled to death] (pp. 12-17). New York: Elsevier.

Bryan, B., Dadzie, S., & Scafe, S. (1985). *The heart of the race.* London: Virago.

Budike, F. (1982). *Surinamers naar Nederland* [Surinamese going to the Netherlands]. Amsterdam: Ivabo.

Buiks, P. E. J. (1983). *Surinaamse jongeren op de Kruiskade* [Surinamese youth at the Kruiskade]. Deventer, the Netherlands: van Loghum Slaterus.

Buis, H. (1988). *Beter een verre buur* [A distant neighbor is better than a close one]. Amsterdam: SUA.

Bullivant, B. M. (1983). *Pluralism: Cultural maintenance and evolution.* Clevedon, England: Multilingual Matters.

Burlew, A. K. (1982). The experiences of Black females in traditional and nontraditional professions. *Psychology of Women Quarterly, 6*(3), 312-326.

Cade, T. (Ed.). (1970). *The Black woman: An anthology.* New York: New American Library.

Canter, D., & Brown, J. (1981). Explanatory roles. In C. Antaki (Ed.), *The psychology of ordinary explanations of social behaviour* (pp. 221-242). London: Academic Press.

Carby, H. V. (1982). White woman listen! Black feminism and the boundaries of sisterhood. In Centre of Contemporary Cultural Studies (Birmingham; Ed.), *The empire strikes back: Race and racism in the 70s* (pp. 212-235). London: Hutchinson.

Carby, H. V. (1987). *Reconstructing womanhood.* New York: Oxford University Press.

Carmichael, S., & Hamilton, C. (1967). *Black power.* New York: Vintage.

Carroll, C. M. (1982). Three's a crowd: The dilemma of the Black woman in higher education. In G. T. Hull, P. B. Scott, & B. Smith (Eds.), *But some of us are brave* (pp. 115-128). Old Westbury, NY: Feminist Press.

Carugati, F. F. (1990). Everyday ideas, theoretical models and social representations: The case of intelligence and its development. In G. R. Semin & K. J. Gergen (Eds.), *Everyday understanding* (pp. 130-150). London: Sage.

Catau, G. (1988). Gemeente Amsterdam laat allochtone woningzoekenden aan hun lot over [The County of Amsterdam leaves nonnative house hunters to fend for themselves]. *LBR Bulletin, 3,* 3-8.

Chase, A. (1980). *The legacy of Malthus: The social costs of the new scientific racism.* Urbana: University of Illinois Press.

Cherribi, O., Fuhr, G. von der, & Niedekker, D. (1989). *Cultuur als visie* [Culture as perspective]. Amsterdam: ACB.

Chesler, M. (1976). Contemporary sociological theories of racism. In P. Katz (Ed.), *Towards the elimination of racism* (pp. 21-71). New York: Pergamon.

Choenni, C., & Zwan, T. van der. (1987a). Meer arbeidsplaatsen voor allochtonen [More jobs for the nonnative]. *LBR Bulletin, 3*(2), 4-9.

Choenni, C., & Zwan, T. van der. (Eds.). (1987b). *Psychologische tests en allochtonen* [Psychology tests for the nonnative] (LBR-Reeks No. 6). Utrecht, the Netherlands: LBR.

Choenni, C., & Zwan, T. van der. (1989). Allochtonen en de arbeidsmarkt [The nonnative and the labor market]. *LBR Bulletin, 1,* 3-10.

Cicourel, A. V. (1964). *Method and measurement in sociology.* New York: Free Press.

Cicourel, A. V. (1973). *Cognitive sociology: Language and meaning in social interaction.* New York: Free Press.

Cicourel, A. V. (1981). Notes on the integration of micro- and macro-levels of analysis. In K. Knorr-Cetina & A. V. Cicourel (Eds.), *Advances in social theory and methodology* (pp. 51-80). Boston: Routledge & Kegan Paul.

Clark, K. (1966, Winter). The civil rights movement: Momentum and organization. *Daedalus,* pp. 239-267.

Clark, R., & Clark, M. (1947). Racial identification and preference in Negro children. In M. Newcomb & L. Hartley (Eds.), *Readings in social psychology.* New York: Holt.

Clarke, J. H., & Garvey, A. J. (1974). *Marcus Garvey and the vision of Africa.* New York: Vintage.

Clay, J. W. (1989). Epilogue: The ethnic future of nations. *Third World Quarterly, 4,* 223-233.

Cock, J. (1980). *Maids and madams: A study in the politics of exploitation.* Johannesburg: Ravan.

Collins, P. H. (1990). *Black feminist thought.* Boston: Unwin Hyman.

Collins, R. (1981a). On the micro-foundations of macro-sociology. *American Journal of Sociology, 86,* 984-1014.

Collins, R. (1981b). Micro-translation as a theory-building strategy. In K. Knorr-Cetina & A. V. Cicourel (Eds.), *Advances in social theory and methodology* (pp. 81-108). Boston: Routledge & Kegan Paul.

Collins, R. (1983). Micro-methods as a basis for macro-sociology. *Urban Life, 12,* 184-202.

Commager, H. S. (1967). *The struggle for equality.* New York: Harper & Row.

Cottaar, A., & Willems, W. (1984). *Indische Nederlanders* [The Indonesian Dutch]. Den Haag, the Netherlands: Moesson.

Cruse, H. (1984). *The crisis of the Negro intellectual.* New York: Quill. (Original work published 1967).

Cruse, H. (1987). *Plural but equal.* New York: William Morrow.

Dabydeen, D. (1987). *Hogarth's Blacks: Images of Blacks in eighteenth century English art.* Manchester: Manchester University Press.

Daniel, W. W. (1971). *Racial discrimination in England.* Harmondsworth, England: Penguin. (Original work published 1968)

Davis, A. (1971). Reflections on the Black woman's role in the community of slaves. *The Black Scholar.* (Reprinted 1981, pp. 3-15)

Davis, A. (1978). Rape, racism and the capitalist setting. *The Black Scholar.* (Reprinted 1981, pp. 39-45)

Davis, A. Y. (1981). *Women, race and class.* New York: Random House.

Davis, A. Y. (1989). *Women, culture, and politics.* New York: Random House.

Dex, S. (1983). The second generation: West Indian female school leavers. In A. Phizacklea (Ed.), *One way ticket: Migration and female labour* (pp. 53-71). London: Routledge & Kegan Paul.

Dijker, A. J. (1989). Ethnic attitudes and emotions. In J. P. van Oudenhoven & T. M. Willemsen (Eds.), *Ethnic minorities* (pp. 77-93). Amsterdam: Swets & Zeitlinger.

Dill, B. T. (1980). The means to put my children through. In L. F. Rodgers-Rose (Ed.), *The Black woman* (pp. 107-123). Beverly Hills, CA: Sage.

Dill, B. T. (1987). The dialectics of Black womanhood. In S. Harding (Ed.), *Feminism and methodology* (pp. 97-108). Bloomington: Indiana University Press.

Diop, C. A. (1974). *The African origin of civilization.* Westport, CT: Lawrence Hill.

Dors, H. (1988). Structurele belemmeringen voor etnische minderheidsgroepen in het onderwijs [Structural obstacles against ethnic minority groups in education]. *Migrantenstudies, 4*(1), 37-49.

Douglas, J. D. (Ed.). (1974). *Understanding everyday life.* London: Routledge & Kegan Paul. (Original work published 1970)

Douglas, J. D. (1976). *Investigative social research.* Beverly Hills, CA: Sage.

Du Bois, W. E. B. (1964). *The world and Africa.* New York: International.

Du Bois, W. E. B. (1969). *The souls of Black folk.* New York: New American Library.

Dummett, A. (1973). *A portrait of English racism.* Harmondsworth, England: Penguin.

Duster, A. (Ed.). (1970). *Crusade for justice: The autobiography of Ida Wells.* Chicago: University of Chicago Press.

Duster, T. (1981). The ideological frame of benign neglect. *Journal of Contemporary Studies, 4*(1), 81-90.

Duster, T. (1990). *Backdoor to eugenics.* New York: Routledge.

Dutton, D. G., & Lake, R. A. (1973). Threat of own prejudice and reverse discrimination in interracial situations. *Journal of Personality and Social Psychology, 28,* 94-100.

Dutton, D. G., & Lennox, V. L. (1974). Effect of prior token compliance on subsequent interracial behavior. *Journal of Personality and Social Psychology, 29,* 65-71.

Eemeren, F. H. van, Grootendorst, R., & Kruiger, T. (1981). *Argumentatietheorie* [Argumentation theory]. Utrecht, the Netherlands: Het Spectrum.

Eiser, R. J. (1980). *Cognitive social psychology.* London: McGraw-Hill.

Eiser, Y. R. (1983). Attribution theory and social cognition. In J. Jaspars, F. Fincham, & M. Hewstone (Eds.), *Attribution theory and research: Conceptual, developmental and social dimensions* (pp. 91-113). London: Academic Press.

Eissien-Udom, E. U. (1962). *Black nationalism.* Harmondsworth, England: Penguin.

Elich, J., & Maso, B. (1984). *Discriminatie, vooroordeel en racisme in Nederland* [Discrimination, prejudice and racism in the Netherlands] (ACOM). s' Gravenhage, the Netherlands: Ministerie van Binnenlandse Zaken.

Ellemers, J. E., & Vaillant, R. E. F. (1985). *Indische Nederlanders en Gerepatrieerden.* Muiderberg, the Netherlands: Coutinho.

Emancipatieraad (Institution). (1988). Zwarte en migrantenvrouwen op de arbeidsmarkt [Black and migrant women on the labor market]. Den Haag, the Netherlands: Author.

Entzinger, H. B. (1984). *Het minderhedenbeleid* [Minority policy]. Meppel, the Netherlands: Boom.

Epstein, C. F. (1973). Positive effects of the multiple negative: Explaining the success of Black professional women. In J. Huber (Ed.), *Changing women in a changing society* (pp. 150-173). Chicago: University of Chicago Press.

Epstein, J. L. (1985). After the bus arrives: Resegregation in desegregated schools. *Journal of Social Issues, 41*(3), 23-43.

Essed, H. A. M. (1984). *De binnenlandse oorlog in Suriname: 1613-1793* [The internal war in Suriname: 1613-1793]. Paramaribo, Suriname: Antom de Kom University.

Essed, P. (1982). *Racisme en feminisme: Socialities Feministiese Teksten 7* (pp. 9-40). Amsterdam: Sara.

Essed, P. (1984). *Alledaags Racisme.* Amsterdam: Sara. [*Everyday racism,* Claremont, CA, Hunter House, 1990]

Essed, P. (1986). *The Dutch as an everyday problem: Some notes on the nature of White racism* (Working paper No. 3). Amsterdam: Centre for Race and Ethnic Studies.

Essed, P. (1987). *Academic racism: Common sense in the social sciences* (Working paper No. 5). Amsterdam: Centre for Race and Ethnic Studies.

Essed, P. (1988). Understanding verbal accounts of racism. *Text, 8*(1), 5-40.

Essed, P. (1989). Black women in White women's organizations. *RFR/DRF, 18*(4), 10-15. (RFR, Resources for Feminist Research, Toronto, Canada)

Essed, P. (1990a). The myth of over-sensitivity about racism. In I. Foeken (Ed.), *Between selfhelp and professionalism, Part III* (pp. 21-36). Amsterdam: Moon Foundation.

Essed, P. (1990b). Against all odds: Teaching against racism at a university in South Africa. *European Journal of Intercultural Studies, 1*(1), 41-56.

European Parliament. (1985). *Report of Committee of Inquiry into the Rise of Fascism and Racism in Europe.* Brussels, Belgium: Author.

European Parliament. (1986). *Zittingsdocumenten* (Hearing documents). Serie A, Document A2-160/85/rev. Bijlagen I-IV. Brussels, Belgium: Author.

European Parliament. (1990). *Report of the Committee of Inquiry into Racism and Xenophobia.* Brussels, Belgium: Author.

Evans, M. (Ed.). (1983). *Black women writers.* London: Pluto.

Evans, S. (1977). Women's consciousness and the southern Black movement. *Southern Exposure, 4*(4), 10-14.

Evans, S. (1979). *Personal politics: The roots of women's liberation in the civil rights movement and the New Left.* New York: Vintage.

Fanon, F. (1967). *Black skins, White masks.* New York: Grove.

Fanon, F. (1985). *The wretched of the Earth.* Harmondsworth, England: Penguin. (Original work published 1963)

Fay, B. (1987). *Critical social science.* Cambridge: Polity.

Fernandez, J. P. (1981). *Racism and sexism in corporate life.* Lexington, MA: Lexington.

Ferrier, J. (1985). *De Surinamers.* Muiderberg, the Netherlands: Coutinho.

Festinger, L. (1976). *A theory of cognitive dissonance.* Stanford, CA: Stanford University Press. (Original work published 1957)

Fielding, N. G. (Ed.). (1988). *Actions and structure.* London: Sage.

Finch, J. (1984). "It's great to have someone to talk to": The ethics and politics of interviewing women. In C. Bell & H. Robert (Eds.), *Social researching* (pp. 70-87). London: RKP.

Fiske, S. T., & Kinder, D. R. (1981). Involvement, expertise, and schema use: Evidence from political cognition. In N. Cantor & J. F. Kihlstrom (Eds.), *Personality, cognition and social interaction* (pp. 171-190). Hillsdale, NJ: Lawrence Erlbaum.

Fiske, S. T., & Taylor, S. E. (1984). *Social cognition.* Reading, MA: Addison-Wesley.

Forgas, J. P. (1982). Episode cognition: Internal representations of interaction routines. *Advances in Experimental and Social Psychology, 15*, 59-101.

Foster-Carter, O. (1984). Racial bias in children's literature: A review of the research on Africa. *Sage Race Relations Abstracts, 9*(4), 1-12.

Fox-Genovese, E. (1988). *Within the plantation household.* Chapel Hill: University of North Carolina Press.

Franklin, J. H. (1952). *From slavery to freedom.* New York: Knopf.

Franklin, V. P. (1984). *Black self determination.* Westport, CT: Lawrence Hill.

Frazier, F. E. (1962). *Black bourgeoisie*. New York: Collier. (Original work published 1957)

Fullbright, K. (1986). The myth of double-advantage: Black female managers. In M. C. Simms & J. Malveaux (Eds.), *Slipping through the cracks: The status of Black women* (pp. 33-45). New Brunswick, NJ: Transaction.

Furnham, A. (1990). Commonsense theories of personality. In G. R. Semin & K. J. Gergen (Eds.), *Everyday understanding* (pp. 176-203). London: Sage.

Furnivall, J. S. (1948). *Colonial policy and practice*. London: Cambridge University Press.

Gaertner, S. L., & Dovidio, J. F. (1986). The aversive form of racism. In J. F. Dovidio & S. L. Gaertner (Eds.), *Prejudice, discrimination, and racism* (pp. 61-89). Orlando, FL: Academic Press.

Garfinkel, H. (1967). *Studies in ethnomethodology*. Englewood Cliffs, NJ: Prentice-Hall.

Genovese, E. D. (1984). *In red and black*. Knoxville: University of Tennessee Press.

Gergen, K. J., & Semin, G. R. (1990). Everyday understanding in science and daily life. In G. R. Semin & K. J. Gergen (Eds.), *Everyday understanding* (pp. 1-18). London: Sage.

Giddens, A. (1979). *Central problems in social theory*. London: Macmillan.

Giddens, A. (1981). Agency, institution, and time-space analysis. In K. Knorr-Cetina & A. V. Cicourel (Eds.), *Advances in social theory and methodology*. Boston: Routledge & Kegan Paul.

Giddens, A. (1984). *The constitution of society*. Cambridge: Polity (in association with Basil Blackwell, Oxford).

Giddings, P. (1986). *When and where I enter: The impact of Black women on race and sex in America*. Toronto: Bantam.

Giddings, P. (1988). *In search of sisterhood*. New York: William Morrow.

Gilkes, C. T. (1982). Successful rebellious professionals: The Black woman's professional identity and community. *Psychology of Women Quarterly, 6*(3), 289-311.

Gilman, S. L. (1985). *Difference and pathology*. Ithaca, NY: Cornell University Press.

Gilroy, P. (1982). Police and thieves. In Centre of Contemporary Cultural Studies (Birmingham; Ed.), *The empire strikes back: Race and racism in the 70s* (pp. 143-182). London: Hutchinson.

Glasgow, D. G. (1980). *The Black underclass*. New York: Vintage.

Glazer, N. (1975). *Affirmative discrimination*. New York: Basic Books.

Glazer, N., & Moynihan, D. P. (1968). *Beyond the melting pot*. Cambridge: MIT Press. (Original work published 1963)

Glazer, N., & Young, K. (Eds.). (1983). *Ethnic pluralism and public policy*. London: Heinemann.

Goffman, E. (1959). *The presentation of self in everyday life*. New York: Doubleday.

Goffman, E. (1961). *Encounters*. Indianapolis: Bobbs-Merrill.

Goffman, E. (1967). *Interaction ritual*. Garden City, NY: Doubleday.

Goffman, E. (1969). *Strategical interaction*. Philadelphia: University of Pennsylvania Press.

Goffman, E. (1974). *Frame analysis*. New York: Harper & Row.

Goffman, E. (1979). *Stigma: Notes on the management of spoiled identity*. Harmondsworth, England: Penguin. (Original work published in 1963)

Goldman, A. (1972). Toward a theory of social power. In S. Lukes (Ed.), *Power* (pp. 156-202). Oxford: Basil Blackwell.

Goldman, A. H. (1979). *Justice and reverse discrimination*. Princeton, NJ: Princeton University Press.

Gordon, M. (1978). *Human nature, class, and ethnicity*. New York: Oxford University Press.

Gossett, T. F. (1963). *Race: The history of an idea in America.* New York: Schocken.

Gowler, D., & Legge, K. (1981). Negation, synthesis and abomination in rhetoric. In C. Antaki (Ed.), *The psychology of ordinary explanations of social behaviour.* London: Academic Press.

Graham, H. (1984). Surveying through stories. In C. Bell & H. Roberts (Eds.), *Social researching* (pp. 104-124). London: Routledge & Kegan Paul.

Gramsci, A. (1971). *Selections from prison notebooks.* London: Lawrence and Wishart.

Grant, J. (1968). *Black protest.* New York: Fawcett Premier.

Greer, G. (1984). *Sex and destiny.* London: Picador.

Griffin, C. (1985). *Typical girls?* London: Routledge & Kegan Paul.

Groeben, N. (1990). Subjective theories and the explanation of human action. In G. R. Semin & K. J. Gergen (Eds.), *Everyday understanding* (pp. 19-44). London: Sage.

Gutman, H. G. (1976). *The Black family in slavery and freedom.* New York: Random House.

Haas, H. de. (1987, February-July). Het *"burgelijk" feminisistische beeld van "Inlanders" en andere "rassen" rond 1900* ["Bourgeois" feministic images of "natives" and other "races"]. Paper presented at the Workshop "Vrouwen en Racisme" [Women and Racism], University of Amsterdam, Center for Race and Ethnic Studies.

Hall, R. M. (1982). *The classroom climate: A chilly one for women?* (Project on the Status and Education of Women). Washington, DC: Association of American Colleges.

Hall, S. (1978). Racism and reaction. In Commission for Racial Equality, *Five views of multi-racial Britain* (pp. 23-35). London: C. R. E..

Hall, S. (1980). Race, articulation and societies structured in dominance. In UNESCO, *Sociological theories: Race and colonialism* (pp. 305-345). Paris: UNESCO.

Hall, S. (1981). Cultural studies: Two paradigms. In T. Bennett, G. Martin, C. Mercer, & J. Woollacott (Eds.), *Culture, ideology and social process* (pp. 19-37). London: Batsford Academic and Educational Ltd.

Hall, S. (1986). Variants of liberalism. In J. Donald & S. Hall (Eds.), *Politics and ideology* (pp. 34-69). Milton Keynes: Open University Press.

Hall, S., Lumlay, B., & McLennan, G. (1977). Politics and ideology: Gramsci. Centre for Contemporary Cultural Studies. *On Ideology* (pp. 45-76). London: Hutchinson.

Hanna, J. L. (1988). *Disruptive school behavior.* New York: Holmes & Meier.

Harmsen, P., van Leeuwen, F., & van Rijen, M. (1988). Wetenschappelijk racisme [Scientific racism]. In H. Hisschemöller (Ed.), *Een bleek bolwerk* [A pale bulwark] (pp. 99-114). Amsterdam: Pegasus.

Harré, R. (1980). Making social psychology scientific. In R. Gilmour & S. Duck (Eds.), *The development of social psychology* (pp. 27-51). London: Academic Press.

Harré, R. (1981). Rituals, rhetoric and social cognitions. In J. P. Forgas (Ed.), *Social cognition* (pp. 212-224). London: Academic Press.

Harré, R., & Secord, P. F. (1972). *The explanation of social behaviour.* Oxford: Basil Blackwell.

Harris, F. R., & Wilkins, R. W. (Eds.). (1988). *Quiet riots.* New York: Pantheon.

Harris, L. (1987). Historical subjects and interests: Race, class and conflict. In M. Davis, M. Marable, F. Pfeil, & M. Sprinker (Eds.), *The year left 2* (pp. 91-106). London: Verso.

Hartmann, P., & Husband, C. (1974). *Racism and the mass media.* London: Davis-Poynter.

Have, P. ten, & Komter, M. (1982). De angst voor de tape [Fearing the tape]. In C. Bouw, F. Bovenkerk, K. Bruin, & L. Brunt (Eds.), *Hoe weet je dat?* [How do you know that?] (pp. 228-242). Amsterdam: de Arbeiderspers.

Heider, F. (1958). *The psychology of interpersonal relations.* New York: John Wiley.

Helle, H. J., & Eisenstadt, S. N. (Eds.). (1985). *Micro sociology.* London: Sage.

Heller, A. (1984). *Everyday life.* London: Routledge & Kegan Paul.

Hemmons, W. M. (1973). *Towards an understanding of attitudes held by the Black woman on the women's liberation movement* (Doctoral dissertation). Ann Arbor, MI: University Microfilms International (No. 74-2521).

Hercules, F. (1972). *American society and Black revolution.* New York: Harcourt Brace Jovanovich.

Hernton, C. C. (1965). *Sex and race in America.* New York: Grove.

Hernton, C. C. (1990). The sexual mountain and Black women writers. In J. M. Braxton & A. N. McLaughlin (Eds.), *Wild women in the whirlwind: Afra-American culture and the contemporary literary renaissance* (pp. 195-212). London: Serpent's Tail.

Hewstone, M. (Ed.). (1983). *Attribution theory: Social and functional extensions.* Oxford: Basil Blackwell.

Hewstone, M. (1989). Intergroup attribution: Some implications for the study of ethnic prejudice. In J. P. van Oudenhoven & T. M. Willemsen (Eds.), *Ethnic minorities* (pp. 25-42). Amsterdam: Swets & Zeitlinger.

Hill, R. B. et al. (1989). *Assessment of the status of African-Americans: Vol 2. Research on the African-American family: A holistic perspective.* Boston: William Monroe Trotter Institute.

Hine, D. C. (1989). *Black women in white.* Bloomington: Indiana University Press.

Hira, S. (1982). *Van Priary tot en met de Kom* [From Priary to de Kom]. Rotterdam, the Netherlands: Futile.

Hoch, P. (1979). *White hero, black beast: Racism, sexism and the mask of masculinity.* London: Pluto.

Hodge, J. L. (1975a). Introduction. In J. L. Hodge, D. K. Struckman, & L. D. Trost (Eds.), *The cultural bases of racism and group oppression* (pp. 1-7). Berkeley, CA: Two Riders.

Hodge, J. L. (1975b). Domination and the will in Western thought and culture. In J. L. Hodge, D. K. Struckman, & L. D. Trost (Eds.), *The cultural bases of racism and group oppression* (pp. 8-48). Berkeley, CA: Two Riders.

Hodge, J. L., Struckman, D. K., & Trost, L. D. (1975). *The cultural bases of racism and group oppression.* Berkeley, CA: Two Riders.

Hofstede, G. (1980). *Culture's consequences.* Beverly Hills, CA: Sage.

Hoogbergen, W., & de Theye, M. (1987). Surinaamse vrouwen in de slavernij [Surinamese women in slavery]. In J. Reijs et al. (Eds.), *Vrouwen in de Nederlandse kolonien* [Women in the Dutch colonies] (pp. 126-151). Nijmegen, the Netherlands: SUN.

Hooks, B. (1981). *Ain't I a woman? Black women and feminism.* Boston: South End.

Hooks, B. (1984). *Feminist theory: From margin to center.* Boston: South End.

Hooks, B. (1989). *Talking back: Thinks feminist—thinking Black.* London: Sheba Feminist.

Hoppe, R. (1987). (Ed.). *Etniciteit, politiek en beleid in Nederland* [Ethnicity, politics and policy in the Netherlands]. Amsterdam: VU Uitgeverij.

Horsman, R. (1981). *Race and manifest destiny.* Cambridge, MA: Harvard University Press.

Huggins, N. I. (1977). *Black odyssey.* London: Allen and Unwin.

Hull, G. T. (Ed.). (1984). *Give us each day: The diary of Alice Dunbar-Nelson.* New York: Norton.

Hull, G. T., Scott, P. B., & Smith, B. (Eds.). (1982). *But some of us are brave: Black women's studies.* Old Westbury, NY: Feminist Press.

Hyman, H. H. (1975). *Interviewing in social research.* Chicago: University of Chicago Press.

Ickes, W. J., & Kidd, R. F. (1976). An attributional analysis of helping behavior. In J. H. Karvey, W. J. Ickes, & R. F. Kidd (Eds.), *New directions in attribution theory.* Hillsdale, NJ: Lawrence Erlbaum.

James, F. J., Mccummings, B. L., & Tynan, E. A. (1984). *Minorities in the sunbelt.* Piscataway, NJ: Rutgers University.

Jaspars, J., Fincham, F., & Hewstone, M. (Eds.). (1983). *Attribution theory and research: Conceptual, developmental and social dimensions.* London: Academic Press.

Jaspars, J., & Fraser, C. (1984). Attitudes and social representations. In R. M. Farr & S. Moscovici (Eds.), *Social representations* (pp. 101-123). Cambridge: Cambridge University Press.

Jaynes, G. D., & Williams, R. M. (Eds.). (1989). *A common destiny.* Washington, DC: National Academy Press.

Jenkins, R. (1986). *Racism and recruitment.* Cambridge: Cambridge University Press.

Jones, B. A. P. (1986). Black women and labor force participation: An analysis of sluggish growth rates. In M. C. Simms & J. M. Malveaux (Eds.), *Slipping through the cracks* (pp. 11-31). New Brunswick, NJ: Transaction.

Jones, E. E., & Davis, K. E. (1965). From acts to dispositions: The attribution process in person perception. In L. Berkowitz (Ed.), *Advances in experimental social psychology* (Vol. 2). New York: Academic Press.

Jones, E. E., & Nisbett, R. E. (1972). The actor and the observer: Divergent perceptions of the causes of behavior. In E. E. Jones et al. (Eds.), *Attribution: Perceiving the causes of behavior.* Morristown, NJ: General Learning Press.

Jones, J. (1985). *Labor of love, labor of sorrow.* New York: Basic Books.

Jones, J. M. (1981). The concept of racism and its changing reality. In B. J. Bowser & R. G. Hunt (Eds.), *Impacts of racism on White Americans* (pp. 27-49). Beverly Hills, CA: Sage.

Jones, J. M. (1986). Racism: A cultural analysis of the problem. In J. Dovidio & S. Gaertner (Eds.), *Prejudice, discrimination and racism* (pp. 279-314). Orlando, FL: Academic Press.

Jones, J. M. (1988). Racism in black and white: A bicultural model of reaction and evolution. In P. Katz & D. Taylor (Eds.), *Eliminating racism.* New York: Plenum.

Jong, W. de. (1989). The development of ethnic tolerance in an inner city area with large numbers of immigrants. In J. P. van Oudenhoven & T. M. Willemsen (Eds.), *Ethnic minorities* (pp. 139-153). Amsterdam: Swets & Zeitlinger.

Jongh, R. de, Laan, M. van der, & Rath, J. (1984). *FNV'ers aan het woord over buitenlandse werknemers* [FNV members speak out about foreign workers]. Leiden: COMT, Rijksuniversiteit te Leiden.

Jordan, W. D. (1968). *White over Black.* New York: Norton.

Joseph, G. (1981). The uncompatible menage a trois: Marxism, feminism, and racism. In L. Sargent (Ed.), *Women and revolution* (pp. 91-109). London: Pluto.

Joseph, G. L., & Lewis, J. (1981). *Common differences.* New York: Anchor.

Kagie, R. (1989). *De eerste Neger* [The first Negro]. Houten, the Netherlands: Het Wereldvenster.

Kanter, R. M. (1977). *Men and women of the corporation.* New York: Basic Books.

Karp, J. B. (1981). The emotional impact and a model for changing racist attitudes. In P. B. Bowser & R. G. Hunt (Eds.), *Impacts of racism on White Americans* (pp. 87-96). Beverly Hills, CA: Sage.

Katz, I., & Prohansky, H. M. (1987). Rethinking affirmative action. *Journal of Social Issues, 43*(1), 99-104.

Katz, J. (1978). *White awareness: Handbook for anti-racism training.* Norman: University of Oklahoma Press.

Katz, P. A. (1976). The acquisition of racial attitudes in children. In P. A. Katz, *Towards the elimination of racism* (pp. 125-154). New York: Pergamon.

Katz, P. A., & Taylor, D. (1988). *Eliminating racism.* New York: Plenum.

Kelley, H. H. (1967). Attribution theory in social psychology. In D. Levine (Ed.), *Nebraska Symposium on Motivation.* Lincoln: University of Nebraska Press.

Kelley, H. H. (1971). *Attribution in social interaction.* Morristown, NJ: General Learning Press.

Kelley, H. K. (1983). Perceived causal structures. In J. Jaspars, F. Fincham, & M. Hewstone (Eds.), *Attribution theory and research: Conceptual, developmental and social dimensions* (pp. 343-369). London: Academic Press.

Kempadoo, K. (1988). *In the name of emancipation: Some aspects of the impact of positive action on Black and migrant women's work in Amsterdam* (CRES Publication Series, Working paper No. 7). Amsterdam: CRES.

Kerner Commission. (1988). *Report of the National Advisory Commission on Civil Disorders.* New York: Pantheon. (Original work published 1968)

Killian, L., & Grigg, C. (1964). Racial crisis in America. Englewood Cliffs, NJ: Prentice-Hall.

Kinder, D. R. (1986). The continuing American dilemma: White resistance to racial change 40 years after Myrdal. *Journal of Social Issues, 42*(2), 151-171.

Klein, R. D. (1983). How to do what we want to do: Thoughts about feminist methodology. In G. Bowles & D. Klein (Eds.), *Theories of women's studies* (pp. 88-104). London: Routledge & Kegan Paul.

KMAN, Horecabond FNV, KGCG. (1985). *Klachtenboek buitenlandse arbeiders in de horeka* [Complaint book of foreign workers in catering]. Amsterdam: Author.

Knorr-Cetina, K., & Cicourel, A. V. (Eds.). (1981). *Advances in social theory and methodology.* Boston: Routledge & Kegan Paul.

Knowles, L., & Prewitt, K. (1969). *Institutional racism in America.* Englewood Cliffs, NJ: Prentice-Hall.

Köbben, A. (1985). Oordeel en discriminatie [Judgment and discrimination]. In G. Cain et al. (Eds.), *Etnische minderheden* [Ethnic minorities] (pp. 53-66). Meppel, the Netherlands: Boom.

Kom, A. de. (1971). *Wij slaven van Suriname* [We the slaves from Suriname]. Amsterdam: Contact.

Komter, M. (1987). *Conflict and cooperation in job interviews.* Unpublished doctoral dissertation, Amsterdam.

Kornalijnslijper, N. (1988). Minderheden en structurele belemmeringen in de volkshuisvesting [Minorities and structural obstacles in public housing]. *Migrantenstudies, 1,* 67-78.

Kovel, J. (1984). *White racism.* New York: Columbia University Press. (Original work published 1970)

Kruglanski, A. W., Baldwin, M. W., & Towson, S. M. J. (1983). The lay-epistemic process in attribution-making. In M. Hewstone (Ed.), *Attribution theory* (pp. 81-95). Oxford: Basil Blackwell.

Labov, W., & Waletzky, J. (1967). Narrative analysis: Oral versions of personal experiences. In J. Helm (Ed.), *Essays on the verbal and visual arts* (pp. 12-44). Seattle: University of Washington Press.

Ladner, J. (1972). *Tomorrow's tomorrow: The Black woman.* New York: Anchor.

Ladner, J. (Ed.). (1973). *The death of White sociology.* New York: Vintage.

Ladner, J. A., & Stafford, W. W. (1981). Defusing race: Developments since the Kerner report. In B. P. Bowser & R. G. Hunt (Eds.), *Impacts of racism on White Americans* (pp. 51-69). Beverly Hills, CA: Sage.

Lakoff, R. T., & Scherr, R. L. (1984). *Face value: The politics of beauty.* Boston: Routledge & Kegan Paul.

Lalljee, M. (1981). Attribution theory and the analysis of explanations. In C. Antaki (Ed.), *The psychology of ordinary explanations of social behaviour* (pp. 119-138). London: Academic Press.

Lalljee, M., & Abelson, R. P. (1983). The organization of explanations. In M. Hewstone (Ed.), *Attribution theory* (pp. 65-80). Oxford: Basil Blackwell.

Landry, B. (1987). *The new Black middle class.* Berkeley: University of California Press.

Larsen, S. (1988). Remembering without experiencing: Memory for reported events. In U. Neisser & E. Winograd (Eds.), *Remembering reconsidered: Ecological and traditional approaches to the study of memory* (pp. 326-355). Cambridge: Cambridge University Press.

Lauren, P. G. (1988). *Power and prejudice.* Boulder, CO: Westview.

Lawrence, E. (1982a). In the abundance of water the fool is thirsty: Sociology and Black "pathology." In Centre of Contemporary Cultural Studies (Birmingham; Ed.), *The empire strikes back: Race and racism in the 70s* (pp. 95-142). London: Hutchinson.

Lawrence, E. (1982b). Just plain common sense: The "roots" of racism. In Centre of Contemporary Cultural Studies (Birmingham; Ed.), *The empire strikes back: Race and racism in the 70s* (pp. 47-94). London: Hutchinson.

Lefebvre, H. (1971). *Everyday life in the modern world.* New York: Harper.

Leinen, K. (1984). *Black police, White society.* New York: New York University Press.

Leiter, K. (1980). *A primer on ethnomethodology.* New York: Oxford University Press.

Lenders, M., & Rhoer, M. van de. (1983). *Mijn God, hoe ga ik doen?* [Oh my god, what am I going to do?]. Amsterdam: SUA.

Lenski, G. (1966). Power and privilege. In S. Lukes (Ed.), *Power* (pp. 241-252). Oxford: Basil Blackwell.

Lerner, G. (1972). *Black women in White America: A documentary study.* New York: Vintage.

Light, I. H. (1972). *Ethnic enterprise in America.* Berkeley: University of California Press.

Lima, J. da. (1988). *Als de nood hoog is.* Den Haag, the Netherlands: Ministerie van Social Zaken en Werkgelegenheid.

Littlewood, R., & Lipsedge, M. (1982). *Aliens & alienists.* Harmondsworth, England: Penguin.

Litwack, L. F. (1979). *Been in de storm so long.* London: Athlone.

Loewenberg, J., & Bogin, R. (1976). *Black women in nineteenth-century American life.* University Park: Pennsylvania State University Press.

Loewenthal, T. (1984). De witte toren van vrouwenstudies [The white towers of women's studies]. *Tijdschrift voor Vrouwenstudies, 17*, 5-17.

Lofland, J., & Lofland, L. H. (1984). *Analyzing social settings.* Belmont, CA: Wadsworth.

Loftus, E. F. (1979). *Eyewitness testimony.* Cambridge, MA: Harvard University Press.

Lomax, L. E. (1962). *The Negro revolt.* New York: Harper & Row.

Lorde, A. (1984). *Sister outsider.* New York: Crossing.

Lorde, A. (1988). *A burst of light.* Ithaca, NY: Firebrand.

Louw-Potgieter, J. (1988). *It wasn't because of me. It was because of me being black: A study of covert racism at Natal University, Durban.* Durban: University of Natal.

Louw-Potgieter, J. (1989). Covert racism: An application of Essed's analysis in a South African context. *Journal of Language and Social Psychology, 8,* 307-319.

Luckmann, B. (1978). The small life-worlds of modern man. In T. Luckmann (Ed.), *Phenomenology and sociology* (pp. 275-290). Harmondsworth, England: Penguin. (Original work published 1970)

Luckmann, T. (Ed.). (1978). *Phenomenology and sociology.* Harmondsworth, England: Penguin.

Lukes, S. (1974). *Power: A radical view.* London: Macmillan.

Luning, M. (1976). *Politie en Surinamers* [The police and the Surinamese]. Amsterdam: University of Amsterdam.

Lutz, H. (1988). *Een brug slaan: over de dilemma's van het "bemiddelen"* [To bridge: About the dilemmas of mediating]. Unpublished paper, CRES, Amsterdam.

Lyman, S., & Scott, M. B. (1970). *A sociology of the absurd.* New York: ACC, Meredith.

Lynch, J. (1986). *Multicultural education.* London: RKP.

Malone, M. (1980). *A practical guide to discrimination law.* London: Grant McIntyre.

Malson, M. (1983). Black women's sex roles: The social context for a new ideology. *Journal of Social Issues, 39*(3), 101-113.

Malveaux, J. (1986). Comparable worth and its impact on Black women. In M. C. Simms & J. M. Malveaux (Eds.), *Slipping through the cracks* (pp. 47-62). New Brunswick, NJ: Transaction.

Malveaux, J. (1987). The political economy of Black women. In M. Davis et al. (Eds.), *The year left 2* (pp. 53-73). London: Verso.

Manning, B., & Ohri, A. (1982). Racism: The response of community work. In A. Ohri, B. Manning, & P. Curno (Eds.), *Community work and racism* (pp. 3-13). London: Routledge & Kegan Paul.

Marable, M. (1980). *From the grassroots.* Boston: South End.

Marable, M. (1983). *How capitalism underdeveloped Black America.* Boston: South End.

Marable, M. (1984). *Race, reform and rebellion.* London: Macmillan.

Marable, M. (1985). *Black American politics.* London: Verso.

Marcuse, H. (1969). Repressive tolerance. In R. P. Wolff, B. Moore, & H. Marcuse (Eds.), *A critique of pure tolerance* (pp. 95-137). London: Jonathan Cape.

Marsh, P., Rosser, E., & Harré, R. (1978). *Rules of disorder.* London: Routledge & Kegan Paul.

Marx, G. T. (1967). *Protest and prejudice: A study of belief in the Black community.* New York: Harper & Row.

Mazrui, A. A. (1986). *The Africans: A triple heritage.* London: BBC Publications.

McAdoo, H. P. (1986). Strategies used by Black single mothers against stress. In M. C. Simms & J. M. Malveaux (Eds.), *Slipping through the cracks* (pp. 153-166). New Brunswick, NJ: Transaction.

McConahay, J. B. (1986). Modern racism, ambivalence, and the modern racism scale. In J. F. Dovidio & S. L. Gaertner (Eds.), *Prejudice, discrimination, and racism* (pp. 91-125). Orlando, FL: Academic Press.

Mehan, H., & Wood, H. (1975). *The reality of ethnomethodology.* New York: John Wiley.

Memmi, A. (1965). *The colonizer and the colonized.* Boston: Beacon.

Memmi, A. (1983). *Racisme hoezo?* [Racism, what do you mean?]. Nijmegen, the Netherlands: Masusa.

Mercer, K. (1986). Racism and transcultural psychiatry. In P. Miller & N. Rose (Eds.), *The power of psychiatry* (pp. 111-142). Cambridge: Polity.

Meulenbelt, A. (1985). *De ziekte bestrijden, niet d patient* [To combat the disease, rather than the patient]. Amsterdam: van Gennep.

Mies, M. (1983). Towards a methodology for feminist research. In G. Bowles & D. Klein (Eds.), *Theories of women's studies* (pp. 117-138). London: Routledge & Kegan Paul.

Miles, R. (1982). *Racism and migrant labour.* London: RKP.

Miller, N., & Brewer, M. B. (Eds.). (1984). *Groups in contact.* Orlando, FL: Academic Press.

Miller, N., Brewer, M. B., & Edwards, K. (1985). Cooperative interaction in desegregated settings: A laboratory analogue. *Journal of Social Issues, 41*(3), 63-79.

Miller, P., & Rose, N. (1986). *The power of psychiatry.* Cambridge: Polity.

Milner, D. (1975). *Children and race.* Harmondsworth, England: Penguin.

Milner, D. (1981). Racial prejudice. In J. Turner & H. Giles (Eds.), *Intergroup behaviour* (pp. 102-143). London: Basil Blackwell.

Mok, I., & Reinsch, P. Q. (1988). *200 jaar Australië, 200 jaar discriminatie van Aboriginals* [200 years Australia, 200 years of discrimination against the Aboriginals] (Parel Publications No. 2). Amsterdam: University of Amsterdam, Department of General Literary Studies.

Montagu, A. (1972). *Statement on race.* London: Oxford University Press.

Montagu, A. (1974). *Man's most dangerous myth: The fallacy of race.* London: Oxford University Press.

Morris, A. D. (1984). *The origins of the civil rights movement.* New York: Free Press.

Morrison, T. (1989, May 22). [Interviewed by Bonnie Angelo]. *Time,* pp. 46-48.

Moscovici, S., & Hewstone, M. (1983). Social representations and social explanations: From the "naive" to the "amateur" scientist. In M. Hewstone (Ed.), *Attribution theory* (pp. 98-125). Oxford: Basil Blackwell.

Moynihan, D. P. (1965). *The Negro family: A case for national action.* Washington, DC: Government Printing Office.

Mueller, C. (1973). *The politics of communication.* New York: Oxford University Press.

Mullard, C. (1982). Multiracial education in Britain: From assimilation to cultural pluralism. In J. Tierney (Ed.), *Race, migration and schooling* (pp. 120-134). London: Holt, Rinehart & Winston.

Mullard, C. (1984). *Anti-racist education: The three O's.* London: National Association for Multi-Racial Education.

Mullard, C. (1985a). *Race, class, and ideology: Some formal notes.* London: University of London, Institute of Education, Centre for Multicultural Education.

Mullard, C. (1985b). *Race, power and resistance.* London: Routledge & Kegan Paul.

Mullard, C. (1986a). *Pluralism, ethnicism and ideology: Implications for a transformative pedagogy* (Publication Series, Working paper No. 2). Amsterdam: CRES.

Mullard, C. (1986b, August 19). *An etharchy in the making.* Paper presented to the International Sociological Association, New Delhi.

Mullard, C., Nimako, K., & Willemsen, G. (1988). *Emancipatie: een kwestie van keuze* (CRES Publication Series, Research paper No. 2). Amsterdam: CRES.

Muraskin, W. A. (1975). *Middle-class Blacks in White society.* Berkeley: University of California Press.

Murray, N. (1986). Anti-racists and other demons: The press and ideology in Thatcher's Britain. *Race and Class, 3,* 1-19.

Myrdal, G. (1972). *An American dilemma.* New York: Random House. (Original work published by Pantheon, 1944)

Nederveen Pieterse, J. (1989). *Empire and emancipation.* London: Pluto.

Negro American, The. (1965, Fall). *Daedalus* [Special issue].

Negro American, The. (1966, Winter). *Daedalus* [Special issue].

Newman, D. K., Amidei, N. J., Carter, B. L., Day, D., Kruvant, W. J., & Russell, J. S. (1978). *Protest, politics and prosperity.* New York: Pantheon.

Omi, M., & Winant, H. (1986). *Racial formation in the United States.* New York: Routledge & Kegan Paul.

Oomens, M. (1987). Veelwijverij en andere losbandige praktijken [Polygamy and promiscuous practices]. In J. Reijs et al. (Eds.), *Vrouwen in de Nederlandse kolonien* (pp. 152-171). Nijmegen, the Netherlands: SUN.

Page, H. E. (1987). *Lessons of the Jackson campaign: Discursive strategies of symbolic control and cultural capitalization.* Unpublished manuscript.

Parekh, B. (1988). Introduction. In SIM, *New expressions of racism: Growing areas of conflict in Europe* (Special publication No. 7, pp. 9-11). Utrecht, the Netherlands: SIM.

Parmar, P. (1982). Gender, race and class: Asian women in resistance. In Centre of Contemporary Cultural Studies (Birmingham; Ed.), *The empire strikes back: Race and racism in the 70s* (pp. 236-275). London: Hutchinson.

Patchen, M. (1982). *Black-White contact in school.* West Lafayette, IN: Purdue University Press.

Patterson, S. (1963). *Dark strangers.* New York: Penguin.

Pattipawae, N. (1986). Verzekeringen en discrminatie [Insurances and discrimination]. *LBR Bulletin, 5,* 9-12.

Pattipawae, N., & Burght, F. van der. (1988). *Discriminatie in the autoverzekeringsbranche* [Discrimination in the area of car insurance] (LBR-Reeks No. 5). Utrecht, the Netherlands: LBR.

Pearson, M. (1986). The politics of ethnic minority health studies. In T. Rathwell & D. Phillips (Eds.), *Health, race and ethnicity* (pp. 100-116). London: Croom Helm.

Penninx, R. (1988). *Minderheidsvorming en emancipatie* [Minority formation and emancipation]. Alphen aan de Rijn, the Netherlands: Samson.

Perkins, L. M. (1983). The impact of the cult of true womanhood on the education of Black women. *Journal of Social Issues, 39*(3), 17-28.

Pettigrew, T. F. (1958). Personality and sociocultural factors in intergroup attitudes: A cross-cultural comparison. *Journal of Conflict Resolution 2,* 29-42.

Pettigrew, T. F. (1971). *Racially separate or together?* New York: McGraw-Hill.

Pettigrew, T. F. (1979). The ultimate attribution error: Extending Allport's cognitive analysis of prejudice. *Personality and Social Psychology Bulletin, 5,*(4), 451-476.

Pettigrew, T. F. (1985). New Black-White patterns: How best to conceptualize them? *Annual Review of Sociology, 11,* 329-346.

Pettigrew, T. F. (1986). The intergroup contact hypothesis reconsidered. In M. Hewstone & R. Brown (Eds.), *Contact & conflict in intergroup encounters* (pp. 169-195). London: Basil Blackwell.

Pettigrew, T. F. (1988). Integration and pluralism. In P. Katz & D. Taylor (Eds.), *Eliminating racism* (pp. 19-30). New York: Plenum.

Pettigrew, T. F., & Martin, J. (1987). Shaping the organizational context for Black American inclusion. *Journal of Social Issues, 43*(1), 41-78.

Pettigrew, T. F., & Martin, J. (1989). Organizational inclusion of minority groups: A social psychological analysis. In J. P. van Oudenhoven & T. M. Willemsen (Eds.), *Ethnic minorities* (pp. 169-200). Amsterdam: Swets & Zeitlinger.

Pheterson, G. (1986). *The whore stigma.* 's Gravenhage, the Netherlands: Ministerie van Sociale Zaken en Werkgelegenheid.

Piliawsky, M. (1982). *Exit 13: Oppression and racism in academia.* Boston: South End.

Pinkney, A. (1984). *The myth of Black progress.* Cambridge: Cambridge University Press.

Pivcevic, E. (1986). *The concept of reality.* New York: St. Martin's.

Pligt, J. van der. (1981). Actors' and observers' explanations: Divergent perspectives or divergent evaluations? In C. Antaki (Ed.), *The psychology of ordinary explanations of social behaviour* (pp. 104-124). London: Academic Press.

Plummer, K. (1983). *Documents of life: An introduction to the problems and literature of a humanistic method.* London: Allen & Unwin.

Polanyi, L. (1981). Telling the same story twice. *Text, 1,* 315-366.

Polenberg, R. (1980). *One nation divisible.* Harmondsworth, England: Penguin.

Polkinghorne, D. (1983). *Methodology for the human sciences.* Albany: State University of New York Press.

Praag, C. van. (1989). Huishoudens en huishoudens-vorming by etnische minderheden in Nederland [Households and household formation among ethnic minorities in the Netherlands]. *Migrantenstudies, 3,* 25-35.

Rainwater, L., & Yancey, W. (1967). *The Moynihan report and the politics of controversy.* Cambridge: MIT Press.

Ramazanoglu, C. (1989). *Feminism and the contradictions of oppression.* London: Routledge.

Ransford, H. E., & Miller, J. (1983). Race, sex and feminist outlooks. *American Sociological Review, 48,* 46-59.

Redmond, R. (1980). *Zwarte mensen in kinderboeken* [Blacks in children's books]. Den Haag, the Netherlands: Nederlands Bibliotheek en Literatuur Centrum.

Reed, W. L. (1989). The role of universities in racial violence on campuses. *Trotter Institute Review, 2*(3-4), 18.

Reid, I. S. (1972). *Together Black women.* New York: Third Press.

Reid, P. T. (1988). Racism and sexism: Comparisons and conflicts. In P. Katz & D. Taylor (Eds.), *Eliminating racism* (pp. 203-221). New York: Plenum.

Reinharz, S. (1983). Experiential analysis: A contribution to feminist research. In G. Bowles & R. D. Klein (Eds.), *Theories of women's studies* (pp. 162-191). London: Routledge & Kegan Paul.

Reinsma, R. (1963). *Een merkwaardige episode uit de geschiedenis van de slavenemancipatie* [A curious episode in the history of slave emancipation]. Den Haag: Van Goor Zonen.

Reubsaet, T. J., & Kropman, J. A. (1985). *Beeldvorming over etnische groepen bij de werving en selectie van personeel* [Opinions about ethnic groups in the recruitment of personnel]. Nijmegen, the Netherlands: ITS.

Reubsaet, T. J. M., Kropman, J. A., & Mulier, L. M. van. (1982). *Surinaamse migranten in Nederland. Deel 2. De positie van Surinamers in de Nederlands samenleving* [The position of Surinamese in Dutch society]. Nijmegen, the Netherlands: ITS.

Reynaert, W. (1988). *Arbeidsmarktperspektief voor allochtonen* [Labor market perspectives for the nonnative]. Assen, the Netherlands: van Gorcum.

Reynolds, E. (1985). *Stand the storm*. London: Allison.

Rich, A. (1979). Disloyal to civilization: Feminism, racism and gynephobia. *Chrysalis, 7,* 9-27.

Riley, K. (1985). Black girls speak for themselves. In G. Weiner (Ed.), *Just a bunch of girls* (pp. 63-76). Milton Keynes: Open University Press.

Robinson, C. (1983). *Black Marxism: The making of the Black radical tradition*. London: Zed.

Robinson, L. S. (1978). *Sex, class, and culture*. New York: Methuen.

Rodgers-Rose, L. F. (1980). Dialectics of Black male-female relationships. In L. F. Rodgers-Rose (Ed.), *The Black woman* (pp. 251-263). Beverly Hills, CA: Sage.

Rodgers-Rose, L. F. (Ed.). (1980). *The Black woman*. Beverly Hills, CA: Sage.

Rodney, W. (1982). *How Europe underdeveloped Africa*. Washington, DC: Howard University Press.

Rogers, M. F. (1983). *Sociology, ethnomethodology, and experience: A phenomenological critique*. Cambridge: Cambridge University Press.

Rollins, J. (1985). *Between women: Domestics and their employers*. Philadelphia: Temple University Press.

Rose, W. L. (Ed.). (1976). *A documentary history of slavery in North America*. New York: Oxford University Press.

Rowe, M. P. (1977). The Saturn's rings phenomenon: Micro-inequities and unequal opportunity in the American economy (Preprint). In P. Bourne & V. Parness (Eds.), *Proceedings*. Santa Cruz: University of California.

Ryan, W. (1971). *Blaming the victim*. New York: Vintage.

Sacks, H., Schegloff, E. A., & Jefferson, G. A. (1974). A simplest systematics for the organization of turntaking for conversation. *Language, 50,* 696-735.

Sanzone, L. (1990). *Lasi Boto* [Lost opportunities]. Amersfoort, the Netherlands: ACO.

Satow, A. (1982). Racism awareness training: Training to make a difference. In A. Ohri, B. Manning, & P.Curno (Eds.), *Community work and racism* (pp. 34-42). London: Routledge & Kegan Paul.

Schank, R. C. (1982). *Dynamic memory*. Cambridge: Cambridge University Press.

Schank, R. C., & Abelson, R. (1977). *Scripts, plans, goals and understanding*. Hillsdale, NJ: Lawrence Erlbaum.

Schenkhein, J. (Ed.). (1978). *Studies in the organization of conversational interaction*. New York: Academic Press.

Schumacher, P. (1987). *De minderheden* [The minorities]. Amsterdam: van Gennep.

Schuman, H., Steeh, C., & Bobo, L. (1985). *Racial attitudes in America: Trends and interpretations*. Cambridge, MA: Harvard University Press.

Schutz, A. (1970). *On phenomenology and social relations*. Chicago: University of Chicago Press.

Schwartz, H., & Jacobs, J. (1979). *Qualitative sociology: A method to madness*. New York: Free Press, Macmillan.

Scott, M. B., & Lyman, S. M. (1972). Accounts. In J. G. Manis & B. N. Meltzer (Eds.), *Symbolic interaction* (2th ed., pp. 404-429). Boston: Allyn & Bacon.

Sears, D. (1988). Symbolic racism. In P. Katz & D. Taylor (Eds.), *Eliminating racism* (pp. 53-84). New York: Plenum.

Sears, D. O., & Kinder, D. R. (1971). Racial tensions and voting in Los Angeles. In W. Z. Hirsh (Ed.), *Los Angeles: Viability and prospects for metropolitan leadership* (pp. 51-88). New York: Praeger.

Seidel, G. (Ed.). (1988). *The nature of the right*. Amsterdam: Benjamins.

Selltiz, C., Wrightsman, L. S., & Cook, S. W. (1976). *Research methods in social relations*. New York: Holt, Rinehart & Winston.

Semin, G. R. (1990). Everyday assumptions, language and personality. In G. R. Semin & K. J. Gergen (Eds.), *Everyday understanding* (pp. 151-175). London: Sage.

Semin, G. R., & Gergen, K. J. (Eds.). (1990). *Everyday understanding*. London: Sage.

Sennett, R., & Cobb, J. (1972). *The hidden injuries of class*. New York: Vintage.

Shadid, W., & Kornalijnslijper, N. (1985). Minderhedenhuisvesting: een terreinverkenning [Housing of minorities: a field orientation]. *Migrantenstudies, 4,* 2-19.

Shadid, W., Kornalijnslijper, N., & Maan, E. (1985). *Huisvesting minderheden* [Housing of minorities]. Leiden, the Netherlands: DSWO Press.

Sharpe, S. (1976). *Just like a girl*. Harmondsworth, England: Penguin.

Shockley, A. A. (1989). *Afro-American women writers 1746-1933*. New York: New American Library.

Shotter, J. (1981). Telling and reporting: Prospective and retrospective uses of self-ascription. In C. Antaki (Ed.), *The psychology of ordinary explanations of social behaviour* (pp. 157-181). London: Academic Press.

Sikking, E., & Brassé, P. (1987). *Waar liggen de grenzen?* [Where are the limits?] (LBR-Reeks No. 4). Utrecht, the Netherlands: LBR.

SIM. (1988). *New expressions of racism: Growing areas of conflict in Europe* (Special publication No. 7). Utrecht, the Netherlands: SIM.

Simms, M. C. (1986). Black women who head families: An economic struggle. In M. C. Simms & J. M. Malveaux (Eds.), *Slipping through the cracks* (pp. 141-151). New Brunswick, NJ: Transaction.

Simms, M. C., & Malveaux, J. M. (Eds.). (1986). *Slipping through the cracks*. New Brunswick, NJ: Transaction.

Simpson, G., & Yinger, M. (1972). *Racial and cultural minorities: An analysis of prejudice and discrimination*. New York: Harper & Row.

Sivanandan, A. (1985). RAT and the degradation of Black struggle. *Race and Class, 26*(4), 1-33.

Skolnick, J. H. (1969). *The politics of protest*. New York: Ballantine.

Slavin, R. P. (1985). Cooperative learning: Applying contact theory in desegregated schools. *Journal of Social Issues, 41*(3), 45-62.

Smit, V. (1985). Barrières voor buitenlanders? Turken en Marokkanen op de woningmarkt [Obstacles against foreigners? Turks and Moroccans on the housing market]. *Migrantenstudies, 4,* 20-35.

Smith, A., & Stewart, A. J. (1983). Approaches to studying racism and sexism in Black women's lives. *Journal of Social Issues, 39,*(3), 1-15.

Smith, A. D. (1981). *The ethnic revival*. Cambridge: Cambridge University Press.

Smith, A. W. (1988). Racial insularity at the core: Contemporary American racial attitudes. *Trotter Institute Review, 2,* 9-13.

Smith, B. (1977). *Toward a Black feminist criticism*. New York: Out & Out Books.

Smith, B. (Ed.). (1983). *Home girls: A Black feminist anthology*. New York: Kitchen Table, Women of Color Press.

Smith, D. E. (1987). *The everyday world as problematic.* Toronto: Toronto University Press.

Smith, D. J. (1977). *Racial disadvantage in Britain.* Harmondsworth, England: Penguin.

Smith, E. J. (1982). The Black female adolescent: A review of the educational, career, and psychological literature. *Psychology of Women Quarterly, 6*(3), 261-288.

Sniderman, P. M., & Tetlock, P. J. (1986). Symbolic racism: Problems of motive attribution in political analysis. *Journal of Social Issues, 42*(2), 129-150.

Snowden, F. M. (1969). *Blacks in antiquity.* Cambridge, MA: Harvard University Press.

Solomos, J. (1986). Varieties of Marxist conceptions of "race," class and the state: A critical analysis. In J. Rex & D. Mason (Eds.), *Theories of race and ethnic relations* (pp. 84-109). Cambridge: Cambridge University Press.

Solomos, J. (1989). *Race and racism in contemporary Britain.* London: Macmillan.

Solomos, J., Findlay, B., Jones, S., & Gilroy, P. (1982). The organic crisis of British capitalism and race: The experience of the seventies. In Centre of Contemporary Cultural Studies (Birmingham; Ed.), *The empire strikes back: Race and racism in the 70s* (pp. 9-46). London: Hutchinson.

Sowell, T. (1981). *Ethnic America.* New York: Basic Books.

Spelman, E. V. (1988). *Inessential woman.* London: Women's Press.

Stampp, K. M. (1956). *The peculiar institution: Slavery in ante-bellum South.* New York: Knopf.

Staples, R. (1970, November-December). The myth of the Black matriarchy. *The Black Scholar,* pp. 26-34.

Staples, R. (1973). *The Black woman in America.* Chicago: Nelson-Hall.

Stasiulis, D. (1987). Rainbow feminism: Perspectives on minority women in Canada. *RFR/DRF, 16*(1), 5-9.

Steady, F. C. (1985). The Black woman cross-culturally: An overview. In F. C. Steady (Ed.), *The Black woman cross-culturally* (pp. 7-41). Cambridge, MA: Schenkman.

Steinberg, S. (1981). *The ethnic myth.* Boston: Beacon.

Stember, C. H. (1976). *Sexual racism.* New York: Harper Colophon.

Stephan, W. G. (1977). Stereotyping: The role of ingroup-outgroup differences in causal attribution for behavior. *Journal of Social Psychology, 101,* 255-266.

Sterling, D. (1979). *Black foremothers: Three lives.* New York: Feminist Press.

Sterling, D. (Ed.). (1984). *We are your sisters.* New York: Norton.

Stichting, A. F. [Anne Frank Foundation]. (Ed.). (1987). *Vreemd gespuis* [Strange scum]. Baarn, The Netherlands: Ambo/Novib.

Stinton, J. (Ed.). (1979). *Racism and sexism in children's books.* London: Writers & Readers.

Stone, M. (1981). *The education of the Black child in Britain.* London: Fontana.

Stuckey, S. (1987). *Slave culture: Nationalist theory and the foundations of Black America.* New York: Oxford University Press.

Tedeshi, J. T., & Reiss, M. (1981). Verbal strategies in impression management. In C. Antaki (Ed.), *The psychology of ordinary explanations of social behaviour* (pp. 271-309). London: Academic Press.

Tennekes, J. (1985). De vage grenzen van tolerantie [The vague limits of tolerance]. *Intermediair, 21*(9), 55-65.

Terborg-Penn, R. (1978). Discrimination against Afro-American women in the woman's movement, 1830-1920. In S. Harley & R. Terborg-Penn (Eds.), *The Afro-American woman.* Port Washington, NY: Kennikat.

Terry, R. W. (1975). *For Whites only* (rev. ed.). Grand Rapids, MI: Eerdmans.

Thomas, W. I. (1928). *The child in America*. New York: Knopf.

Tobin, G. A. (Ed.). (1987). *Divided neighborhoods*. Newbury Park, CA: Sage.

Tomlinson, S. (1983). Black women in higher education: Case studies of university women in Britain. In L. Barton & S. Walker (Eds.), *Race, class and education* (pp. 66-80). London: Croom Helm.

Trost, L. D. (1975). Western metaphysical dualism as an element in racism. In J. L. Hodge, D. S. Struckmann, & L. D. Trost (Eds.), *Cultural bases of racism and group oppression* (pp. 49-89). Berkeley, CA: Two Riders.

Troyna, B., & Williams, J. (1986). *Racism, education and the state*. London: Croom Helm.

Turner, J. (1987). Analytical theorizing. In A. Giddens & J. Turner (Eds.), *Social theory today* (pp. 157-194). Cambridge: Polity.

Tuttle, W. M. (1984). *Race riot*. New York: Atheneum.

Uyl, R. den, Choenni, C., & Bovenkerk, F. (1986). *Mag het ook een buitenlander wezen* [Will a foreigner also do?] (LBR-Reeks No. 2). Utrecht, the Netherlands: LBR.

van Dijk, T. A. (1983). *Minderheden in de Media* [Minorities in the media]. Amsterdam: SUA.

van Dijk, T. A. (1984). *Prejudice in discourse*. Amsterdam: Benjamins.

van Dijk, T. A. (1987a). *Communicating racism*. Beverly Hills, CA: Sage.

van Dijk, T. A. (1987b). *Schoolvoorbeelden van Racisme* [Textbook examples of racism]. Amsterdam: SUA

van Dijk, T. A. (1987c). Elite discourse and racism. In I. Zavala, T. A. van Dijk, & M. Dìaz-Diocaretz (Eds.), *Approaches to discourse, poetics and psychiatry* (pp. 81-122). Amsterdam: Benjamins.

van Dijk, T. A. (1988). *News analysis: Case studies of international and national news in the press—Lebanon, ethnic minorities, refugees and squatters*. Hillsdale, NJ: Lawrence Erlbaum.

van Dijk, T. A. (1989). Structures and strategies of discourse and prejudice. In J. P. van Oudenhoven & T. M. Willemsen (Eds.), *Ethnic minorities* (pp. 115-138). Amsterdam: Swets & Zeitlinger.

van Dijk, T. A. (1991). *Racism and the press*. London: RKP.

van Dijk, T. A., & Kintsch, W. (1983). *Strategies of discourse comprehension*. New York: Academic Press.

Van Sertima, I. (Ed.). (1985). *African presence in early Europe*. New Brunswick, NJ: Transaction.

Vermeulen, H. (1984). Etnische groepen en grenzen [Ethnic groups and boundaries]. In *Surinamers, Chinezen en Turken*. Weesp, the Netherlands: Het Wereldvenster.

Vuijsje, H. (1986). *Vermoorde onschuld* [Murdered innocence]. Amsterdam: Bakker.

Wallace, M. (1978). *Black macho and the myth of the superwoman*. London: Calder.

Wallace, P. A. (1980). *Black women in the labor force*. Cambridge: MIT Press.

Walton, S. F. (1969). *The Black curriculum*. East Palo Alto, CA: Black Liberation Publishers.

Weigel, R. H., & Howes, P. W. (1985). Conceptions of racial prejudice: Symbolic racism reconsidered. *Journal of Social Issues, 41*(3), 117-138.

Weitz, S. (1972). Attitude, voice and behavior: A repressed affect model of interracial interaction. *Journal of Personality and Social Psychology, 24*, 14-21.

Wellman, D. T. (1977). *Portraits of White racism*. Cambridge: Cambridge University Press.

West, C. (1987). Race and social theory: Towards a genealogical materialist analysis. In M. Davis, M. Manning, F. Pfeil, & M. Sprinker (Eds.), *The year left 2* (pp. 74-90). London: Verso.

White, D. G. (1985). *Ar'n't I a woman?* New York: Norton.

Wicklund, R. A., & Frey, D. (1981). Cognitive consistency: Motivational vs non-motivational perspectives. In J. Forgas (Ed.), *Social cognition* (pp. 141-163). London: Academic Press.

Wilkerson, M. B. (1986). A report on the educational status of Black women during the un decade of women, 1976-85. In M. Simms & J. Malveaux (Eds.), *Slipping through the cracks* (pp. 83-96). New Brunswick, NJ: Transaction.

Wilkinson, D. Y., & Taylor, R. L. (Eds.). (1977). *The Black male in America.* Chicago: Nelson-Hall.

Wilkinson, S. (1981). Personal constructs and private explanations. In C. Antaki (Ed.), *The psychology of ordinary explanations of social behaviour* (pp. 205-219). London: Academic Press.

Willemsen, G. (1988). Minderheden op de arbeidsmarkt: de gevolgen van een verkeerd geïnspireerde politiek [Minorities on the labor market: The consequences of wrongly inspired politics]. *Migrantenstudies, 4*(1), 50-66.

Willemsen, T. M., & van Oudenhoven, J. P. (1989). Social psychological perspectives on ethnic minorities: An introduction. In J. P. van Oudenhoven & T. M. Willemsen (Eds.), *Ethnic minorities* (pp. 11-21). Amsterdam: Swets & Zeitlinger.

Williamson, J. (1984). *The crucible of race.* New York: Oxford University Press.

Willie, C. V. (1981). *The ivory and ebony towers.* Lexington, MA: Lexington.

Wilmore, C. S. (1983). *Black religion and Black radicalism.* New York: Orbis.

Wilson, A. (1987). *Mixed race children.* London: Allen & Unwin.

Wilson, W. J. (1978). *The declining significance of race.* Chicago: Chicago University Press.

Wilson, W. J. (1987). *The truly disadvantaged.* Chicago: Chicago University Press.

Woodward, C. V. (1957). *The strange career of Jim Crow.* New York: Oxford University Press.

WRR. (1989). *Allochtonenbeleid.* 's Gravenhage, the Netherlands: SDU.

Wubben, H. (1986). *Chineezen en ander Aziatisch ongedierte* [Chinese and other Asian vermin]. Zutphen, the Netherlands: de Walburg Pers.

Zee, J. van der. (1988). *Zwarte Studenten aan de Rijksuniversiteit Groningen.* Groningen, the Netherlands: Andragogisch Instituut.

Zeven, B. (1987). *Van Chineezen reserves en pindamannen* [About Chinese reserves and peanut men]. In Anne Frank Stichting (Ed.), *Vreemd gespuis* (pp. 77-91). Baarn, the Netherlands: Ambo/Novib.

Zimmerman, D. H., & Pollner, M. (1970). The everyday world as a phenomenon. In J. D. Douglas (Ed.), *Understanding everyday life* (pp. 80-103). London: RKP.

Index

319

About the Author

Philomena Essed (University of Amsterdam) works within an interdisciplinary framework, combining various fields of study, such as race relations theory, sociology, social psychology, and feminist theory. Her research interests include the development of cross-cultural perspectives on the experience and empowerment of Black women. She also studies and advises on intercultural management and team building in organizations. She has lectured on women's everyday experiences of racism in various European countries. She has contributed a number of articles to international journals. Her work has appeared in four different languages and was published, apart from the Netherlands, in the United States, the United Kingdom, Canada, Germany, and Italy. She is the author of *Everyday Racism* (1984/1988; 1990).